THE FLORIDA EDITION
OF THE WORKS OF LAURENCE STERNE

VOLUME VII

The Letters, Part 1: 1739–1764

VOLUME VIII

The Letters, Part 2: 1765–1768

UNIVERSITY PRESS OF FLORIDA

Florida A&M University, Tallahassee
Florida Atlantic University, Boca Raton
Florida Gulf Coast University, Ft. Myers
Florida International University, Miami
Florida State University, Tallahassee
New College of Florida, Sarasota
University of Central Florida, Orlando
University of Florida, Gainesville
University of North Florida, Jacksonville
University of South Florida, Tampa
University of West Florida, Pensacola

THE FLORIDA EDITION OF THE WORKS OF LAURENCE STERNE

Melvyn New, General Editor

VOLUMES I AND II. *The Life and Opinions of Tristram Shandy, Gentleman: The Text*, edited by Melvyn New and Joan New (1978)

VOLUME III. *The Life and Opinions of Tristram Shandy, Gentleman: The Notes*, edited by Melvyn New, with Richard A. Davies and W. G. Day (1984)

VOLUME IV. *The Sermons of Laurence Sterne: The Text*, edited by Melvyn New (1996)

VOLUME V. *The Sermons of Laurence Sterne: The Notes*, edited by Melvyn New (1996)

VOLUME VI. *A Sentimental Journey through France and Italy and Continuation of the Bramine's Journal: The Text and Notes*, edited by Melvyn New and W. G. Day (2002)

VOLUMES VII AND VIII. *The Letters*, edited by Melvyn New and Peter de Voogd (2009)

THE FLORIDA EDITION OF THE WORKS OF LAURENCE STERNE

VOLUME VIII

The Letters, Part 2: 1765–1768

Laurence Sterne

The Florida Edition of the Works of Laurence Sterne

VOLUME VIII

The Letters

PART 2: 1765–1768

Edited by Melvyn New and Peter de Voogd

University Press of Florida

GAINESVILLE · TALLAHASSEE · TAMPA · BOCA RATON

PENSACOLA · ORLANDO · MIAMI · JACKSONVILLE · FT. MYERS · SARASOTA

Printed in the United States of America. This book is printed on Glatfelter Natures Book, a paper certified under the standards of the Forestry Stewardship Council (FSC). It is a recycled stock that contains 30 percent post-consumer waste and is acid-free.

14 13 12 11 10 09 6 5 4 3 2 1

Library of Congress Cataloging-in-Publication Data
Sterne, Laurence, 1713-1768.
[Correspondence. Selections]
The letters, part 2: 1765-1768 / Laurence Sterne,
edited by Melvyn New and Peter de Voogd.
p. cm. — (The Florida edition of the works of Laurence Sterne ; v. 8)
Includes index.
ISBN 978-0-8130-3237-5 (acid-free paper)
1. Sterne, Laurence, 1713-1768.—Correspondence. 2. Novelists, English—18th century—Correspondence. I. New, Melvyn. II. Voogd, Peter Jan de. III. Title.
PR3716.A6 2009
823.6—dc22 2008038639

The University Press of Florida is the scholarly publishing agency for the State University System of Florida, comprising Florida A&M University, Florida Atlantic University, Florida Gulf Coast University, Florida International University, Florida State University, New College of Florida, University of Central Florida, University of Florida, University of North Florida, University of South Florida, and University of West Florida.

University Press of Florida
15 Northwest 15th Street
Gainesville, FL 32611-2079
www.upf.com

CONTENTS OF PART 2

ILLUSTRATIONS IN PART 2

LIST OF LETTERS IN PART 2

LETTERS IN PART 2

* Letters not in Curtis.

** Letters in Curtis for which we had access to a ms. (in whole or in part) not available to Curtis.

Letter Book indicates letters pasted in the so-called *Letter Book,* now at the Pierpont Morgan Library, New York.

No.	*Date of Composition*	*Addressee*	*Source*	*Page*
1765				
144	March 16	David Garrick	Medalle	401
145*	March 23	Thomas Astle	Ms., Houghton Library	404
146	April 6	David Garrick	Ms., National Library of Scotland	405
147	April 15	Robert Foley	Medalle	409
148	April	Mrs. F——	Ms., *Letter Book*	411
149	?April 23	Lady P.	Medalle	416
150	May 6–13	dear Lady	Ms., *Letter Book*	421
151**	May 29	Viscount Effingham	Ms., Beinecke Library	425
152	June 11	William Combe	*Daily Universal Register*	430
153	June 18	Countess ******/Eliza	Ms., *Letter Book*	435
154	July 5	Thomas Hesilrige	Ms., Houghton Library	442
155	July 13	Robert Foley	Medalle	444

1766

continued

continued

No.	*Date of Composition*	*Addressee*	*Source*	*Page*
213	June 30	A. L——e, Esq.	Medalle	595
214	June 30	Ignatius Sancho	Ms., Monkman Collection, Shandy Hall	597
215	July 6	Anne and William James	Medalle	599
216*	July 18	Reverend Sir	Ms., York Minster Library	600
217	July 28	Isaac Panchaud	Medalle	601
218	August 2	Anne and William James	Medalle	603
219*	August 7	John Clough	Ms., York Minster Library	605
220	August 10	Anne James	Ms., British Library	606
221	August 11	John Hall-Stevenson	Medalle	609
222	August 24	Lydia Sterne	Medalle	612
223	September 3	Thomas Becket	Ms., Princeton University Library	616
224	September 12	Hannah	Ms., Houghton Library/Medalle	616
225	September 19	Sir W.	Medalle	618
226	September 27	Sir W.	Medalle	621
227	October 1	Isaac Panchaud	Medalle	623
228	October 2	Mrs. F——	Medalle	624
229	October 3	Anne and William James	Medalle	625
230	November 12	Anne James	Medalle	628
231*	?November	Hannah	Ms., Monkman Collection, Shandy Hall	630
232	November 15	Hannah	Curtis	631

Appendix: Letters Pertaining to Sterne and His Family

No.	*Date of Composition*	*From*	*To*	*Source*	*Page*
1740					
i	?1740	Laurence Sterne	Elizabeth Lumley	Medalle	663
1750					
ii	December 6	Jaques Sterne	Francis Blackburne	Ms., British Library	668
1751					
iii	1751	Elizabeth Sterne	Theophilus Garencieres	Ms., Princeton University Library	671
1753					
iv	March 9	Elizabeth Sterne	Elizabeth Montagu	Ms., Huntington Library	672
1757					
v*	May 13	Laurence Sterne	Stephen Croft	Ms., Princeton University Library	674
1758					
vi*	1758	Elizabeth Sterne	John Blake	Ms., Monkman Collection, Shandy Hall	675

1760					
vii	March 7	William Warburton	David Garrick	*Private Correspondence of Garrick* (1831)	676
viii	March 8	Laurence Sterne	James Dodsley	Ms., New York Public Library	678
ix	March 8	Laurence Sterne	Richard Berenger	Ms., *Letter Book*	679
x	March 28	Lord Fauconberg	John Gilbert	Ms., British Library	680
xi	April 15	Anonymous		Cross, *Letters* (1904)	681
xii	June 15	William Warburton	Laurence Sterne	Medalle	686
xiii	June 16	William Warburton	David Garrick	*Private Correspondence of Garrick* (1831)	688
xiv	June 26	William Warburton	Laurence Sterne	*Unpublished Papers of Warburton* (1841)	689
xv	July 25	Robert Brown	John Hall-Stevenson	Transcription, *Letter Book*	691
xvi	November	Elizabeth Sterne	Elizabeth Montagu	Ms., Huntington Library	693
1765					
xvii	?April	"Jenny Shandy"	Laurence Sterne	Transcription, *Letter Book*	695
1766					
xviii	July 13	John Hall-Stevenson	Laurence Sterne	Transcription, *Letter Book*	696
xix(a)*	July 21	Ignatius Sancho	Laurence Sterne	*Letters of Sancho* (1782)	696
xix(b)	July 21	Ignatius Sancho	Laurence Sterne	Transcription, *Letter Book*	699
xx	July 27	Laurence Sterne	Ignatius Sancho	Ms., *Letter Book*	701

continued

No.	*Date of Composition*	*From*	*To*	*Source*	*Page*
1767					
xxi	January 21	Laurence Sterne	Thomas Becket	Ms., Houghton Library	703
xxii	?November	John Eustace	Laurence Sterne	*Life and Correspondence of James Iredell* (1857)	703
1768					
xxiii*	March 26	Robert Hay Drummond	Elizabeth Montagu	Ms., Huntington Library	705
xxiv	April	Elizabeth Montagu	Sarah Scott	Ms., Huntington Library	707
xxv	April 5	Lydia Sterne	Elizabeth Montagu	Ms., Huntington Library	708
xxvi	June 6	Robert Hay Drummond	Elizabeth Montagu	Ms., Huntington Library	710
xxvii	June 17	Robert Hay Drummond	Elizabeth Montagu	Ms., Huntington Library	711
xxviii	August 31	Lydia Sterne	Elizabeth Montagu	Ms., Huntington Library	713
xxix	September 4	Elizabeth Montagu	Sarah Scott	Ms., Huntington Library	716
xxx	?September	Elizabeth Montagu	Leonard Smelt	Ms., Huntington Library	717
xxxi	?September	Lydia Sterne	Thomas Becket	Curtis	720
xxxii	October 6	Lydia Sterne	Thomas Becket	Curtis	721
xxxiii	November 18	John Hall-Stevenson	Lydia Sterne	Curtis	722
xxxiv*	November	Lydia Sterne	Thomas Becket	Ms., Houghton Library	724
xxxv*	December	Lydia Sterne	Thomas Becket	Ms., Houghton Library	727
xxxvi**	?December	Lydia Sterne	Thomas Becket	Ms., Hyde Collection, Harvard University	728
xxxvii	December 15	Lydia Sterne	Elizabeth Montagu	Ms., Huntington Library	729

1769					
xxxviii	?January	Lydia Sterne	Elizabeth Montagu	Ms., Huntington Library	732
xxxix	?March	Lydia Sterne	William Strahan	Ms., Beinecke Library	735
xl	?May	Elizabeth & Lydia Sterne	John Wilkes	Ms., British Library	736
xli	?May	Elizabeth & Lydia Sterne	John & Mary Wilkes	Ms., British Library	738
xlii*	?June	Lydia Sterne	David Garrick	Ms., Pusey Library, Harvard University	738
xliii	July 22	Lydia Sterne	John Wilkes	Ms., British Library	741
xliv	October 24	Lydia Sterne	John Wilkes	Ms., British Library	745
1770					
xlv	February 13	Lydia Sterne	John Hall-Stevenson	Ms., British Library	746
xlvi	March 2	Lydia Sterne	Elizabeth Montagu	Ms., Huntington Library	748
xlvii*	March 23	Lydia Sterne	Jane Fenton	Ms., Monkman Collection, Shandy Hall	750
1771					
xlviii	September 26	Lydia Sterne	Elizabeth Montagu	Ms., Huntington Library	753
1772					
xlix	March 23	Lydia Sterne	Elizabeth Montagu	Ms., Huntington Library	755
l	April	Elizabeth Montagu	Lydia Sterne	Transcription, Huntington Library	757
li	April 15	Eliza Draper	Anne James	British Library	758

continued

No.	*Date of Composition*	*From*	*To*	*Source*	*Page*
1775					
lii*	?June	Lydia Sterne de Medalle	David Garrick	Dedication to *Letters of Sterne* (1775)	768

Note

1. A printed version in the *European Magazine* (1825) was not known to Curtis; the ms. has not been located.

WORKS FREQUENTLY CITED

All journals are abbreviated as in the *PMLA* Bibliography. The place of publication before 1800 is understood to be London, unless otherwise indicated. Classical quotations and translations are taken from the editions of the Loeb Classical Library, Harvard University Press, unless otherwise indicated.

For *Tristram Shandy,* indicated as *TS,* reference is keyed by volume, chapter, and page number in the *Florida Edition,* 2 vols., ed. Melvyn New and Joan New (University Press of Florida, 1978). For the annotations to *Tristram Shandy,* the notes refer to volume 3 of the *Florida Edition,* ed. Melvyn New, with Richard A. Davies and W. G. Day (University Press of Florida, 1984), designated *Notes.*

For Sterne's sermons, indicated as *Sermons,* reference is keyed to volume 4 of the *Florida Edition,* ed. Melvyn New (University Press of Florida, 1996). For annotations to *Sermons,* the notes refer to volume 5 of the *Florida Edition,* ed. Melvyn New (1996).

For *A Sentimental Journey,* indicated as *ASJ,* reference and annotations are keyed to volume 6 of the *Florida Edition,* ed. Melvyn New and W. G. Day (University Press of Florida, 2002).

For *Continuation of the Bramine's Journal,* indicated as *BJ,* reference and annotations are also keyed to volume 6 of the *Florida Edition.*

Short Titles

1780	*The Works of Laurence Sterne in Ten Volumes Complete* (London: Printed for W. Strahan, J. Rivington, et al., 1780).
Brookes	R. Brookes, M.D., *The General Dispensatory* (1753).
Cash, *EMY*	Arthur H. Cash, *Laurence Sterne: The Early and Middle Years* (London: Methuen, 1975).

Cash, *LY*	Arthur H. Cash, *Laurence Sterne: The Later Years* (London: Methuen, 1986).
Cervantes, *Don Quixote*	Miguel de Cervantes, *Don Quixote,* trans. Peter Motteux, rev. John Ozell, 7th ed., 4 vols. (1743).
Cross, *Letters*	Wilbur L. Cross, ed., *Letters and Miscellanies,* 2 vols. in *The Works and Life of Laurence Sterne,* 12 vols. (New York: J. F. Taylor, 1904).
Cross, *Life,* 1909	Wilbur L. Cross, *The Life and Times of Laurence Sterne* (New York: Macmillan, 1909).
Cross, *Life,* 1925	Wilbur L. Cross, *The Life and Times of Laurence Sterne, A New Edition,* 2 vols. (New Haven: Yale University Press, 1925).
Cross, *Life,* 1929	Wilbur L. Cross, *The Life and Times of Laurence Sterne,* 3d ed. (New Haven: Yale University Press, 1929).
Curtis	Lewis Perry Curtis, ed., *Letters of Laurence Sterne* (Oxford: Clarendon Press, 1935).
Fitzgerald, 1864	Percy Fitzgerald, *The Life of Laurence Sterne,* 2 vols. (London: Chapman and Hall, 1864).
Fitzgerald, 1896	Percy Fitzgerald, *The Life of Laurence Sterne,* 2 vols. (London: Downey & Co., 1896); rpt. ed., 2 vols. in *The Works and Life of Laurence Sterne,* 12 vols. (New York: J. F. Taylor, 1904).
Letters of Garrick	*The Letters of David Garrick,* ed. David M. Little and George M. Kahrl (Cambridge: Belknap Press of Harvard University Press, 1963).
London Past and Present	Henry B. Wheatley, *London Past and Present: A Dictionary of Its History, Associations, and Traditions* (London: John Murray, 1891).
Medalle	*Letters of the Late Rev. Mr. Laurence Sterne, to His Most Intimate Friends,* ed. Lydia Medalle, 3 vols. 1775.
Memoirs	*Sterne's Memoirs*, intro. and commentary by Kenneth Monkman (Privately printed for The Laurence Sterne Trust, 1985).
Namier and Brooke	Sir Lewis Namier and John Brooke, *House of Commons, 1754–1790,* 3 vols. (London: History of Parliament Trust, 1964).

ODEP	*The Oxford Dictionary of English Proverbs,* 3d ed. rev., F. P. Wilson, ed. (Oxford: Clarendon Press, 1970).
OED	*The Oxford English Dictionary* (Oxford: Oxford University Press, 1992) (online edition).
OL	[William Combe], *Original Letters of the Late Reverend Mr. Laurence Sterne* (1788).
Oxford DNB	*The Oxford Dictionary of National Biography* (Oxford: Oxford University Press, 2004) (online edition).
Pope	Alexander Pope, *The Twickenham Edition of the Poems of Alexander Pope,* ed. John Butt, et al., 12 vols. (London: Methuen, 1939–69).
Shakespeare	*The Riverside Shakespeare*, ed. G. Blakemore Evans, et al. (Boston: Houghton Mifflin, 1974).
Smollett, *Travels*	Tobias Smollett, *Travels through France and Italy,* 2 vols. (1766).
Tilley	Morris Palmer Tilley, *A Dictionary of the Proverbs in England in the Sixteenth and Seventeenth Centuries* (Ann Arbor: University of Michigan Press, 1950).
VO	[William Combe], *Sterne's Letters to His Friends on Various Occasions* (1775).
Walpole, *Correspondence*	*The Yale Edition of Horace Walpole's Correspondence,* ed. W. S. Lewis, et al., 48 vols. (New Haven: Yale University Press, 1937–83).
Walpole, *Memoirs . . . George II*	Horace Walpole, *Memoirs of King George II,* ed. John Brooke, 3 vols. (New Haven: Yale University Press, 1985).
Walpole, *Memoirs . . . George III*	Horace Walpole, *Memoirs of King George III,* ed. Derek Jarett, 4 vols. (New Haven: Yale University Press, 2000).
Whitefoord Papers	John Croft, "Anecdotes of Sterne," in *The Whitefoord Papers,* ed. W.A.S. Hewins (Oxford: Clarendon Press, 1898).

NOTE ON THE TEXT

In our textual and annotational presentation of Sterne's correspondence, we have tried to keep in mind the first six volumes of the *Florida Edition of the Works of Laurence Sterne,* so that one can now read Sterne's fictions, sermons, and letters in a format that provides the comfortableness of uniformity. At the same time, however, collections of letters, and especially, it seems, a collection of Sterne's letters, where almost every letter can be found to offer its own special textual problems, demands a certain flexibility in textual presentation not required by his other writings. The fact that many of the letters printed herein are holographs not immediately (if ever) intended for publication, while others are based on printed versions of quite varying authority and accuracy, necessitated a number of formatting decisions for a single printed edition; the alternative, a facsimile edition, did not seem appropriate, although at some point it might be a legitimate project, especially of the manuscript letters, if only to give us as much access to Sterne's handwriting as can possibly be gathered together in one place.

The letters appear in chronological order, as best we could establish it. For each letter we have supplied as much information as we could determine concerning the date—thus in the dateline we have often interpolated information, based on what Sterne has written, so that place, day, and the full date are all provided, with interpolations in square brackets; at times, of course, the information in the copy-text of the letter was insufficient to deduce additional information. We have not italicized any of the dateline, although at times Sterne seems to have drawn a line of underscoring; we have read such lines as marks of division (slashes), and have not reproduced them, neither after the date nor at any other division of the letter (e.g., after the salutation or the PS indicating a postscript).

The salutation is offered as in the copy-text, although we have almost uniformly set it on a separate line from the text; at times in both holographs and printed versions, the text begins on the same line as the salutation, but that is not Sterne's dominant habit.

We have tried to reproduce the texts available in manuscript with scrupulous faithfulness, indicating all the deletions, insertions, additions, scribal oddities, and the like. In transposing the manuscript to print, we used certain symbols to indicate the state of the manuscript:

< > a deletion from the text
~ ~ written over a deletion
∨∨ an insertion in the line of text
∧∧ an addition to the text
| end of the line
|| end of the page
? a conjectural reading

Sterne's long "s" and double "m" written as m̄ have been silently normalized. Obviously inadvertent repetitions of words have been silently emended; a dash at the end of one line and repeated at the beginning of the next line has been altered to one dash, the length of the longer of the two. We have tried to approximate Sterne's dash length, at least by providing 1em, 2em, and 3em lengths—and in a few cases, an even longer dash. Where Sterne opens or closes quoted or parenthetical material without a match, we have silently provided it where it seemed most appropriate. At times Sterne leaves a long space between the end of a sentence and the beginning of a new sentence, indicating perhaps a change of topic, or more likely a break in his writing time; we have indicated that space in this edition. Where Sterne has superscript letters to indicate currency, we have normalized them to standard type-size equivalents. We have retained all of the other superscript abbreviations he used, although we have omitted the periods he often included under them—they tend to interrupt the normal punctuation of the sentence.

We have indicated the end of a line (|) or page (||) only when doing so helps clarify the text. In her own letters (see appendix), Lydia Medalle often omits periods when her sentence and the line end together, and we have used the vertical to indicate the probable end of her sentence, especially where her new sentence begins with a lowercase letter, as was her wont. Ampersands have been preserved, along with Sterne's capitalization, although it is often difficult—if not impossible—to know Sterne's intention in this regard. We have tried to be accurate enough to avoid using [*sic*] after every odd spelling; if a word is misspelled, it is as it appears in the manuscript. No other substantive or accidental changes have been made to the readings of the manuscripts without being recorded in the collation list following each letter. When our reading of the manuscript differs from Curtis's reading, we have noted it in the same collation list with a *C*.

Where only a printed version of a letter exists, we have reproduced it as accurately as possible; the only silent substantive emendation we have made is to alter Medalle's "Anthony" to Sterne's spelling, "Antony," when referring to Hall-Stevenson. Where several printed versions of the same letter exist, we have tried to determine the version with the closest claim to the manuscript itself and have used it as our copy-text. Emendations to the printed copy-text have been noted in the collation list following each letter. Where Medalle uses an initial for a name, Curtis would often fill it in with bracketed letters: hence "Mrs. S[terne]"; we have instead simply printed the name, when obvious, without brackets. Most important, for both letters based on manuscripts and those based on printed versions, we have tried to make certain that our decisions concerning the text of each letter and its collation details are self-contained in the apparatus beneath each letter, in the collation itself, in the listing of previous publications, in the *Status* section, or in the annotations.

The letter closings are particularly troublesome because they are so often a function of the size of the writing paper being used and the space available at the bottom of the page. Still, because Sterne seems at times to have an intention in the divisions of his closing, we have imitated his manuscripts in their distinct line-division, placing his signature flush right and the lines above it progressively indented in a tier effect down to the signature. In printed versions, the closings seem more arbitrary, and we have not duplicated italics or the capitalization (or use of small caps) often used for his name, where Sterne did not customarily use either. Medalle uniformly has a period after her signature line, but we have omitted it.

We have silently altered Sterne's various indications of a postscript to "PS" without punctuation and set it flush left; the slant he sometimes includes to set off the text (sometimes misread as indicative of underscoring) has been ignored. Longer postscripts have been indented on a new line.

After the letter we have listed, first, the extra-textual items where they exist: *Address, Postmark, Docket,* and *Endorsement*. Following that we have an indication of the manuscript available (*MS*), the previous publication(s) of the letter (*Pub.*), and, if necessary, a *Status* section in which the textual problems of a particular letter are discussed at some length. We have indicated the appearance of all letters in Medalle and Curtis by letter number.

The collation follows this information. Each entry is keyed by superscript bold letters in the text; after the letter in the collation list there follows the relevant word or words in our text, followed by a bracket; to the right of the bracket are the alternative readings, the source(s) indicated by abbreviations (Medalle = *M;* Curtis = *C*), or a clear indication of the authority (*Cross-1925*); the sources for variant readings will all be found in the publication section above the collation. In instances where we are reading the same manuscript, all variants between our text and Curtis's text are noted, excepting variants in dash lengths, spacing between sentences (as noted above), and places where we have read emendations and deletions that he failed to record. We have tried, as did Curtis, accurately to reproduce all Sterne's elided openings and past-tense elisions, with or without apostrophes (i.e., 'tis or tis, griev'd or grievd), but have not included our different readings in the collation.

Annotations are keyed in the text by superscript numerals. The relevant word or words are provided to indicate the subject of the annotation. We have, as throughout the Florida edition, erred on the side of copiousness rather than conciseness, although we have tried to keep genealogical and antiquarian information to a minimum, while emphasizing the context for the letters provided by Sterne's own writings and by other authors of the same era, undergoing similar experiences. Hence, for example, our shadowing of Sterne's letters during his travels with Smollett's *Travels through France and Italy* (1766). As with the annotations in other volumes, we have held to a bare minimum citations without texts. In this regard, it was pleasant to find in Earl Miner's final posthumous publication, *Paradise Lost, 1668–1968: Three Centuries of Commentary* (Lewisburg: Bucknell University Press, 2004), a strong defense of the practice: "The second major innovation is provision in quotation of the passage cited rather than simply identifying a passage and leaving to the reader the task of discovering the passage referred to. . . . Modern readers of Milton, we believe, are highly unlikely to take the pains to verify the existence of a bare citation in an obscure work . . . ." So, too, modern readers of Sterne might not even feel compelled to return to *Tristram Shandy* when told there is a parallel passage in II.17. We have, instead, quoted the relevant passage.

We have consulted a variety of sources for the historical and social background of the 1760s, when most of the letters were written, but more and more found ourselves drawn to Horace Walpole's *Correspondence* and *Memoirs of King George II and King George III.* Sterne's encounter with the public life of the times was brief and rather superficial—he flamed across London and Paris and Florence and was far too soon extinguished. Somehow, ponderous historical analyses did not seem to capture his encounter as usefully as Walpole's magnificent—albeit biased—mixture of perceptive insight and popular gossip. We found a comment in Walpole for almost every occasion and every personality that Sterne thought fit to write about, an overlap that does not strike us as unexpected. When we consulted the *Oxford DNB,* we used the new edition of 2004–5, online. Similarly, *OED* references are to the online version. Classical sources are quoted from the Loeb Classical Library text and translations unless otherwise indicated.

We have translated all foreign language passages, with apologies to those for whom this was an unnecessary task. We particularly thank Anne Bandry and Brigitte Friant-Kessler for their advice in this, and also for their geographical expertise as we attempted to track Sterne though France and Italy on the basis, at times, of very confusing allusions to places and routes.

We are not happy with the number of unidentified personages remaining or the several occasions on which we admit to having no understanding of a passage in a letter. Letters are, of course, derived from immediate events, including the just preceding exchange of correspondence, and without sufficient context private allusions can often be undecipherable—and most especially when Sterne is writing to a friend like Hall-Stevenson and a shorthand language of hints and innuendo are sufficient for both writers to understand one another. We have tried to hold conjectures to a minimum, simply admitting to ignorance as occasion warranted.

144. *To David Garrick*

Text: Medalle

London, [Saturday,] March 16, 1765.

Dear Garrick[a]

I threatened you with a letter in one I wrote a few weeks ago to Foley, but (to my shame be it spoken) I lead such a life of dissipation I have never had a moment to myself which has not been broke in upon, by one engagement or impertinence or another—and as plots thicken towards the latter end of a piece, I find, unless I take pen and ink just now, I shall not be able to do it, till either I am got into the country, or you to the city.[1] You are teized and tormented too much by your correspondents, to return to us, and with accounts how much your friends, and how much your Theatre[2] wants you—so that I will not magnify either our loss or yours—but hope cordially to see you soon.—Since I wrote last I have frequently stept into your house—that is, as frequently as I could take the whole party, where I dined, along with me—This was but justice to you, as I walk'd in as a wit—but with regard to myself, I balanced the account thus—I am sometimes in my friend Garrick's[b] house, but he is always in Tristram Shandy's[3]—where my friends say he will continue (and I hope the prophecy true for my own immortality) even when he himself is no more.

I have had a lucrative winter's campaign here—Shandy sells well[4]—I am taxing the publick with two more volumes of sermons,[5] which will more than double the gains of Shandy—It goes into the world with a prancing list of *de toute la noblesse*[6]—which will bring me in three hundred pounds, exclusive of the sale of the copy—so that with all the contempt of money which *ma façon de penser*[7] has ever impress'd on me, I shall be rich in spite of myself: but I scorn you must know, in the high *ton*[8] I take at present, to pocket all this trash—I set out to lay a portion of it in the service of the world, in a tour round Italy, where I shall spring game, or the duce is in the dice.[9]—In the beginning of September I quit England, that I may avail myself of the time of vintage, when all nature is joyous,[10] and so saunter philosophically for a year or so, on the other side the Alps.—I hope your pilgrimages have brought Mrs. Garrick[a] and yourself back *à la fleur de jeunesse*[11]—May you both long feel the sweets of it, and your friends with you.—Do, dear friend, make my kindest wishes and compliments acceptable to the best and wisest of the daughters of Eve[12]—You shall ever believe and ever find me affectionately yours,

L. Sterne

MS: Not located.
Pub.: Medalle, no. 53; Curtis, no. 137.

[a]Garrick] G. *M* [b]Garrick's] ——'s *M*

1. I am got . . . the city] Sterne departed London in late March, soon after writing this letter, but his destination was Bath; he would not return to Coxwold until late in May (Cash, *LY* 206–17). For an account of the Garricks' sojourn on the continent, 1763–65, see George Winchester Stone, Jr., ed., *The Journal of David Garrick Describing His Visit to France and Italy in 1763* (New York: Modern Language Association of America, 1939), xiii–xiv; and *Letters of Garrick*, 1:xli–xlii. Both accounts agree that Garrick left London as the result of a disappointing 1762–63 season and stayed abroad from September 1763 (they departed on September 18, the day the new season opened, an obviously *dramatic* gesture) to April 1765. After a trip to Italy, they had returned to Paris in November 1764—Sterne is writing to them there.

2. your Theatre] Drury Lane Theatre, where Sterne had the freedom of the house (see letter 47). Cf. *Letters of Garrick,* xli: "After nearly fifteen years as the mainstay of Drury Lane, Garrick had exhausted himself and satiated the London audience"; and cf. the comments they quote from the *London Chronicle* (September 15–17, 1763, 270), ironically lamenting his departure (1:386, n. 4). The trip, they suggest, was very important to him: the French admired him greatly, and this helped make him "more of a conscious artist, a critic, with a sense of greater values. On his return to England his better acting was noticed by all his contemporaries" (xliii).

3. in Tristram Shandy's] Garrick in fact appears in *TS* four times: *TS,* III.12.213 ("And how did *Garrick* speak the soliloquy last night?"), III.24.246 ("my dear friend *Garrick,* whom I have so much cause to esteem and honour"), IV.7.333 ("O *Garrick!* what a rich scene of this would thy exquisite powers make!"), and VI.29.549 ("my dear friend *Garrick*"). The friendship hit a snag, however, soon after this letter; see letter 146.

4. Shandy sells well] See letter 141, n. 2.

5. two more volumes of sermons] Volumes III and IV of the *Sermons* appeared on January 18, 1766, "Price 5*s.* sewn, or 6*s.* bound" (*Public Advertiser*). There were some 690 subscribers, who paid a crown (5 shillings) each, which would have yielded more than £170. If all subscribers took one set only, which is not necessarily the case (see letter 151), the subscription would have brought in just over half of what Sterne anticipated. For his publisher, Sterne, as he had with *TS*, now went to Becket and Dehondt; but see letter 157, where he seems to contemplate a return to Dodsley's fold. William Strahan did the actual printing; his invoice reads "Sterne's Sermons Vols 3 and 4. 27½ Sheets No. 4000 @ £2:10:0 [=] 68:15:0" (British Library, Add. MSS. 48800, 153), so Sterne's profit from the subscriptions alone was not bad. For an account of the composition of these volumes, see *Sermons*, 5:4–5.

6. *de toute la noblesse*] All of the nobility. The list of subscribers is "prancing" indeed: one can find more than 130 persons of title, including six dukes, many members of parliament and the military establishment, fellow clerics, and some very well known names: Crébillon, Diderot, Garrick, d'Holbach, Reynolds, and Voltaire. Foley, Panchaud, and William Combe also subscribed. But, as Cash, *LY*, 214, notes, where six bishops subscribed in 1760, none did for this installment—the quarrel with Warburton would seem to have taken its toll.

7. *ma façon de penser*] My way of thinking. Sterne's correspondence would seem to argue in quite another direction, even if we justify his concern about money by pointing to the two establishments he was now financing. At best, we might suggest that Sterne shared an attitude toward wealth with most of the educated elite of the eighteenth century; in sermon 13 ("Duty of setting bounds to our desires") he criticizes "the cynical stale trick of haranguing against the goods of fortune,—they were never intended to be talked out of the world.—But as virtue and true wisdom lie in the middle of extremes,—on one hand, not to neglect and despise riches, so as to forget ourselves,—and on the other, not to pursue and love them so, as to forget God;—to have them sometimes in our heads,—but always something more important in our hearts" (*Sermons* 4:130–31).

8. high *ton*] See letter 86, n. 6. *OED*'s first entry for the separate use of *ton* is dated 1769, from *Lloyd's Evening Post:* "The present fashionable *Ton* (a word used at present to express every thing that's fashionable) . . . ."

9. I shall . . . the dice] One hopes Sterne means a successful search for materials for his fiction. The second clause is proverbial; see Tilley, D250, and *ODEP*, 182 (*the Devil is in the dice*).

10. the time . . . joyous] See letter 95, n. 4.

11. *à la fleur de jeunesse*] To the flower of youth; as Little and Kahrl point out in their introduction, "Mrs. Garrick suffered a severe attack of rheumatism [in

the summer of 1764]; next Garrick contracted a near-fatal fever in Munich . . ." (*Letters of Garrick* xlii).

12. daughters of Eve] For Eva Maria Garrick, see letter 81, n. 1. Cf. *TS*, VIII.8.664: "A daughter of Eve, for such was widow Wadman, and 'tis all the character I intend to give of her—"; *Sermons*, 4:179, and letter 210.

145. *To Thomas Astle*[1]

Text: Ms.

[London, Saturday, March 23, 1765][2]

My dear Sir

a perpetual round of engagements, wherein, every moment of my time has been mortgaged—together with Some Days Illness, the natural fruits of so much dissipation[3]—ha<s>~d~[a] put out of my power, what was so oft in my head—to wait upon You—I will do my self the pleasure of being <at Y>~an~ hour or two with You on Tuesday morning—being determined at noon to set out for Bath for a week to break this magic Circle—If I sh^{d} not be with You by half an hour after nine—will You suppose, I have been obliged to decamp sooner—& will You suffer me to see You upon my return?

Be assured of the Sense I have of y^{r} great civility to me, & that

I am dear Sir
most truely Yr
obliged
L. Sterne

Saturday

Address: To / T. Astle Esqre

Endorsed: Tristram Shandy / to Mr Astle / [in another hand:] Revd Mr Sterne (Tristram Shandy.) / No. 120.

MS: Houghton Library, Harvard University, Amy Lowell Collection.

Pub.: Cash, *LY*, 361–62.

[a]ha<s>~d~] has *LY*

1. *Thomas Astle*] The *Oxford DNB* slightly revises Cash's account, *LY*, 362, n. 1 (derived from the original entry):

> Thomas Astle (1735–1803), archivist and collector of books and manuscripts, was born on 22 December 1735 at Yoxall, on the edge of Needwood Forest, Staffordshire, the eldest son of Daniel Astle (*d.* 1775), keeper of the forest . . . . He was perhaps educated at Eton College. He was articled to an attorney at Yoxall, but, despite having lost one eye in an accident at school, chose instead to spend his life in the world of ancient manuscripts and records.
>
> In 1761 Astle was engaged by the British Museum to compile the index to the catalogue of the Harley manuscripts; he was probably also responsible for the long and very useful preface. In the same year that this was published, 1763, he was elected FSA; he was elected FRS in 1766.

His chief work, *The Origin and Progress of Writing,* appeared in 1784; it was, again quoting *Oxford DNB,* "an authoritative source for the history of writing well into the nineteenth century, and was last reprinted in 1876." Astle's interest in Sterne, or Sterne's in Astle, remains unknown, beyond this rather uninformative letter; perhaps Astle wanted to show him the copy of Ernulphus's curse in the Harleian collection (see *TS* 2:952).

2. Date] Cash, *LY*, 362, writes: "(. . . Since this letter was written on a Saturday before a Tuesday when Sterne planned to set out for Bath, it can be tentatively dated 23 March 1765. The exact date of Sterne's departure is not known, but he was planning to leave by the 23rd. On that date Elizabeth Montagu wrote to her sister in Bath, Sarah Scott, introducing Sterne, who would soon be arriving [Huntington Library MS, MO 5819].)"

3. dissipation] Cf. letter 144, where one week earlier Sterne had admitted to Garrick his "life of dissipation." Lord Fauconberg's daughter, Lady Mary Belasyse, wrote to her father on February 25, 1765: "I saw Mr. Sterne yesterday, he looks rather better than he did, has prodigious spirits, & leads a life of perpetual Rackett, I wonder how he bears it" (*LY* 204–5; quoting the Wombwell Papers, North Yorkshire Record Office, Northallerton).

146. *To David Garrick*

Text: Ms.

Bath—[Saturday,] Ap—6—1765

I scalp You![1]—my dear Garrick! my dear friend!—foul befall the man who hurts a hair of y[r] head!—and so full was I of that very Sentiment,—that my Letter had not been sent to the Office[a2] ten minutes, before <I> My heart smote me; & I sent to recall it—but fail'd. You are sadly to blame, Shandy! for this; quoth I, ˅&˅ leaning with my head on my hand, as I recriminated upon my false delicasy in the affair—Garricks nerves (if he has any left) are as fine and delicately spun, as thy own—his Sentiments as honest & friendly—thou knowest, Shandy, that he loves thee—why wilt thou hazard him a moment's pain? Puppy! Fool, Coxcomb, Jack Asse &c &c—& so I ballanced the acc^{t} to Y^{r} favour, before I rec^{d} it drawn up in *your Way*—I say *your way*—for it is not stated so much to y^{r} honour & Credit, as I had pass'd the acc^{t} before—for twas a most lamented Truth, that I never rec^{d} one of the Letters, your friendship meant me—except <at>—whilst in Paris——O! how I congratulate you<r> for the Anxiety the world <c> has & continues to be under, for y^{r} return—Return—return to the few who love you and the thousands who admire You—The moment you set y^{r} foot upon y^{r} Stage—Mark! I tell it You—by some magick, irresisted power, every Fibre ab^{t} y^{r} heart will vibrate afresh & as strong & feelingly as ever: Nature with Glory at her back, will <foment the f> light up the torch within you—& There is enough of it left, to heat and enlighten the World these many many, many Years.[3]

God[b] be praised! I utter it from my Soul, that y^{r} Lady, & my Minerva <?> is in a condition to Walk to Windsor[4]—full rapturously will I lead the graceful Pilgrim to the Temple, where I w$^{\langle d\rangle ll}$ sacrifise ∧with∧ the purest Insense, to her—but you may worship with me—or not—twil make no difference either in the truth or Warmth of my Devotion——<I> still, (after all I have seen)—I still maintain her peerlesse.

Powel![5]—Lord God![c]—give me some one with less smoak & more fire—There are, who like the Pharisees, still think they shall be heard for *much* speaking[6]—come—come away my dear Garrick, <—>~&~ teach us another Lesson—

adieu!—I love you dearly—and Y^{r} Lady better.—not hobbihorsically—but most sentimentally & affectionately.

for I am Y^{rs} (that is, if you never say another word ab^{t} this scoundrel 20 p^{ds})[d][7]

with al' the Sentim^{ts} of <f>~L~ove & friendliness[e] you deserve from me—

L. Sterne——

I am playing the devil at Bath—shall be in Town to hail y^{r} coming. __[f][8]

Address: A Monsr / Monsieur Garrick / chez Monsr Foley Banquier / rue St Sauveur / a Paris. / par Calais
Postmark: 8 AP BATH PD
MS: National Library of Scotland, MS. 582, no. 593.
Pub.: Medalle, no. 54; Curtis, no. 138.

[a]sent to the Office] put into the post-office *M* [b]God] Heaven *M* [c]Lord God!] good Heav'n! *M* [d]ab^{t} this scoundrel 20 p^{ds})] about ——) *M* [e]friendliness] friendship *M* [f]postscript] *om. M*

1. I scalp You] Cash, *LY,* 214, reconstructs the occasion of this letter: "The difficulty arose over the £20 which Sterne had borrowed from Garrick when he went abroad in 1762 [see letter 76]. . . . When a gentleman brought Garrick the news that Sterne was seriously ill in Paris [in the spring of 1764], Garrick got worried about the money owed him. He wrote to George Colman from Rome on 11 April 1764 . . . [see above, letter 126, n. 7]. Hearing nothing, Garrick, now in Paris, wrote several times to Sterne in London. The letters miscarried, said Sterne. When one finally reached him, Sterne was so offended by the tone that he scribbled an angry reply. Garrick shot back that Sterne was scalping him." This account gains additional credence from Garrick's reputation for avariciousness (see Boswell, *Life of Johnson* 770, 925), although, as noted earlier (letter 76, n. 3), £20 was a considerable sum in Sterne's day.

2. the Office] Medalle's emendation to "post-office," where letters were franked and collected for the next post, helps clarify Sterne's sentence; posts were run three times a week, and Sterne's letter went out with the Monday post on April 8.

3. Return—return . . . many Years] Garrick's first appearance after his continental absence, as Benedick in *Much Ado about Nothing,* on November 14, 1765, was a success. Thomas Davies, *Memoirs of the Life of Garrick* (1781), 2:98–99, describes the occasion: "The joy of the audience was expressed, not in the usual methods of clapping of hands and clattering of sticks, but in loud shouts and huzzas." It was a command performance, and, despite his fears of being ill-received, "he was given

a cordial and enthusiastic welcome, with the King in the royal box and the house crammed" (*Letters of Garrick* 2:478, n. 2). Indeed Sterne's comments are prescient in that Garrick's theatrical career reached new heights after his European excursion.

In the midst of Sterne's compliment is his familiar language of fibers and vibrations; see *ASJ,* 6:370, n. to 153.6–9; and 6:372, n. to 155.15, where, significantly enough, Johnson is quoted on Addison's *Cato:* "its hopes and fears communicate no vibration to the heart." Sterne's language of sensibility was not a private vocabulary but the discourse of the age, and most particularly in relation to theatrical performance.

4. Minerva . . . Walk to Windsor] Minerva is the Roman goddess of wisdom and patroness of the arts. Sterne's "walk to Windsor" may take into account the Garricks' home in Hampton (Fuller House), on the Thames, some twelve miles west of the heart of London; a walk from there to Windsor would be about eight miles further west.

5. Powel] See *Letters of Garrick,* 1:388, nn. 2–3: "William Powell (1735–1769), the actor, whom Garrick had met shortly before his departure. Recognizing his abilities, Garrick had carefully coached him, hoping that he might in some measure serve to compensate for his own absence. Powell proved a brilliant success, performing no less than eighteen capital parts during his first season at Drury Lane. Powell made his debut at Drury Lane on Oct. 8 as Philaster in Colman's alteration of the tragedy by Beaumont and Fletcher. His triumph on this occasion rivaled the initial appearances of Garrick and Barry." In March 1765, Sterne could have seen him play Lear and Othello; Curtis, 237, n. 2, quotes Davies, 2:93, who qualifies his opinion that "few actors have for these twenty years displayed such talents for tragick passion as Powell" with the observation that Powell also had "an inclination sometimes to rant and bluster, and sometimes a propensity to whine and blubber." Still, Powell was a worthy rival of Garrick, and Sterne's comments have a bit of sycophancy about them—he is, after all, trying to repair the damage caused by his intemperate letter, now unfortunately lost.

6. Pharisees . . . *much* speaking] See Matthew 6:7: "But when ye pray, use not vain repetitions, as the heathen do: for they think that they shall be heard for their much speaking"; Sterne probably misremembered the verse, rather than deliberately altering it.

7. if you never . . . 20 p^{ds}] As indicated, Medalle, typically enough, omits this phrase. Cash, *LY,* 214–15, suggests that Sterne probably paid the debt, but also that the friendship between them cooled after this exchange: "he and Sterne ceased writing to one another, so far as we know, and no further compliments to Garrick appeared in Sterne's books. The friendship, such as it was, had grown cold."

8. y[r] coming] As Curtis notes, 238, n. 5, the Garricks reached London on Thursday, April 25, 1765 (*London Evening Post* for April 25–27). For Sterne's time at Bath, see letter 148.

147. *To Robert Foley*

Text: Medalle

Bath, [Monday,] April 15, 1765.

My dear Foley[a]

My wife tells me she has drawn for one hundred pounds, and 'tis fit that you should be paid it that minute—the money is now in Becket's hands—send me, my dear Foley[a] my account, that I may discharge the balance to this time, and know what to leave in your hands.—I have made a good campaign of it this year in the field of the literati—my two volumes of Tristram, and two of sermons, which I shall print very soon,[1] will bring me a considerable sum.—Almost all the nobility in England honour me with their names, and 'tis thought it will be the largest, and most splendid list which ever pranced before a book, since subscriptions came into fashion.[2]—Pray present my most sincere compliments to lady H[3]——whose name I hope to insert with many others.—As so many men of genius favour me with their names also, I will quarrel with Mr. Hume[b], and call him deist, and what not, unless I have his name too.[4]—My love to Lord W.[5]——Your name, Foley[a] I have put in as a free-will offering of my labours—your list of subscribers you will send—'tis but a crown for sixteen sermons[6]—Dog cheap! but I am in quest of honour, not money.—Adieu, adieu,—believe me, dear Foley[a]

Yours truly,
L. Sterne

MS: Not located.
Pub.: Medalle, no. 55; Curtis, no. 139.

[a]Foley] F. / F— *M* [b]Hume] H——e *M*

1. two volumes . . . very soon] See letters 141, n. 2, and 144, n. 5, for details concerning these publications. Sterne's optimism about publishing the sermons "very soon" was misplaced; they did not appear for another nine months.

2. subscriptions came into fashion] See letter 144, nn. 5 and 6. Curtis, 239, n. 3, mentions that Sterne's list was "greatly surpassed by that of Zachary Grey in his edition of *Hudibras*, published in 1744." A few years after Sterne's death, *Antiquity; or, The Wise Instructor*, compiled by John Bodenham and Nicholas Ling, was published in Bristol in 1770, and again in York in 1773; the 1773 edition lists 3,500 subscribers to the two editions!

3. lady H] *1776* has "lady H—— whose" but *1775* is as here; as with "Lord W." below ("Lord W——" in *1776*), we have taken the dash as punctuation rather than an indication of missing characters. Curtis, 239, n. 4, suggests Isabella, Lady Hertford (1726–1782), who with Lord Hertford would subscribe to *Sermons* in 1769, but not to this installment. We really have no way of knowing if other Lady H's were in Foley's circle of acquaintance during this time, but the Duchess of Hamilton (1733–1790), Lady Caroline Hervey (1736–1819), Lady Dorothea Hotham (*d.* 1798), Lady Elizabeth Howard (1746–1813), and Lady Lucy Wentworth Howard (*d.* 1771) all subscribed in 1766; Foley, the person one did banking with when traveling on the continent, might well have been acquainted with them all. And it is at least possible that Sterne's letter to Lady Hervey (letter 156)—assuming, as Curtis and we do, that it is not a Combe forgery—is a thank-you note indicating Foley's success in soliciting her subscription.

4. his name too] David Hume did not subscribe.

5. Lord W.] Curtis, 239, n. 6, suggests Hugh Percy (1742–1817), Lord Warkworth, who did indeed subscribe. If we follow the long tradition that identifies the recipient of letter 149 with his wife, Lady Anne Stuart, it would mean that a week after sending his "love" to the husband, he was flirtatiously courting the wife; that is not, of course, impossible, but see our discussion of letter 149, *Status*. Lord Viscount Wenman (1742–1800) also subscribed in 1766; he had completed his studies at Oxford in 1760 and married in 1766—possibly he was on the Grand Tour in 1763–64, and Sterne had met him in Paris. And we might also suggest Lord Viscount Weymouth (1734–1796), who subscribed in 1760, and who was, according to Walpole, *Memoirs . . . George III*, an "inconsiderable debauched young man . . . but so ruined by gaming, that the moment before [being named Governor of Ireland in 1765] . . . he was setting out for France to avoid his creditors" (2:154–55).

6. sixteen sermons] Volumes III and IV contain only twelve sermons.

148. *To Mrs. F——*[1]

Text: Letter Book

[?London, April 1765]

To M^{rs} F——

——and pray what occasion, (either real or ideal,) have You Madam, to write[a] ∨a∨ ∧Letter∧ from Bath to Town, to enquire whether <[two illegible words]>[2] Tristram Shandy is a married Man or no?[3]—and You may ask in Your turn, if you please, What occasion has Tristram Shandy gentleman to sit down and answer it?

for the first, dear Lady (for we are begining to be a little acquainted)[4] You must answer to your own conscience—as I shall the 2^{d}, to mine; for from an honest attention to my internal workings in that part where the Conscience of a gallant man resides,[5] I perceive plainly, that such fair advances from so fair a Princesse—(freer & freer still) are not to be withstood by one of Tristram Shandy's make and complexion—Why my dear Creature (—we shall soon be got up to the very climax of familiarity)—If T. Shandy had but one single spark of galantry-fire[b] in any one apartment of his whole Tenement,[6] so kind a tap at the dore would have <lighted> ∧call'd∧ it <up>~all~ ∧forth∧ to have <seen> ∧enquired∧ What gentle Dame it was that stood without——good God! is it You Mrs F....! what a fire have You lighted up! tis enough to set the whole house in a flame

"*If Tristram Shandy was a single Man*"——(o dear!)—"from the Attacks of Jack, Dick[c] and Peter I am quite secure"—(this by the by Madam, requires proof)—But my dear Tristram! *If* thou wast a single Man—bless me, Mad^{m}, this is downright wishing for I swear it is in the *optative Mood* & no other—well! but my dear T. Shandy wast thou a single Man, I should not know what to say—& may I be Tristram'd to death, if I should know what to do———

do[d] You know my dear Angel[e] (for you may feel I am creeping still closer to you and before I get to the end of my letter I forsee the freedome betwixt us will be kept within no decent bounds)—do You know I say to what a devil of a shadow of a tantalizing Helpmate[7] you must have fallen a victime on that supposision—why my most adorable! except that I am tolerably strait made, and near six feet high, and that my Nose, (whatever as an historian I say to the contrary),[8] is an inch at least longer than most of my neighbours—except that—That I am a two footted animal without one Lineament[9] of Hair of the beast upon me, totally spiritualized out of all form for conubial purposes[10]——let me whisper, I am now 44[11]—and shall this time twelve-month be 45—That I am moreover of a thin, <?>∧dry—∧, hectic, unperspirable habit of Body—so sublimated and rarified in all my parts[12] That a Lady of yr <penetration> Wit[13] would not give a brass farthing for a dozen such: next May when I am at my best, You shall try me—tho I tell You before hand I have not an ounce & a half of carnality about me—& what is that for so long a Journey?

In such a Land of scarsity, I well know, That Wit profiteth nothing—all I have to say is, That as I shd have little else to give, what I had, should be most plenteously shed upon you.—but then, the devil an' all is, You are a Wit Yrself, and tho' there might be abundance of peace so long as the *Moon* endured[14]—Yet when that luscious period was run out, I fear we shd never agree one day to an end;∧—∧there would be such ∧Satyre &∧ sarcasm <&>~——~scoffing & flouting—rallying & reparteeing of it, <&>~———~thrusting & parrying in one dark corner or another, There wd be nothing but mischief———but then—as we shd be two people of excellent Sense, we shd make up matters as fast as they went wrong—What tender reconciliations!—<?O> byf heaven! it would be a Land of promise—milk & Honey![15]

—Honey! aye there's the rub[16]—
——I once got a surfiet of it
I have the honour
to be with the utmost
regard
Madm Yr most
obedt humble Servt
T. Shandy.

MS: Letter Book, Pierpont Morgan Library, New York.
Pub.: Cross, *Life* (1925), 2:243–45; Curtis, no. 140.

[a]to write] to a write *MS* [b]galantry-fire] galanty-fire *MS* [c]Jack, Dick] Jack | Dick *MS* [d]do—— ¶do] *MS, Cross-1925;* do—do *C* [e]Angel] Angle *MS* [f]<?O> by] *MS;* O by *C*

1. *Mrs. F*——] In the *Letter Book,* this letter is attributed—in a hand not Sterne's—"To Mrs. Ferguson of Bath—1765? ('my witty widow')," but as Cross, *Life* (1925), 2:243, indicates, "She could not have been Mrs. Ferguson, for Sterne had been acquainted with that 'witty widow' for many years. . . . Was she Mrs. Fenton? and did Sterne first meet her at Bath? The questions may be asked but not answered." Curtis, 241, n. 1, refers us to letter 41 (see n. 1; cf. letters 63, n. 1, and 127, n. 1), where he had indicated the difficulty of identifying Sterne's several Mrs. F's. Cash, *LY,* 211, makes no effort to identify the recipient of this letter, pointing out also that "we cannot know whether it is a copy of a letter Sterne actually posted or some literary exercise or fantasy. Nevertheless, it gives us a notion of the comic pruriency of which he was capable . . . ." Finally, as New and Day point out apropos the Marquesina di F*** (*ASJ* 6:310, n. to 77.15), "Sterne's female admirers had an uncomfortable penchant for being named F——."

Whoever the recipient, both Curtis, 238, n. 4, and Cash, *LY,* 206–8, make much of Sterne's playing the bachelor at Bath, based primarily on correspondence between Elizabeth Montagu and her sister, the novelist Sarah Scott. Montagu had written to her, introducing Sterne as a man "full of the milk of human kindness, harmless as a child, but often a naughty boy, and a little apt to dirty his *frock.*" This warning was, at the beginning, insufficient to prevent Scott from enjoying Sterne's company, even his wooing of her companion, Mrs. Cutts. But Sterne seems to have overplayed his hand, and by April 30, Montagu was writing to Scott that she was "ashamed to hold long converse" with him, and had more or less not been "at home" to him on his return to London. Curtis provides extensive passages from Montagu's letters. Finally, we might call attention to another document in the *Letter Book,* Sterne's transcription of a coy letter supposedly received from an admirer at Bath (see appendix, letter xviii).

2. two illegible words] Curtis indicates the deletion with "[the]" but clearly there are two words, separated by the end of the line. One might see "she | shall" or, less likely, "the | auth[or]" or yet other alternatives, but Sterne's overscoring has made any certainty impossible.

3. a married Man or no] The question of Tristram's marital status is raised early and comically in *TS,* I.18.56: "I must beg leave, before I finish this chapter, to enter a caveat in the breast of my fair reader;—and it is this:——Not to take it absolutely for granted from an unguarded word or two which I have dropp'd in it,——'That I am a married man.'"

4. dear Lady . . . acquainted] Sterne plays self-consciously with this motif of increasing familiarity or intimacy, commenting each time on his encroachment, as the century would have labeled his advances: "dear Lady," "Princesse," "dear Creature," and, finally, "dear Angel." See also letter 149, "O my dear lady, etc."

5. where the . . . man resides] Sterne's bawdiness here is obvious, but he had spoken sharply against just such "gallantry" in "Abuses of conscience": "A man shall be vicious and utterly debauched in his principles; . . . shall live shameless, in the open commission of a sin which no reason or pretence can justify;—a sin, by which, contrary to all the workings of humanity, he shall ruin for ever the deluded partner of his guilt;—rob her of her best dowry . . . . Surely, you will think conscience must lead such a man a troublesome life . . ." (*TS* II.17.148–49).

6. his whole Tenement] A commonplace for the body, usually, as in Dryden's famous phrase, "Tenement of Clay"; cf. *TS,* I.23.83: "the tenements of their souls" and n. to the passage, 3:120, n. to 83.13. "Galantry-fire" seems to be Sterne's invention.

7. Helpmate] Cf. *BJ,* 172: "O my Bramine! my Friend! my——Help-mate!—for that . . . is the Lot mark'd out for thee . . . ." Sterne had originally written "my future wife"; see *ASJ,* 6:507, t.n. to 172.15. "Helpmate" has its origin, of course, in Genesis 2:18, the creation of Eve as "an help meet" for Adam.

8. whatever . . . to the contrary] The "history" of Tristram includes the information that during his birthing, Dr. Slop "with his vile instruments . . . crushed his nose . . . as flat as a pancake to his face" (*TS* III.27.253). In light of the equation of nose and phallus in *TS,* Sterne seems eager to set the record straight.

9. Lineament] Cf. *BJ,* 212: "tell me, have I varied in any one Lineament, from the first Sitting—to this last . . . ." *OED* (s.v., 1.b): "A minute portion, a trace . . . Obs."

10. totally spiritualized . . . purposes] Cf. *ASJ,* 128, where Yorick declares his innocence with the *grisset* by asserting that he has paid "as many a poor soul has *paid* before me for an act he *could* not do, or think of." In an extensive note to this passage (6:355–56), New and Day suggest it marks that tendency in Sterne's life and writings neatly summed up by James A. Work: "with a curiously perverse and possibly self-revelatory sense of the incongruous [Sterne] grins again and again over sexual impotence, the suspicion of which hovers like a dubious halo over the head of every Shandy male, including the bull" (introduction to *Tristram Shandy*

[Odyssey Press, 1940], lx). We should recall that in the just published volume VII of *TS,* Tristram stands "garters in my hand," reflecting on a bout of impotency (VII.29.624); and in *BJ,* he will assure Eliza that, despite being treated for venereal disease, he has had "no commerce whatever with the Sex—not even with my wife . . . these 15 years" (176.28ff.). See below, n. 12.

11. I am now 44] The "*optative Mood*": Sterne was 52.

12. That I am . . . my parts] Cf. *BJ,* 180: "I shall be sublimated to an etherial Substance by the time my Eliza sees me—she must be sublimated and uncorporated too, to be able to see me—but I was always transparent & a Being easy to be seen thro' . . . ." And see *TS,* I.11.27, where Yorick is said to have a character that exhibits "as mercurial and sublimated a composition . . . as the kindliest climate could have engendered."

13. a Lady of y[r] <penetration> Wit] Cf. *ASJ,* 74–75: "she had a quick black eye, and shot through two such long and silken eye-lashes with such penetration, that she look'd into my very heart and reins." Sterne's boldness fails him here, but he returns to the notion in letter 177, where Elizabeth Vesey is complimented as "the most penetrating of her sex." M. New makes much of this in "Proust's Influence on Sterne: Remembrance of Things to Come," *MLN* 103 (1988): 1038: "Perhaps Sterne's major insight into the nature of human desire is the idea that the most satisfying human union is achieved when the female penetrates and the male receives."

14. abundance of peace . . . endured] See Psalm 72:7: "In his days shall the righteous flourish; and abundance of peace so long as the moon endureth."

15. we sh[d] never . . . Honey] This entire passage is based on *TS,* III.20.229—were this letter not in Sterne's hand, we would suspect a Combe usurpation of a Shandean text. Given an abundance of wit, Tristram argues, "we should never agree amongst ourselves, one day to an end:——there would be so much satire and sarcasm,——scoffing and flouting, with raillying and reparteeing of it,——thrusting and parrying in one corner or another,——there would be nothing but mischief amongst us." On the other hand, "as we should all of us be men of great judgment, we should make up matters as fast as ever they went wrong . . . milk and honey,——'twould be a second land of promise." Interestingly enough, Sterne's two primary alterations for turning the passage into a billet doux is to modify "corner" with "dark" and add "tender reconciliations." "Milk and honey" is a biblical commonplace, although Sterne seems to subvert the phrase; see next note.

16. there's the rub] *Hamlet,* III.i.65 (cf. letter 131, n. 9). Sterne's meaning here is obscure, perhaps intentionally; is he referring to a surfeit of judgment? Or of sexual contact that resulted in sexual malfunction? It is the same question that hovers over his affair with Eliza.

149. *To Lady P.*

Text: Medalle

Mount Coffee-house,[1]
Tuesday 3 o'Clock. [?April 23, 1765]

There is a strange mechanical effect produced in writing a billet-doux within a stone-cast of the lady who engrosses the heart and soul of an inamorato—for this cause (but mostly because I am to dine in this neighbourhood) have I, Tristram Shandy, come forth from my lodgings to a coffee-house the nearest I could find to my dear Lady ———[a]'s house, and have called for a sheet of gilt paper, to try the truth of this article of my creed—Now for it—

O my dear lady—what a dishclout of a soul hast thou made of me?[2]—I think, by the bye, this is a little too familiar an introduction, for so unfamiliar a situation as I stand in with you—where heaven knows, I am kept at a distance—and despair of getting one inch nearer you, with all the steps and windings I can think of to recommend myself to you—Would not any man in his senses run diametrically from you—and as far as his legs would carry him, rather than thus causelessly, foolishly, and fool-hardily expose himself afresh—and afresh, where his heart and his reason tells him he shall be sure to come off loser, if not totally undone?—Why would you tell me you would be glad to see me?—Does it give you pleasure to make me more unhappy—or does it add to your triumph, that your eyes and lips have turned a man into a fool, whom the rest of the town is courting as a wit?—I am a fool—the weakest, the most ductile, the most tender fool, that ever woman tried the weakness of—and the most unsettled in my purposes and resolutions of recovering my right mind.—It is but an hour ago, that I kneeled down and swore I never would come near you—and after saying my Lord's Prayer for the sake of the close, of not being led into temptation—out I sallied like any Christian hero, ready to take the field against the world, the flesh, and the devil; not doubting but I should finally trample them all down under my feet[3]—and now am I got so near you—within this vile stone's cast of your house—I feel myself drawn into a vortex, that has turned my brain upside downwards, and though I had purchased a box ticket to carry me to Miss ******* benefit,[4] yet I know very well, that was a single line directed to me, to let me know Lady ———[a] would be alone at seven, and suffer me to spend the evening with her, she would infallibly see every thing verified I have told her.—I dine at Mr. C——r's in Wigmore-street,[5] in this neighbourhood, where I shall stay till seven, in hopes you purpose to put me to this proof. If[b] I hear nothing by that time I shall conclude you are better disposed of—and shall take a sorry hack, and sorrily jogg on to the play—Curse on the word. I know nothing but sorrow—except this one thing, that I love you (perhaps foolishly, but)

most sincerely,

L. Sterne

MS: Not located.

Pub.: Medalle, no. 110; Curtis, no. 141.

Status: Letters 149 and 150 are placed together here, as in Curtis, although both their addressees and their dates are still very much in question. The identification of Medalle's "Lady P." as Lady Anne Stuart (*b.* 1746) is a long-standing one; Fitzgerald, *Life* (1896; rpt. ed., *Works* [1904], 2:115), says there can be "no reasonable doubt," and Cross, Curtis, and Cash all have accepted the identification, even though, as Cash notes, after her marriage to Lord Warkworth in July 1764 (see above, letter 147, n. 5), Lady Anne referred to herself as Lady Warkworth until October 1766, when her husband was created Lord Percy and she changed accordingly. Hence we must assume, given the 1765 dating, that the original was addressed to Lady Warkworth, but that Medalle learned that she was now Lady Percy and thus altered the manuscript reading to Lady P.

Two arguments can be made to support this identification: first, the subsequent career of Lady Warkworth/Percy as an unfaithful wife, and second, her husband's name (as Lord Warkworth) on the 1766 subscription list (though her own name did not appear). Appeals to these lists are, however, as noted previously, a two-edged sword. For example, Lady Lepell Phip[p]s (1723–1780), daughter of Lord Hervey (Pope's Sporus) and wife of Constantine Phipps (*c.*1722–1775), of Mulgrave Castle, Yorkshire, also subscribed in 1766. Their son was in the Beauchamp circle in Paris in 1764 (see letter 130, n. 15), which may have led to Sterne's introduction to Lady Phipps in London; Sterne recounts a story about his conduct at her table in letter 152. (He names her as "*Lady*

Lepel," and Combe as "the late Lady Mulgrave," but in the subscription list for 1766, she is listed as "Lady Lepele Phips.")

We also find in that list Lady Anna Maria Palmer, Lady Pole, second wife of Sir John Pole (*d.* 1766); nothing more is known of her except that she not only subscribed in 1766, but again, and for *two* sets, in 1769. Also worth mentioning is Elizabeth Spencer, Lady Pembroke (1737–1831), who is not listed, but her husband, Henry Herbert, Earl Pembroke, is, both in 1766 and for *ASJ*. A year earlier (May 1764) she had been involved in her husband's scandal, according to Walpole, *Memoirs . . . George III*, 2:49: "Lord Pembroke, one of the wildest young men of the times, had been dismissed from the King's Bedchamber for debauching and eloping with a young lady of distinction, though married to a more beautiful woman, sister of the Duke of Marlborough." In her "sad story" are elements that certainly would have appealed to Sterne.

With these alternative possibilities in mind, we can return to Lady Warkworth/Percy. Curtis, 243, n. 1, noting first that Sterne may have met her at the York races in August 1764, provides the details of the behavior that elevated her to primacy as a candidate: "Possessing great charm of person, she was, as Lady Caroline Lamb might have said of her, 'mad, bad, and dangerous to know.' She quarrelled with her husband and mother-in-law, suffered discovery of letters from admirers, and in March 1768 brought disaster and banishment about her ears by making an assignation . . . with a certain Mr. F—— [!], telling him 'he might come with safety, for that her Lord was to be out of Town the whole day' . . . . Because of an intrigue with a young gentleman of Cambridge Lord Percy divorced her in 1779." Whether or not this well-documented, infamous history (*Town and Country Magazine* [1772] called her "a notoriously promiscuous adulteress" [*Oxford DNB*]) makes her a likely candidate for Sterne's advances remains the question; it is worth noting that she was only 19 years old in 1765, while Lady Pembroke was 28, a somewhat more likely age for seduction by a man of 52—and especially a seduction by means of the sentimentalism of this letter.

Curtis, 245–46, on the basis of this letter, makes Lady Warkworth/Percy the addressee of letter 150, which he is able to date with some certainty: "The fact that the flirtatious tone of the letter resembles that of the letter addressed in Apr. of this year to Lady Warkworth leads me to believe it was written to her . . . ." The fact is, however, that the tone is quite different, one plaintive, the other playful. The letters would seem to have little to do with one another except that the dating, if correctly argued, does put them in some proximity.

The date of letter 149 is of particular importance because of the malicious use made of it by Thackeray, *English Humorists* (1851; New York: Thomas Y. Crowell, 1902), 148. Dating it April 21, 1767, based on the allusion to the benefit performance (and its position in the Medalle edition), he attacked Sterne unmercifully for deceiving *poor* Eliza. Cross, in *Letters,* 2:82, argued that Sterne was too ill to write it in the spring of 1767, and that he was abroad in 1766. Hence, 1765 was the probable year, and on April 23 of that year, benefits were given for two unmarried actresses, Miss Wright at Drury Lane and Miss Wilford at Covent Garden: "The seven stars correspond to the letters in the name of Miss Wilford. She was a beautiful dancer who made her first appearance as an actress on that evening" (quoting John Genest, *History of the Stage,* vol. v). This supposition is supported by the fact that Sterne would not have needed to buy a ticket at Drury Lane, since he had the freedom of the house. Curtis accepts this date without question; Cash, *LY,* 211–12, n. 75, suggests that months other than April need to be considered, and that the benefit seasons from 1760, 1761, and 1766 are also possible, although he admits that even if we found some likely candidates, the results would be inconclusive.

Based on internal evidence, Curtis dates letter 150 in the period of May 6–13, 1765, and, as mentioned, links it to letter 149 on the basis of style. While the two letters are quite different to our ears, it nevertheless is apparent that Sterne's springtime in London and Bath in 1765 was, as he himself called it, "a life of dissipation" (letter 144). Without evidence to establish a more definitive dating for letter 149, it seems to find its appropriate niche between letters 148 and 150, all three forming sufficient documentation of that dissipation.

One additional problem must be addressed. In *ASJ,* 58, Yorick mentions that "It had ever . . . been one of the singular blessings of my life, to be almost every hour of it miserably in love with some one; and my last flame happening to be blown out by a whiff of jealousy . . . I had lighted it up afresh at the pure taper of Eliza but about three months before." New and Day, *ASJ,* 6:293–94, n. to 58.3, suggest, "without making any strong claim," the possibility that "my last flame" is Lady Warkworth/Percy, and tie this passage to Sterne's report in *BJ,* 184, of a meeting with "Sheba" in Hyde Park on May 1, 1767 (arisen from his sickbed, it should be noted), where the two bandy remarks about old and new loves; Curtis tentatively suggests that "Sheba" is Lady Warkworth/Percy, and New and Day pursue the notion: "it does seem possible that Sterne is recording his own flirtation with Lady Warkworth and its demise. That it took place or reawakened while he was pursuing Eliza (and even with her knowledge) seems quite in keeping with the tone of the *BJ* entry; and, one additional bit of evidence, no love letter in Sterne's canon is in fact quite as *miserable* [as letter 149]." It is possible, of course, to believe that Sheba is connected to letter 149, without accepting the recipient as Lady Warkworth/Percy.

The summation of New and Day, 6:294, is worth repeating: "Amidst this play of conjectures . . . one might draw the conclusion that when Yorick tells us he has 'been in love with one princess or another' almost all his life (*ASJ* 44), he is only partially capturing Sterne's own practice, which was to be in love with as many women as possible, as often as possible. The language of love for Sterne—the language permeating *BJ*—was the inherited one of faithfulness, possession, and jealousy . . . but his practice was characterized most of all by Sterne's ironic awareness of fugaciousness."

[a]———] [Warkworth] *C*   [b]proof. If] proof‸ If *MS*

1. Mount Coffee-house] Situated in Mount Street, Grosvenor Square, running from Davies Street to Park Lane halfway between Oxford Street and Piccadilly. *London Past and Present,* 2:564–65, quotes a poem by William Mason: "In Coffee-house of good account, / Not far from Bond Street, called *The Mount,* / Soame Jenyns met the Dean of Gloucester" ("The Dean and the Squire," 1782); and notes that John Westbrook, father of Shelley's Harriet, was formerly its landlord. Grosvenor Square was "one of the most aristocratic and fashionable places of residence in London"; not only did Warburton live there, but both the Pembroke and Percy families had houses on the square. See Lillywhite, *London Coffee Houses,* 375–76.

2. what a dishclout . . . of me] Sterne had compared his complexion to that of a "dishclout" in letter 83, but here he seems closer to *OED*'s "taken as a type of limpness and weakness." His play on "familiarity" is similar to that in letter 148 (see n. 4 to that letter).

3. It is but . . . under my feet] Cf. *ASJ,* 122 ("The Temptation. Paris"): "I know as well as any one, he [the devil] is an adversary, whom if we resist, he will fly from us—but I seldom resist him at all; from a terror, that though I may conquer, I may still get a hurt in the combat—so I give up the triumph, for security; and instead of thinking to make him fly, I generally fly myself." Sterne plays with the idea of flight again in letter 150.

Sterne's "the world, the flesh, and the devil" derives from the litany in the *BCP;* he would have known well the entire verse: "From fornication, and all other deadly sin; and from all the deceits of the world, the flesh, and the devil, *Good Lord, deliver us.*"

4. a box ticket . . . benefit] See *Status* above.

5. Mr. C——r's in Wigmore-street] Cross, *Letters,* 2:84, has "C[owpe]r's," but without explanation; Curtis leaves it as here, unidentified. Wigmore Street runs parallel to and north of Oxford Street, from Portman Square (where Elizabeth Montagu had her London home) to Cavendish Square. The only subscriber (under "C") to *Sermons* in 1766, of sufficient wealth to live in that neighborhood, was Anthony Chamier, Esq. (1725–1780), a London financier and founding mem-

ber of the Literary Club; he was at this time secretary to the Duke of Grafton (Namier and Brooke, 2:208), but we have no idea where in London he lived, and it remains a stab in the dark.

150. *To "dear Lady"*[1]

Text: Letter Book

York. [?May 6–13, 1765][2]

Do You think, <my> dear <***> <,>~L~ady,—shandy-headed as I am, that I could be served with a Letter de Cachet,[3] without instantly obeying the summons, or sending some lawful excuse by the return of the Courier?

—fugitive as I am——I have not run away from my loyalty—I fled with a Militia-captain:[4] it was not <out> ‸from Principles‸ of rebellion,—but ‸of‸ virtue, that we made our escapes: The Goddess of Prudence and Self-denial bears witness to our Motives—We ran headlong like a Telemachus and a Mentor from a Calypso & her Nymphs,[5] hastening as fast as our members[6] would let us, from the ensnaring favours of an enchanting Court, the delights of which, <in> we forefelt in the end, must have un-*captain'd* the Captain——& dis-*Order'd* the Priest. We beseech You, to think of both of us, as we are——nothing extenuate, or set down aught in malice.[7]

To begin, (in good manners) with myself. think not, dear ****, when I fled,—think not, ‸that‸ I could <l[*?*eave]>~r~un away from the remembrance of past kindnesses, or the expectation of future ones——Good God! Is it possible I could forget my red leather pocket-book with silver clasps?——my two sticks of seal wax——my Scissars, (which by the bye want<ing> grinding) & my pen-knife.[8] Unhappy man! wander where I may, have I not the *trioptick* hibernian pair of Spectacles,[9] wch *** gave me, ever upon my nose, <to> magnifying every crooked step I take? do I not carry about me the golden headed pencil & pinch-beck ‸Ruler‸[10] which the truely virtuous & open hearted Princess Micomicon,[11] put into my hands at parting—hallowed & mystick Gifts convey'd by a heavenly hand, to mark & measure down my back-slidings and my fore-slidings[12]—*les egarments de mon coeur, & mon esprit pendent mon exile!*[13]

As for my Militia-Captain, my thrice worthy fellow wanderer, and the kind contriver & coadjutor of my escape—Let not my pen—but let his own Atchievements write his elogy. This moment that I am writing is he preparing to plunge himself into dangers, to forget himself—his friends—& think only of his country—<[several illegible words]>now does the drum beat——& the shril Fife shriek in his ears[14]—his pulse quickens——mark how he girds on his sword——for heaven's sake! where will this end?

he is going, with his whole Batallion to Leeds[15]——to Leeds?—yes <—>~M^{dm}~ he is going to root out the manufactures—to give the spinsters & Weavers[16] no elbow room—to compliment Industry with ∧a∧ Jubil<a>~ee~——by all that is good! He will do the State some service; & they shall know it.[17]

I am
&c &c—
L.S.

MS: Letter Book, Pierpont Morgan Library, New York.
Pub.: Cross, *Life* (1925), 2:240–41; Curtis, no. 142.

1. *dear Lady*] There is no addressee in the *Letter Book;* we derive "*dear Lady*" from the opening sentence. Cross, *Life* (1925), 2:240, suggests the letter was addressed to Emma Gilbert, Baroness Edgcumbe (see letters 68, n. 2, and 77, n. 14), based solely on her name being on the very short list of correspondents presumably wrapped around the contents of the *Letter Book* (see letter 63, n. 1); no other argument for her has surfaced, and it seems rather unlikely that such a letter would be sent to the married daughter of an archbishop, even a deceased archbishop. At the bottom of the leaf of the *Letter Book* on which this letter is pasted, in a hand not Sterne's, is written "?To the Countess of Edgcombe? unpublished." The identification was rejected by Curtis in favor of Lady Warkworth, but Cash, *LY,* 215, n. 79, is not at all convinced by Curtis's argument that letters 149 and 150 are similar in style; see our own demur concerning Curtis's argument in the *Status* section of letter 149. The intended recipient of this letter remains unknown.

2. Date] The ms. is undated. Curtis, 246–47, n. 9, by way of explaining the final

paragraph, astutely reconstructs the events of May 1765 that led to riots in the north among the weavers, and the stationing of Sir George Savile's militia regiment in Leeds in the week of May 13, 1765; see n. 4 below.

3. Letter de Cachet] See letter 6, n. 10.

4. a Militia-captain] Cross, 2:240, suggests William Combe, but Curtis, 246, n. 1, makes a convincing case for Sir George Savile (1726–1784), of Thornhill, an MP representing Yorkshire since 1759, and captain of a regiment in the West Yorkshire militia. Namier and Brooke call him "one of the most respected men in the Commons": "upright, disinterested, independent, 'a pattern of excellence in a British senator'" (3:406). He never married. Cash, *LY*, 215–16, accepts Curtis's argument, although he notes that Sterne "knew many men who were active in northern militia regiments" (n. 80). Savile subscribed to *Sermons* (1760).

5. Telemachus . . . Nymphs] Sterne alludes to the popular continuation of the *Odyssey* by François de Salignac de la Mothe Fénelon (1651–1715), *Les Aventures de Télémaque fils d'Ulysse* (1699). In book 6, Telemachus, attended by Mentor (the goddess Minerva in disguise), visits the temptress Calypso. Seeing Telemachus enamored of her, Mentor tosses him from a cliff to the sea below and the two make their escape. Smollett's translation would appear six years after his death, in 1776.

6. members] A word that probably is not innocent in Sterne. Cf. *TS*, I.7.11: "*rights, members, and appurtenances whatsoever*" (repeated, *TS* I.15.45); and IV.17.350: "*Nature* . . . in all *provoking cases,* determines us to a sally of this or that member—or else she thrusts us into this or that place, or posture of body, we know not why . . . ." See John S. Farmer and W. E. Henley, *Slang and Its Analogues* (1894), s.v. *member:* "The *penis.*" The remainder of the sentence is equally suspect.

Sterne puns again on priestly *(dis-)orders* in letter 177, a bawdy *tour de force:* "You perceive I should be left naked . . . if not quite dis-*Orderd.*"

7. nothing . . . in malice] The continuation of these lines from Othello's last great speech is very apt: "Speak of me as I am; nothing extenuate, / Nor set down aught in malice. Then must you speak / Of one that lov'd not wisely but too well" (*Othello,* V.ii.342–44).

8. my red leather . . . pen-knife] Sterne will return to this trope of gratitude in *BJ*, 200–201, where he thanks Eliza for "Every Trincket you gave or exchanged" and again: "I have a present of a portrait . . . [and] a gold Stock buccle & Buttons . . . [and] the Sculptures upon poor Ovid's Tomb . . . ." To be sure, the gifts in this letter are somewhat suspect, in keeping with its bawdy tenor; cf. the little purse of "green taffeta, lined with a little bit of white quilted sattin, and just big enough to hold the crown" in *ASJ*, 123 ("The Temptation. Paris"); and the several plays with "knives" in *TS* (e.g., VIII.8.664–65: "a daughter of Eve . . . had better be fifty leagues off—or in her warm bed—or playing with a case-knife . . ."; see also

nn. to 198.16–19 and 665.1–2, 3:214 and 3:504). The "Scissars" that want "grinding" also seem a bit too Shandean.

9. *trioptick* hibernian pair of Spectacles] Curtis, 246, n. 5: "In effect like our trifocal glass, these spectacles had three sets of lenses, one stationary and two movable by side hinges." Where Curtis found this information is unknown. We have not been able to find another usage in the eighteenth century; *OED* has no entry. We are similarly stymied by "hibernian," unless it is meant to indicate that the donor of these spectacles (i.e., the addressee) was Irish. Cf. Chambers, *Cyclopædia,* s.v. *spectacles:* "F. Cherubin [François Lassere, Father Cherubin D'Orléans (1613–1697), author of *La Dioptrique oculaire* (1671)], a capuchin, describes a kind of spectacle telescopes, for the viewing of remote objects with both eyes; hence called binoculi. . . . The same author invented a kind of spectacles, with three or four glasses, which performed extraordinarily."

Cross is convinced that "***" indicates someone other than the addressee: "The girl who at parting" gave these gifts is not the Calypso of the first part of the letter. However, although the first addressee is indicated with four asterisks, and this one with only three, Sterne is often careless in this way; the clear thrust of the passage is that Sterne has received a multitude of gifts from the person to whom he writes his comic appreciation.

10. pinch-beck Ruler] "Pinchbeck," named after its inventor Christopher Pinchbeck (*d.* 1732), is an alloy "containing a high proportion of copper and a low proportion of zinc which is used chiefly in making cheap jewellery, on account of its resemblance to gold" (*OED*). Pinchbeck snuffboxes and watches were common, and in Sterne's time seem to have been valued almost as much as gold and silver. Hence Sterne's equation of the "golden headed pencil" with the pinch-beck ruler would be without irony, whereas by the mid-nineteenth century "pinchbeck" had become a word of contempt for the counterfeit and spurious; but see also letter 167, n. 6, where Walpole is quoted abusing a "pinchbeck principality."

11. Princess Micomicon] In *Don Quixote,* I.IV.2.3.10, the witty Dorothea, at the instigation of the curate and the barber, acts the part of the Princess Micomicona, "only heiress in a direct line to the vast kingdom of Micomicon" (2:27), in an effort to restore Don Quixote to his senses.

12. back-slidings and my fore-slidings] Cf. *TS,* I.21.76: "The backslidings of *Venus* in her orbit fortified the *Copernican* system . . . and the backslidings of my aunt *Dinah* in her orbit, did the same service in establishing my father's . . . ." "Fore-slidings" is a nonce word, unrecorded in *OED;* it perhaps echoes "forefelt" in the paragraph above.

13. *les egarments . . . exile!*] *The wanderings of my heart and spirit during my exile!* Once again Sterne refers to the novel by Crébillon, fils, *Les égarements du cœur et de l'esprit* (1736); see above, letter 45, n. 5, and letter 86.

14. now does . . . his ears] Sterne returns to *Othello,* III.iii.351–54: "Farewell the neighing steed and the shrill trump, / The spirit-stirring drum, th' ear-piercing fife, / . . . / Pride, pomp, and circumstance of glorious war!"

15. he is . . . Leeds] In May 1765 English silk weavers rioted in protest against government measures that favored the French silk industry. The Riot Act was read on May 21, and troops were stationed on the highways as unrest spread from Manchester to the woolen industry of Leeds. It was common practice to use militia regiments to quell industrial riots, and sending Savile's second battalion of the West Riding militia on maneuvers in Leeds seems to have been sufficient, since no riots are known to have occurred there, although Sterne would not have known that when he wrote the letter. Walpole, *Memoirs . . . George III,* 2:142ff., gives a good account of the disturbances in London, which soon spread to the North; see also W. J. Shelton, *English Hunger and Industrial Disorders* (Toronto: University of Toronto Press, 1973), 192–97.

16. spinsters & Weavers] Cf. *TS,* V.16.445: "My father spun his, every thread of it, out of his own brain,—or reeled and cross-twisted what all other spinners and spinsters had spun before him . . ."; and VII.10.591: "but the carders and spinners were all gone to bed." *Spinster* was a legitimate usage for someone (usually a woman) whose occupation was spinning, but a pun is always a possibility with Sterne.

17. He will . . . know it] Sterne again returns to *Othello,* a line just before the lines quoted in n. 7: "I have done the state some service, and they know't" (V.ii.339). Sterne alludes to *Othello* again in *ASJ,* 37.17–19, and *BJ,* 222.25, and possibly, as well, 201.16–17 and 210.2; see nn. to those passages.

151. *To Thomas Howard, Earl of Effingham*[1]

Text: Ms.

Coxwould near Easingwould
[Wednesday,] May 29. 1765

My good Lord

(for I believe you from my heart to be so,——or my pen would not have belied my opinion of You——& since <upon> ‸I've begun with‸ an Article of belief—give me leave to add, That *I believe* You have power to be any thing—but no thanks to You—so I hope you render them to whom they are due—& so god prosper You) as all this is included in a parenthesis—your Lords[p] has a right to leave it out—it will not hurt the Sense——I mean your own——for as for mine—the point has been some years ago, settled by the world—tho' by the by—I intend to puzzle it—by some feeble Efforts in the work I am ab^{t}—tho' was I to tell you the subject of the first Sermon[2] I've begun with—you would think it so truely Shandean, that no after-Wit would bring me off[a]—nothing venture—nothing have[3]—all which being duely perpended & consider'd by y^{r} Lordship; I return y^{r} Lordship thanks for your Subscriptions—as I do to the *aimable Contesse votre chere Mere*[4]—for the honour of her name &c— — —

Hall left me bleeding to death at York, of a small Vessel in my Lungs—the duce take these bellows of mine; I must get 'em stop'd, or I shall never live to *persifler*[5] Lord Effingham again.——apropos! will you be at York races[6]—for next to the pleasure of getting my five and fourty Shillings[7] out of Y^{r} hands—I know nothing will give me more delight than to ∧see∧ you in the *flesh*—who's?[b] What?——cura valetudinem tuam diligenter[8]—as a means to w^{ch}, keep y^{r} body in temperance, Soberness & chastity—wch is a quotation from ye church catechism,[9] w^{ch} <I> with all y^{r} good memory, ∧I fear∧ y^{r} Lordship sometimes forgets. Greet Scroope[10] & Blaquiere[11] in my name—present—(not my brotherly Love—but) my fraternal pity to Dean Wrotsly[12]—)—What sh^{d} make such a fool <?co>~p~op into my head?—my own vile passions. & that's the truth of the matter—& so I cross it all out

If the whole Letter had been served the same way; it would not have fared the worse with y^{r} Lordship—but I should have lost the <p>~H~onour and satisfaction of saying

That I am
with the highest esteems
for y^{r} Character & Talents
my Lord
Y^{r} most faithful
& obliged humb^{l} Servt
L. Sterne

Address: To / The Right Honble / Lord Visc^t Effingham / St James's Coffee house[13] / London.

Postmark: 31 MA

MS: Beinecke Rare Book and Manuscript Library, Yale University.

Pub.: European Magazine 33 (May 1798): 313–14; Curtis, no. 143.

Status: Curtis did not have access to the manuscript, but indicates he took his text not from the first printing of the letter in *European Magazine* (1798), but from "a more faithful printing of the letter in a London newspaper in June 1822"; we have not tried to locate that version, given the reappearance of the manuscript, a gift of C. B. Tinker to the Beinecke Library.

The *European Magazine* version introduces Sterne to the reader as "this once popular writer," then proceeds to misdate the letter 1766, and to omit that section of it from "in the *flesh*" to "Greet Scroope," replacing the missing passage with three asterisks, and "great" for "Greet"; its reading is thus rendered: ". . . delight than to see you * * * great Scroope and Blaquiere." Curtis's version restored this passage.

Sterne does joke that what he has just written should be deleted, and we can assume he meant from "in the *flesh*" to "all out," although the actual "x" mark he drew extends only from "(not my brotherly" to the end of the paragraph. However, it is so faintly drawn that it is clear he intended the earl to read every word. *EM* brackets this smaller section and in a footnote indicates that "the enclosed sentence between crotchets is crossed out in the original." Curtis's newspaper version would seem to have indicated the same, and Curtis actually draws an "x" over the same portion of text.

Other variants in the *EM* version are puzzling: "some years ago, settled" becomes "long settled"; "y^r Lordship thanks" becomes "you thanks"; "out of Y^r hands," "out of my hands"; and "What sh^d make such a fool . . . ," "What should not such a fool . . . ." The editor was either very careless or very intrusive.

[a]off] of *MS*   [b]*flesh*—who's?] flesh [ms. patched] who's? *MS*

1. *Earl of Effingham*] Thomas Howard (1747–1791), 3d Earl of Effingham, who after his years at Eton had entered the army in 1762, married in 1766, and would rise to the rank of lieutenant colonel in 1782. He later became Governor of Jamaica, 1789–*d.* Curtis, 248, n. 1, quotes Nathaniel Wraxall, *Historical and Posthumous Memoirs, 1772–1784* (1884), to the effect that he was a person of "great eccentricity of deportment." He did indeed subscribe to *Sermons* (1766), as did

his mother, Elizabeth Beckford Howard (1718–1791), Countess of Effingham. It is well to keep in mind that the earl was not yet twenty years old when he received this letter.

2. first Sermon] Volume III of the published *Sermons* opens with "The character of Shimei" (*Sermons* 4:150–56). In his headnote to that sermon, New suggests that "while there is much that is interesting in 'Shimei,' one is tempted to believe that another sermon, 'The Levite and the [sic] concubine' (18), might more readily be labeled 'truly Shandean.' Perhaps Sterne had intended it for the initial offering of volume III but allowed discretion to rule the day" (*Sermons* 5:187). We may add that sandwiched between these two sermons is sermon 17, "The case of Hezekiah and the messengers," which Sterne might also have deemed "Shandean" for the reasons outlined in letter 133.

3. nothing venture—nothing have] Proverbial; see Tilley, N319, and *ODEP*, 581.

4. *aimable Contesse votre chere Mere*] I.e., kind Countess, your dear mother; see n. 1. Correctly: *Comtesse.*

5. *persifler*] See letter 86, n. 17. The French verb (meaning to rally, banter, joke) never entered the English language, as did *persiflage* and *persifleur (OED).*

6. York races] As Curtis notes, 249, n. 6, Lord Effingham's name is not among the subscribers to the Assembly Rooms listed in the *York Courant* of August 27, 1765, where he found other acquaintances of Sterne—Dr. Burton, the Chaloners, Crofts, Thornhills, and Turners, the Marquis of Rockingham, the Earl of Scarborough, and Lord and Lady Warkworth.

7. five and fourty Shillings] This sum would seem to imply that Lord Effingham ordered no fewer than nine sets, which is not indicated in the list. It is also possible that the earl was soliciting subscriptions for Sterne among his acquaintances; several Howards in Surrey, where Lord Effingham had his estate, subscribed in 1766.

8. cura . . . diligenter] A conventional Roman salutation, not unlike the "take care!" of American usage, but in context with perhaps a bawdy innuendo concerning venereal disease.

9. keep . . . church catechism] Among the duties set forth in the required answer to the catechist's question, "What is thy duty towards thy Neighbour?" is "To keep my body in temperance, soberness, and chastity." Behind the response is Titus 2, and especially verse 12: "Teaching us that, denying ungodliness and worldly lusts, we should live soberly, righteously, and godly, in this present world." Sterne had given much the same advice to Hall-Stevenson and his brothers; see letter 72, n. 14.

10. Scroope] Curtis identifies him, 249, n. 8, as Thomas Scrope (1723–1792), of Colby, Yorkshire, one of the Demoniacs, among whom he was called the "Cardinal." Hall-Stevenson assigned "Thomas of Colby's Tale" to him in *Crazy Tales*. Scrope probably subscribed to *Sermons* (1766), although the two entries are "J. Scroop, Esq." and "—— Scroop, Esq.," so we cannot be certain. See Cash's account of Thomas Scrope, *EMY*, 187–88, and also Namier and Brooke; among other tidbits, we are told by them that "in May 1764 Scrope was declared insane by a commission of lunacy, and the administration of his estates was vested in his half-brother Gervase Scrope; but he was released 30 Nov. 1764" (3:418). The possibility that greetings are being sent to Gervase rather than Thomas must be kept in mind (and "J." in the subscription list can as easily indicate a phonetic error for "G." as a scribal error for "T."); one link between Gervase Scrope and Blaquiere (see next note) is that both subscribed to George Thompson's translation *A Description of the Royal Palace and Monastery of St. Laurence* (1760). Sterne was among the subscribers to this work by a fellow Yorkshireman. But "Scrope" was a common name in Yorkshire (and neighboring Lincolnshire), and appears often in subscription lists for Yorkshire authors, so identifying any particular one is always problematic.

11. Blaquiere] Curtis, 249, n. 9, identifies him as John Blaquiere (1732–1812), the son of a French emigrant, "who rose to become Lieut.-Col. of the 17th Dragoons and secretary of the legation under Lord Harcourt at Paris in 1771–2. He was appointed Chief Secretary of Ireland in 1772, entered the Irish Parliament, and in 1800 was created Baron de Blaquiere." He and his wife subscribed to *Sermons* (1766).

12. Wrotsly] Sir Richard Wrottesley (1721–1769) of Wrottesley Hall, Staffordshire, chaplain to the King since 1763 and appointed to the "lucrative Deanery of Worcester" on April 13, 1765 (Curtis, 249, n. 10; *EM* leaves the name blank). Walpole offers some of his choicest vituperation: "[He] turned parson from a mad fondness for preaching, [and] was to the last degree debauched and disreputable, and treated his wife inhumanly" (*Memoirs . . . George III* 4:82). This might be sufficient reason for Sterne's obvious dislike, without Curtis's suggestion that Sterne may have been jealous of his advancement in the church. Wrottesley subscribed to *Sermons* (1760), and one of his unmarried daughters subscribed in both 1766 and 1769: Mary (*d.* 1769) was maid-of-honour to Queen Charlotte; Elizabeth (1745–1822) was described by the indefatigable Walpole as a "young lady . . . uncommonly void of beauty, grace, or insinuation" (4:82; he provides a softer view in *Correspondence* 23:121).

13. St James's Coffee house] See letter 70, n. 3.

152. *To William Combe*

Text: Daily Universal Register

Coxwould, [Tuesday,] June 11, 1765.

So *Burton*[1] really told you, with a grave face and an apparent mortification, that I had ridiculed my Irish friends at Bath for an hour together, and had made a large company merry at *Lady Lepel*'s[2] table during an whole afternoon at their expence. By Heavens, 'tis false as misrepresentation can make it. It is not in my nature, I trust, to be so ungrateful, as I should be, if absent or present, I should be ungracious[a] to them. That I should make *Burton* look grave, whose countenance is formed to mark the smiles of an amiable and an honest heart, is not within my chapter of possibilities;—I am sure it is not in that[b] of my intentions to say any thing that is unurbane[c3] of such a man as he is:—for, in my life, did I never communicate with a gentleman of qualities more winning, and dispositions more generous. He invited me to his house with kindness, and he gave me a truly graceful welcome, for it was *with all his heart.*[d] He is as much formed to make society pleasant as any one I ever saw; and I wish he were as rich as Crœsus,[4] that he might do all the good an unbounded generosity would lead him to do. I never passed more pleasant hours in my life than with him and his fair countrywomen; and foul befall the man[5] who should let drop a word in dispraise of him or them!—And there is the charming widow *Moor,*[6] where, if I had not a piece of legal meadow of my own, I should rejoice to *batten*[e] the rest of my days;—and the gentle elegant *Gore,*[7] with her fine form and Grecian face, and whose lot I trust it will be to[f] make some man happy who knows the value of a tender heart:—Nor shall I forget another widow, the interesting Mrs. Vesey,[8] with her vocal and fifty other accomplishments.—I abuse them!—it must not be told,—for it is false,—and it should not be believed, for it is unnatural.—It is true I did talk of them, for an hour together, but no sarcasm or unlucky sallies mingled with my speech:—Yes, I did talk of them, as they would wish to be talked of,—with smiles on my countenance, praise on my tongue, hilarity in my heart, and the goblet in my hand.—Besides, I am myself of their own country:—My father was a considerable time on duty with his regiment in Ireland;[9] and my mother gave me to the world when she was there,[10] on duty with him.—I beg of you, therefore, to make all these good people believe that I have been at least misunderstood, for it is impossible that *Lady Barrymore*[11] could mean to misrepresent me.

Read *Burton* this letter if you have an opportunity, and assure him of my most cordial esteem and respect for him and all his social excellencies; and whisper something kind and gentle for me, as you well know how, to my fair countrywomen; and let not an unmerited prejudice or displeasure against me remain any longer in their tender bosoms.—When you get into disgrace of any kind, be assured that I will do as much for you.

I am here as idle as ease of heart can make me; I shall wait for you till the beginning of next month; when, if you do not come, I shall proceed to while away the rest of the summer at *Crazy Castle* and *Scarborough*. In the beginning, the very beginning of October, I mean to arrive in Bond-street[12] with my *Sermons;* and when I have arranged their publication, then hey go mad for Italy:[13] whither you would do well to accompany me.—In the mean time, however, I hope and wish to see you here; it will, after all, be much better than playing the *Strephon*[14] with phtisical nymphs at the Bristol Fountain.[15] But do as you may—

I am,
Most sincerely, your's,
L. Sterne

MS: Not located.

Pub.: Daily Universal Register (April 24, 1787); *European Magazine* 12 (November 1787): 339–40; Combe, *Original Letters* (1788), 39–44; Curtis, no. 144.

Status: See the *Status* commentary for letter 133. As with that letter to Combe, Curtis bases his text of this letter on the version in *Original Letters* (*OL*), letter 8, but again, there are numerous differences between that version and the two that preceded it in print, first in the *Daily Universal Register* (*DUR*), second, seven months later, in *European Magazine.* The *EM* version seems most unreliable because of obvious in-house editing: italics are dropped at will, as are Sterne's characteristic dashes. Combe's version has some twenty-one variants from the *DUR* version, most suggesting his own attempts to correct the punctuation. The more significant variants are listed in the collation below. Although this letter is more suspect than letter 133, so much so that Curtis omits the final paragraph, we believe that the tinkering of *EM* and *OL* remove us even further from whatever original material Combe first presented to his printer, and hence have used the *DUR* text. We have also included the final paragraph, no more or less suspect than the rest of the letter, which does seem to be derived—however corrupted—from a Sterne text (Hamilton, "William Combe" 426, and Cash, *LY* 201, concur with this judgment). Indeed, the only sentence we believe almost certainly a Combe invention is the forced parallelism of "smiles on my countenance, praise on my tongue, hilarity in my heart, and the goblet in my hand"; did Sterne ever write so stilted a sentence? But as Hamilton notes, letters 8, 23, and 35 of *OL* "do not display indebtedness to Sterne's writings for phrase or substance, and they are consistent with the known facts.... Indeed, the concluding flourishes of all three are rather in the 'empty' style and may well be interpolations, but otherwise these letters bear little resemblance to Combe's usual manner. They are in no sense empty of thought or concrete detail" (426).

[a]I should be ungracious] *DUR, EM;* I were to be ungracious *OL* [b]not in that] *DUR, OL;* not that *EM* [c]unurbane] *DUR, EM;* inurbane *OL* [d]*with all his heart*] *DUR, EM;* with all his heart *OL* [e]*batten*] *DUR, EM;* batten *OL* [f]trust it will be to] *DUR, OL;* I trust to *EM*

1. *Burton*] In *DUR* and *EM, "Burton"* is footnoted as the "present amiable and excellent Lord Cunningham"; by 1788, however, when Combe published *OL,* he had become the "late amiable and excellent Lord Cunningham." Francis Pierpoint Burton, Esq. (*d.* 1787), of Buncraggy, Co. Clare, Ireland, succeeded his uncle as Baron Conyngham of Mount Charles in 1781 (Curtis, 251, n. 2). He subscribed to *Sermons* (1766).

2. *Lady Lepel's*] *OL* provides the identification: "The late Lady Mulgrave." Lady Lepell Phipps, daughter of John, Lord Hervey of Ickworth (Pope's Sporus); see letter 149, *Status.* Curtis, 251, n. 4, quotes Walpole, *Correspondence,* 17:274 (to Mann in 1742): "a fine black girl, but as masculine as her father should be." She subscribed to *Sermons* (1766), as did her husband Constantine Phipps (created first Baron Mulgrave of New Ross, Co. Wexford, in 1767) and her son. The connection of both Burton and Phipps to Ireland should be noted.

3. unurbane] Cf. *TS,* II.2.97: "'Tis language unurbane." *OED* cites this passage as its sole illustration. While the use of the word here might seem typical of

Combe's exploitation of Sterne's texts for his forgeries, the fact that he "corrected" the word to "inurbane" in *OL* is, perhaps, an indication that *DUR* did indeed have Sterne's holograph in hand.

4. rich as Crœsus] A proverbial expression (see Tilley, C832, and *ODEP,* 674), based on the last king of Lydia (560–546 B.C.), whose wealth became legendary. Sterne is usually more inventive in his use of commonplaces—perhaps we see Combe's signature here.

5. foul befall the man] Another suspicious Combe-like echo; cf. *ASJ,* 89 (addressing the *fille de chambre*): "I see innocence, my dear, in your face—and foul befal the man who ever lays a snare in its way!"

6. widow *Moor*] Perhaps, as Curtis suggests, 251, n. 5, the "M[rs] Moore of Bath" mentioned in letter 237, the list of correspondents found with the *Letter Book.* A "Mr. More" subscribed to *Sermons* (1769), but no Mrs. Mo[o]re is to be found in any of the lists. Deborah Heller, editor of the Montagu-Vesey correspondence, has graciously provided us with the text of a letter (*c.*1763) from Montagu to Vesey, which discusses a Mrs. Moore of Limerick, "a most amiable Woman who out of regard for her children retired in her early Widowhood to the cave of Malvina, there the lonely watcher of the night sat listening [to] winds when she might have given an ear to the softer sighing of lovers. She has been a perfect Penelope in constant love & solitary woe." Whether she left her retreat at times to take the waters of Bath is not known, but Montagu's romantic description of her certainly suggests the sort of inaccessible woman Sterne found attractive; and it is worth recalling that this letter specifically addresses Sterne's conduct toward his "Irish friends."

7. elegant *Gore*] Curtis, 251, n. 6, tentatively suggests Letitia Gore, who subscribed to *Sermons* (1766, 1769), and to *ASJ* as well. She is perhaps the daughter of Nathaniel Gore and Letitia Booth, of Lissadell Castle, Co. Sligo, born in 1726 (see Burke, *Irish Peerage;* PRO, Northern Ireland, Lissadell Papers, D/4131), but nothing is known of her other than this scanty information.

8. Mrs. Vesey] See letter 177. Cash, *LY,* 208, n. 67, doubts that Elizabeth Vesey was at Bath during this season; she certainly was not a widow in 1765 (her husband died in 1785). It is very likely that Combe fabricated this passage, especially since it echoes a passage in a more obviously forged *OL* letter (19): "I saw the charming *Mrs. Vesey* but for a moment, and she contrived with her voice and her thousand other graces to *dis—order* me" (*OL* 103).

9. My father . . . Ireland] Roger Sterne was stationed in Ireland intermittently between 1713 and 1727; see Cash, *EMY,* chs. 1 and 2, passim.

10. gave me . . . there] Laurence Sterne was born at Clonmel near Waterford, Co. Tipperary; in writing his *Memoirs* for Lydia, Sterne misspelled the town: "The family, if any left, live now at Clo<m>nwel in the South of Ireland—at w[ch]

Town I was born, ‸Nov. 24. 1713‸ a few Days after my Mother arrived with the Regiment from Dunkirk—My Birth Day was not ominous to my poor Father, who was that Day with <the> many other Brave Officers broke & sent a Drift into the wide world . . ." (1, 3; Sterne's usage of *ominous* is considered obs. by *OED*, with its last example dated 1662—i.e., "of good omen, auspicious").

11. *Lady Barrymore*] Margaret Davys (*d.* 1788), daughter of Paul Davys, 1st Viscount Mountcashell of Ireland, was the widow of James Barry, 5th Earl of Barrymore. She subscribed to *Sermons* (1766), as did her son, Richard Barry (1745–1773), 6th Earl of Barrymore, a captain in the 9th Dragoons; he also subscribed to *ASJ*.

12. Bond-street] This is the earliest reference in Sterne's correspondence to the London lodgings he would maintain until his death, on the first floor of a house in Old Bond Street, then the first on the left from Piccadilly, on the site of the present no. 48 (see Curtis, 293, n. 1, and Cash, *LY*, 201–3). Curtis does not print this final paragraph, believing it a Combe invention, most particularly because he does not believe Sterne lived in Bond Street before January 1767. Cash, on the other hand, accepts the paragraph and hence that Sterne established his Bond Street residence before May 1765. He believes "the very beginning" sounds like "Combe's padding," but "the elliptical clause, 'hey go mad for Italy' has a Sterneian ring and sounds not at all like Combe's prose" (201–2, n. 52). We would argue just the contrary, that nothing in the passage sounds more typical of Combe's dipping into Sterne's fiction for phrasing than this usage, borrowed from the opening chapter of *TS* (I.1.2), and by no means a commonplace phrase at the time (*OED* cites it as the first usage; but see D. W. Patrick, "Gastripheres, Mundungus, and 'The Hey-go-mad,'" *Shandean* 12 [2001]: 119–21). Hence, while we provide the entire letter, we suspend judgment as to whether Sterne did indeed already have a residence in Bond Street in 1765. Among other residents of note, Gibbon lived in Old Bond Street in 1758, and Boswell in 1769 (*London Past and Present* 1:219).

Sterne's landlady was Mary Fourmantel (*d.* 1776), "Hair Bag Maker to his Majesty" (the "bag" was a silken pouch designed to hold the back-hair of a wig); it is not known if she was directly related to Catherine Fourmantel, but considering the rareness of the name, it is at least possible.

13. Italy] Sterne set out for Italy in October 1765, well before the *Sermons* appeared on January 18, 1766. He had had the sermon-writing project in mind at least since March 1763 (see letter 109), but as New (*Sermons* 5:4–5) suggests, it is likely that Sterne simply "worked over existing manuscripts and fragments in a rather desultory fashion . . . . Rather than creating anything new from whole cloth, the sermons of volumes III and IV . . . have roots in . . . a sermon-writing career that coincides with the start of Sterne's clerical career in 1737 and ended

probably in 1765 with his final acts of revision." His Italian journey had been on his mind since at least November 1764 (see letter 143). And see also letter 157.

14. *Strephon*] One of the characters in *Arcadia* (*pub.* 1590) by Sir Philip Sidney (1554–1586), the name became commonplace in pastoral poetry; Pope uses it in "Spring: The First Pastoral."

15. phtisical nymphs at the Bristol Fountain] The Bristol Hotwells, where Combe spent some time in the 1770s, and published *The Philosopher in Bristol* (1775). The phrasing here is echoed in the second paragraph of the entirely spurious letter 33 in *OL,* 183 ("The very same spirit that has led thee from hence to the Bristol Fountain, for no other earthly purpose, but to let a Phthysical maiden lean upon thine arm . . ."), and is almost certainly Combe's invention; see Hamilton, *Doctor Syntax,* 33–36.

153. *To the Countess ******/Eliza*

Text: Letter Book

<———To the Countess of ******>

<Coxwould June> ∧18∧ [?Tuesday, June 18, 1765]

∨My dear Bramine.∨

I have some time forboded I should think of you too much; and behold it is come to pass; for there is not a day in which I have not of late, detected myself a dozen times at least in the fact <in>~of~ <*?*th> thinking and reflecting some way or other <upon you> with pleasure upon you; but in no time or place <*?*dearst Lady>, do I call your figure <up> so strongly up to my imagination and enjoy so much of y^{r} <sweet converse> good heart and sweet converse as when I am in company with my Nuns: tis for this reason, since I have got down to this all-peaceful and romantick retreat,[1] that my Love and my Devotion are ever taking me and leading me gently by the hand to these delicious Mansions of our long-lost Sisters: I am just now return'd from one of my nightly visits; & tho' tis late, for I was detain'd there an hour longer than I was aware of, by the sad silence and breathlessness of the night, and the delusive[a] subject (for it was yourself) which took up the conversation—yet late as it is, I cannot go to bed without writing to you & telling you how much, and how many kind things we have been talking about you these two hours——Cordelia! said I as I lay half

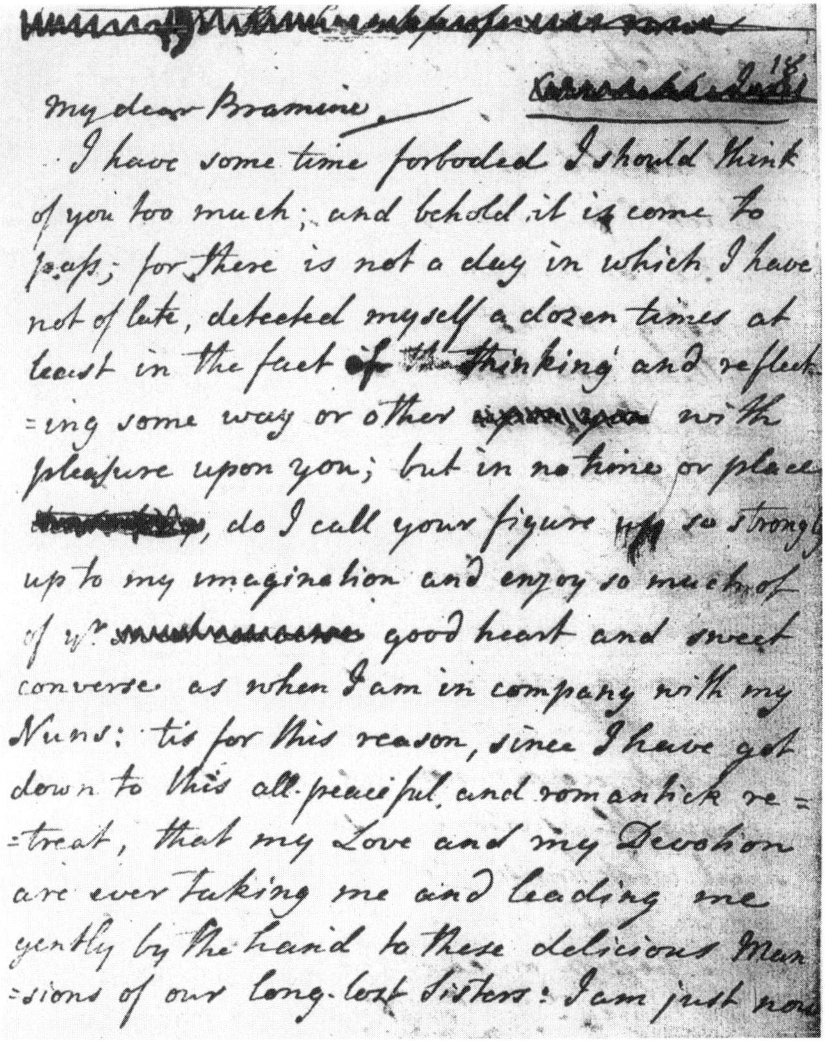

18

My dear Bramine,

I have some time forboded I should think of you too much; and behold it is come to pass; for there is not a day in which I have not of late, detected myself a dozen times at least in the fact of thinking and reflect=ing some way or other with pleasure upon you; but in no time or place, do I call your figure so strongly up to my imagination and enjoy so much of of yr. good heart and sweet converse as when I am in company with my Nuns: tis for this reason, since I have got down to this all-peaceful and romantick re=treat, that my Love and my Devotion are ever taking me and leading me gently by the hand to these delicious Man=sions of our long-lost Sisters: I am just now

Figure 5. Opening page of letter of June 18, 1765, to Countess******/Eliza, *Letter Book*, Pierpont Morgan Library, New York.

reclined upon her grave—long—long, has thy spirit triumphed over these[2] infirmities, and all the contentions to w^{ch} <the> human hearts are subject—alas! thou hast had thy share——for she look'd, <me th> I thought, down upon me with such a pleasurable sweetness—so like a delegated Angel[3] whose breast glow'd with fire, that Cordelia could not have been a stranger to the passion on earth——poor, hapless Maid! cried I—Cordelia gently waved her head——it was enough—I turn'd the discourse to the object of my own disquietudes—I talk'd to her of <Lady ******>~[my Bramine]~: I told her, how kindly nature had formd you—how gentle—how wise—how good—Cordelia, (me thought) was touchd with my description, and glow'd insensibly, as sympathetic Spirits do, as I went on—This Sisterly kind Being with whose Idea I have inflamed your Love, Cordelia! has promissed, that she will one night or other come in person, and in this sacred Asylum pay your Shade a sentimental Visit along with me——when? when? said she, animated with desire—God knows, said I, pulling out my handkerchief & dropping[b] tears faster than I could wipe them off—<When> God[c] knows! said I, crying bitterly as I repeated the words—God knows! but I feel something like ∧a∧ prophetic[d] conviction within me, which says, that this gentlest of her Sex will some time take sanctuary from the cares and treachery of the world and come peacefully & live amongst You——and why not sleep amongst us too?—O heaven! said I, laying my hand upon my heart—— and will not you, Yorick, mix your ashes with us too?—for ever my Cordelia! and some kind hearted Swain[4] shall come and weed our graves, as I have weeded thine,[5] and when he has done, shall sit down at our feet and tell us the Stories of his passions and his disappointments.

<my dear Lady>~My dear Bramine~, tell me honestly, if you do not wish from your soul to have been of this party—aye! but then as it was dark and lonely, I must have been taken by the hand & led home by you to your retired Cottage—and what then?[6] But I stop here—& leave you to furnish the answer.—*a propos*—pray when you first made a conquest of T. Shandy did it ever enter your head what a visionary, romantic, <?[one word]> kind of a Being you had got hold of? When <Lady ***>~the Bramine~ sufferd so careless and laughing a Creature

to enter her <?roof>,[7] did she dream of a man of Sentiments, and that ∧She∧ was opening the door to such a one, to make him prisoner for Life—O Woman! to what purpose hast thou exercised this power over me? or, to answer what end in nature, was I led by so mysterious a path to know you,—<I Love You>,∨—to love You—∨—and fruitlessly to lament and sigh that I can only send my spirit after you, as I have done this night to ∧my∧ Cordelia—poor! spotless Shade! the world at least is so merciful as not to be jealous of our Intercourse—I can paint thee, blessed Spirit all-generous and kind as hers I write to——I can <lay>~lie~ besides thy grave, and drop tears of tenderness upon the Turf wch covers thee, and not one passenger[8] turn his head aside to remark or envy me[e]——But for thee, dear <Countess>~Bramine~, (for alas! alas! what a world do we live in)—it tells me, I must not approach your Shrine, even were it <with> to worship you with the most unspotted Sacrifise—at this distance, it will give me leave to offer it up upon yr altar—and at present I must be content with that Licence—then Let <me>, my[f] dear Goddesse, accept it kindly—let me swear before her Altar That She never <had> heard[g] a prayer from a warmer heart, or recd Insense from a more honest Votary—Let me tell her once more I love her; and as a good Christian is *taught*[h] to love his maker—that is, for his own sake and the excellencies of his Nature.[9]

now in answer to all this, why ∧have∧ I never recd—one gracious nod, <conveyed thro'>[i] from You? why do you not write to me? is writing painful? or is it only so, to me? dear Lady write any<how>~thin~g and write it any how, so it but comes from yr heart, twil be better than the best Letter that ever came from Pope's head[10]——In short, write yr Nonsense, if you have any—write yr Chit Chat—your pleasures, your pains, yr present humours and present feelings (would to God I had just now hold of yr hand).—I want to hear you are well—I want to hear You say, you have something more[j] than cold esteem for me—in short I know not What I want <I want>——

I have the honour to
be, dear <Lady ******>~Bramine~
&c &c &c — — — —
∨*The Bramin*—∨

MS: Letter Book, Pierpont Morgan Library, New York.
Pub.: Cross, *Life* (1925), 2:252–54; Curtis, no. 201.
Status: When Cross first published this letter in the second edition of *Life* (1925), along with the other contents of the *Letter Book,* he headed it with a most innocuous note: "This, I infer from the erasures, is a draft rather than a copy of a letter to the Bramine, i.e., Mrs. Elizabeth Draper, then on the way to India. The superscription, which Sterne tried to blot out with his pen is 'Coxwould, June 18.' The year, not given, must be 1767. Towards the close of the letter, Sterne asks the Bramine why she has not yet written to him. Her first letter awaited him when he came to York on July 27 [see *BJ* 222]." Cross was equally reticent in the third edition (1929), leaving it to Curtis, 362, to describe the manuscript more precisely: "The MS. of this letter is the most compromising document that remains to us in Sterne's autograph. It is apparently the draft of a letter that may have been posted and is addressed to the Bramine, Mrs. Draper. . . . Examination . . . shows us at once, if indeed the bantering tone of a good portion of the letter has not suggested the like conclusion, that the letter was originally addressed to a woman whom Sterne calls the 'Countess ******.' We observe that Sterne has in every instance substituted his pet name for Mrs. Draper for that of the unknown 'Countess,' and that the superscription and signature, 'The Bramine,' are additions of another date."

Curtis then accepts Cross's dating of the letter as 1767, whether directed to the Countess or to Eliza (the ghostly Cordelia "was especially occupying his thoughts and leisure during the spring and summer of 1767"), reviving the charge that Sterne seems to have courted two women simultaneously; see our discussion above, letter 149, *Status.* Cash, on the other hand, argues that the original letter to the Countess was written on June 18, 1765, basing his argument on the fact that Sterne had told Eliza about "Cordelia" on first meeting her in the winter of 1767, and thus that the fantasy he describes must have taken place earlier; since Sterne was not in Coxwold in June 1762, 1763, 1764, or 1766, Cash opts for the date 1765 (*LY* 218–19, n. 2).

We have accepted this reasoning, but *cum grano salis.* Cash argues that for Sterne to "carry on simultaneously two public sentimental courtships with well-bred women is out of keeping with his character," and hence that the letter could not have been written to the Countess in 1767, and immediately redirected to Eliza. But Eliza had been gone for two months, and, writing from Coxwold, Sterne was rather out of the public eye; that he would attempt to fill the emptiness left by her departure by opening a correspondence with an old interest (Lady Warkworth? but see our discussion of letter 149) or a new one seems as likely as not. That Sterne recycled material in his correspondence (and his romances) is a theory pursued by the editors of *ASJ;* see in particular,

6:385, n. to 171.25–26; and, indeed, Sterne had written about Cordelia to Eliza as early as April 16 (172), in an entry that may have originated twenty-seven years earlier in his courtship of Elizabeth.

At some time then, probably two years after first writing the letter, but possibly only a day or two later, Sterne crossed out "Countess," and wrote in "Bramine," his pet name for Eliza Draper; see letter 192. Perhaps he planned to use some or all of it in the journal; he does return to Cordelia in entries on June 12, July 27, and August 3 (*BJ* 200, 223, 224).

[a]delusive] delusiv *MS* [ms. defective]; delusive *Cross-1925;* <delusio[n]> *C* [b]dropping] droping *MS* [c]<When> God] when God *Cross-1925* [d]like ∧a∧ prophetic] like prophetic *Cross-1925* [e]envy me] envy one *Cross-1925* [f]Let <me>, my] Let me, my *Cross-1925* [g]never <had> heard] never had heard *Cross-1925* [h]*taught*] taught *Cross-1925* [i]nod, <conveyed thro'>] nod conveyed thro' *Cross-1925* [j]more] mor *MS* [ms. defective]

1. my Nuns . . . retreat] See Curtis, 363, n. 1: "The 'delicious Mansions of our long-lost Sisters' and of the ghostly 'Cordelia' are the ruins of Byland Abbey, built about the year 1177 by Cistercian monks from Furness Abbey and abandoned at the Dissolution. To this spot, which lies about two miles north-east of Coxwold, Sterne would wander, there to indulge his reveries, people it with nuns, and contemplate the ivy-covered walls, the brushwood, and purling stream. He was trespassing upon the property of the Stapyltons, of Myton." Sterne's "romantick retreat" is, of course, Shandy Hall, from the rear garden of which it is possible to glimpse the few remaining heights of the abbey; a photograph of the place is provided by Thomson, *Wild Excursions,* facing 211.

"Cordelia" would seem to have nothing to do with King Lear's daughter (but see *ASJ* 386–87, n. to *BJ* 172.20–23); Sterne may have thought it an appropriate "monastic" name, based on *cordeliers* (a French term for Franciscans; Sterne would introduce a Franciscan monk into the early pages of *ASJ*). Alternatively, he perhaps had had access to an unpublished poem by Mark Akenside, "To Cordelia" (1740): "From pompous life's dull masquerade, / From Pride's pursuits, and Passion's war, / Far, my Cordelia, very far, / To thee and me may Heaven assign / The silent pleasures of the shade . . . ." The poem continues in this vein for several more stanzas (see Robin Dix, ed., *The Poetical Works of Mark Akenside* [Madison, NJ: Fairleigh Dickinson University Press, 1996], 409, 521). We have not been able to establish any relationship between Akenside and Sterne, but the poem seems to have been in the possession of Israel Wilkes, John Wilkes's older brother, who spent much of his life in Europe. We thank Professor Dix for his detailed response to our queries concerning Akenside's poem, a short lyric certainly very much in the tradition Sterne evokes with his sentimental visitations to the abbey.

2. these] ?those (the difference between Sterne's "e" and "o" is at times, as here, impossible to establish).

3. delegated Angel] Cf. Elizabeth Carter, "Written at Midnight in a Thunder Storm" (in *Poems on Several Occasions,* 1762): "Thy Life may all the tend'rest Care / Of Providence defend / And delegated Angels round / Their guardian Wings extend." Whether or not Sterne actually alludes to Carter or Akenside (see n. 1), it is clear that his musings show more than a casual familiarity with the poetic idiom of the "graveyard school" (see n. following).

4. some kind hearted Swain] Cf. Thomas Gray, "Elegy Written in a Country Church Yard," ll. 93–97: "For thee, who mindful of th' unhonour'd Dead / Dost in these lines their artless tale relate; / If chance, by lonely contemplation led, / Some kindred Spirit shall inquire thy fate, / Haply some hoary-headed Swain may say . . . ." As Cash, *LY,* 219, notes, "Sterne (as the figure in the fantasy) behaves more like the poet in Gray's *Elegy* than Tristram or Yorick."

5. weed our graves . . . thine] A favorite image for Sterne, beginning with Tristram's homage to Trim in *TS* VI.25.544–45: "Weed his grave clean, ye men of goodness,—for he was your brother . . ."; see also *ASJ,* 27, Yorick's visit to the grave of Father Lorenzo: "I sat by his grave, and plucking up a nettle or two at the head of it . . . I burst into a flood of tears." In *BJ,* 200, Sterne returns to the scene: "I have return'd from a delicious Walk of Romance [to Byland Abbey] . . . & I have pluckd up a score Bryars by the roots wch grew near the edge of the foot-way . . . ."

6. as it was dark . . . what then?] As usual, Sterne's irrepressible bawdiness twines itself around his sentimentalism. The ambiguity of "and why not sleep amongst us too?" is here concretized into an invitation to spend the night; as Sterne inevitably recognizes, he cannot sustain a separation between Yorick and Tristram.

7. enter her <?roof>] Sterne's overscoring is particularly heavy, and while we have accepted Cross's "roof," as did Curtis and Cash, "room" would be the more ready guess and perhaps is overwritten on "roof" (i.e., "<roof>~room~"). If, on the other hand, Sterne deleted the word completely, whatever it might have been, he leaves the sentence with a rather compromising—and characteristic—aposiopesis. Finally, if he did indeed intend "roof," we may have a somewhat sacrilegious echo of Luke 7:6, where the centurion tells Jesus, "I am not worthy that thou shouldest enter under my roof."

8. passenger] Cf. *TS,* I.12.35–36: "a foot-way crossing the church-yard close by the side of his grave,—not a passenger goes by without stopping to cast a look upon it . . . ." This is, of course, Yorick's grave. Once a primary definition of *pas-*

senger ("a person who passes by or through a place; a traveller, *esp.* a traveller on foot" [*OED*]), the usage is probably obsolete today.

9. as a good Christian . . . Nature] If Sterne had a specific text in mind, we have not located it; the closest we could discover is an unlikely source, the Puritan John Owen's *Christologia* (1679): "When the soul hath a view by faith (which nothing else can give it) of the *goodness* of God as manifested in Christ, that is, of the essential excellencies of his nature as exerting themselves in him, it reacheth after him with its most earnest embraces, and is restless until it comes to perfect fruition" (rpt. ed., [Edinburgh, 1772], 211). The entire chapter 13 is filled with similar observations.

10. from y^r heart . . . Pope's head] Cf. letter 62, n. 9; Sterne gave this advice to several correspondents, including his daughter. See also letter 77 (and n. 5), where he distinguishes his own letters from those of Pope or Voiture, because his were never written "to be printed."

154. *To Thomas Hesilrige*[1]

Text: Ms.

York. [Friday,] July 5. [1765]

My dear dear Sir

I made a thousand enquiries after you all this last winter and was told I should see you some part of it, in town—pray how do you do? and how do you go on, in this silly world? have you seen my 7 & 8 graceless Children[2]—but I am doing penance for them, in begetting a couple of more ecclesiastick ones—which are to stand penance (again) in their turns—in Sheets[3] ab^t the middle of Sept^r—they will appear in the Shape of <2> the 3^d & 4 Vol^s of Yorick. These you must know are to keep up a kind of balance, in my shandaic character,[4] & are push'd into the world for that reason by my friends with as splendid & numerous a List of Nobility &c—as ever pranced before a book, since subscriptions came into fashion—I should grieve not to have your name amongst those of my friends—& in so much good company as it has a right to be in—so tell me to set it down—and if you can Lord Maynards[5]—I have no designe my dear Hesselridge upon y^r purse—tis but a crown—but I have a design upon the Credit of[a] Ld Maynard's name—& that of a person I love & esteem so much as I do

You. If any occasions come in y[r] Way of adding 3 or 4 more to the list; y[r] friendship for me, I know will do it——N.B.—You must take their crowns—& keep them for me till fate does me the courtesy to throw me in y[r] Way. This will not be, I fear, this year—for in September, I set out *Solus* for Italy—& shall winter at Rome & Naples: L'Hyvere <de> a Londres ne vaut ‸pas‸ rien, pour les poumones—a cause d'humiditè et la fumè dont l'aire est chargèe[6]—Let me hear how you do soon—and believe me ever your devoted & affect[te]

friend & wellwisher
L. Sterne

Address: To / — Hesselridge Esqre / at Lord Maynards, / Essex
MS: Widener Collection, Houghton Library, Harvard University, 11.4.1.
Pub.: Cross, *Life* (1909), 349; Curtis no. 145.

[a]upon the Credit of] up the Credit *MS* [ms. defective]; upon the credit [of] *Cross-1909;* up[on] the credit of *C*

1. *Thomas Hesilrige*] Curtis, 253, n. 1, identifies him as Thomas Hesilrige (*c.*1741–1817), a great-nephew of Lord Maynard (see n. 5, below); he subscribed to *Sermons* (1766, 1769) and to *ASJ*. When first publishing the letter in 1909 (with a heavy editorial hand almost worthy of Medalle), Cross added the comment: "If all the letters sent forth from Shandy Hall were as gay and courteous as this one, we may easily understand their success .... Mr. Hesselridge, almost needless to say, forwarded his subscription along with Sir William's" (350). Cross erred somewhat in this; Sir William Maynard (1721–1772) and Lady Maynard did indeed subscribe in 1766, but not his distant cousin, Lord Maynard, to whom Sterne seems to be alluding.

2. graceless Children] Sterne alludes to volumes VII and VIII of *TS*, published six months earlier, in January 1765.

3. in Sheets] A punning reference to the paper on which volumes III and IV of *Sermons* were to be printed and the white sheet in which a person found guilty of adultery did public penance (see letter 14, n. 3); cf. Pope, *Dunciad* (1742), I.229–30: "Unstain'd, untouch'd, and yet in maiden sheets; / While all your smutty sisters walk the streets." The two volumes appeared on January 18, 1766; see above, letter 152, n. 13.

4. balance, in my shandaic character] From the onset of *TS* to its final volume, Sterne sought to find a balance between "Tristram" and "Yorick"; see, e.g., letter

35A; and *TS,* IX.12.761: "it is necessary, that . . . a good quantity of heterogeneous matter be inserted, to keep up that just balance betwixt wisdom and folly, without which a book would not hold together a single year . . . ."

5. Lord Maynards] Charles Maynard (*c.*1690–1775), 6th Baron Maynard, and lord-lieutenant of Suffolk (1763–69). Sterne uses this colorful image of the list "prancing" before his book on several occasions; see letters 144, nn. 5, 6, and 147, n. 2.

6. L'Hyvere . . . chargèe] Winters in London are bad for one's lungs because of the humidity and heavy smoke in the air. Sterne's misguided accents, preserved here, would indicate this is his own diagnosis, and not copied from a medical textbook; why he felt the urge to use French is not known.

155. *To Robert Foley*

Text: Medalle

York, [Saturday,] July 13, 1765.

My dear Sir,

I wrote some time in spring,[1] to beg you would favour me with my account. I believe you was set out from Paris, and that Mr. Garrick brought the letter with him—which possibly he gave you. In the hurry of your business you might forget the contents of it; and in the hurry of mine in town (though I called once) I could not get to see you. I decamp for Italy in September, and shall see your face at Paris, you may be sure—but I shall see it with more pleasure when I am out of debt[2]—which is your own fault, for Becket has had money left in his hands for that purpose.—Do send Mrs. Sterne her two last volumes of Tristram; they arrived with your's in spring, and she complains she has not got them.—My best services to Mr. Panchaud.—I am busy composing two volumes of sermons—they will be printed in September, though I fear not time enough to bring them with me. Your name is amongst the list of a few of my honorary subscribers—who subscribe for love.—If you see Baron D'Holbach, and Diderot, present my respects to them[3]—If the Baron wants any English books, he will let me know, and I will bring them with me—Adieu.

I am truly your's,

L. Sterne

MS: Not located.
Pub.: Medalle, no. 57; Curtis, no. 146.

1. I wrote . . . in spring] On April 15 (see letter 147).

2. out of debt] Cash, *LY,* 214–15, argues that the phrasing here "suggests that his other debts had already been paid," meaning his debt to Garrick, which had caused a breach between them (see letter 146); we find the phrasing less specific, although clearly Sterne was trying to meet all his obligations before departure.

3. If you see . . . to them] D'Holbach and Diderot did in fact subscribe to *Sermons* (1766).

156. *To Lady Caroline Hervey*[1]

Text: Combe, *Original Letters*

[Coxwold,] Saturday Noon. [?July 1765]

Here am I now actually at my writing table,—shall I divulge the secret?—in something between the fortieth and forty-fifth year of my life,[2]—I shall leave your Ladyship, if you please, to imagine all the rest;—and, in this advancing state of my age, am I to address myself to all those charms which are composed by the happiest combination of youth and beauty.—

But if you should consider this as a presumption, I will quit those beauties which belong only to early life, and make my application to qualities, which are of every period, and possess that lengthened charm, which makes one overlook the wrinkles of age, and turns the hoary hair into Auburn Tresses.[3] That you will always possess the one as you now do the other, I have heard acknowledged wherever I have heard your name mentioned: nor do I remember that your praise was ever accompanied with the exception of a single *but*—from any of the many various forms and shapes, which envy plants in every corner to snarl at excellence.

But while your Ladyship, by a kind of miraculous power, can subdue envy with respect to yourself,—you may sometimes, without meaning it, encourage its attacks upon others.—For my part, nothing can be more certain than that I shall be envied with a vengeance, when it is known with what a gracious condescension you have indulged my request: but envy, on such an occasion, will add to my laurels instead of withering them:—it is like the scar of glory; and, I am as proud of the one, as the patriot hero has reason to be of the other.

To confine myself, however, to the purpose of this paper.

Permit me to thank your Ladyship most cordially, for permitting me to solicit the honour of your protection[4]—as for attempting to thank you for having granted it, that is not in my power; both my pen and my lips find it impossible to obey the impulse of my heart on the occasion.—Perhaps the time may come, when some of the *Shandy* family may possess a sufficient eloquence, to offer you that homage, which is very devoutly felt, but cannot be adequately expressed,—indeed it cannot, by

Your Ladyship's most faithful,
and obedient humble servant,
L. Sterne

MS: Not located.

Pub.: Combe, *Original Letters* (1788), 192–95; Curtis, no. 147.

Status: Curtis and Hamilton accept this letter as genuine, but the usual caution is recommended; see esp. n. 3. While the letter does not have Combe's usual expropriation of Sternean phrasing, and while it does address a specific issue that can be verified elsewhere (i.e., Lady Caroline's subscription to *Sermons* in 1766), the language and images do seem more labored than Sterne's usual efforts at letters of gratitude.

1. *Lady Caroline Hervey*] Curtis, 255, n. 1: "Lady Caroline Hervey (1736–1819), the youngest daughter of John, Lord Hervey of Ickworth." Her older sister, Lady Lepell Phipps (later Lady Mulgrave), was also acquainted with Sterne (see letter 152, n. 2), and she also subscribed to *Sermons* (1766). Their father was, of course, Pope's Sporus; he had married Mary Lepell, maid of honor to Princess (later Queen) Caroline. Curtis quotes Charles Churchill's "The Times" (*Poems*, 3d ed., 1766), 2:284–85, a description of Lady Caroline and her mother: "That Face, that Form, that Dignity, that Ease, / Those pow'rs of pleasing with that will to please, / By which Lepel, when in her youthful days, / E'en from the currish Pope extorted praise, / We see, transmitted, in her daughter shine / And view a new Lepel in Caroline."

2. in something . . . life] Cf. letter 148, where Sterne provides the same misinformation to the ubiquitous Mrs. F——.

3. hoary hair into Auburn Tresses] One can hope these are Combe's interpolations, and, indeed, he used both phrases in his other writings, the first in "A Poetical Epistle to Sir Joshua Reynolds" (1777), and the second in both *Dance of Life* (1817) and *Second Tour of Doctor Syntax in Search of Consolation* (1820).

4. your protection] Lady Caroline subscribed to *Sermons* in 1766.

157. *To Mr. Dodsley*[1]

Text: Ms.

Coxwould [Monday,] July 19. 1765

Sir

I give you the trouble of a letter merly to rectify a mistake you are under, from supposing I want to reprint a sermon out of the 2 Vol^{s} of Yoricks wch you have purchased—the doing this, I think, would hurt you—& therefore I w^{d} be the last person to do it: the Sermon I meant is <?o>~i~n Shandy which on the contrary will do you good but no hurt.[2]

As for y^{r} uncertainty whether you <should> ∧ought to∧ bid for these Sermons I am going to print—I really see no obstacle from our not agreeing upon our last bargain—I never took that amiss—All I ever took ill was ∧of∧ the gen^{l} report—that You said, you was a loser by my works, wch I am morally sure you never w<ere>~as~—however even that is long since gone out of my mind—for thank God I have yet to learn what the pain of a long [ms. cropped with loss of top line of text] less on small ones.[3]

You say truely, that continuations of Works seldom keep up their sale—the fault I fear is oftener in the author, than in the publick—for want of keeping up variety and the attention of the world with it.

These 2 I am ab^{t}—I trust will be equal in all resp^{ts} to the others—but in some better—as they will have more characters in them[a]—& be something more spirited—they[b] will be the last of Yorick's sermons—that <?I may> will[c] ever be printed—and I suppose[d] will be bought to compleat the Set—or [illegible word] the set of ∧the smaller∧ social duties to wch they are confin'd[4]—& indeed twas by ^a^ gen^l cry for them, that I was led to write them.[5] I shall however print but 5000—in Case the Copy is not sold—& go directly to Italy, & leave them to their fate.[6]

I am Sir
y^r very humble & ob^t
Servt
L. Sterne

Address: To Mr Dodsley / Bookseller / Pell Mell / London
Postmark: 24 IV YORK
MS: Pierpont Morgan Library, MA 4500.
Pub.: Shandean 17 (2006): 80–84.

acharacters in them] characte [ms. damaged] them *MS* **b**spirited—they] spirite [ms. damaged] they *MS* **c**sermons—that will] sermons— [ms. damaged] <?I may> will *MS* **d**suppose] supp [ms. damaged] *MS*

1. *Mr. Dodsley*] James Dodsley; Robert Dodsley had died ten months earlier on September 23, 1764. See letters 36 and 47, n. 4, and appendix, letter viii, for Sterne's financial dealings with the Dodsley firm. The date of this letter is erroneously given as July 29 in the *Shandean* rather than July 19—the number is cropped, but the earlier date is established by the postmark.

2. the Sermon . . . no hurt] In volume IV of *Sermons* (1766), the final sermon is "Abuses of conscience," first published in 1750, and again in *TS*, II.17, where it is delivered by Trim (see *TS* 2:946–51, Appendix Seven, for a detailed account of the three versions). Had Sterne reprinted a sermon from the first two volumes of *Sermons,* Dodsley would have been correct to raise the copyright question.

3. I never . . . small ones] This comment would seem to explain, at long last, the motives that caused Sterne to abandon Dodsley as his publisher (see letter 72, n. 16). Despite his disclaimer, partially obliterated by the loss of a line of text due to cropping, Sterne seems to have remained resentful, and to have allowed his irritation to govern subsequent publishing arrangements, beginning with a failure to come to terms with Dodsley for volumes V and VI of *Tristram,* his turning instead to Becket and Dehondt for their publication in December 1761, and, finally, his continued use of that firm to the end of his life, despite his offering Dodsley at this time the opportunity to bid on the second installment of *Sermons.*

4. These 2 . . . confin'd] The twelve sermons comprising volumes III and IV confirm Sterne's description—namely, that they are about *characters* (e.g., Shimei, Hezekiah, the Levite and his concubine, Felix, the prodigal son, Jacob, and, finally, the rich man and Lazarus); and about the social duties, both those inherent in the "character" sermons, as well as in several others. "National mercies considered. On the Inauguration of his present Majesty," clearly urges civic obedience to and gratitude for one's government, as does "Advantages of Christianity to the world"; "Pride" and "Humility" both discuss social virtues. Sterne's comment might also imply that the first installment of fifteen sermons concentrated on our "larger duties," which in the eighteenth century would have meant "spiritual" duties (the typical distinction made, for example, between the two tablets constituting the ten commandments).

5. & indeed . . . write them] Perhaps the cry was from his congregation, since most of the sermons seem to have been written well before 1760.

6. I shall . . . fate] *Sermons,* 5:469–83 (Appendix Three), and Kenneth Monkman, "Towards a Bibliography of Sterne's Sermons," *Shandean* 5 (1993): 32–109, could discover only that William Strahan printed 4,000 copies of the first edition of volumes III–VII of *Sermons* (see Monkman 75, 88). Perhaps Sterne again lowered his expectations; he does seem to imply that more than 5,000 copies were printed of the first edition of the first two volumes, which went through two more editions before the end of 1760. Sterne departed for Italy in October 1765 (see Cash, *LY* 229), three months before these sermons appeared (January 18, 1766); these two volumes were the only publications of Sterne that he did not personally see through the press.

158. *To John Wodehouse*[1]

Text: Medalle

Coxwould, [Friday, August][2] 23, 1765.

At this moment am I sitting in my summer house with my head and heart full, not of my uncle Toby's amours with the widow Wadman, but my sermons—and your letter has drawn me out of a pensive mood—the spirit of it *pleaseth me*[3]—but in this solitude, what can I tell or write to you but about myself—I am glad that you are in love—'twill cure you (at least) of the spleen,[4] which has a bad effect on both man and woman—I myself must ever have some dulcinea in my head[5]—it harmonises the soul—and in those cases I first endeavour to make the lady believe so, or rather I begin first to make myself believe that I am in love—but I carry on my affairs quite in the French way, sentimentally—"*l'amour*" (say they) "*n'est rien sans sentiment*"[6]—Now notwithstanding they make such a pother about the *word*, they have no precise idea annex'd to it[7]—And so much for that same subject called love—I must tell you how I have just treated a French gentleman of fortune[8] in France, who took a liking to my daughter—Without any ceremony (having got my direction[9] from my wife's banker) he wrote me word that he was in love with my daughter, and desired to know what *fortune* I would give her at present, and how much at my *death*—by the bye, I think there was very little *sentiment* on *his side*—My answer was "Sir, I shall give her ten thousand pounds the day of marriage—my calculation is as follows—she is not eighteen, you are sixty-two—there goes five thousand pounds—then Sir, you at least think her not ugly—she has many accomplishments, speaks Italian, French, plays upon the guittar, and as I fear you play upon no instrument whatever, I think you will be happy to take her at my terms, for here finishes the account of the ten thousand pounds"—I do not suppose but he will take this as I mean, that is—a flat refusal.—I have had a parsonage house burnt down by the carelessness of my curate's wife[10]—as soon as I can I must rebuild it, I trow—but I lack the means at present—yet I am never happier than when I have not a shilling in my pocket—for when I have I can never call it my own. Adieu my dear friend—may you enjoy better health than me, tho' not better spirits, for that is impossible.

Yours sincerely,
L. Sterne

My compliments to the Col.[11]

MS: Not located.
Pub.: Medalle, no. 56; Curtis, no. 148.

1. *John Wodehouse*] See letter 112, n. 3. Medalle merely has "To Mr. W." Cross, *Letters*, 2:86, Curtis, 257, and Cash, *LY*, 221–23, all agree in identifying the addressee as Wodehouse, though none offers a reason. Almost certainly this letter

and letter 160—also addressed by Medalle "To Mr. W."—were written to the same person, but nothing in either letter helps to establish his identity; we accept "Wodehouse" simply because we can find no evidence against him. His multiple subscriptions in 1768 and 1769 suggest a close friendship toward the end of Sterne's life, but why then did he not subscribe in 1766, especially since we know Sterne was very active in soliciting his friends precisely at the time this letter was written?

2. August] Medalle has "May 23, 1765," which is obviously incorrect because the fire described in the letter occurred on August 1–2; see n. 10 below.

3. *pleaseth me*] Sterne's underscoring perhaps indicates a quotation. Wodehouse seems to have announced in his letter an affair of the heart (he would not marry until 1769); in *Pericles,* II.v., King Simonides reads a letter from his daughter in which she declares her love for Pericles, and the scene (and act) ends with their agreement to wed and the King's declaration: "It pleaseth me so well that I will see you wed, / And then with what haste you can, get you to bed" (ll. 92–93).

4. cure you . . . spleen] Cf. *TS,* IV.22.360: "If [my book is] wrote against any thing,——'tis wrote, an' please your worships, against the spleen." For a useful summary of the tradition behind the phrase, see Kay Himberg, "'Against the Spleen': Sterne and the Tradition of Remedial Laughter," *A History of English Laughter from Beowulf to Beckett and Beyond,* ed. Manfred Pfister (Amsterdam: Rodopi, 2002), 69–82. Swift had ironically labeled *Tale of a Tub* "A dangerous treatise writ against the spleen" in his "The Author upon Himself" (see *Scholia* in *Scriblerian* 24.2 [1992]: 241–42).

5. dulcinea in my head] Cf. *ASJ,* 44, where Yorick responds to the "misfortune" of La Fleur's being "always in love": "I am heartily glad of it, said I . . . . In saying this, I was making not so much La Fleur's eloge, as my own, having been in love with one princess or another almost all my life, and I hope I shall go on so, till I die, being firmly persuaded, that if ever I do a mean action, it must be in some interval betwixt one passion and another . . . ." And cf. *TS,* VIII.26.709: "I call not love a misfortune, from a persuasion, that a man's heart is ever the better for it." *OED*'s first illustration of the name of Don Quixote's imagined mistress being used metaphorically is from Smollett's *Roderick Random* (1748).

6. *l'amour . . . sentiment*] Love is nothing without sentiment. Sterne will return to this expression and expand it in *ASJ,* 63: "L'amour n'est *rien* sans sentiment. / Et le sentiment est encore *moins* sans amour" (And sentiment is still *less* without love). If Sterne had a particular source for the sentiment (i.e., "say they"), we have not located it.

7. Now notwithstanding . . . annex'd to it] Sterne repeats this notion in his two fictions; see *TS,* IX.25.787, where Tristram sets about correcting an error, "which

the bulk of the world lie under——but the French, every one of 'em to a man, who believe in it, almost as much as the REAL PRESENCE, '*That talking of love, is making it*'"; and *ASJ*, 33, where he questions the French reputation as lovers:

> how it has come to pass . . . I know not; but they have certainly got the credit of understanding more of love, and making it better than any other nation upon earth: but for my own part I think them errant bunglers, and in truth the worst set of marksmen that ever tried Cupid's patience.
>
> —To think of making love by *sentiments!*

Cash, *LY*, 221–23, exhibits an uncharacteristic distaste for the sentiments of this letter, finding in them a style of "lovemaking he has picked up in France" but not very "apt to win his lady." In declaring his "innocence" to Wodehouse, however, Sterne is contradicting—perhaps mocking—his fictional passages, where, in both instances, he is critical of the French; as to whether or not Sterne's affairs were themselves *sentimental*, one might note the opposed views of Cash and New in *Age of Johnson* 12 (2001): 291–360.

Sterne's final phrase is Lockean; cf. *TS*, V.32.470, where Walter doubts that Trim "has any one determinate idea annexed to any one word he has repeated" in his rote recitation of the Ten Commandments; and see the note to this passage, *TS*, 3:382–83, quoting Locke's prefatory "Epistle to the Reader" (*ECHU* 13).

8. gentleman of fortune] Unidentified.

9. direction] I.e., address.

10. a parsonage . . . curate's wife] The vicarage at Sutton was destroyed by fire on August 1–2, 1765. Curtis, 257, n. 2, quotes the account from the *York Courant* of August 6, repeated in the *London Chronicle*, August 8–10: "Last Thursday . . . in the afternoon, the end of the parsonage house of Sutton in the Forest, next the church, was discovered to be on fire: but by timely assistance, it was extinguished without much damage, and some men sat up all night to watch it. Next day every thing was thought to be safe, but in the afternoon the other end of the house was found to be on fire, which burnt so furiously, that its progress could not be stopp'd, and the whole building was consum'd, but the greatest part of the furniture was saved. How these fires happened is not known." Cash, *LY*, 224–25, provides an elaborated account of the fire based on a letter in *OL*, 45–50, that would seem to be closer to Sterne in a few passages than to Combe: "an affrighted messenger, on a breathless horse . . . arrived to acquaint me, that the parsonage house at ——— was on fire, when he came away, and burning like a bundle of faggots . . . . In short, by the carelessness of my curate, or his wife, or some one within his gates, I am an house out of pocket—I say, literally, out of pocket; for I must rebuild it at my own costs and charges . . ." (cf. *VO* 20–21).

The curate was Marmaduke Callis (see letter 74, n. 4). Cash, *LY*, 225, notes that he had "received an invitation to become the assistant curate of Walsby and

Wellow, Nottinghamshire, at a salary higher than Sterne paid him. He had gone so far as to get testimonial letters from the neighbouring clergy. Sterne, no doubt, had declined to release him. Given this history, most people were going to suppose—as indeed we too suppose—that Callis or his wife or both, their patience worn out, had set fire to the house." Callis remained under Sterne until the fall of 1765, when he did indeed take the position at Walsby and Wellow; Sterne, on his way abroad, nominated Lancelot Colley (*b.* 1740), the parish clerk of nearby Alne, to replace him—at a salary, Cash comments, "£6 above that which he had been giving Callis" (see also Curtis, 144, n. 3).

11. the Col.] Unidentified. Given that Wodehouse resided in Norfolk, we might suggest Lord George Townshend (1724–1807), of Raynham, Norfolk, MP for Norfolk, 1747–64, and a colonel in the army (28th Foot); he subscribed to *Sermons* (1760, 1766). Col. Townshend was the older brother of Charles Townshend (see above, letter 69, n. 11).

159. *To Dear Sir*[1]

Text: Ms.

Coxwould Munday [?August 1765][2]

Dear Sir

I am this moment obliged wth Y^{rs}—I am a vile casuist; but I verily believed, there was no impropriety, (excepting that of the great Liberty I took with you in writing upon my own concerns to you) in telling one Brother, the wants of another, when the supplying them, would give bread to a third[a]——& could you have accomplish'd it—I know y^{r} heart (which is a better casuist than both y^{rs} & my head put together—w^{d} have determined this point on the side ‸of‸ me and my Curate—I gave my last Curat 32 p^{ds}—but if he is a quiet & good subject and <w>~S~hould prefer 34 to it—with all my heart—I am a little incommoded wth spitting of blood to day—but if it stops, shall not be incommoded with the honour & great pleasure of paying my resp^{ts} to his Grace[3] next Sunday—& saying dear Sir, how

much I'm obliged to You.

L. Sterne

MS: Private collection.

Pub.: Kenneth Monkman, "Two Sterne Letters, and Some Fragments," *Shandean* 1 (1989): 123 (fragmentary transcription from *Quaritch Catalogue* 263 [1918]); *Michael Silverman (London) Catalogue* 16 (Summer 1997), item 46 (transcription and facsimile); Christie's online facsimile, lot 0175, auction sale (7411) of the Albin Schram Autograph Collection, July 3, 2007.

[a]a third] *MS;* another *Shandean*

1. *Dear Sir*] Other than that the addressee must be a fellow cleric, his identity is unknown.

2. Date] Cf. Monkman, 123: "Quaritch suggests a date of 1761, but I think 1765 is more likely, and 'my last Curate' would be Marmaduke Callis, whose sudden departure from Sutton after the disastrous fire at the vicarage [see letter 158, n. 10] led Sterne, on the eve of a visit to the Continent, to employ one John Armistead as a stop-gap. Or, after his return to England in 1766, the new curate could have been Lancelot Colley." Monkman found his alternatives in Curtis, 144, n. 3; Cash, *LY,* 225, n. 11, believes, however, that Armistead was a neighboring cleric, who might have filled in from time to time, but was not Sterne's curate. Rather, he suggests, Sterne made arrangements before his departure to Italy in October for Colley to replace Callis. On the other hand, the fact that Colley received £38, £6 more than Callis (see letter 74, n. 4), and not the £2 suggested in this letter, may indicate Sterne was indeed writing about Armistead (or another stop-gap appointment); the letter fails to provide sufficient information for a conclusive identification of its subject.

Additional evidence for dating the letter is perhaps found in Sterne's again spitting blood; see letter 160, where the understated "incommoded" becomes "the most violent spitting of blood that ever mortal man experienced."

3. his Grace] I.e., Archbishop Drummond; see above, letter 78, n. 3.

160. *To John Wodehouse*

Text: Medalle

Coxwould, [Friday,] [?September] 20, 1765.[1]

Thanks, my dear W. for your letter—I am just preparing to come and greet you and many other friends in town—I have drained my ink standish to the bottom, and after I have published, shall set my face, not towards Jerusalem,[2] but towards the Alps—I find I must once more fly from death[3] whilst I have strength—I shall go to Naples and see whether the air of that place will not set this poor frame to rights[4]—As to the project of getting a bear to lead,[5] I think I have enough to do to govern myself—and however profitable it might be (according to your opinion) I am sure it would be unpleasurable—Few are the minutes of life, and I do not think that I have any to throw away on any one being.——I shall spend nine or ten months in Italy, and call upon my wife and daughter in France at my return—so shall be back by the King's birth-day[6]—what a project!—and now my dear friend am I going to York, not for the sake of society—nor to walk by the side of the muddy Ouse, but to recruit myself of the most violent spitting of blood that ever mortal man experienced; because I had rather (in case 'tis ordained so) die there, than in a post-chaise on the road.—If the amour of my uncle Toby do not please you, I am mistaken—and so with a droll story I will finish this letter[7]—A sensible friend of mine, with whom not long ago, I spent some hours in conversation, met an apothecary (an acquaintance of ours)—the latter asked him how he did? why, ill, very ill—I have been with Sterne, who has given me such a dose of *Attic salt*[a8] that I am in a fever—Attic salt, Sir, Attic salt! I have Glauber salt—I have Epsom salt in my shop, &c.—Oh! I suppose 'tis some French salt—I wonder you would trust his report of the medicine, he cares not what he takes himself—I fancy I see you smile—I long to be able to be in London, and embrace my friends there—and shall enjoy myself a week or ten days at Paris with my friends, particularly the Baron d'Holbach, and the rest of the joyous sett—As to the females—no I will not say a word about them—only I hate borrowed characters taken up (as a woman does her shift) for the purpose she intends to effectuate. Adieu, adieu—I am yours whilst

L. Sterne

MS: Not located.
Pub.: Medalle, no. 59; Curtis, no. 149.

[a]*Attic salt*] *M-1776; Atticsalt M-1775*

1. Date] Medalle dates the letter "December 20, 1765," and in the second edition, "December 20, 1766," which was copied by *1780*, and perpetuated by Cross in *Letters*, 2:129. Sterne was in Italy by December 1765 and back in England by the end of June 1766, so neither date is possible; the letter must certainly have been written before the second week in October, when Sterne embarked for the continent. Curtis suggests September 20, 1765, and we concur. Medalle also has the addressee as simply "Mr. W."; see letter 158, n. 1.

2. towards Jerusalem] See Ezekiel 21:1–2: "And the word of the Lord came unto me, saying, Son of man, set thy face toward Jerusalem . . . ."

3. fly from death] Cf. *TS*, VII.1.577: "had I not better, whilst these few scatter'd spirits remain . . . had I not better, Eugenius, fly for my life?"

4. set this poor frame to rights] Sterne had, ironically enough, used exactly the same phrase in letter 127 (February 1764, from Montpellier), when he suggested that "every step I take that brings me nearer England, will . . . help to set this poor frame to rights."

5. getting a bear to lead] See letter 72, n. 9.

6. the King's birth-day] On June 4; see letter 176. As Cash notes, *LY*, 249, "probably Sterne did not reach London as early as 4 June, the king's birthday, which he had hoped to celebrate with Hall; his arrival was not noticed until 17 June, in the *St. James's Chronicle* . . . . By 28 June Sterne was in York and home to Shandy Hall a few days later."

7. a droll story . . . this letter] John Croft, *Scrapeana* (1792), 12–13, tells the story as happening between "Mr. F." and an apothecary in Coney-street, which runs into the Minster Yard; it has been assumed by Cross (1929), 367–68, and Curtis, 258, n. 3, that the friend was Marmaduke Fothergill (see letter 17, n. 5) and the apothecary, Theophilus Garencieres (see letter 9, n. 1); the attributions are not defended, although both seem probable enough.

8. *Attic salt*] "Refined, delicate, poignant wit" (*OED*, which cites Sterne's usage in *TS*, V.3.421, where a witty triumph at Obadiah's expense is reflected in Walter's eyes: "the *Attic* salt brought water into them"). See *Notes* to *TS*, 3:347, n. to 421.2. *Scrapeana* is basically a jest-book, and if Sterne/Fothergill had not told the story himself, we might think of Croft's record simply making use of Sterne's name to retail a commonplace joke. And indeed, some suspicion must be voiced that Sterne is here merely rehearsing a witticism rather than an actual experience.

161. *To John Spencer, Viscount Spencer of Althorp*

Text: Letter Book

Coxwould [Tuesday,] Oct. 1. 1765

My Lord

I wish I knew how to thank You properly for your obliging present;[1] for to do it with all the sense I have of your goodness to me, would offend You; and to do it with less—would offend myself. I can only say to Lord Spencer "*That I thank him*" and promise him at the same time what I know will be more acceptable, That I will make his kind Wish in the Inscription * <upon his present> as prophetic as the singularity of so odd a composition as I am made up<on> of, will let me.[2]

I will trouble your Lordship with nothing more upon this subject—but this—That When the Fates—or Follies of the Shandean family have melted down every ounce of silver belonging to it—

—That this shall go last to the Mint,[3]—but I blush at the thought; for in the worst wreck that can happen, I hereby ordain and decree, That the rest of the Shandeans retire philosophically into some corner of the world with this Testimony of Lord Spencer's Kindness to their Ancestor.

I have, my Lord, the
honour to be, with the
truest regard
Y^{r} Lord^{ps}
faithful Servant
L. Sterne

*Laurentio Sterne A.M: / Joannes Comes Spencer / Musas, charitasque omnes / propitias precatur.

MS: Letter Book, Pierpont Morgan Library, New York.
Pub.: Cross, *Life* (1925), 2:245–46; Curtis, no. 150.

1. present] Cf. *BJ,* 200–201: "This has been a year of presents to me—my Bramine—How many presents have I rec^{d} from You, in the first place?—Ld Spencer has loaded me with a grand Ecritoire of 40 Guineas . . ." (June 13, 1767).

Cash, *LY,* 226–27, believes both passages refer to the same gift from John Spencer (see above, letter 69, n. 8), despite the discrepancy of dates, and that this is the "Ink Standish" that John Croft mentions in his "Anecdotes of Sterne": "what with Presents from the Nobility on which he plumed himself highly (and particularly a Silver Ink Standish from Earl Spencer which he boasted of) . . . his Vanity mounted on his slowest Hobby Horse ran away with him beyond all bounds" (*Whitefoord Papers* 228).

2. That I will . . . let me] Rather oddly, Sterne appends the inscription to his letter (one assumes Spencer had ordered it, and did not need to have it copied out); its difficult phrasing might be translated as "To Laurence Sterne, A.M., John, Earl Spencer, prays to all the Muses and in his love wishes that they may be propitious to you." Although, as Curtis notes (260, n. 5), the title of Earl was expected as early as August 1765, it was not bestowed until October 2; possibly, Sterne copied out the inscription in order to add, by way of compliment, "Comes" (i.e., Earl).

The self-description, "singularity of so odd a composition," echoes the account of Yorick in *TS,* I.11.27, "as mercurial and sublimated a composition,----as heteroclite a creature in all his declensions"; cf. letter 148, n. 12.

3. When the Fates . . . the Mint] Curtis, 260, n. 4, compares Sterne's compliment here to Tristram's tribute to Uncle Toby: "Whilst I am worth one [shilling], to pay a weeder,——thy path from thy door to thy bowling green shall never be grown up.——Whilst there is a rood and a half of land in the *Shandy* family, thy fortifications, my dear uncle *Toby,* shall never be demolish'd" (*TS,* III.34.265).

162. *To Robert Foley*

Text: Medalle

London, [Monday,] October 7, 1765.

Dear Sir,

It is a terrible thing to be in Paris without a perriwig to a man's head![1] In seven days from the date of this, I should be in that case, unless you tell your neighbour Madame Requiere to get her *bon mari de me faire une peruque à bourse, au mieux—c'est à dire—une la plus extraordinaire—la plus jolie—la plus gentille—et la plus——*

—Mais qu' importe? jai l'honneur d'etre grand critique—et bien difficile encore dans les affaires de peruques[2]—and in one word that he gets it done in five days after notice—

I beg pardon for this liberty, my dear friend, and for the trouble of forwarding this by the very next post.—If my friend Mr. F.[3] is in Paris—my kind love to him and respects to all others—in sad haste—

Yours truly,
L. Sterne

I have paid into Mr. Becket's hands six hundred pounds, which you may draw upon at sight, according as either Mrs. Sterne[a] or myself make it expedient.

MS: Not located.
Pub.: Medalle, no. 60; Curtis, no. 151.

[a]Sterne] S—— *M*

1. It is . . . man's head] Cf. Tristram's comment on his entrance into Paris: "the French love good eating——they are all *gourmands*——we shall rank high; if their god is their belly——their cooks must be gentlemen: and forasmuch as *the periwig maketh the man,* and the periwig-maker maketh the periwig——ergo, would the barbers say, we shall rank higher still—we shall be above you all . . ." (*TS* VII.17.600). He returns to the theme in *ASJ,* 67 ("The Wig. Paris."): "When the barber came, he absolutely refused to have any thing to do with my wig: 'twas either above or below his art: I had nothing to do, but to take one ready made of his own recommendation." As Curtis, 260, n. 2, observes, "even Johnson, while travelling in France in 1775, 'was furnished with a Paris-made wig, of handsome construction'"; cf. *ASJ,* 300–301, n. to 67.1ff., quoting Smollett's wry comments on the "total metamorphosis" an English traveler must undergo to be fashionable in Paris. And see letter 86, n. 3.

2. *bon . . . peruques*] "to get her good husband to make me a bag wig, at least—that is to say—one of the most extraordinary—the jolliest—the most genteel—and the most——

But what does it matter? I have the honor to be quite critical—as well as very difficult in the matter of wigs."

Sterne's French is quoted as it appears in Medalle, with all its errors preserved, several of which she corrected in the second edition. Cf. *TS,* IV.S.T.297: "I have been at the promontory of Noses; and have got me one of the goodliest and jolliest, thank heaven, that ever fell to a single man's lot."

3. Mr. F.] Curtis, 260, n. 3, suggests the comedic actor and playwright Samuel

Foote (1720–1777); Sterne mentions Foote by name in letter 163 as being in Paris when he arrived there. Curtis, 261, n. 4, repeats an anecdote from Croft's *Scrapeana* (1792), in which Foote, being asked his opinion of Sterne, supposedly replied, "that with all his *Stars* he was but an *obscure writer*" (130). Sterne and Foote had been linked together in an anonymous epigram published in *Gentleman's Magazine* (November 1760):

> Two choice spirits of late have serv'd up to the town,
> Two dishes high-season'd to make them go down,
> How improv'd are our minds? How enlighten'd our age?
> By Shandy at home, and by Foote on the stage!
> One gives them broad hints of what stuff they are made,
> T'other gives them the cue how to set up the trade.

We thank W. B. Gerard for calling these lines to our attention. Foote subscribed to *Sermons* (1769).

163. *To Thomas Becket*

Text: Notes & Queries

Paris, [Saturday,] Oct. 19, 1765.

Dear Sir,

—I had left a parcel of small draughts the highest not above 50 p^{ds}, with Mr. Panchaude[a] when I rec^{d} yrs, which I shewd. he desired me to tell you He w^{d} never send one of 'em except to Selvin—so they might lay in his hands till you had time to pay 'em—it making no difference; as he w^{d} not negoesiate[b] them to any one else—as you will re^{ve} never have[1] but one at a time, & that not often, drawn upon—you might be easy ab^{t} it.

I have been considering the preface, & indeed have wrote it;[2] but upon reflecting upon it more than when I saw you; I think tis better the Sermons go into the world without Apology—let them speak for themselves. If I change this opinion I will send it you in time—if not, go on without it.

I got here[3] in 5 days, much recovered by my Journey; and set out in few days for Italy. Mr. Wilks and Foot[4] are here.

I am, dear Sir, truely y^{rs},

L. Sterne

Address: To Mr. Becket Bookseller in the Strand London.
MS: Not located.
Pub.: N&Q, 4th ser., 12 (September 1873): 244–45; Curtis, no. 152.

[a]Panchaude] Pancharde *N&Q* [b]negoesiate] *N&Q* [thus spelled]

1. will re^{ve} never have] Thus printed in *N&Q;* we may assume Sterne deleted or intended to delete "re^{ve} [i.e., receive]." The letter as it first appeared in *N&Q* differs in many accidentals from Cross's version in *Letters,* 2:96. Curtis, 261, indicates that Fitzgerald owned the manuscript in 1904, which may indicate that Cross had access to it; Cross was, however, freehanded in normalizing accidentals, and thus we have based our text, as did Curtis, on the first printing. Cross also has the reading "will re^{ve} never have . . . ."

The *N&Q* version is prefaced with an editorial comment: "The following is a *verbatim* copy of a letter addressed by Sterne to his publisher, Becket. The handwriting is excellent, but the orthography and composition are more than usually careless." The submission is signed "C." and "Inverness." Curtis, 261, suggests "Robert Carruthers, of Inverness"; he was a scholar of eighteenth-century literature, publishing a life of Pope in 1853, and an edition of Boswell's *Journal of a Tour to the Hebrides* in 1860.

2. the preface . . . wrote it] Volumes III and IV of *Sermons,* 1766, appeared without a preface; Sterne's draft has not survived.

3. here] Cf. *ASJ,* 68: "so taking down the name of the Hotel de Modene where I lodged, I walked forth . . . ." John Poole, "Sterne at Calais and Montreuil," *London Magazine and Review* 1 (March 1825): 591, locates this hotel in the Rue Jacob, Faubourg St. Germain (see *ASJ* 302, n. to 68.13–14). It is quite possible that Sterne resided there during this stay in Paris, if not on earlier visits, although Cash, *LY,* 229, reminds us that we really do not know if he "stayed there at all, but simply used it in his fiction."

4. Wilks and Foot] John Wilkes (see letter 130, n. 1) was at the Hôtel de Saxe, in the Rue du Colombier, one block away from the Hôtel de Modene. For "Foot" see letter 162, n. 3. Curtis cites Walpole's rather reluctant participation in their company: "You will think it odd that I should want to laugh, when Wilkes, Sterne, and Foote are here; but the first does not make me laugh, the second never could, and for the third, I choose to pay five shillings when I have a mind he should divert me" (to Thomas Brand, October 19, 1765; *Correspondence* 40:386).

164. *To Isaac Panchaud*

Text: Medalle

Beau Pont Voisin,[1] [Thursday,] November 7, 1765.

Dear Sir,

I forgot to desire you to forward whatever letters came to your hand to your banker at Rome,[2] to wait for me against I get there, as it is uncertain how long I may stay at Turin, &c. &c. at present I am held prisoner in this town by the sudden swelling of two pitiful rivulets from the snows melting on the Alps—so that we cannot either advance to them, or retire back again to Lyons—for how long the gentlemen who are my fellow-travellers, and myself, shall languish in this state of vexatious captivity, heaven and earth surely know, for it rains as if they were coming together to settle the matter.—I had an agreeable journey to Lyons, and a joyous time there; dining and supping every day at the commandant's—Lord F. W.[3] I left there, and about a dozen English—If you see lord Ossory,[4] lord William Gordon,[5] and my friend Mr. Crawfurd,[6] remember me to them—if Wilkes is at Paris yet,[7] I send him all kind wishes—present my compliments as well as thanks to my good friend Miss Panchaud[a], and believe me, dear Sir, with all truth, yours,

L. Sterne.

MS: Not located.
Pub.: Medalle, no. 61; Curtis, no. 153.

[a]Panchaud] P—— *M*

1. Beau Pont Voisin] As Curtis, 262, n. 2, notes, Sterne means Pont de Beauvoisin, nine posts (some 54 miles) from Lyon, on the border between France and Savoy. The "bridge" is over the river Guier, which runs into the Rhône at this point; Sterne's "two rivulets" may be a witticism.

2. banker at Rome] The Marquis Belloni, who was also Garrick's banker (*Letters of Garrick* 2:389, 391) and Giacomo Casanova's (*History of My Life,* trans. W. R. Trask [Baltimore: Johns Hopkins University Press, 1997], 7:101, 195). Nothing

more seems to be known about him, although Curtis, 268, n. 5, quotes Wilkes, without citation, to the effect that he was "a great banker." Walpole alludes to an earlier banker, taken by the editors to be Girolamo Belloni (*d.* 1761), author of a treatise on commerce (1750), perhaps the father of the Belloni these figures were dealing with (*Correspondence* 17:23 [to Mann]).

3. Lord F. W.] Identified by Cash, *LY,* 231–32, as William Wentworth, 2d Earl Fitzwilliam (1748–1833), who would have been no more than eighteen years old in 1765. He subscribed to *Sermons* (1766), as did his mother Anne Watson-Wentworth (*d.* 1769), daughter of the 1st Marquis of Rockingham; she had subscribed in 1760 as well. Cash offers no reason for the attribution (in the lists the name is given as "Earl Fitz-William" and "Lady Fitz-William"); Earl Fitzwilliam was the nephew of the 2d Marquis of Rockingham, who had befriended Sterne in 1760 (see letter 52, n. 1).

4. lord Ossory] John Fitzpatrick (1745–1818), 2d Earl of Upper Ossory, Ireland, who subscribed to *Sermons* (1766) and *ASJ* and later purchased the 1760 Reynolds portrait of Sterne (Cash, *EMY* 301; *LY* 230); he entered Parliament in 1767 and is frequently mentioned by Boswell as a member of the Literary Club. In the same letter to Thomas Brand cited in letter 163, n. 4, Walpole goes on to say, anticipating Sterne's observation in *ASJ,* 17 ("*As an English man does not travel to see English men,* I retired to my room"): "Besides, I certainly did not come in search of English; and yet the man I have liked the best in Paris is an Englishman, Lord Ossory, who is one of the most sensible amiable young men I ever saw . . ." (40:386).

5. Gordon] Lord William Gordon (1744–1823), brother of Lord George Gordon, who gave his name to the Gordon riots in 1779. He subscribed to *ASJ.* It is worth noting the extraordinary youthful ages of Sterne's companions. According to Namier and Brooke, 2:519, Lord William "resigned from the army in January 1769 when he eloped to Scotland with Lady Sarah Bunbury, wife of Sir Charles Bunbury . . . ." Well might Sterne's critics argue that he corrupted the morals of his age!

6. Crawfurd] John Craufurd (*c.*1742–1814), of Errol, Perth, "nicknamed at Eton 'The Fish' for his avid curiosity . . . . From 1760 . . . he made annual visits abroad and was as well known in French as in English society. A little man of weak physique but exceptional intelligence, he had a mercurial temperament, in which gaiety, wit, and restless activity alternated with melancholy, hypochondria and indolence. Notorious as a gambler, he was one of the founders of Almacks in 1764" (Namier and Brooke 2:269–70). According to John Macdonald's *Travels in Various Parts of Europe, Asia, and Africa* (1790), Craufurd told Sterne the story that is transformed into "The Case of Delicacy" concluding *ASJ* (see 160ff. and

n.). Craufurd subscribed to *Sermons* (1766) and probably for a large-paper copy of *ASJ* ("Mr. Crawford").

7. if Wilkes is at Paris yet] Wilkes had slipped off to Paris in December 1763 to escape imprisonment for seditious libel after his attacks on Lord Bute's foreign policy in the *North Briton,* and was in the process of negotiating his return, although his request for a full pardon, £5,000 compensation for imprisonment, and £1,500 annual pension fell on deaf ears. He finally returned to London in early February 1768, and reentered Parliament as the representative of Middlesex (see Namier and Brooke 3:639–40; Peter D. G. Thomas, *John Wilkes: A Friend to Liberty* [Oxford: Clarendon Press, 1996], 55–69; and Arthur H. Cash, *John Wilkes,* chs. 8–9).

165. *To Isaac Panchaud*

Text: Ms.

Turin. [Friday,] <D> Nov: 15—1765

Dear Sir

After many difficulties I have got safe & sound—tho eight days in passing the Mountains of Savoy.[1] I am stop'd here for ten days by the whole Country betwixt here[a] & Milano[b] being[c] under Water by continual rains—but I am very happy—and have found my <en>~W~ay into a dozen houses already—to morrow I am to be presented, ^to the King[2]—^ and when that Ceremony is over, have my hands full of Engagements—no english here but S[r] James Macdonald,[3] who meets with much respect.—and M[r] Ogilby[4]—we're[d] all together; and shall depart in peace together. my kind Services to all—& be so good as to forward the inclosed

Y[rs] most truely.
L— Sterne

PS my Comp[s] to[e] Miss Panchaude——

Address: A / Messrs— / Messieurs Foley & Panchaude / Banquiers / Rüe S[t] Sauveur / a Paris.

Endorsed: Turin 15. Nov. 1765 / L. Sterne recu le— /rep le 11 Mars 17

MS: Pierpont Morgan Library, New York (tipped in *Letter Book).*
Pub.: Medalle, no. 62 (with usual "corrections" and without the postscript); facsimile in *Autographic Mirror* 4 (April 7, 1866), 108, item 133; Curtis, no. 154.

[a]here] her *MS* [b]Milano] Milan *M;* Milane *C* [c]being] [ ] *MS* [ms. torn] [d]we're] were *C* [e]Comp[s] to] Comp[t] to *C*

1. passing the Mountains of Savoy] Sterne describes this journey far more dramatically in *ASJ,* 160:

> When you have gained the top of mount Taurira, you run presently down to Lyons—adieu then to all rapid movements! 'Tis a journey of caution; . . . .
>
> Let the way-worn traveller vent his complaints upon the sudden turns and dangers of your roads—your rocks—your precipices—the difficulties of getting up—the horrors of getting down—mountains impracticable—and cataracts, which roll down great stones from their summits, and block his road up . . . .

See the notes to this passage, 6:380, nn. to 160.4 and 5, wherein the editors offer conflicting views of this journey across the Alps from Lyon through the Duchy of Savoy, over the pass of Mount Cenis to Susa, and thence to Turin. Dr. Samuel Sharp, *Letters from Italy* (1767), 289, was awed by the dangers; on the other hand, Giuseppe Baretti, *An Account of the Manners and Customs of Italy* (1768), 2:314, argues that "Those dangerous precipices exist nowhere, but in the imagination of the timorous." Dangerous or not, the passes were often unsuitable for wheeled vehicles, which were dismantled and carried in pieces on mules, while the travelers were carried by porters in a contraption described by Boswell: "I mounted the Alps machine, which consisted of two trees between which were twisted some cords on which I sat. There was also a kind of back and arms, and a board hung before on which I put my feet. In this machine did four fellows (six I should say), changing two and two, carry me over the *saevas Alpes*" (*Boswell on the Grand Tour* [1955], 23). See Cash, *LY,* 233; Cash errs in saying that such scenes "were of no interest to Sterne, and he described them in neither letters nor novels."

2. the King] I.e., Charles Emmanuel III (1701–1773), King of Savoy and Sardinia, considered one of the more enlightened emperors of the House of Savoy. Cash, *LY,* 233–34, quotes Peter Beckford, *Familiar Letters from Italy to a Friend in England,* 2 vols. (Salisbury, 1805), 1:68, on Sterne in Turin: "I met that eccentric genius STERNE—Alas, poor YORICK! many a merry hour have I passed in thy company, admired thy wit, and laughed at thy vagaries!—hours that might have been more profitably employed, but never more agreeably." Beckford (1740–1811), the cousin of the author of *Vathek,* subscribed to *Sermons* (1766).

3. S[r] James Macdonald] Sir James Macdonald (1742–1766), 8th Bart. of Slate, Isle of Skye. Curtis, 264, n. 3, provides samplings of the high praise Macdonald

won, despite his youth, from his contemporaries, both as a scholar and social presence. Boswell lauded him in *Life of Johnson* as the "*Marcellus* of Scotland" (Oxford, 1980), 1129, n. 2; and in *Boswell on the Grand Tour*, 200, wrote that he "wished to be a Sir James Macdonald." Cash, *LY*, 179 and 234, notes that he was part of the Beauchamp circle in Paris in 1764 (see letter 130, n. 15); and also a favorite of Elizabeth Montagu and her circle (see Lord Lyttelton's epitaph in the parish church of Slate, quoted by Boswell in *Journal of a Tour to the Hebrides*, ed. G. B. Hill, rev. L. F. Powell [Oxford: Oxford University Press, 1950], 5:151–53). Macdonald accompanied Sterne from Turin to Rome and Naples, where he fell seriously ill and died in July 1766. See also Hume, *Letters*, ed. Greig, 1:477, 501, 518; 2:76 ("a very extraordinary young Man in all Respects"); and Walpole (to Mann, September 26, 1765): "a very extraordinary young man; for variety of learning. He is rather too wise for his age, and too fond of showing it . . ." (*Correspondence* 22:343–44).

4. M[r] Ogilby] Curtis, 264, n. 4, suggests William Ogilvie (1740–1832), of Banff, "who attended the University of Aberdeen from 1756 to 1760, became Preceptor of a school in Dublin, and married in 1774 the Duchess of Leinster, sister of Lady Sarah Lennox." We might suggest, as a more likely possibility, John Ogilvie (1733–1813), author, cleric, and Fellow, Edinburgh Royal Society, who praised Sterne in his *Philosophical and Critical Observations on the Nature, Characters, and Various Species of Composition* (1774), 1:338–42; quoted in part in Howes, *The Critical Heritage*, 240–41: "In this kind of fable Mariveaux [*sic*], Crébillon, and we may add, our late ingenious countryman Sterne, in his Sentimental Journey, excel all other writers whatever . . . . [His] merit . . . lies in his happy talent of exciting the tenderest and most affecting sensations from the most trifling occurrences . . . ." A "Mr. Ogilby" is listed as subscribing to five large-paper copies of *ASJ;* and a "Mr. Ogilvy" to *Sermons* (1766); one might assume they are the same person.

166. *To Isaac Panchaud*

Text: Ms.

Turin [Thursday,] Nov: 28. 1765

Dear Sir

pray put the inclosed in the post as soon as they[a] arrive at Ruè St Sauveur.

I am just leaving this place with S[r] James Macdonald for Milan &c.

We have spent a Joyous fortnight here, & met with all kinds of honours—& with regret do we both bid adieu but Health on my side, & good sense on his say tis better to be at Rome.

My Comp^s to all friends, to my friend Foley, if at Paris, &c &c . . .

Y^rs most[b] truely
L. Sterne

My best resp^ts to Miss Panchaude.

Address: A Messrs / Foley et Panchaude / Banquiers Rue de St Saveur / a Paris

Endorsed: Turin, 28 Nov. 1765 / L Sterne—— / recu le 3 ?Dec[c] / repl. 11 Mar 1766 / M. / [?]

MS: Pierpont Morgan Library, New York, MA 2984.

Pub.: Medalle, no. 63; Curtis, no. 155.

Status: The manuscript indicates that Curtis's text, taken "from a nineteenth-century copy of the original MS." in his possession, was basically accurate. It also indicates the typical freedoms Medalle took with her father's letters; we provide here the full text of her version of this short letter:

> I am just leaving this place with Sir James Macdonald for Milan, &c.—We have spent a joyous fortnight here, and met with all kinds of honours—and with regret do we both bid adieu—but health on my side—and good sense on his—say 'tis better to be at Rome—you say at Paris—but you put variety out of the question.—I intreat you to forward the inclosed to Mrs. Sterne—My compliments to all friends, more particularly to those I most value (that includes Mr. F. if he is at Paris.)
>
> I am yours most truly,

[a]they] the *MS* [b]most] m[ ] [ms. torn] [c]?Dec] [ms. illegible]

167. *To Isaac Panchaud*

Text: Ms.

Florence [Wednesday,] 18. ^Dc^r^ 1765

dear Sir

I have been a month passing the plains of Lombardie, stopping[a] in my Way at Milan, Parma, Plaenza,[1] Bolognia with Weather as delicious, as a kindly April in England[2]—& have been 3 days in crossing a part of the Apenines coverd with thick snow—sad transition!—I stay here three days[3] to dine with our Plenipo[4]—L^{ds} Tithfield[5] & Cowper[6]—and in 5 days shall tread the Vatican, and be introduced to all the Saints in the Pantheon[7]—I stay but 14 Days to pay these <Common> Civilities & then decamp for Naples.

send the Inclosed to my Wife—& Beckets Letter to London—

Y^{rs} truly
L. Sterne

Address: A Monsieur / Monsr Foley et Panchaud / Banquères Rüe de / St Sauveur / a Paris.

Endorsed: Florence 18 X^{b} 1765 / L. Sterne / recu le 2 Janv. 1766 / rep. Le 11 Mars / M. / [?]

MS: Fitzwilliam Museum, Cambridge.

Pub.: Medalle, no. 64; facsimile in *Isographie des hommes célèbres; ou, Collection de fac-similé de lettres autographes et de signatures* . . . (Paris: T. Delarue, 1828–30, vol. 3, as cited by Curtis); Curtis, no. 156.

[a]stopping] stoping *MS*

1. Plaenza] Sterne's misspelling for Piacenza. Curtis accepts Medalle's "Placenza," printing it as "Plac[e]nza." Piacenza is actually between Milan and Parma on the road to Bologna.

2. as a kindly April in England] Robert Browning was not, then, the first English traveler to Italy whose thoughts turned toward an April day in England.

3. three days] Curtis, 266, n. 4, and Cash, *LY*, 237, note that they actually stayed a few extra days in Florence; see Macdonald's letter to William Weller Pepys, January 5, 1766: "I remain only six days at Florence on account of the excessive cold which I regret less as I mean to return thither in summer. The Venus de Medici herself did not prevent my teeth from chattering when I was looking at her, you may judge from thence of the rest" (*A Later Pepys*, ed. Alice C. C. Gaussen [London: John Lane, 1904], 1:279). The wit of this correspondence suggests why Sterne enjoyed Macdonald's company—and vice versa.

It was during this stay that Sterne "sat for a portrait—the amusing caricature in oil of Sterne and Death which now hangs in Jesus College. The artist was Thomas Patch [1725–1782], who made his home in Florence. Patch was a favourite of Mann [see n. 4 below] . . . and often made cartoons of the English guests—but always with their permission. One cannot but wonder whether Sterne himself suggested that Patch might paint him as Tristram Shandy greeting Death . . ." (*LY* 237). For a full account, see *EMY,* 310–11, and plates VII and VIII; and see also Duncan Patrick, "Tristram's Dialogue with Death and Thomas Patch's 'Sterne and Death,'" *Shandean* 16 (2005): 118–36.

4. our Plenipo] Sir Horace Mann (1701–1786), envoy extraordinary and minister plenipotentiary at the court of Florence from 1740 until his death. His correspondence with Walpole ran into thousands of letters and has served us, as it has all scholars of the eighteenth century, as an invaluable source of fact and gossip concerning the age. Mann was not a completely favorable reader of *TS;* in response to the first two volumes, he wrote to Walpole: "You will laugh at me, I suppose, when I say I don't understand *Tristram Shandy,* because it was probably the intention of the author that nobody should. It seems to me *humbugging,* if I have a right notion of an art of talking or writing that has been invented since I left England. It diverted me, however, extremely, and I beg to have as soon as possible the next two volumes" (*Correspondence* 21:446); he was less enthusiastic after reading them, however: "Nonsense pushed too far becomes unsupportable" (21:521). Nonetheless, as Cash notes, *LY,* 236–38, Mann hosted Sterne at the embassy and provided him with a letter of introduction to Cardinal Alessandro Albani in Rome.

5. Tithfield] Sterne's misspelling and error, noted by both Curtis, 266, n. 6, and Cash, *LY,* 236. It was Lord Titchfield's younger brother, Lord Charles Edward Bentinck (1744–1819), who was in Florence at this time. Lord William Henry Cavendish Bentinck, Lord Titchfield (1738–1809), had returned from his Grand Tour in late 1761 and assumed the title of 3d Lord Portland on the death of his father in 1762. The younger brother, aptly enough for Sternean tastes, was nicknamed "Jolly Heart" (Namier and Brooke 2:82), but although both father and mother, the Duke and Duchess of Portland, were among the subscribers to *Sermons* (1760), the brothers never subscribed to Sterne; the Duchess (or her daughter-in-law) also subscribed in 1769.

6. Cowper] George Nassau Clavering-Cowper (1738–1789), Viscount Fordwich, had become 3d Earl Cowper in 1765. He had arrived in Florence in June 1759, quickly thereafter "losing his whole time by acting the cicisbeo to the Marchesa [Corsi], and entertaining all her dependants" (Mann to Walpole, June 14, 1760; *Correspondence* 21:415; see also 22:361 and 363). Not even the entreaties of his dying father could get him to return to England (Namier and Brooke 2:265–66), and he stayed on in Florence, becoming a leading member of Florentine society. Cf. Gibbon (*Letters,* ed. Norton, 1:182; June 20, 1764): "I hope we shall avoid the fate of Lord Fordwich . . . . The charms of a superanuated beauty have captivated

Figure 6. Caricature of Sterne greeting Death (1765), by Thomas Patch, Jesus College, Cambridge.

him to such a degree as to make him totally forget his country and to fix him at Florence these five or six years without the least prospect of his ever leaving it."

Still, Walpole's scathing descriptions of him ("To tell you the truth, the Earl I conclude is a madman" and "an English Earl, who has never seen his earldom, and takes root and bears fruit at Florence, and is proud of a pinchbeck principality in a third country, is as great a curiosity as any in the Tuscan collection" [*Correspondence* 24:187, 529; letters to Mann, 1776, 1779]) seem unfair; he became a member of the Florentine Academy, encouraged Count Volta in his researches in electricity, and was admitted to the Royal Society. His collection of scientific instruments is now at the University of Bologna; and as an art collector he was able to offer George III Raphael's self-portrait and *Madonna and Child* in 1780 in a vain attempt to be awarded the Garter (Namier and Brooke 2:266). Like Bentinck, he was related to the Egertons (see letter 79, n. 1).

7. the Pantheon] In *ASJ*, 37, Sterne would turn his visit to the Pantheon into an obviously bawdy joke at Smollett's expense: "I met Smelfungus in the grand portico of the Pantheon—he was just coming out of it—'*Tis nothing but a huge cock-pit*, said he—I wish you had said nothing worse of the Venus of Medicis, replied I . . . ." As the editors note, Smollett was already back in England when Sterne was in Rome; similarly, the assertion that he met Smelfungus in Turin (*ASJ* 37) is also untrue if we insist on reading literally.

168. *To Lydia Sterne*

Text: Medalle

Naples, [Monday,] February 3, 1766.

My dear Girl,

Your letter, my Lydia, has made me both laugh and cry—Sorry am I that you are both so afflicted with the ague, and by all means I wish you both to fly from Tours, because I remember it is situated between two rivers, la Loire, and le Cher—which must occasion fogs, and damp unwholesome weather—therefore for the same reason go not to Bourges en Bresse[1]—'tis as vile a place for agues.—I find myself infinitely better than I was—and hope to have added at least ten years to my life by this journey to Italy—the climate is heavenly, and I find new principles of health in me, which I have been long a stranger to—but trust me, my Lydia, I will find you out wherever you are, in May. Therefore I beg you to direct to me at Belloni's at Rome,[2] that I may have some idea where you will be then.—The account you give me of Mrs. C——[3] is truly amiable, I shall ever honour her—Mr. C. is a diverting companion—what he said of your little French admirer was truly droll—the Marquis de ——[4] is an impostor, and not worthy of your acquaintance—he only pretended to know me, to get introduced to your mother—I desire you will get your mother to write to Mr. C. that I may discharge every debt, and then my Lydia, if I live, the produce of my pen shall be yours—If fate reserves me not that—the humane and good, part for thy father's sake, part for thy own, will never abandon thee!—If your mother's health will permit her to return with me to England, your summers I will render as agreeable as I can at Coxwould—your winters at York——you know my publications call me to London.—If Mr. and Mrs. C—— are still at Tours, thank them from me for their cordiality to my wife and daughter. I have purchased you some little trifles, which I shall give you when we meet, as proofs of affection from

Your fond father,
L. Sterne

MS: Not located.
Pub.: Medalle, no. 65; Curtis, no. 157.

1. Bourges en Bresse] Sterne's misspelling confuses Bourges, in central France, some 90 miles east of Tours, and Bourg-en-Bresse, about 200 miles southeast of Bourges and 60 miles southeast of Chalon sur Saône. Clearly, Elizabeth and Lydia were on the move from the south of France, where Sterne had left them two years earlier; Tours is 400 miles northeast of Montpellier; see letter 176, n. 6.

2. find you . . . at Rome] Sterne changed his plans several times in the next few weeks; see letters 169, 170, 173, and 174, where he sets forth and reiterates a plan to return to England with Henry Errington (see letter 169, n. 1), via Austria and Germany rather than through France. This plan never materialized, however, and Sterne eventually caught up with his wayward family in late spring on his way back to England (see letter 176). For "Belloni," see letter 164, n. 2.

3. Mrs. C——] Both Mrs. and Mr. C—— remain unidentified.

4. Marquis de ——] Unidentified.

169. *To Robert Foley*

Text: Medalle

Naples, [Saturday,] February 8, 1766.

Dear Sir,

I desire Mrs. Sterne[a] may have what cash she wants—if she has not received it before now: she sends me word she has been in want of cash these three weeks—be so kind as to prevent this uneasiness to her—which is doubly so to me.—I have made very little use of your letters of credit, having since I left Paris taken up no more money than about fifty louis at Turin, as much at Rome—and a few ducats here—and as I now travel from hence to Rome, Venice, through Vienna to Berlin, &c. with a gentleman of fortune,[1] I shall draw for little more till my return—so you will have always enough to spare for my wife.—The beginning of March be so kind as to let her have a hundred pounds to begin her year with.—

There are a good many English here,[2] very few in Rome, or other parts of Italy.—The air of Naples agrees very well with me[3]—I shall return fat—my friendship to all who honour me with theirs—Adieu my dear friend—I am ever yours,

L. Sterne

MS: Not located.
Pub.: Medalle, no. 66; Curtis, no. 159.

[a]Sterne] S—— *M*

1. gentleman of fortune] Cf. Curtis, 270, n. 6: "Henry Errington (?1738–1819) of Sandhoe, Northumberland, was the son of John Errington, of Beaufront. With inclinations towards Roman Catholicism he had spent at least a year upon the Continent, during which time he met Sterne at Rome and journeyed with him to Naples. From a passage in Lady Mary Coke's *Letters and Journals* (Edinburgh 1889–96, i. 104) it is clear that he would have gone on to Vienna, possibly in company with Sterne as already agreed, had not the death of Lady Stormont, wife of the English Ambassador to the Imperial Court, on 16 March 1766, obliged him to change his plans. He appears to have met Sterne again at York Races in Aug. of this year . . . ." Cash adds that Sterne had known Errington in England (cf. letter

170: "I have known him these three years"), and that he "turned out to be another Thomas Thornhill: he thought it such a privilege to be in Sterne's company that he was willing to pay the bills for most of Sterne's travel expenses" (*LY* 240).

2. There are . . . English here] Cf. Cash, *LY*, 241: "Sterne shared his lodgings with Errington and Macdonald. They must have gone together to call upon William Hamilton, the British envoy to the Court of Naples [see letter 172]. . . . Among the twenty-five Englishmen in Naples [see letter 171] that winter was John Symonds, soon to be appointed Professor of Modern History at Cambridge, for whom Sterne wrote a letter of introduction to Dr Richard Gem in Paris [see letter 174]. Another was Sir William Stanhope, the younger brother of Lord Chesterfield [see letters 225 and 226]."

3. The air . . . with me] As Curtis, 268, n. 4, points out, "Sterne for the sake of a *mot* reversed his opinion of Naples before the abbé Galiani whom he met at the house of d'Holbach in Paris during the spring: 'La seule bonne chose qu'ait dite cet ennuyeux M. Sterne, est lorsqu'il me dit: Il vaut mieux mourir à Paris que vivre à Naples'" (The only good thing this tedious M. Sterne has said is when he told me: it's better to die in Paris than live in Naples) (quoting Ferdinando Galiani, *Correspondance* [Paris, 1881], 2:328).

170. *To John Hall-Stevenson*

Text: Medalle

Naples, [Tuesday,] February 11, 1766[1]

My dear Hall[a]

'Tis an age since I have heard from you—but as I read the London Chronicle, and find no tidings of your death, or that you are even at the point of it, I take it, as I wish it, that you have got over thus much of the winter free from the damps, both of climate and spirits, and here I am, as happy as a king after all, growing fat, sleek, and well liking[2]—not improving in stature, but in breadth.—We have a jolly carnival of it[3]—nothing but operas—punchinellos—festinos[4] and masquerades—We (that is *nous autres*)[5] are all dressing out for one this night at the Princess Francavivalla,[6] which is to be superb.—The English dine with her (exclusive) and so much for small chat—except that I saw a little comedy[7] acted last week with more expression and spirit, and true character than I shall see one hastily again.—I stay here till the holy week, which I shall pass at Rome, where I occupy myself a month—My plan was to have gone from thence for a fortnight to Florence—and then by Leghorn to Marseilles directly home—but am diverted from this by the repeated proposals of accompanying a gentleman, who is returning by Venice, Vienna, Saxony, Berlin, and so by the Spaw,[8] and thence through Holland to England—'tis with Mr. Errington.[b9] I have known him these three years, and have been with him ever since I reach'd Rome; and as I know him to be a good hearted young gentleman, I have no doubt of making it answer both his views and mine—at least I am persuaded we shall return home together, as we set out, with friendship and good will.—Write your next letter to me at Rome, and do me the following favour if it lies in your way, which I think it does—to get me a letter of recommendation to our ambassador (Lord Stormont[10] at Vienna) I have not the honour to be known to his lordship, but Lords P —— or H ——,[11] or twenty you better know, would write a certificate for me, importing that I am not fallen out of the clouds. If this will cost my cousin little trouble, do inclose it in your next letter to me at Belloni.[12]—You have left Skelton I trow a month, and I fear have had a most sharp winter, if one may judge of it from the severity of the weather here, and all over Italy, which exceeded any thing known till within these three weeks here, that the sun has been as hot as we could bear it.—Give my kind services to my friends—especially to the houshold of faith—my dear Garland[13]—to Gilbert[14]—to the worthy Colonel[15]—to Cardinal Scrope[c],[16] to my fellow labourer Pantagruel[17]—dear cousin Antony, receive my kindest love and wishes.

Yours affectionately,
L. Sterne

PS

Upon second thoughts, direct your next to me at Mr. Watson[d] banker at Venice.[18]

MS: Not located.
Pub.: Medalle, no. 67; Curtis, no. 158.

[a]Hall] H. *M* [b]Mr. Errington.] Mr. E ...... *M* [c]Scrope] S—— *M* [d]Mr. Watson] Mr. W. *M*

1. Date] Medalle and Curtis have "February 5, 1766," but see Louis T. Milic, "A Sterne Letter Re-dated," *N&Q,* n.s. 3 (1956): 212–13; Milic argues convincingly that the Principessa di Francavilla's ball was given on Shrove Tuesday, February 11, 1766, and hence that February 11 is also the correct date for this letter. To be sure, Sterne may have started the letter on February 5 with the first few sentences, then put it off for another week—as we know he did on several other occasions.

2. fat, sleek, and well liking] Cf. "good liking," letter 184, n. 3. Now considered archaic, "well liking" was a phrase often connected with "fat" and "flourishing," indicating "in good condition and of lusty appearance; thriving, healthy, plump" (*OED*). Cf. *Love's Labor's Lost,* V.ii.268: "Well-liking wits they have—gross gross, fat fat."

3. jolly carnival of it] Curtis, 270, n. 2, quotes from a letter Gibbon wrote from Naples the year earlier (January 29, 1765): "We are at present in the midst of a most brilliant Carnaval, and shall scarce be able to breath between balls, Operas[,] Assemblies and dinners" (*Letters,* ed. Norton, 1:191). These are, of course, pre-Lenten celebrations. Holy Week in 1766 would be from Palm Sunday, March 23, to Easter, March 30.

4. festinos] An entertainment or feast; Sterne's letter is the second illustration cited in *OED,* the first being Walpole to Mann, 1741.

5. *nous autres*] We others. I.e., the English, specifically, foreigners, more generally.

6. Princess Francavivalla] Curtis, 270, n. 3: "The Principessa Eleonora Borghese [*d.* 1779] had married Michele Imperiali, Principe di Francavilla [*d.* 1782], in 1740. . . . With the prestige of great fortune and Court posts the Principe and his wife had reigned among the first hosts of Naples from the time of their marriage." Curtis quotes from Samuel Sharp's *Letters from Italy . . . in the Years 1765, and 1766,* 2d ed. (1767): "The Prince of *Franca Villa* keeps a kind of open table every night, with twelve or fourteen covers, where the *English* of any figure are at all times received with the greatest politeness. Though it be not the custom to dine or sup with one another . . . yet, during the Carnival, some few exert themselves so far as to give balls . . . ; but the Princess of *Franca Villa* this season gave three in one week, where the company amounted to seven or eight hundred people each time" (110–11; here and in n. 7 below, we have added material from Sharp not included by Curtis).

7. a little comedy] Curtis, 270, n. 4, again cites Sharp, 98: "during the Carnival, there are three or four plays represented several nights, by private persons, and by

Convents, at their own expence, which meet with great applause; and, amongst others, there is one given by the *Cœlestine* Monks, which is extremely celebrated. They perform with remarkable humour and exactness, nor do the Fathers scruple to wear womens dresses, and appear in very lascivious characters."

8. the Spaw] I.e., Spa, Belgium, a famous resort some twenty miles southwest of Liege; it gave its name to all such resorts throughout Europe. The waters had been known since the fourteenth century, and in Sterne's day Spa was considered one of the most fashionable of all bathing places on the continent.

9. Mr. Errington] See letter 169, n. 1.

10. Stormont] David Murray (1727–1796), 7th Viscount Stormont, served as the English ambassador to the Imperial court in Vienna from 1763 to 1772 (Curtis, 271, n. 7).

11. Lords P —— or H ——] Unidentified. Curtis's guess of Lord Hertford (see letter 133, n. 5) is unconvincing since Sterne is obviously thinking of persons Hall-Stevenson would see in London (Sterne assumes he has departed Skelton to winter in town). The subscribers' lists offer too many possible candidates, including Lords Pembroke (1734–1794) and Portmore (1700–1785), both of whom subscribed to *Sermons* (1766) and to *ASJ;* Lords Pigot (1719–1777) and Powlett (1720–1794), subscribers to *Sermons* in 1766 and 1769, 1760 and 1769, respectively; and Henry Temple, Lord Palmerston (1739–1802), MP for East Looe, 1762–68, and a member of the Literary Club. He is one of the very few who took all four opportunities to subscribe to Sterne's works. Lord Huntingdon (1729–1789) is a possible candidate for "Lord H ——"; he was lord lieutenant of the West Riding, almost certainly acquainted with Hall-Stevenson, and subscribed to *Sermons* (1760, 1766); but Lord Hinchingbrooke (1744–1814), MP for Brackley at this time, is also possible, and the fact is that Hall-Stevenson would almost certainly have known every lord who subscribed to Sterne's works, as did Hinchingbrooke in 1766. And, needless to say, there is always the possibility that Sterne named lords who had not subscribed.

12. Belloni] The banker; see letter 164, n. 2.

13. Garland] Traditionally assumed to be Nathaniel Garland (*c.*1721–1770), of Epsom, who subscribed to *Sermons* (1760 and 1769), and may also be the Mr. Garland who subscribed to *ASJ.* Tollot mentions a Mr. Garland in his letter to Hall-Stevenson in 1764 (*Seven Letters,* ed. Cooper [1844], 1, 2, 7), and Cash, *EMY,* 188, n. 2, cites another letter in which Tollot sends greetings to Lascelles, Garland, and Gilbert (the Cooper papers, Beinecke Library, no. 22). Still, the identification is tenuous at best, especially since an equal candidate presents himself in the subscription lists, James Garland, Esq. (*b. c.*1717), a London attorney, who was an enthusiastic supporter of Sterne, subscribing to four sets of *Sermons* in 1760

and to a large-paper copy of *ASJ*. His name appears in subscription lists where Hall-Stevenson also appears—e.g., George Thompson's *A Description of the Royal Palace . . . called the Escurial* (1760) and Francis Fawkes, *Theocritus* (1767), a work to which Sterne also subscribed (see letter 151, n. 10). What makes these lists particularly telling is that Thomas Gilbert (see letter 137, n. 8), Colonel Thomas Hall (see below, n. 15), and Robert Lascelles (see letter 73, n. 7) were all subscribers to both works; Nathaniel Garland is not listed.

Here and elsewhere, alternative identifications based on the subscription lists are intended to suggest only that "traditional identifications" are not always justified.

14. Gilbert] See letter 137, n. 8.

15. Colonel] Curtis suggests George Lawson Hall, but without comment. Hall-Stevenson had two brothers, however, who were colonels, Thomas Hall and George Lawson Hall; see letter 72, n. 13. For a lone "Colonel" the more likely candidate is probably Colonel John Hale; see letter 142, n. 10.

16. Cardinal Scrope] See letter 151, n. 10. The sobriquet "Cardinal" does support the assumption that this is Thomas Scrope, of Colby, as Curtis, 271, n. 13, asserts.

17. Pantagruel] Rev. Robert Lascelles, or "Panty" to his fellow Demoniacs; see letter 73, n. 7.

18. Mr. Watson . . . Venice] See letter 172. Cf. Boswell's address in Venice: "My address is *Chez M. Jean Watson à Venise*" (*Boswell on the Grand Tour*, 94; letter of June 15, 1765).

171. *To Isaac Panchaud*

Text: Medalle

Naples, [Friday,] February 14, 1766.

Dear Sir,

I wrote last week to you, to desire you would let Mrs. Sterne[a] have what money she wanted—it may happen as that letter went inclosed in one to her at Tours, that you will receive this first—I have made little use of your letters of credit, as you will see by that letter, nor shall I want much (if any) till you see me, as I travel now in company with a gentleman—however as we return by Venice, Vienna, Berlin, &c. to the Spaw, I should be glad if you will draw me a letter of credit upon some one at Venice, to the extent of fifty louis—but I am persuaded I shall not want half of them—however in case of sickness or accidents, one would not go so long a rout without money in one's pocket.—The bankers here are not so conscientious as my friend Panchaud. They[b] would make me pay twelve per cent. if I was to get a letter[1] here.—I beg your letters, &c. may be inclosed to Mr. Watson at Venice[2]—where we shall be in the Ascension.[3]—I have received much benefit from the air of Naples—but quit it to be at Rome before the holy week.—There are about five and twenty English here—but most of them will be decamp'd in two months—there are scarce a third of the number at Rome—I suppose therefore that Paris is full—my warmest wishes attend you—with my love to Mr. Foley[c] and compliments to all—I am, dear Sir, very faithfully,

Yours,
L. Sterne

Sir James Macdonald is in the house with me, and is just recovering a long and most cruel fit of the rheumatism.[4]

MS: Not located.
Pub.: Medalle, no. 68; Curtis, no. 160.

[a]Sterne] S—— *M* [b]Panchaud. They] P. they *M* [c]Foley] F. *M*

1. a letter] I.e., a letter of credit.
2. Mr. Watson at Venice] See letter 170, n. 13.
3. the Ascension] Cf. Macdonald to Pepys (May 3, 1766): "All the English are gone to Venice for the Ascension" (*A Later Pepys* 1:284). Ascension Day, one of the chief festivals of the Christian church, is celebrated forty days after Easter; in 1766 it would have been on Thursday, May 7. By that date, Sterne was on his return trip to England, probably already in France.
4. Sir James . . . rheumatism] Macdonald did not accompany Sterne and Errington to Rome, but stayed in Naples; cf. his letter to Pepys, from Rome on May 3, 1766: "I returned from Naples three weeks ago. Having suffered so severely from the dreadful rhumatism I had had in that place, I was far from having recovered all my strength at the time of my return" (1:283). See also 1:286, where, after describing his appalling symptoms—written July 5, 1766—he strikes a Sternean tone: "However I keep up my spirits as well as I can, and jog on soberly

in hopes of better days"; those better days never came, and Macdonald died of an aneurism of the heart at Frascati, outside of Rome, on July 26, 1766, at the age of 24.

172. *To William Hamilton*[1]

Text: Ms.

Rome [Monday,] March 17. 1766.

Dear Sir.

I could not be at ease in my Conscience, If I did not do by Letter, what I was not able to do in words the Eve of my departure; & that was to thank you and M[rs] Hamilton for the many civilities and attentions paid me by you both, during my Stay at Naples; which upon looking back upon at this distance, I estimate higher, and <?mo><and> feel the pleasure I partook of more sensibly, than I did, w[<th>n] I was actually enjoying them——This is contrary to Nature's Etiquette—I feel it true however this bout, and with all the Sensibility of a temper not ungrateful I return You both all I am able; & that is my best thanks.[2] My friend & self had a voyage of it by Mount Cassino,[3] full of cross accidents;[4] but all was remedied along the road by sporting and Laughter—<I>~W~e dined & suppd and[a] lay at the Monastery of Cassino where we were rec[d] and treated like Sovereign Princes <?at>~——~and on Saturday[5] by eleven o clock in the Morning got here without bodily hurt except that a Dromedary of a beast fell upon me in full Gallop, and by rolling[b] over me crushd me as flat as a Pankake[6]— but I am growing round again. Cox[c] and Hyat[7] leave me nothing to tell you ab[t] the news of Rome, They will be arrived <b>~a~t Naples before this. However there is an Acc[t] here that <G> the great Rock of Giberaltor is overthrown by an earthquake[8]—tant pis pour nous:[9] we could only defend the place ag[st] Men.

M[r] Errington presents his respects to You & M[rs] Hamilton in the best manner—I beg to add mine.

When You see Miss Tuting[10] pray present my most friendly good wishes <t>~f~or her—as well as respects to her—I have the Honour Dear Sir to be with all warmth and <go>~T~ruth

Y^{r} most faithful & most obliged
L. Sterne

PS

my Service to all friends[d]—not omitting the Countesses de Rouget & Mahong.[11]

Address: A / Sua Excelleza[e] / Il Sig^{n} Hamilton / Envoyè de sa / Majestè Britanique / a Naples
Endorsed: Mr Sterne March 17th / 1766.
MS: University of Rochester Library, Mss. Collection.
Pub.: W. H. Arnold, *Ventures in Book Collecting* (New York: Charles Scribner's, 1923), 173–74; Curtis, no. 161.

[a]and] at *MS;* at Cuy *Arnold* [b]rolling] roling *MS* [c]Cox] Core *Arnold, C* [d]friends] frieds *MS* [e]Excelleza] Exceltera *C*

1. *William Hamilton*] Sir William Hamilton (1730–1803), a grandson of the 3d Duke of Hamilton, was appointed British envoy extraordinary and plenipotentiary to the court of Naples in 1764. He and his wife, Catherine, *née* Barlow (*d.* 1782), were well known for their hospitality and interest in art and antiquities. Cf. Gibbon's notice: "I have not yet seen Mr Hamilton our Minister but he is extremely liked by the English here" (*Letters,* ed. Norton, 1:191; January 29, 1765); and Sharp's: "Mr. *Hamilton,* the Envoy, a very polite Gentleman, receives company every evening, which conduces much to the pleasure of the *English* residing here. It is the custom, when neither the Opera, nor any particular engagements prevent, to meet at his house, where we amuse ourselves as we are disposed, either at cards, the billiard-table, or his little concert; some form themselves into small parties of conversation" (*Letters from Italy* 76; November 1765). Unfortunately, Hamilton's fame now rests largely on Admiral Nelson's affair with his second wife, Lady Emma Hamilton; see n. 11.

2. all I . . . best thanks] Sterne uses a similar formula several times in his letters; see, e.g., letter 60 (to Warburton), written six years earlier: "I return your lordship all I am able—my best thanks."

3. Mount Cassino] Arnold and Curtis misread Sterne's hand as "Cussino," but Sterne often left his "a" opened. The Benedictine Abbey of Monte Cassino was "the traditional stopping place for travellers making the Rome-Naples journey

via Capua. Some fifty years earlier the monks had added a handsome wing to the monastery in which they housed guests 'of distinction.' Meals were excellent and the monks themselves waited at table" (Cash, *LY* 244). In 1944 the monastery had to be destroyed by Allied forces when the German army used its elevated situation to control the valleys below; the present building is a reconstruction. What Arnold thought might be meant by "supped at Cuy" eludes us, and probably was only his errant attempt to make sense of Sterne's hand.

4. cross accidents] Cf. *TS,* I.5.9: "a set of as pitiful misadventures and cross accidents as ever small HERO sustained." The note to this passage, 3:53, n. to 9.1, indicates the frequency of the phrase in Sterne's sermons.

5. on Saturday] As Curtis, 274, n. 5, suggests, Sterne arrived on March 15, planning, as did many travelers, to spend Holy Week, March 23–30, in Rome. Sharp arrived on March 20 for the same purpose, and gives a full account of the events, *Letters from Italy,* 191–203, concluding "these things are worth seeing once, and were a man to chuse a month in the year to spend at *Rome,* I would recommend that month, in which the Holy Week is included."

6. flat as a Pankake] Cf. *TS,* III.27.253, apropos Slop's forceps and Tristram's nose: "he has crush'd his nose . . . as flat as a pancake to his face." The phrase is proverbial; see Tilley, P39, and *ODEP,* 267; and *Notes* to *TS,* 3:261, n. to 253.9–10.

7. Cox and Hyat] Curtis reads "Core," but fails to identify him. John Ingemells, *A Dictionary of British and Irish Travellers in Italy, 1701–1800* (New Haven: Yale University Press, 1997), 248, lists a Mr. Coxe traveling with a companion whose name is variously spelled as "Hiet[?]" or "Monsu Hijet," and of whom nothing else is known. A Mr. Hyatt subscribed to *Sermons* (1760), as did a John Cox; Capt. Cox subscribed in 1766, and Rev. Mr. Cox in 1769, but of course we have no idea whether any of these subscribers can be identified with Sterne's Italian acquaintances.

8. the great . . . earthquake] Curtis, 274, n. 7: "Sterne may have received an exaggerated account of the violent hurricane that caused damage to the amount of £140,000 at Gibraltar on 30 Jan. 1766; *St. James's Chronicle,* 8–11 March 1766 [p. 4]." Sterne's pride in the defense of Gibraltar may reflect the fact that his father was stationed there between 1727 and 1730.

9. tant pis pour nous] Too bad for us. Sterne plays with the phrase *tant pis* (as opposed to *tant mieux*) in *ASJ,* 39; see 6:277, nn. to 39.19 and 39.21. Cf. letter 187, n. 4.

10. Miss Tuting] I.e., Sarah Tuting, for whom see letter 135, n. 1. Cf. Cash, *LY,* 243: "Sterne may have danced that night [at the masked ball mentioned in letter 170] with Sarah Tuting, that attractive consumptive with whom he had been so sentimentally smitten at York in 1764. But the greeting he sent to her through Hamilton . . . does not suggest an intimacy." In fact, it is even possible, given the

phrasing, that Tuting was expected in Naples and had not arrived before Sterne's departure.

11. Countesses de Rouget & Mahong] Curtis, 274, n. 9, suggests Rouget may be "Marie de Croy-Havré (*b.* 1737), who married in 1760 Gabriel François, Comte de Rougé (1729–86)." Mahong (correctly, Mahony) is Lady Anne Clifford (1715–1793), the widow of Count James Joseph Mahony (1699–1757), a soldier of fortune at the court of Naples (see Ingemells, *Dictionary* 629). Curtis's summary of her career is worth quoting: "In her youth the Countess Mahony met Horace Walpole, in her middle years Sterne, and [she] lived on at Naples to caress for nine days on end in 1787 the illiterate and irresistible Emma Lyon, lately arrived to become the mistress of Sir William Hamilton" (274–75, n. 10). Emma Lyon is probably better known under her adopted name, Emma Hart, soon to become the mistress of Admiral Nelson.

173. *To Richard Chapman*[1]

Text: Ms.

Rome—[Monday,] March 17. 1766.

Dear Sir

I am return'd from Naples to this City; where I stay a fortnight in my way to Venice, being engaged to travel with a Gentleman of fortune thro' all Germany homewards—this Journey, as we must stay some time at Vienna and 8 weeks at the King of Prussia's Court where I am invited; ^it^ will hold me so long that I shall not have occasion for the ground adjoining to my house ^this summer^, so you will let it to M[r] Scot[2] for the rent I pay; begging[a] only that he will have an eye to the house, and that whatever wants repairing may be done as it happens—I am greatly mended in my health:—the whole winter at Naples having ^been^ warm as Spring; and tis now so hot here, we can scarse be out of doors in the middle of the day—I hope by this long round home to be set up for ever—as I we pass thro' the longest Cut of all Germany, then traverse thro' the Kingdome of Bohemia—the Electorate of Saxony, Prussia, Hanover, Brunswick &c then thro Holland and Flanders; so that if exercise will strengthen a man I shall have enough of that Remedy. The Duke ^Prince^ of Mecklenbourg,[3] our Queen's Brother, has been here these six months; and as we lodge next door <?with> to him, we have the honour to be much with him & every evening with him at his Chambers; he is a very good natured young Creature. We have some[b] english Nobility here, & some of great fashon & fortune, with one of wch it is, I make this long Journey wch will not be accomplished till about Christmas; <w>~b~y which time we shall be both got to London; & the April after, I shall see you I hope all well and in good Spirits: Mrs Sterne & my girl are leaving Tours where they have had but bad health; and are advised to return again into the Southernmost part of France to recover their health[c] again which there is no doubt but they will accomplish. as I shall not be at Coxwould this Summer, & consequently shall not stand in need of a Servant, I shd be obliged if you would Let Nanny Write[4] know as much—that if She shd chuse to go to Service till my return she may have time to fix herself—on my return if She is not better placed, I should be very glad to hire her.

give my Service[d] to Mrs Chapman & to yr Brother & Sister[5]—to Fetherston,[6] S[?][7] and all friends

I am truly Yrs
L. Sterne

Address: To / Mr Chapman / Newborough near / Coxwould Yorkshire. / Ingleterra. / [another hand:] via milano

MS: Kenneth Monkman Collection, Shandy Hall.

Pub.: Kenneth Monkman, "Two More Unpublished Sterne Letters," *Shandean* 2 (1990): 143–48 (facsimile fig. 43).

[a]begging] beging *MS* [b]some] som *MS* [ms. defective] [c]health] heath *MS* [d]Service] Services *Shandean*

1. *Richard Chapman*] Lord Fauconberg's steward; see letter 15, n. 5.

2. Mr Scot] Identified by Monkman, 145, n. 4, as Francis Scott, one of Lord Fauconberg's principal tenants in Coxwold. No subletting is recorded in the Fauconberg Rentual 1755–1771, now in the Beinecke Library, Yale University. Doubtless, Sterne's earlier-than-expected return to Yorkshire at the end of June, the result of Errington's change of plans, made subletting unnecessary (see letter 169, n. 1).

3. Mecklenbourg] George August (1748–1785), Prince of Mecklenburg-Strelitz. Monkman, 145, n. 7, leads us to Horace Mann's comments on the prince, who was in Florence later in 1766: "We have here a very good little Prince, who pretends to nothing, but whose very civil behaviour attracts respect. I mean the youngest Prince Mechlembourg, to whom in the light of the Queen's brother this Court shows great attentions" (*Correspondence* 22:437–38; letter dated July 19, 1766).

4. Nanny Write] Unidentified. Monkman, 145, n. 9, reminds us of *TS*, IX.17.769, where Tristram mentions, apropos of his household arrangements, the "thin poor piece of a Vestal (to keep my fire in) and who has generally as bad an appetite as myself." The vestal priestesses were virgins responsible for keeping the eternal fire in the Temple of Vesta, goddess of home and hearth.

5. Brother & Sister] Monkman, 145, n. 10, identifies the brother as William Chapman (1721–1781), of Wildon Grange, a mile northwest of Coxwold. We have not been able to find information on their sister—or, possibly, a sister-in-law.

6. Fetherston] Unidentified. A Mr. Fetherston subscribed to *Sermons* in 1766; Thomas Fetherston (*c.*1684–1772) is mentioned by Curtis, 7, n. 13, as related to Sterne's mother and is mentioned in Sterne's "Memoirs." However, as Monkman notes, 145, n. 11, it was "a common enough name locally." William Featherston subscribed to Thompson (see above, letter 170, n. 13), as did a goodly number of Yorkshire inhabitants.

7. S[?]] The ms. is badly damaged at the fold.

174. *To Dr. Richard Gem*[1]

Text: Curtis

Rome Easter Sunday [March 30, 1766]

Dear Sir

The Gentleman who gives you this is Mr Symonds[2] a person of Learning & Character; he has spent most of the winter at Naples whilst I was there, and returns thro' Paris to England; an Acquaintance with Dr Jemm during his short stay at Paris will make him happy—and I hope you so too, & therefore I have wrote to bring you together

—I am much recover'd in my health, by the Neapolitan Air—I have been here in my return 3 Weeks, seeing over again wt I saw first in my way to Naples—In a few days I leave this place for Venice from whence with Mr. Errington whom I accompagny home I proceed to

Vienna, Dresden, Berlin, Hanover, Holland &c. Whether we come back to Paris is not yet settled. I have so many worthy men I esteem there, I shd be very happy, if it can be brought to pass—We have pass'd a jolly laughing winter of it—and having changed the Scene for Rome; We are passing as merry a Spring as hearts could wish. I wish my friends no better fortune in this world, than to go at this rate—haec est Vita dissolutorum[3] (what a vile pen?) my comp^s^ to Foley to Baron Holbach—Diderot—Panchaude—but say something civil on my part to my old good friend Miss Panchaude whom no one wishes better to—

I am dear Sir
Very truly yrs.
L. Sterne

Address: To Dr. Jemm at Paris / N.B. To be given to Mr. Symonds when he pass'd by Rome.
MS: Not located.
Pub.: Cross, *Life* (1909), 380–81 (in part); Curtis, no. 162.

1. *Richard Gem*] Richard Gem (*c.*1716–1800), spelled "Jemm" by Sterne, and "Jamme" (emended to "Jemm" in the 2d ed.) by Cross, was physician to the British Embassy in Paris since 1762, and an intimate of the *philosophes;* see W. P. Courtney, *N&Q,* 11th ser. 2 (1910): 121–23. Cross had quoted portions of the letter in 1909. Curtis worked from a transcription provided by Cross, and notes that the manuscript, formerly in the possession of Frederick Locker-Lampson, a Victorian poet, had not been traced.

2. Mr Symonds] John Symonds (1729–1807), like Richard Gem a graduate of St. John's College, Cambridge (BA 1752, MA 1754), would succeed Thomas Gray as Professor of Modern History at Cambridge in 1771. His publications include *Remarks on an Essay on the History of Colonisation* (1778); *Observations upon the Expediency of Revising the Present Edition of the Gospels and Acts of the Apostles* (1789); *Observations upon the Expediency of Revising the Epistles* (1794); and numerous articles in Young's *Annals of Agriculture.*

3. haec est Vita dissolutorum] Thus the life of the dissolute. Sterne's parenthetical comment is a puzzle. An inkblot on the ms. would fully explain it, although not the question mark. Perhaps an exclamation point is intended instead—and

perhaps not "pen" but "pun," referring to "go at this rate" and the idea of death that hovers around "dissolutio."

175. *To Mrs. T——*

Text: Curtis/Sotheby Auction Catalogue

Lanoüe near Dijon,[1] [Saturday,] *May* 24, 1766

Miss T—— having gone out of the room (but upon what occasion god[a] knows) Tristram Shandy has thought meet,[b] to profit by her absence,[c] and the temptation this *Void*[d] has laid in his way—of[e] sending his best respects to the mother—not[f] altogether for the sake of the daughter,[g] (for that wd be uncivil)[h] but in Testimony[i] of his esteem for Mrs. T—— and her worthy character, and at the same time, in[j] Homage to the Graces of her fair Offspring[k], which appear so lovely in the eyes of Tristram Shandy—that[l] 'tis well[m] for the fair Goddesse[n] that he is under a slight pre-engagement—indeed 'tis only Marriage.[o]

MS: Not located.

Pub.: Sotheby Catalogue of Valuable Books, June 15–16, 1897, 21; Curtis, no. 163; *The Library of H. Bradley Martin, Sotheby (New York),* (Auction, April 30–May 1, 1990, item 3232).

Status: Curtis based his text on that reproduced in the Sotheby catalogue of 1897, which differs considerably from the text reproduced by Sotheby in 1990. Clearly, the copyists were not as careful as one might wish. We have based our text on the *1990* version, but retained several readings from Curtis that seemed to us more accurate. Our efforts to locate the manuscript after its 1990 sale have been unsuccessful.

On the key question of the addressee, we have altered Curtis's "Triste" to "T——" because the *1990* copyist records "Tutte," and suggests a misspelling of Tuting, hence Sarah Tuting (see above, letters 135, n. 1, and 172, n. 10). Curtis identified Mrs. Triste as Agnes Hore Trist, wife of Browse Trist (*c.*1698–1777), MP for Totnes, Devonshire, 1754–63, and the mother of three daughters, Agnes, Elizabeth, and Susanna; no other link has ever been established between this family and Sterne. On the other hand, we know Tuting was on the Continent at this time, although it seems unlikely, even for Sterne, to misspell the name of an old Yorkshire family.

Curtis, 276, provides a partial text of the letter Miss T—— wrote to her mother, a text based, we must assume, on the *1897* Sotheby description (he says that this was the first half "of a sheet of paper" beneath which Sterne wrote his note); the rather garbled *1990* description indicates that Sterne's note "is written on the following page," and that Miss T—— wrote on both sides of a half-sheet. Miss T——, we might note, indicates that Sterne wrote on "the otherside." Curtis's text of Miss T——'s letter differs from that reproduced in *1990;* Curtis, 276:

> *Lanoüe near Dijon, May* 24, 1766. My ever dearest Madam. . . . You will see by the date of this that we are not at Dijon. We found the town but unpleasant to live any time in, . . . all the people of any fashion has been to see us . . . : We have had a visit of three days from they [*sic*] famous Docr. . . . pleasing, agreeable man as well as the most sensible that I ever was in company with. I was obliged to go out of the room, and in the meantime Tristram Shandy took up my pen & wrote what you see on the other side; he goes to England to-morrow, and takes this letter to put in the office in London.

The *1990* version is quite different:

> We have had a visit of three days from the famous doc[to]r Sterne. He is one of the most agreeable men, as well as the most senceable men that I was ever in company with. . . . I was obliged to go out of the room and in the meantime, Tristram Shandy took up my pen, and wrote what you see on the otherside, he goes for England tomorrow and takes this letter to put in the office in London.

That Sarah Tuting would call Sterne a doctor seems as highly unlikely as her description of the "doctor"; Curtis's version would seem to indicate that the doctor and Sterne are two different people.

[a]god] *1990;* God *C* [b]meet,] *1990;* meet *C* [c]absence,] *1990;* absence *C* [d]*Void*] *1990;* void *C* [e]way—of] *1990;* way, of *C* [f]mother—not] *1990;* mother, not *C* [g]daughter,] *1990;* daughter *C* [h]uncivil)] *1990;* uncivil), *C* [i]Testimony] *1990;* testimony *C* [j]same time, in] same in *C;* same, in *1990* [k]Offspring] *1990;* offspring *C* [l]Shandy—that] *1990;* Shandy, that *C* [m]'tis well] *C;* his will *1990* [n]the fair Goddesse] *C;* the Goddesse *1990* [o]Marriage] *1990;* marriage *C*

1. *Lanoüe near Dijon*] We have taken both the place and the date from Curtis's transcription of Miss T——'s letter (see *Status* above). In letter 176, Sterne writes that he is staying "near Dijon" at "a delicious Chateau of the Countess

of M———." Curtis, 278, n. 2, suggests this is Lydia's error for the comtesse la Noüe, and argues that Sterne and Miss T—— were guests of Gabriel-François de la Noüe-Vieuxpont (1714–1779), comte de Vair, comte de la Noüe, and his wife, Marie-Marguerite Chevalier, comtesse de Vair et de la Noüe. The town was, in all likelihood, Fontette, where la Noüe's good friend, Jean-Baptiste-Antide Fevret (1713–1796), chevalier de Fontette, resided. Miss T——'s "*Lanoüe*" would, as Cash notes, indicate the house, not a town (*LY* 246, n. 58).

176. *To John Hall-Stevenson*

Text: Medalle

[Saturday,] May 24,[1] near Dijon [1766]

Dear Antony,

My desire of seeing both my wife and girl has turn'd me out of my road towards a delicious Chateau of the Countess of M———,[2] where I have been patriarching it[3] these seven days with her ladyship, and half a dozen of very handsome and agreeable ladies—her ladyship has the best of hearts—a valuable present not given to every one.—Tomorrow, with regret, I shall quit this agreeable circle, and post it night and day to Paris, where I shall arrive in two days, and just wind myself up, when I am there, enough to roll on to Calais[4]—so I hope to sup with you the king's birth day, according to a plan of sixteen days standing.[5]—Never man has been such a wildgoose chace after a wife as I have been—after having sought her in five or six different towns, I found her at last in *Franche Comté*[6]—Poor woman! she was very cordial, &c. and begs to stay another year or so—my Lydia pleases me much——I found her greatly improved in every thing I wish'd her—I am most unaccountably well, and most accountably nonsensical—'tis at least a proof of good spirits, which is a sign and token given me in these latter days[7] that I must take up again the pen.—In faith I think I shall die with it in my hand, but I shall live these ten years, my Antony, notwithstanding the fears of my wife, whom I left most melancholy on that account.—This is a delicious part of the world; most celestial weather, and we lie all day, without damps, upon the grass—and that is the whole of it, except the inner man (for her ladyship is not stingy of her wine) is inspired twice a day with the best Burgundy that grows upon the mountains, which terminate our lands here.—Surely you will not have decamp'd to Crazy Castle before I reach town.—The summer here is set in good earnest—'tis more than we can say for Yorkshire—I hope to hear a good tale of your alum works—have you no other works[8] in hand? I do not expect to hear from you, so God prosper you—and all your undertakings.—I am, my dear cousin,

Most affectionately yours,

L. Sterne

Remember me to Mr. Gilbert[a], Cardinal Scrope[b], the Col. &c. &c. &c.[9]

MS: Not located.
Pub.: Medalle, no. 69; Curtis, no. 164.

[a]Gilbert] G—— *M* [b]Scrope] S—— *M*

1. Date] Medalle dates the letter "May 25," but the date and content of letter 175 to "Mrs T——" make it more probable that it was written on the eve of Sterne's setting out for Paris, as argued by Curtis, 277–78.

2. M———] See letter 175, *Status,* for the likely identification of the countess.

3. patriarching it] *OED* records this passage as its last example of a nonce-word for playing the patriarch; Sterne may be thinking of himself as an elder among these half dozen "handsome and agreeable ladies" or perhaps as a Solomon or David figure: "In pious times, e're Priestcraft did begin / Before *Polygamy* was made a sin" (Dryden, *Absalom and Achitophel,* ll. 1–2).

4. to Calais] Dijon to Paris took 38 posts, Paris to Calais another 34. One "post" was about six miles.

5. sixteen days standing] Sterne indicated his plan to be back in England in time for the King's Birthday (June 4) as early as letter 160, to Wodehouse (September 20, 1765)—i.e., before his departure. Here he is probably referring to the new itinerary worked out when the planned excursion with Errington collapsed, sometime after March 16 (see letter 169, n. 1); perhaps he had shared that itinerary in an earlier May letter to Hall-Stevenson, now lost.

6. *Franche Comté*] It is unknown where precisely Sterne found his family. Franche Comté is a region along the Swiss border comprising Haute Saône, Doubs, and Jura. Elizabeth and Lydia had moved across France, from the Pyr-

enees north to Montauban and then further north to Tours, before moving east toward the Swiss border. Sterne possibly found them in or near Bourg-en-Bresse (see letter 168), some 90 miles south of Dijon, and just west of the Franche Comté; or perhaps a more northern town (e.g., Dole) in the Franche Comté, which would explain why Elizabeth and Lydia would stop at Chalon sur Saône on their way south (see letter 178, n. 3).

7. sign . . . latter days] As so often in his letters to Hall-Stevenson, Sterne slips into a mock-scriptural tone. He probably knew that "sign" and "token" were considered interchangeable translations; see Cruden, *Concordance,* s.v. *sign.* "Latter days" is an Old Testament commonplace—e.g., Numbers 24:14, Hosea 3:5, etc.

8. alum works . . . no other works] See letter 137, n. 10. Hall-Stevenson does not seem to have had any "other works in hand," assuming Sterne means literary works; he had published *A Pastoral Puke* in 1764 and would publish his *Makarony Fables* in 1768; see, however, letter 179 for another possible effort at this time, a pamphlet attacking Warburton, published in 1766.

9. Remember me . . . &c.] Cf. letter 170, nn. 14, 15, and 16, for the probable identifications of these friends.

177. *To Elizabeth Vesey*[1]

Text: Letter Book

London. [Friday,] June 20; [1766][2]

To M[rs] <Vesey>.

of the two bad cassocs,[3] fair Lady, which I am worth in the world, I would this moment freely give the better of 'em to find out by what irresistable force of magic it is, that I am influenced to write a Letter to you upon so short an Acquaintance—*short,* did I say—I unsay it again: I have had the happiness to be acquainted with M[rs] Vesey almost time immemorial—surely the most penetrating of her sex[4] need not be told that intercourses of this kind are not to be dated by hours, days or months, but by the slow or rapid progress of our intimacies which can be measured only by the degrees of penetration by w[ch] we discover Characters at first sight, or by the openess and frankness of heart w[ch] lets the by-stander into it, without the pains of reflection; either of these spares us, what a short life can ill afford and that is, that long and unconscionable time in forming Connections, which had much better be spent in tasting the fruits of them—now, I maintain, that of this frame & contexture is the fair Mrs Vesey——her character is to be read at once; I saw it before I had walk'd ten paces besides <you> her.—I believe in my Conscience, dear Lady, that you have absolutely no inside at all——

That you are graceful, & elegant & most desirable &c &c. every common beholder, who only stares at You as a dutch Boore does at the Queen of Sheba[5] <,> ∧in a puppit Show∧ can readily find out; But that You are sensible, and gentle and tender—& from one end[a] to the other of you full of the sweetest tones & modulations, requires a Connoisseur of more taste & feeling—in honest truth You are a System of harmonic Vibrations[6]—You are the sweetest and best tuned ∧of all∧ Instruments—∧O∧ Lord! I would give away my other Cassoc to touch you——but in giving this <my> last rag of ∧my∧ Priesthood[b] for this pleasure You perceive I should be left naked—<nay> if not quite dis-*Orderd*:[7]—so divine a hand as y^{rs} would presently get me into Order<s> again—but if You[c] suppose, this would leave me, as You found me—∧believe me∧ dear Lady, You are mistaken.

all <this> which being weigh'd and put together, let me ask you <d>~m~y dearest Mrs V. what business you had to come here from Ireland—or rather, what business have You to go back again——the deuce take you[8] w^{h} your musical and other powers—could nothing serve you but you must turn T. Shandys head, as if it was not turn'd enough already: as for turning my heart; I forgive You, as you have been so good as to turn ∧it∧ towards so excellent & heavenly an Object—

now, dear Mrs Vesey, if You can help it, dont think of Y^{r}self. but believe me wth great Esteem for y^{r} Character & self.

Y^{rs}
L— S.

MS: Letter Book, Pierpont Morgan Library, New York.
Pub.: Sterne's Letters to His Friends on Various Occasions (1775), no. 9 (*VO*); Curtis, no. 76.

Status: A version of this letter was first published in Combe's *Sterne's Letters to His Friends on Various Occasions* (1775; letter 9), surrounded by forgeries and hence long considered with dubiety until the discovery of a copy in the *Letter Book.* This copy, in Sterne's hand, is addressed to Mrs. Vesey, whose name is then lined through, although it is spelled out several times in the text itself. The large number of substantive variants between the *Letter Book* and *VO* versions may suggest the very free hand Combe exercised as an editor or the possibility that he had access to another version. We can hope that no letter was actually sent to Mrs. Vesey, who would not have been amused. In fact, on a quite conjectural level, we might wonder if Combe and Sterne collaborated to write a humorously insinuating (if somewhat sophomoric) letter, and added piquancy to their project by pretending Mrs. Vesey was the addressee. The possibility that Sterne met Combe in London at this time is at least suggested by an allusion to him in letter 179 as having provided a post chaise for Sterne's use in July.

We list the substantive variants between the two versions here for the convenience of comparison:

Letter Book	*VO*
• the better of 'em	the latter of them
• I have had the happiness to be acquainted with M[rs] Vesey almost time immemorial—surely	I have been acquainted with Mrs. V—— this long and many a day: for, surely,
• which can be measured	which are measured
• at first sight	at once
• by-stander	observer
• can ill afford	could ill afford
• that long	the long
• fruits	sweets
• now, I maintain, that of	Now of
• ten paces besides	twenty paces beside
• Lady, that you have absolutely no inside at all	lady, if truth was known, *that you have no inside at all*
• graceful, & elegant & most desirable	graceful, elegant, and desirable
• who only stares	who can stare
• in a puppit Show	*om.*
• readily	easily
• sensible, and gentle	sensible, gentle

• requires a Connoisseur of more taste & feeling	requires a deeper research.
• in honest truth	*om.*
• Vibrations—You are the sweetest and best tuned	vibrations—the softest and best attuned
• O Lord	Lord
• giving this <my> last rag ‸my‸ of Priesthood for this pleasure You perceive I	giving my last rag of priesthood for that pleasure, I
• if not quite	to say nothing of being quite
• presently get me	presently put me
• dear Lady, You are mistaken	dear Mrs. V——, you are much mistaken
• all <this> which being weigh'd and put together, let me ask you <d>~m~y dearest Mrs V. what business	All this being duly put together, pray, dear lady, let me ask you, What business
• from Ireland—or rather, what	from ———? or, to speak more to the purpose, what
• go back	return back
• T. Shandys head	*Tristram Shandy*'s head
• as for turning my heart	as for your turning my heart
• of Y^{r}self. but believe me wth great Esteem	of *yourself*—¶But believe me to be, / With the highest esteem

There are a corresponding number of variants in the accidentals, including capitalization and punctuation.

[a]from one end] *Combe;* from end *MS* [b]of ‸my‸ Priesthood] ‸my‸ of Priesthood *MS* [c]You] Yo *MS* [edge of ms.]

1. *Elizabeth Vesey*] For the problem of the addressee, see *Status.* Elizabeth Vesey (*c.*1715–1791) was a good friend of Elizabeth Montagu since the early 1750s and, with her, one of the first to host Bluestocking parties "at which the entertainment consisted of conversation on literary subjects" (Anna Miegon, "Biographical Sketches of Principal Bluestocking Women" in *Reconsidering the Bluestockings,* ed. Pohl and Schellenberg, 36). Miegon notes that Vesey was probably born in Ireland, the daughter of Mary Muschamp and Sir Thomas Vesey, Bishop of Ossory, and that her first husband, William Handcock of Willbrook in Westmeath, a member of Parliament, died in 1741. Her second marriage, to Agmondesham Vesey, an Anglo-Irish landowner and politician, occurred before

1746. Her social circle was the subject of two poems, Charles Hoole's "Modern Manners" and Hannah More's *Bas Bleu; or Conversation,* and, again according to Miegon, included Johnson, Burke, Garrick, Gibbon, Reynolds, Warton, Adam Smith, Percy, and Sheridan; the absence of Sterne's name is indicative of the fact that we simply have no idea how well Sterne knew her.

On December 30, 1761, she was in Reynolds's studio when the Earl of Bath was sitting for his portrait. The occasion had been organized by Elizabeth Montagu, who had also invited Sterne to be there (Cash, *LY* 116); if true, however, then the comment in this letter, that they have had "so short an Acquaintance," might seem to make the 1766 dating incorrect. But the letter is clearly addressed from London, and in June 1760 and also June 1761, Sterne was already back in Yorkshire; the only time Sterne was in London in June was in 1766.

There is but one other reference to Elizabeth Vesey in Sterne's correspondence, and that is found in letter 152, itself of doubtful provenance, from which it appears that Sterne erroneously thought that she was a widow (if indeed he, and not William Combe, wrote that part of the letter). See Myers, *The Bluestocking Circle,* 7–9, 251–53, 265–66, a convincing portrayal of Vesey as a "self-abnegating wife"; and Deborah Heller, "Subjectivity Unbound: Elizabeth Vesey as the Sylph in Bluestocking Correspondence," in *Reconsidering the Bluestockings*, 215–34. Heller analyzes Vesey's nickname, the "Sylph," in language that at times makes her sound almost Shandean: "The ability to be different, to do something new, to transcend the bounds of convention" (221); and she also notes the concern that Montagu and Elizabeth Carter had about the precarious state of Vesey's health, of body and mind, at least from the 1770s: "Indeed she is formed for enjoyments much superior to that *foolish* world, which too much engages her mind, and leads it on by the dancing phantom of an *ignus fatuus* of pleasure, which she wearies her spirits in pursuing, and which she never is able to overtake" (230; quoting a letter from Carter to Montagu). See also Felicity A. Nussbaum, *The Limits of the Human: Fictions of Anomaly, Race, and Gender in the Long Eighteenth Century* (Cambridge: Cambridge University Press, 2003), 84–108, and esp. 98–100, where several similarities between the characters of Sterne and Vesey are posited; Nussbaum leaves undocumented, however, her claim that "rumors of an illicit liaison between [them] abounded after a series of apocryphal obscene amorous letters from Sterne to Vesey surfaced" (100). In all that has been uncovered about Vesey, there is no indication that she would have been at all receptive to Sterne's letter if indeed it was posted to her; no other Sterne letter addressed to Vesey—apocryphal, obscene, or amorous—has survived.

2. Date] Curtis, 137, dates the letter "?1761," based on the Reynolds's studio visit; Cash, *LY,* 25–27, seems to agree that the letter was written at this early date, although he fails to account for the fact that June 1766 was the only June Sterne

was in London. Cash also suggests that "her assemblies were more like the literary salons of Paris than those of any other British woman" (26), but provides no evidence; and he debunks the tradition of a relationship between Sterne and Vesey by noting the gossip originated with Combe. Finally, whether sent in 1761 or 1766 (when Vesey was 50 years old), we can agree with Cash, 27, that "if Sterne had been foolish enough actually to send his letter, it would have instantly put an end to any budding romance or friendship."

3. two bad cassocs] Cf. *TS,* III.11.211: "I vow and protest, that of the two bad cassocks I am worth in the world, I would have given the better of them, as freely as ever *Cid Hamet* offered his,——only to have . . . heard my uncle *Toby*'s accompanyment." See *Notes* to *TS,* 3:218, n. to 211.18–21, where the allusion to Cervantes is traced; and cf. letter 222.

4. most penetrating of her sex] For the importance of Sterne's notion of "female penetration," see letter 148, n. 13. The bawdiness of the entire passage is obvious enough, but the possible echo of Wycherley's Horner is perhaps worthy of note: "ask but all the young Fellows of the Town, if they do not lose more time like Huntsmen, in starting the game, than in running it down . . ." (*The Country Wife,* I.i; ed. Arthur Friedman [Oxford: Clarendon, 1979], 253).

5. dutch Boore . . . Sheba] Sterne's "dutch Boore" would seem to indicate some awareness of the origin of "boor" as a generalized uneducated rustic in the Dutch word for *peasant* (see *OED,* s.v. *boor;* cf. *boer*). The Queen of Sheba visits Solomon with great pageantry and precious gifts (1 Kings 10); it was a popular subject in puppet shows.

6. harmonic Vibrations] A favorite image both for Sterne and for the century; see *ASJ,* 6:370, n. to 153.6–9, for a record of its occurrences elsewhere in the Sterne canon.

7. quite dis-*Orderd*] For an earlier play on being "dis-ordered," see letter 150, n. 6.

8. the deuce take you] Cf. *TS,* VIII.11.669–70, where Tristram discusses his varying attitudes toward his mistress:

> Brightest of stars! thou wilt shed thy influence upon some one———
> The duce take her and her influence too . . . .
> I would not touch it for the world . . . .

There is sufficient similarity between the tone of this chapter and Sterne's letter to provide a bit of additional support for the 1766 dating.

178. *To Isaac Panchaud*

Text: Medalle

York, [Saturday,] June 28, 1766.

Dear Sir,

I wrote last week to Mr. Becket to discharge the balance due to you—and I have receiv'd a letter from him telling me, that if you will draw upon him for one hundred and sixty pounds, he will punctually pay it to your order—so send the draughts when you please—Mrs. Sterne[a] writes me word, she wants fifty pounds—which I desire you will let her have—I will take care to remit it to your correspondent—I have such an entire confidence in my wife, that she spends as little as she can, tho' she is confined to no particular sum—her expences will not exceed three hundred pounds a year,[1] unless by ill health, or a journey—and I am very willing she should have it—and you may rely, in case it ever happens that she should draw for fifty or a hundred pounds extraordinary, that it and every demand shall be punctually paid—and with proper thanks; and for this the whole Shandean family are ready to stand security.—'Tis impossible to tell you how sorry I was that my affairs hurried me so quick thro' Paris, as to deprive me of seeing my old friend Mr. Foley[b] and of the pleasure I proposed in being made known to his better half[2]—but I have a probability of seeing him this winter.—Adieu dear Sir, and believe me

Most cordially yours,
L. Sterne

PS

Mrs. Sterne[a] is going to Chalon, but your letter will find her I believe at Avignon[3]—she is very poorly—and my daughter writes to me with sad grief of heart that she is worse.

MS: Not located.
Pub.: Medalle, no. 70; Curtis, no. 165.

[a]Sterne] S. *M* [b]Foley] F. *M*

1. three hundred pounds a year] A generous stipend, usually considered sufficient for a gentleman to live a gentleman's life.

2. better half] Curtis, 279, n. 2, cites the *Register of Marriages,* St. Anne's, Soho, for the marriage of Foley to an heiress, Dorothy Hinchliff, daughter of Thomas Hinchliff, merchant of London (1677–1741), on December 21, 1765. The bride was unkindly described by Lady Hervey in a letter to Horace Walpole as "that old fool of forty who chooses to present him [Foley] with sixty-five thousand pounds which her father old Hinchliff cheated half England out of to enable his daughter to buy a master" (letter of December 19, 1765; *Correspondence* 31:86).

3. Chalon . . . Avignon] Chalon sur Saône is some 40 miles south of Dijon, 30 miles south of Dole (see letter 176, n. 6). This would favor the notion that the Sternes met somewhere north of Chalon (perhaps Dole), and that as Elizabeth and Lydia began their journey south to Avignon, where they would eventually settle, it was their first stop before entering the Saône valley.

179. *To John Hall-Stevenson*[1]

Text: Letter Book

Coxwould [Tuesday,] July 15. 1766

To J. Hall Esqre

Thou hast so tender a conscience my dear Cosin Antonio, and takest on so sadly for thy sins, that thou wast certainly meant and intended to have gone to heaven—if ever Wit went there—but of that, I have some slight mistrusts, inasmuch as we have all of us (accounting myself, thou seest, as one) had, if not our good things, at least our good sayings in this life; & the Devil <?Yo>~tho~u knowest, who is made up of spight,[2] will not let them pass for nothing: and now I am persuaded in my mind, that it was by the suggestions of Satan, which, I trust my dear Antonio, we shall live finally to beat down under our feet, That thou gavest heed unto these Reviewers, & didst not rather chuse to cut them, as Jehudi did the role, with a penknife,[3] than vex and pucker[4] thy conscience at the rate thou doest. Heaven forgive me! for I said [?twice[a]] as much both of <Dr> Kunastrokius and Solomon too—but every footman and chamber maid in town knew both their Stories before hand[5]—& so there was an end of the matter.

These poor Devils, as well as thou and I, will have "*their Say.*"—or else they cannot have their supper;[6] & the best way I trow <?wd> is to let them stop their own mouths—[7]

A thousand nothings, or worse than nothings, have <snatch'd> been every day snatching my pen out of my hands since I parted with you; I take it up to day in good earnest & shall not let it go till York races[8]—<unless ‸the Devil‸ dear Antony, should tempt thee [word(s) illegible] thy [word(s) illegible] before thee, and so drive thee out of the nobleness of thy Contritions> unless the devil should tempt you in yr Contritions to Scarborough—If you would profit by yr misfortunes, & laugh away misery <for>~there~ for a week—ecco lo il vero Punchinello![9] I am your man. only send me Letter of <?the time> "*Ifs*, and *hows*, and *whens*" for you know I have reformd[b] my Cavalry—<Combes[10]> ‸B — — —‸ has left me his post chaise, & when I say my Lord's prayer, I always think of it—to understand wch it will put thee Antony, to runing over thy *Pater noster*[11] wch I fear thou hast not done these many years.

may god give you grace[12]
& believe me, dear Cosin
most Affly Yrs
L.S

MS: Letter Book, Pierpont Morgan Library, New York.
Pub.: Cross, *Life* (1925), 2:247–48; Curtis, no. 167.

[a] ?twice] [ms. torn] [b] reformd] reform *MS* [on right-hand edge]

1. *John Hall-Stevenson*] This letter answers a short note sent by Hall-Stevenson two days earlier, and surviving in Sterne's transcription (Curtis, no. 166; here printed in appendix, no. xviii). In it, Hall-Stevenson laments an attack on him by "the Reviewers" and avers contrition for his "bestiality with the Bishop of Gloucester"—i.e., William Warburton (see above, letter 46, n. 1). An anonymous pamphlet, *The First Chapter of Prophecies of the Prophet Homer. With A Letter to the B[ishop] of G[loucester],* had been published in London by J. Wilkie on April 7, 1766, and had been promptly vilified by both the *Critical Review* 21 (April 1766): 319 and *Monthly Review* 34 (May 1766): 398–99. Curtis, 280, n. 1, describes the

affair thus: "This satire, which ridiculed the bishop's attempt in the second book of his *Divine Legation* to prove that in the sixth book of the *Aeneid* Virgil had represented the initiation of Aeneas to the Eleusinian mysteries, might have received from the reviewers the praise due to its wit had they not been enraged by an allusion to Mrs. Warburton's alleged affair with Thomas Potter . . . . In consequence the reviewers were quick to have a stroke at the writer," the *Monthly Review* calling him "an object of detestation and abhorrence . . . and an utter stranger to the first principles of decency and good-breeding."

Curtis was not quite ready, however, absolutely to assign the pamphlet to Hall-Stevenson, concluding finally that it was "not impossible that he was the author." Hartley, "Sterne's Eugenius," 444, n. 21, adds some additional "circumstantial evidence," but also demurs: "There is not, however, enough to make the attribution entirely defensible." Cash, *LY,* 251–52, recounts the episode, but seems mistaken in believing Hartley rejected Hall-Stevenson's authorship (see 251, n. 5). That the pamphlet does not appear in Hall-Stevenson's 1795 *Works* may well be the result of the contrition he expresses here. We conclude, as does Cash, that in the absence of any other writing to which this exchange between Sterne and Hall-Stevenson might refer, the April 7 pamphlet must be considered the subject.

Cash, 252, n. 7, suggests that Hall-Stevenson's letter of contrition is the result of something Sterne wrote to him after reading the pamphlet, but we have no documentation for that. While it is true that they do not seem to have discussed these reviews when they had opportunity in May and June, it can easily be assumed that contrition took its time lodging in Hall-Stevenson's conscience.

2. Devil . . . of spight] Sterne repeats an aspect of Satan emphasized by Milton; see, e.g., *Paradise Lost,* 2.384–85: "done all to spite / The great Creator"; and 9.176–78: "this Man of Clay, Son of despite, / Whom us the more to spite his Maker rais'd / From dust: spite then with spite is best repaid."

3. as Jehudi . . . penknife] See Jeremiah 36:21 and 23: "So the king sent Jehudi to fetch the roll . . . . And it came to pass, that when Jehudi had read three or four leaves, he cut it with the penknife, and cast it into the fire . . . ."

4. vex and pucker] *OED* does not record *pucker* as Sterne uses it here; it does record the colloquial figurative use of the substantive: "a state of agitation or excitement; a flutter, a fuss," citing Richardson's *Pamela* as its first illustration: "Mrs. Jewkes . . . seem'd in a great Pucker."

5. I said . . . before hand] See letter 45 (and n. 9), where Sterne defended himself in much the same language for exposing Dr. Richard Mead as Kunastrokius in *TS,* I.7.12.

6. will have . . . their supper] Sterne probably glances at the proverbial expression, "No song, no supper" and its variants; see Tilley, S1003*a,* and *ODEP,* 574.

7. let them stop their own mouths] A scriptural phrase; see, e.g., Psalms 63:11: "the mouth of them that speak lies shall be stopped" and 107:42: "all iniquity shall stop her mouth"; Romans 3:19, Job 5:16, and Titus 1:11. Sterne uses the phrase in sermon 23 ("The parable of the rich man and Lazarus"): "when every man's case shall be reconsidered,——then wilt thou be fully justified in all thy ways, and every mouth shall be stopped" (*Sermons* 4:218); and again in sermon 44 ("The ways of Providence justified to man").

8. York races] Sterne was busy writing volume IX of *TS*, but he had perhaps not gotten very far; toward the end of the first chapter, Tristram describes himself "sitting, this 12th day of August, 1766, in a purple jerkin and yellow pair of slippers, without either wig or cap on . . ." (IX.1.737). Perhaps, in true Shandean fashion, he had simply returned to the first chapter after writing other parts of the volume; see letter 181, n. 3. The York Races in 1766 were held between August 18 and 23.

9. ecco lo il vero Punchinello!] Sterne alludes to a story he would have heard while in Naples, recorded in Sharp's *Letters from Italy* (1767), 183–84:

> At *Naples* there is a place called the *Largo del Castello,* not unlike our *Tower-Hill,* the resort of the idle populace. Here, every afternoon, Monks and Mountebanks, Pick-pockets and Conjurors, follow their several occupations. . . . It happened one day, that Punch succeeded marvellously, and the poor Monk preached to the air, for not a living creature was near him: Mortified and provoked that a puppet-shew, within thirty yards of him, should draw the attention of the people from the Gospel, to such idle trash, with a mixture of rage and religion, he held up the crucifix, and called aloud, *Ecco il vero Pulcinella;—"Here is the true* Pulchinello,—*come here,—come here!"*——The story is so well known in *Naples* to be true, that the most devout people tell it . . . .

10. Combes] "Combes" is heavily crossed out, but we accept Curtis's reading as the correct one. It is conjectured that Combe, who was soon to go abroad (see letter 188), visited Sterne and left his post-chaise with him (Curtis, 282, n. 9; Cash, *LY* 250–51), but that does not account for the deletion of "Combes" and the substitution of the unidentified "B— — —" in his place; we, too, have no explanation for one or the other. Sterne "reformed" his "cavalry" by purchasing two long-tailed horses (see letter 211).

11. my Lord's prayer . . . *noster*] One assumes Sterne means that the post-chaise leads him into temptation—i.e., the means of transport to the places (e.g., Scarborough) that tempted him.

12. may god give you grace] In his benediction Sterne paraphrases part of 2 Corinthians 13:14, which always concludes an Anglican service. Cf. the close of letter 184. Cash, *LY,* 253, calls attention to both conclusions: "Sterne the priest is . . . evident in the benediction with which he concluded . . . ."

180. *To Dear Sir*[1]

Text: Medalle

Coxwould, [Wednesday,] July 23, 1766.

Dear Sir,

One might be led to think that there is a fatality regarding us—we make appointments to meet, and for these two years have not seen each others face but twice—we must try, and do better for the future—having sought you with more zeal, than C.... sought the Lord,[2] in order to deliver you the books you bad me purchase for you at Paris—I was forced to pay carriage for them from London down to York—but as I shall neither charge you the books nor the carriage—'tis not worth talking about.—Never man, my dear Sir, has had a more agreeable tour than your Yorick—and at present I am in my peaceful retreat, writing the ninth volume of Tristram—I shall publish but one[3] this year, and the next I shall begin a new work of four volumes,[4] which when finish'd, I shall continue Tristram with fresh spirit.—What a difference of scene here! But with a disposition to be happy, 'tis neither this place, nor t'other that renders us the reverse.—In short each man's happiness depends upon himself—he is a fool if he does not enjoy it.[5]

What are you about, dear S———? Give me some account of your pleasures—you had better come to me for a fortnight, and I will shew, or give you (if needful) a practical dose of my philosophy; but I hope you do not want it—if you did—'twould be the office of a friend to give it—Will not even our races tempt you? You see I use all arguments—Believe me yours most truly,

Laurence Sterne

MS: Not located.
Pub.: Medalle, no. 71; Curtis, no. 169.

1. *Dear Sir*] Medalle identifies the recipient only as "Mr. S." Curtis, 284, tentatively identifies him as Edward Stanley (1718–1789), a fellow of the Royal Society who subscribed to *Sermons* (1760) and to *ASJ* (a large-paper copy), and to whom,

Curtis believed, Sterne had given a portrait of himself, painted by Reynolds in 1764. Cash, *EMY,* 305–6, convincingly argues that no such portrait exists. His comment, however, that there "is no evidence to link Sterne with . . . Stanley" overlooks Stanley's subscriptions.

Unfortunately, the subscription lists offer many other candidates for "Mr. S," none of whom rises beyond the realm of possibility, although, simply to offset Mr. Stanley, we might guess Jennison Shafto, Esq. (*c.*1728–1771), who subscribed to *Sermons* in 1766 and possibly in 1760 (listed as Mr. Shaftoe) and 1769 (as Jennings Shaftoe, Esq.), and to a large-paper copy of *ASJ* (as Mr. J. Shaftoe). Sterne's comment, "Will not even our races tempt you?" suggests someone who might be susceptible to such temptation; Shafto, of Wrattling Park, Cambridgeshire, and MP for Leominster, 1761–68, was a well-known sportsman and owner of race horses. In fact, he owned and raced a horse called "Yorick" in 1760 and 1761; Kenneth Monkman, "Shandean Race Horses," *Shandean* 10 (1998): 24–25, notes that Sterne and Shafto almost certainly met, suggesting the York races in 1765, because the Shaftos are listed as subscribers to the Assembly Rooms during Race Week. Sterne's comment that they have met twice in the past two years might then refer in part to that meeting. Monkman also notes that Shafto—if all the entries indeed refer to Jennison Shafto—was one of only four persons who subscribed to Sterne at every opportunity (25–26).

2. C.... sought the Lord] Medalle's "C" is a mystery. David is usually considered the primary seeker of the Lord in Scripture (see, e.g., Psalms 27:8, 34:4, 77:2, 105:4, 119:10, etc.), but even for Medalle, reading a "D" as a "C" seems a stretch. Others in Scripture seek the Lord (e.g., Jehoshaphat in 2 Chronicles 22:9), but the only "C" who does so would be Caiaphas ("a searcher; *or* he that seeks with diligence" [Cruden]), which would give a somewhat different twist to the passage (see Matthew 26, John 18).

3. but one] All previous volumes of *TS* had come out in pairs. Volume IX is not only single, it is also the shortest of them all, padded out by Sterne's decision to start all chapters on a new page. On the other hand, see letter 182 (to Becket), where Sterne indicates he will have two volumes ready for him. Whether or not Sterne completed *TS* will always be a critical rather than biographical question; we may at least suggest, on the one hand, that volume IX concludes many themes opened earlier, and, on the other, that Sterne's work was such that it could always be *reopened* (a more accurate word, perhaps, than *continued).* See Wayne Booth, "Did Sterne Complete *Tristram Shandy,*" *MP* 48 (1951): 172–83; R. F. Brissenden, "'Trusting to Almighty God': Another Look at the Composition of *Tristram Shandy,*" in *Winged Skull,* ed. Cash and Stedmond, 258–69; and Peter de Voogd, "The Design of *Tristram Shandy,*" BJECS 6 (1983): 159–62. See also the introduction to *ASJ,* 6:xviii–xix.

4. four volumes] Sterne sold subscriptions to *ASJ* as a four-volume work, but accompanying the subscribers' copies was an inserted apology for his failure to deliver on that commitment:

> THE Author begs leave to acknowledge to his Subscribers, that they have a further claim upon him for Two Volumes more than these delivered to them now, and which nothing but ill health could have prevented him, from having ready along with these.
>
> The Work will be compleated and delivered to the Subscribers early the next Winter.

Sterne died before he could fulfill this promise, but, as with *TS,* the conclusion to volume II is both an ending and an opening.

5. But with . . . enjoy it] The idea is commonplace, but the sermon Sterne placed first when he published *Sermons* in 1760 was "Inquiry after happiness," which begins: "The great pursuit of man is after happiness: it is the first and strongest desire of his nature—in every stage of his life, he searches for it, as for hid treasure . . . runs after and enquires for it afresh—asks every passenger who comes in his way *Who will shew him any good?*—who will assist him in the attainment of it, or direct him to the discovery of this great end of all his wishes?" (*Sermons* 4:3). His conclusion: "there is a plain distinction to be made betwixt pleasure and happiness. For tho' there can be no happiness without pleasure—yet the converse of the proposition will not hold true.—We are so made, that from the common gratifications of our appetites, and the impressions of a thousand objects, we snatch the one, like a transient gleam, without being suffered to taste the other, and enjoy that perpetual sunshine and fair weather which constantly attend it. This, I contend, is only to be found in religion—in the consciousness of virtue—and the sure and certain hopes of a better life, which brightens all our prospects . . ." (10–11).

181. *To Ignatius Sancho*[1]

Text: Letters of Ignatius Sancho (facsimile)[2]

Coxwould near York [Sunday,] July 27. 1766.

There is a strange coincidence, Sancho, in the little events (as well as in the great ones) of this world: for I had been writing a tender tale of the sorrows of a friendless poor negro-girl;[3] and my eyes had scarse done smarting ^with it^, when your Letter[4] of recommendation in behalf of so many of her brethren and sisters, came to me——but why *her brethren?*——or your's, Sancho! any more than mine? It is by the finest tints, and most insensible gradations, that nature descends from the fairest face about St James's, to the sootiest complexion in africa: at which tint of these, is it, that the ties of blood are to cease? and how many shades must we descend lower still in the scale, 'ere Mercy is to vanish with them?[5]——but 'tis no uncommon thing, my good Sancho, for one half of the world to use the other <?w> half of it like brutes, & then endeavour to make 'em so. for my own part, I never look *Westward* (when I am in a pensive mood at least) but I think of the burdens which our Brothers & Sisters are *there* carrying—& could I ease their shoulders from <an> ∧one∧ ounce of <S>~'e~m, I declare I would set out this hour upon a pilgrimage to Mecca for their sakes—wch by the by, Sancho, exceeds your Walk of ten miles, in about the same proportion, that a Visit of Humanity, should one, of mere form——however if you meant <the Corporal> ∧my Uncle Toby,∧ more——he is y^{r} Debter,

If I can weave the Tale I have wrote into the Work I'm ab^{t}—tis at the service of the afflicted—and a much greater matter; for in serious truth, it casts a <melancholy> ∧sad∧ Shade upon the World, That so great a part of it, are and have been so long bound in chains of darkness[6] & in Chains of Misery; & I cannot but both respect & felicitate You, that by so much laudable diligence you have broke the one—& that by falling into the hands of so good and merciful a family,[7] Providence has rescued You from the other.

and so, good hearted Sancho! adieu! & believe me, <I have always> I will not forget y^{r} Letter.

Y^{rs}
L Sterne

MS: Not located. A second version of this letter appears in the *Letter Book* (see appendix, no. xx).

Pub.: Medalle, no. 85; facsimile in *Letters of the Late Ignatius Sancho* ([4th ed.], 1802; 5th ed., 1803); Curtis, no. 170A; facsimile in *Shandean* 3 (1991), insert between 152–53.

1. *Ignatius Sancho*] A fine brief account of the life of Ignatius Sancho (*c.*1729–1780) is provided in the introduction to Vincent Carretta's modern edition of *Letters of the Late Ignatius Sancho, An African* (London: Penguin, 1998). What is known about him is based primarily on Joseph Jekyll's biographical introduction to the first edition of *Letters* (1782), reprinted in subsequent editions. Sancho was born around 1729 on a slave ship bound for the West Indies. By the age of two he was orphaned and "taken by his owner to England and given to three maiden sisters in Greenwich, who believed that keeping the child ignorant would render him submissive" (Carretta ix). Fortunately, he was noticed by a neighbor, John, 2d Duke of Montagu, who had an interest in educating ex-slaves. The duke died in 1749, but his widow took Sancho under her wing, and when she died in 1751, she left him with a pension that was soon spent. Having left the three Greenwich sisters by this time, he reentered service for the family of the late duke's son-in-law, George Brudenell-Montagu (1712–1790), 4th Earl of Cardigan, created 3d Duke of Montagu in 1766. The duke and duchess (Mary) subscribed to *ASJ* and again to *Sermons* (1769).

Some six years after Sterne's death, Sancho was released from the duke's service and opened a grocery store in the vicinity of Parliament; Carretta notes that his social circle was vast, as "reflected in the subscription list for the first edition of *Letters,* which includes men and women, aristocrats, servants, artists, businessmen, country squires, and prominent politicians" (xiii). He was the "first African to be given an obituary in the British press" when he died on December 14, 1780, and the "only eighteenth-century Afro-Briton accorded an entry" in the old *DNB* (ix).

When Medalle published Sterne's letter (no. 85), she preceded it with Sancho's (no. 84), which was soon thereafter reprinted in the *Gentleman's Magazine* (January 1776). We have included this letter in the appendix (letter xix[a]), but have used the text published by Frances Crewe in her collection of Sancho's *Letters* (1782); it is very close to the Medalle version in its wording, but the differences in accidentals suggest Lydia's usual "corrections," and we have given precedence to Sancho's editor over Sterne's in this instance. Letter xix(b) is Sterne's rewritten version, found in the *Letter Book.* Crewe's first edition was quickly followed in the next two years by a second and third; and in 1802 and 1803, they were again republished (the fourth [undesignated] and fifth editions), this time by Sancho's son, William, who had become a bookseller. The enthusiastic reception of Sancho's letters, and their Sternean qualities, is discussed by Carretta, xv–xx (who follows the 1782 text), and by Madeleine Descargues, "Ignatius Sancho's *Letters,*" *Shandean* 3 (1991): 145–62.

2. *Text*] We have based our text on the facsimile copy inserted just after San-

cho's letter in the 5th edition of *Letters of Ignatius Sancho* (1803), and that first appeared in the undesignated 4th edition of 1802. It is reproduced in *Shandean* 3 (1991). Medalle's version is taken from the original of this facsimile (now lost), with her usual changes of punctuation and capitalization, but otherwise uncharacteristically verbatim in substantives. Curtis's version is clearly based on the facsimile. Carretta published both the facsimile version and the *Letter Book* version in appendix B of his edition of Sancho's *Letters,* 332–34.

3. a tender tale . . . negro-girl] Although Sterne provides the date of August 12 for Tristram writing in his study in IX.1 (see above, letter 179, n. 8), it is quite likely that he did not write the volume sequentially. In chapter 6 (747), where Trim tells the story of Tom and the sausage-maker's widow, he mentions "a poor negro girl, with a bunch of white feathers . . . flapping away flies—not killing them," to which Toby responds, "'Tis a pretty picture! . . . she had suffered persecution, Trim, and had learnt mercy——." Trim goes on to promise "the story of that poor friendless slut that would melt a heart of stone," but it is never told. Whether Sterne's "tender tale" consisted of this passage or Trim's untold story we do not know.

4. your Letter] See above, n. 1. In the letter, Sancho indicates he "would walk ten miles in the dog days, to shake hands with the honest corporal" (no small task, given Sancho's obesity), but centers his attention on the question of slavery and Sterne's call in sermon 10 ("Job's account of the shortness and troubles of life") to "consider slavery——what it is,——how bitter a draught, and how many millions have been made to drink of it" (*Sermons* 4:99). Sancho asked Sterne to give "one half-hour's attention" to the subject; the passage in *TS,* IX.6, is perhaps Sterne's immediate response, but he would address slavery again in *ASJ,* 96–97: "Disguise thyself as thou wilt, still slavery! said I—still thou art a bitter draught; and though thousands in all ages have been made to drink of thee, thou art no less bitter on that account. . . . I was going to begin with the millions of my fellow creatures born to no inheritance but slavery, etc."

5. It is . . . with them?] Sterne's attitude reflects, perhaps, the notions of one of his favorite authors, Montaigne, as evinced in his famous essay "Of Cannibals."

6. chains of darkness] The phrase is taken from 2 Peter 2:4: "For if God spared not the angels that sinned, but cast them down to hell, and delivered them into chains of darkness, to be reserved unto judgment." Sterne had used the phrase in sermon 21 ("National mercies"), but to allude to nations "strongly bound in chains of darkness,—and chains of power," almost certainly referring, in the sermon's context, to governments dominated by Roman Catholicism (4:201).

7. good and merciful a family] See above, n. 1, and appendix, letter xix(b), n. 9.

182. *To Thomas Becket*

Text: Curtis

Coxwould [Saturday,] Augst 30. / 66

Dear Sir

I send you very small Bills—but they are such as I can pick up in the Country.

I shall publish the 9th & 10 of Shandy[1] the next winter—but sh^{d} be glad to know, how many of the 4 last have moved off in the Compass of almost a Year, since We last settled.[2]

Is Mr Combes[3] in Town? If you see him, tell him to write to me.

Y^{rs}

L— Sterne

MS: Not located; Curtis indicates it was in the hands of Alwin J. Scheuer, Esq., New York City.

Pub.: Sotheby's *Catalogue of Printed Books*, May 5, 1930, 27 (not located); Curtis, no. 171.

1. 9th & 10 of Shandy] See letter 180, and n. 3. Cash, *LY*, 259, suggests that Sterne had "second thoughts about publishing only a single volume this time .... But, beset by illness and anxiety, he never wrote a tenth volume." See also letter 188, which implies that Sterne did at least begin writing an additional volume.

2. how many ... settled] On Sterne's continued interest in his sales, see letter 89, n. 15. Sterne's inquiry here would be about volumes V and VI, which sold very slowly, and volumes VII and VIII, 4,000 copies of which had appeared some twenty months earlier. A concealed second edition, dated 1765, without Sterne's signature and with the errata corrected, may be evidence that Sterne had regained his popularity (see *TS* 2:830); or it may represent a later printing (1770), indicating that booksellers at that time had a need for additional copies to make up sets (see 2:934). That only 3,500 copies of volume IX were printed (2:937) may suggest that the sales of VII and VIII did not measurably improve over V and VI.

3. Mr Combes] I.e., William Combe; see above, letter 179, n. 10.

183. *To Isaac Panchaud*

Text: Medalle

Coxwould, [Sunday,] September 21, 1766.

My dear Friend,

If Mrs. Sterne[a] should draw upon you for fifty louis d'ors, be so kind as to remit her the money—and pray be so good as not to draw upon Mr. Becket for it (as he owes me nothing) but favour me with the draught, which I will pay to Mr. Selwin.——A young nobleman[1] is now negociating a jaunt with me for six weeks, about Christmas, to the Fauxbourg de St. Germain—I should like much to be with you for so long—and if my wife should grow worse (having had a very poor account of her in my daughter's last) I cannot think of her being without me—and however expensive the journey would be, I would fly to Avignon[2] to administer consolation to both her and my poor girl—Wherever I am, believe me

Dear Sir, yours,
L. Sterne

My kind compliments to Mr. Foley[b]: though I have not the honour of knowing his rib,[3] I see no reason why I may not present all due respects to the better half of so old a friend, which I do by these presents—with my friendliest wishes to Miss Panchaud[c].

MS: Not located.
Pub.: Medalle, no. 72; Curtis, no. 172.

[a]Sterne] S—— *M* [b]Foley] F—— *M* [c]Panchaud] P— *M*

1. A young nobleman] Unidentified; as was always the case (see letter 72, n. 9), Sterne's hopes for funding his travels by accompanying a young gentleman to Europe came to naught.

2. Avignon] See letter 178.

3. his rib] Sterne refers to Foley's recent marriage (see letter 178, n. 2); on "rib" as a colloquialism for "wife," see letter 17, n. 6.

184. *To John Hall-Stevenson*

Text: Ms.

Coxwould [Friday,] <D>~O~ct. 17. 1766[1]

My dear Cosin

I consider thee as a bank note in a corner draw'r of my bureau—I know it is there (I wish I did)—& its value, tho' I seldome take a peep at it—if a comparison will excuse my idlenesses <of> and neglects of all kind to thee—so be it——tho' I must take further shame, & own I had not wrote now, but that I profited by the *transit* of a Craselite,[2] by my door—of whom I have learn'd all welcome Acc^{ts} of thee—that thou farest well—and art good liking[3]——for my own part I have had my Menses[4] thrice this month, which is twice too often——and am not altogether according to my feelings, by <spending> being so much, <ab>~w~hich I cannot avoid, at Lord Fauconberg[a], who oppress me to death with civility[5]——so Tristram goes on busily——what I <f>~c~an find appetite to write—is so so——You never read such a chapter of evils from me——I'm tormented to death & the devil, by my Stillington Inclosure[6]—and am every hour threatend with a Journey to Avignion, where Mrs Sterne is very bad—and by a series of Letters Ive got from Lydia, I suppose is going the way of us all—

I want to know from yourself how you do—and You go on——I mean allum.[7] full gladly would I see you—but whilst Im tied neck & heels[8] as I am—tis impracticable——remember me sometimes in y^{r} Potations——bid Panty pray for me ∧when he prays for the holy catholic Church—[9]∧ —present my compliments to Mrs Ferguson[10]—& be in peace and charity with all mankind

& the blessing of God the Father
——Son——
&
holy ghost be with you
Amen.

L Sterne[b]

PS

Greet Hales[11]—& his houshold—

Address: To / J. Hall Stevenson Esqre / Skelton Castle / near / Guisbro
Endorsed: Sterne / Letter
MS: Skelton Castle.
Pub.: Cooper, *Seven Letters*, 10–11; Curtis, no. 175.

[a]Fauconberg] <F>~—~—— *MS;* F———'s [Falconbridge] *Cooper;* F[auconberg]'s *C* [b]L Sterne] [doubly underscored] *MS*

1. Date] Cooper misdated the letter "Dec. 17," probably misled by Sterne's inadvertent "D," which is then overwritten. Curtis, 290, without access to the manuscript, followed Cooper's dating. Cooper had seen the letter in Skelton Castle, and it is still there.

2. Craselite] The word is not in *OED;* it is almost certainly Sterne's neologism, alluding to Crazy Castle, and would thus refer to one of the Demoniacs. For this spelling of their haunt, see Hall-Stevenson's letter to Sterne in appendix, no. xviii. Sterne played in much the same way in *TS,* V.33.472: "What have we Moonites done?" and again in *ASJ,* 45–46, with the inhabitants of Abdera, "every Abderite . . . and every Abderitish woman."

3. good liking] Cf. "well liking," letter 170, n. 2. Sterne seems to be straining for an archaism. See *OED,* s.v. *liking,* vbl. sb. I.6, "Bodily condition, esp. good or healthy condition" (*obs.,* with the last example from 1768–74); cf. *Good-liking,* 4, and especially the last illustration (1656): "plump and in a good liking."

4. Menses] Sterne's rueful bit of humor marks the increasingly bad health that would accompany the last fifteen months of his life; cf. *TS,* IX.24.779: "It is one comfort at least to me, that I lost some fourscore ounces of blood this week in a most uncritical fever which attacked me at the beginning of this chapter . . . ."

5. Lord Fauconberg . . . civility] Cooper's "Falconbridge" is an obvious slip for "Fauconberg," for whose kindnesses to Sterne, see letter 15, n. 4, and passim.

6. Stillington Inclosure] See letters 92, n. 8, 96, n. 3, and 142, n. 1. Curtis, 291, n. 1, has a lengthy discussion, only part of which seems relevant: "Sterne, both as Vicar of Stillington and as landowner, was liable to many wearisome meetings held for the purpose of signing the petition, defending the interests of the several landowners, selecting the solicitor and surveyor, nominating the Commissioners, and agreeing to their awards. For Sterne the chief benefit of enclosure was the commutation of the tithes of wool and lamb to allotments of land. In all about fourteen hundred acres were enclosed in 1766 (Stillington Enclosure Act, *Private Acts of Parliament,* 6 George III, c. 16)."

7. allum] See letters 137, n. 10, and 176, n. 8.

8. neck & heels] A commonplace phrase derived from a method of punishment for criminals; Philip Francis, *Poetical Translation of the Works of Horace,*

vol. 2 (3d ed., 1749), 235, 237, uses it twice in translating *Satire II.7:* "he, who next engages you to drink, / Must tie you Neck and Heels" (ll. 44–45), and "Or by the conscious Chamber-Maid are prest / Quite double, Neck and Heels, into a Chest" (ll. 79–80). Cf. Mary Davys, *The Reform'd Coquet*, 110: "the other they tied neck and heels in the Barge . . ." (1724; New York: Garland, 1973).

9. bid Panty . . . catholic Church] The Apostles' Creed, read at morning and evening service, contains the lines: "I believe in the Holy Ghost; The holy Catholick Church; The communion of Saints; The forgiveness of sins; The resurrection of the body, And the life everlasting." For "Panty" (Rev. Robert Lascelles) see letter 73, n. 7.

10. M[rs] Ferguson] See letter 148, n. 1. Nothing is known about this woman who must have lived in the neighborhood of Skelton Castle.

11. Hales] I.e, Colonel John Hale; see letter 142, n. 10.

185. *To Robert Foley*

Text: Medalle

Coxwould, [Saturday,] October 25, 1766.

My dear Foley[a]

I desired you would be so good as to remit to Mrs. Sterne[b] fifty louis, a month ago[1]—I dare say you have done it—but her illness must have cost her a good deal—therefore having paid the last fifty pounds into Mr. Selwin's hands, I beg you to send her thirty guineas more—for which I send a bank bill to Mr. Becket by this post—but surely had I not done so, you would not stick at it—for be assured, my dear Foley[a] that the first Lord of the Treasury[2] is neither more able or more willing (nor perhaps half so punctual) in repaying with honour all I ever can be in your books.—My daughter says her mother is very ill—and I fear going fast down by all accounts—'tis melancholy in her situation to want any aid that is in my power to give—do write to her—and believe me, with all compliments to your Hotel,[3]

Yours very truly,
L. Sterne

MS: Not located.
Pub.: Medalle, no. 73; Curtis, no. 173.

[a]Foley] F. *M* [b]Sterne] S—— *M*

1. a month ago] See letter 183, to Panchaud.

2. first Lord of the Treasury] In *TS*, IX.11.760, Walter is compared to "the first Lord of the Treasury thinking of *ways and means* . . . ." Perhaps the mention here provides a clue to Sterne's progress, although see letter 184, n. 4.

3. to your Hotel] A rather odd usage, reminding us that in French, *hôtel* can mean simply a large house—here extended, it would seem, to Foley's household, as is common enough in English, *house* = *household.*

186. *To Isaac Panchaud*[1]

Text: Medalle

York, [Tuesday,] November 25, 1766.

Dear Sir,

I just received yours——and am glad that the balance of accounts is now paid to you—Thus far all goes well—I have received a letter from my daughter with the pleasing tidings that she thinks her mother out of danger—and that the air of the country is delightful (excepting the winds)[2] but the description of the Chateau my wife has hired is really pretty—on the side of the Fountain of Vaucluse[3]—with seven rooms of a floor, half furnished with tapestry, half with blue taffety, the permission to fish, and to have game; so many partridges a week, &c. and the price—guess! sixteen guineas a year—there's for you Panchaud[a]—about the latter end of next month my wife will have occasion for a hundred guineas—and pray be so good, my dear sir, as to give orders that she may not be disappointed—she is going to spend the Carnival at Marseilles at Christmas—I shall be in London by Christmas week, and then shall balance this remittance to Mrs. Sterne[b] with Mr. Selwin[c]. I am going to ly in of another child of the Shandaick procreation, in town—I hope you wish me a safe delivery[4]——I fear my friend Mr.

Foley[d] will have left town before I get there—Adieu dear Sir—I wish you every thing in this world which will do you good, for I am with unfeigned truth,

Yours,
L. Sterne

Make my compliments acceptable to the good and worthy Baron D'Holbach—Miss Panchaud[a] &c. &c.

MS: Not located.
Pub.: Medalle, no. 74; Curtis, no. 174.

[a]Panchaud] P. *M* [b]Sterne] S. *M* [c]Selwin] S—— *M* [d]Foley] F. *M*

1. *Isaac Panchaud*] Medalle erroneously has "To the same," which would be the "Mr. F[oley] at Paris" of the previous letter. *1780* corrects this to "Mr. Panchaud."

2. excepting the winds] Sterne had alluded to the proverbial winds of Avignon in *TS,* VII.41.644, "and hearing moreover, the windyness of Avignion spoke of . . . as a proverb"; the Florida editors, 3:492, n. to 644.25–26, note that this refers to the "mistral, the northwest wind that sweeps down the Rhone valley . . . ." They were able to locate only one proverb, "Avignon venteuse, sans vent contagieuse" (Avignon is windy, without being contagious), but we can offer another, more apropos suggestion: "Avenie ventosa, sine vento venenosa, cum vento fastidiosa" (windy Avignon, pest-ridden when there is no wind, wind-pestered when there is") (*Encyclopaedia Britannica,* 1911, s.v. *Avignon*).

3. Fountain of Vaucluse] Fontaine-de-Vaucluse, a village east of Avignon, at the springs of the river Sorgue. Petrarch lived in the vicinity in exile from Florence from 1313; he met Laura there in 1327, and ten years later settled in Vaucluse itself (see letter 194, nn. 3, 4, and 5). Combe, *Original Letters,* 185, gives Sterne a rather unhappy allusion to the place in what we hope is a forgery: "And so we will go next spring, if you please, to the fountain of *Vauclusa,* and think of *Petrarch,* and, which is better, apostrophise his *Laura.*—By that time, I have reason to think my wife will be there, who, by the bye, is not *Laura;*—but my poor dear *Lydia* will be with her, and she is more than a *Laura* to her fond father." See also *OL,* 190.

4. I am going . . . delivery] The intermingling of artistic creation and procreation was one of Sterne's favorite tropes from the very beginning of his writing career; see, e.g., the letter he attached to *Political Romance* (1759), advising his printer, Caesar Ward (see letter 32, n. 4), that he intends "That the Child be fili-

ated upon me, *Laurence Sterne* . . . . And I do, accordingly, own it for my own true and lawful Offspring" (49). See also the penultimate paragraph of letter 188, and, very dramatically, letter 235.

187. *To Thomas Belasyse, Lord Fauconberg*

Text: Ms.

London [Tuesday,] Jan: 6. 1767.
Bond Street[1]

My Lord.

Before I left York I had the Honour to dine with Lord Fairfax[2] & talk over the Affair of the Turnpike:—upon the whole I find he thinks as y^{r} Lords^{p} does, that the ingrafting the Craik & Oulston turn pike[3] upon the other, would only be burthensome to their own plan of going directly from York to Helmsly &c— —His motive in offering it you, being merely, that he might not ∧be∧ guilty of an Act of Omission & ∧in∧civility to Your Lords^{p};—in going on with their plan, wth paying you the proper Compliment thereupon—So when we are all of a mind—tant mieux.[4]

I left York on Saturday in such a terrible Hurricane of Wind & snow, as no one but a Captain of the *blues,* & a Parson of the *true blues,*[5] would have ventured out in—twas one continued storm all the way, & many stages had we to plough through Snow up to the horses bellies, so that with the utmost perseverence (or obstinacy if y^{r} Lordship pleases)[6] We could get but to Barnet[7] the third night—The Storm began here 24 hours after it began at York. It has now begun to thaw in this Metropolis—& I suppose the Kingdome round—for as it has come together—tis likely to Go a way (I hope) as it came.

I inclose the Ladies a Letter with acc^{t} of what kind of Weather there is in the theatrical World[8]—and shall beg leave to continue my Advertisements to them two or three times a week—till I have the pleasure to see them

I am my Lord.
y^{r} most Obliged & faithful Servt
L. Sterne

MS: Private collection, UK; Curtis may have had access to it or to a careful transcription.
Pub.: Curtis, no. 176.

1. Bond Street] See letter 152, n. 12, and Curtis, "Sterne in Bond-street," *TLS* (March 24, 1932): 217. Cash, *LY*, 261, notes that Sterne left Coxwold on January 1 or 2 (and this letter makes clear that he left York on January 3), and Curtis, 293, that he wrote this letter "upon the day of his arrival in London."

2. Lord Fairfax] Charles Gregory Fairfax (*d.* 1772), since 1738, 9th Viscount Emley. Fairfax House in York (built between 1750 and 1753) was his city residence, but he lived primarily at Gilling Castle near Helmsley. As Curtis notes, 293, n. 2, as lord of the manors of Walton and Gilling he had to inform his neighbor Lord Fauconberg about "the Affair of the Turnpike," Newburgh Priory being about a mile and a half from Oulston.

3. Craik & Oulston turn pike] Oulston and Craik (Crayke) are villages just south-southeast of Coxwold, approximately three miles apart; the turnpike from York to Helmsley, approximately twenty-four miles, was completed, but the plan to connect Crayke and Oulston did not materialize—perhaps because, as Fairfax is said to have thought, it would have meant a detour from a direct line between York and Helmsley. A "turnpike" was a kind of tollgate, originally a gate or bar set across a road to stop carriages and people in order to make them pay for keeping the road in repair. During Sterne's day, the landscape of rural England was transformed by the building and improving of minor roads on an unprecedented scale; see William Albert, *The Turnpike Road System in England, 1663–1840* (Cambridge: Cambridge University Press, 1972), esp. chapters 2–3, which describe in detail "the 'Turnpike Mania' of the years 1751–72" (14; see 13–56).

4. tant mieux] So much the better. Yorick gives a lesson on the use of *tant pis* and *tant mieux* in *ASJ*, 39–40; see nn. to the passage, 6:277–78; and cf. letter 172, n. 9.

5. Captain . . . *true blues*] Curtis, 293, n. 3, believes this is "a whimsical allusion not to the Royal Horse Guards, who were known as the *Blues*, but to the regiment of militia, commanded by Colonel William Thornton [see letter 30, n. 2], and called the '*Yorkshire Blues* . . . a company of men who were clothed in blue in the time of the rebellion'" (quoting Tate Wilkinson, *Memoirs of his Own Life* [York, 1790], 4:274). Cash, 261, reads Sterne's metaphor as indicating that he actually traveled to London with a militia captain, but we have no evidence of that—or, indeed, that he was alluding to the Yorkshire Blues. The play on "*blues*" continues with "*true blues*," a derogatory expression for dissenters, as in Samuel Butler's *Hudibras*, part I, canto 1, ll. 191–94: "'Twas *Presbyterian* true Blue, / For he was of that stubborn Crew / Of Errant Saints, whom all men grant / To be

the true Church *Militant*" (ed. Zachary Grey, 2d ed. [1764], 1:25–26; in annotating another occurrence in part III, canto 2, l. 870, Grey points to the wearing of blue aprons by Presbyterian preachers [2:296–97]).

6. perseverence . . . pleases] The phrasing has a proverbial ring; see, e.g., Sir Thomas Browne, *Religio Medici* (1642), part 1, section 25: "for obstinacy in a bad cause, is but constancy in a good" (*Works,* ed. Geoffrey Keynes [Chicago: University of Chicago Press, 1964], 1:36); and *TS,* I.17.50: "My father was a gentleman of many virtues,—but he had a strong spice of that in his temper which might, or might not, add to the number.----'Tis known by the name of perseverance in a good cause,—and of obstinacy in a bad one" (see also n. to 50.3–4, 3:84).

7. Barnet] Eleven miles from London, just south of Potters Bar.

8. I inclose . . . World] Lady Fauconberg had died in 1760; Sterne was writing to the two daughters still living at home, Lady Catherine (see letter 85, n. 2) and Lady Mary (see Curtis, 296, n. 6, and Cash, *LY* 55, 60–61); letters 189 and 190 are the only two surviving installments on this promise.

188. *To William Combe*

Text: Letter Book

London Bond street
Jan. 6. 1767[1]

To —— ——

I arrived here but yesterday, where, (after a terrible journey <of>~in~ most inhospitable weather) I was met agreeably with your Letter from Paris—I first sympathize for the unkind greeting upon french-ground which you met with by your overthrow[2]——may it be the last shock you receive in this world!—this reflection, costs me a deep Sigh—& alas! my friend! I dread it will let you go off no cheaper—I fear some thing has gone wrong with you;[3] if so; why would not you make me a partner? I am a dab at giving <[illegible word] councils; & in finding out ways & means> advice,[4]—& I esteemd and loved you—& you knew it.

If I am wrong; my friendship has only been too quick sighted and perhaps too easily alarm'd by false appearances; only there were some little mysterious turns & windings in the manner of your leaving England, which mark'd the steps of an entangled man. is it some nasty scrape of gallantry?—or a more cleanly one of simple Love? If it is the latter, I'll put off my Cassoc & turn Knight Errant for you, & say the kindest things of you to Dulcinea that Dulcinea ever heard ∧—if she has a Champion∧—and <?>~if~ words will not atchieve it—Ill enter the Lists with him and break a spear in your behalf; tho by the by, mine is half rusty, and should be hung up in the old family hall amongst Pistols without Cocks, and Helmets which have lost their Vizards[5]—

I miscarried of my tenth Volume by the violence of a fever, I have just got thro'—I have however gone on to my reckoning with the ninth, <in>~of~ w[ch] I am all this week in Labour pains; & if ∨to∨ <?>~Da~ys Advertiser is to be depended upon shall be safely deliver'd by tuesday.[6]

adieu. I heartily wish your happiness—seek it where you will, my dear Sir, You will find it no where, but in Company with Virtue and Honour.

I am &c ——

L.S.

MS: Letter Book, Pierpont Morgan Library, New York.
Pub.: Cross, *Life* (1925), 2:251–52; Curtis, no. 177.

1. Date] Curtis, 293, alters the manuscript date of January 6 to "?7–9 Jan." Since we know Sterne left York on January 3 (see letter 187, and n. 1) and had come as far as Barnet on Monday, January 5, he would have entered London on the 6th. He must have begun this letter on Wednesday, January 7, and in view of the penultimate paragraph concluded it later in the week. Although the *Letter Book* copy does not have an addressee, we agree with Cross and Curtis that echoes of the letter in Combe's imitations make it almost certain that he was the recipient of the original (see next note).

2. your overthrow] Combe would appear to have had a fall from his horse; in both *Various Occasions* (1775) and *Original Letters* (1788) he returns to the episode, repeating Sterne's sentiments in this letter: "I have been much concerned at your overthrow; but our roads are ill contrived for the airy vehicles now in fashion. May it be the last fall you ever meet with in this world!—but this reflection costs me a deep sigh—and I fear, my friend, you will get over it no cheaper" (*VO* 26); and again: "I am grieved for your downfall, though it was only out of a park-

chair—May it be the last you will receive in this world; though, while I write this wish, my heart heaves a deep sigh, and I believe it will not be read by you, my friend, without a similar accompaniment" (*OL* 17). This second version is actually dated August 8, 1764. In both instances, the fall takes place in England, not France, as in Sterne's letter. The incident serves as a useful illustration of Combe's inventive (and highly unreliable) system of imitation.

3. gone wrong with you] Curtis, 294, n. 1, suggests Combe went to France to avoid his London creditors, but Hamilton, *Doctor Syntax*, 23–24, argues convincingly that "although he was living extravagantly, he could scarcely have exhausted by December" a legacy of £2,000 he had inherited in March. Rather, Hamilton suggests that Sterne's guess of "an amorous entanglement" is not implausible, although finally he admits that "we are not likely to discover what sent Combe in haste to France in December 1766." He returned sometime in 1767.

4. I am a dab . . . advice] Cf. *OL*, 72: "though I think myself a dab at giving good counsel in such cases as his, I cannot bring myself to prescribe on the occasion . . . ." The illegible word is definitely not "good" in the original.

5. I'll put off . . . Vizards] The entire passage alludes, of course, to *Don Quixote*, although it is Sancho and not Quixote who acts as a go-between. For another allusion to Dulcinea, see letter 158, n. 5. Sterne makes use of several of the jokes in this passage in *ASJ*, 65, when he looks out of his Paris hotel window at the "old with broken lances, and in helmets which had lost their vizards . . . all tilting at it like fascinated knights in tournaments of yore for fame and love." As the note indicates (6:298–99, n. to 65.15–17), the vizardless helmets almost certainly refer to the "damage wrought to noses by the chemical treatment of venereal disorders"; one suspects Sterne is merely retailing a hoary witticism.

Combe makes use of the passage in *VO*, 16: "But wherefore do I think of arms and *Dulcineas*,—when, alas, my spear is grown rusty, and is fit only to be hung in the old family hall, among pistols without *cocks*, and helmets that have lost their vizard"; and again, *OL*, 163, "My *Knight Errant* spirit has already told her that she is a *Dulcinea* to me—but I would most willingly take off my armour and break my spear, and resign her as an *Angel* to you"; and, tiresomely, a third time: "would have made thee the veriest Knight Errant, that ever brandished a spear, or wore a vizard" (*OL* 182).

6. my reckoning . . . tuesday] For Sterne's birthing metaphor, see letter 186, n. 4. Curtis, 295, n. 4, provides information on the advance notices of the forthcoming publication of volume IX in the *Gazetteer and New Daily Advertiser* for January 8, 1767, and the *Public Advertiser* for January 9, which helps him date the letter as indicated in n. 1. Volume IX did not, in fact, appear until January 29, when 3,500 copies were published by Becket and Dehondt.

189. *To Thomas Belasyse, Lord Fauconberg*

Text: Ms.

London Friday. [January 9, 1767]

My Lord

When we got up yesterday morning, the Streets were 4 inches deep in snow—it has set in, now, with the most intense cold[1]—I could scarse lay in bed for it; & this morning more snow again—tho' the roads after all, are extreamly good near Town & I suppose every where else—the Snow has been very deep in Kent.

No news. I dined yesterday with Lord Marsh[2] & a large Company of the duke of Yorks people[3] &c— — —and came away just as wise as I went—the King—at Cimon,[4] the new Opera last night—no body at Covent garden[5] but the Citizen's children & apprentices—— The Duke of York was to have had a play house of his own, & had studied his part—in the fair penitent and made Garrick act it twice on purpose to profit by it—but the King tis said; has desired the Duke to give up the part & the project with it—[6]

☞(all this is for the Ladies) to whom, wth all Comp^s^ to the party at Quadrille & Lady Catherine[7]

I am, my Lord
y^r^ most unworthy Gazetteere
that ever wrote—
but most faithfully
y^r^ ever Obliged
L Sterne

MS: Newburgh Priory; now in North Yorkshire County Council Archives, Northallerton.

Pub.: Fitzgerald, *Life* (1864), 2:330; Curtis, no. 178.

1. deep in snow . . . cold] Curtis, 295, n. 1, quotes from Lady Mary Coke, *Letters and Journals*, 1:112, entry for January 9: "It has snow'd great part of the night, & is one of the coldest days I ever felt." Cf. Walpole, *Correspondence*, 22:479 (letter

dated January 21, 1767): "We have a most dreadful winter, the coldest I ever remember"; the editors supply the additional information that the thermometer in London fell to F17° on January 10 and F15½° on the 19th. The following January, when the ailing Sterne returned to London for his fatal visit, would be even more frigid; see *Correspondence,* 22:578–79, n. 8.

2. Lord Marsh] William Douglas (1725–1810), Earl of March and Ruglen, later 4th Duke of Queensberry, notorious for his womanizing and gambling. Sterne knew him from the York Races. His father, Charles Douglas (1698–1778), 3d Duke of Queensberry, subscribed to *Sermons* (1766) and to a large-paper copy of *ASJ.*

3. duke of Yorks people] Sterne had been feted by the Duke of York on his triumphal 1760 visit to London (see letter 53, n. 5) and had preached before him at the York Minster on August 24, 1766, following the York Races, which the Duke had attended (see Cash, *LY* 256). Which of the duke's friends attended this particular dinner has not been ascertained, but clearly his circle gave rigorous support to Sterne, if we may base our supposition on hints in the subscription lists. Thus, his master of horse, Sir William Boothby (1721–1787), subscribed to *Sermons* (1760, 1766) and to a large-paper *ASJ;* his groom of the bedchamber, Hon. Robert Brudenell (1726–1768), to *Sermons* (1760, 1766); and his treasurer, Charles Sloane Cadogan (1728–1807), to *Sermons* (1766) and a large-paper *ASJ;* we may almost suspect Sterne of soliciting subscriptions between courses. See n. 6 below.

4. Cimon] Garrick's dramatic romance *Cymon,* with music by Michael Arne (*c.*1740–1786), the illegitimate son of Thomas Arne (1710–1778) of "Rule, Britannia!" fame, was first performed on January 2, 1767. A performance by royal command was given on Thursday, January 8, 1767. The play was a "great success" (*Letters of Garrick* 2:552, n. 4).

5. Covent garden] Susanna Centlivre's *The Busy Body,* Sterne's old favorite (see letter 104, n. 2), was playing at Covent Garden. In correspondence, Robert Hume has pointed out to us that Sterne was a "bit over-gloomy" about Centlivre's play, which grossed £147 versus *Cymon's* £228 on January 8, the night of its command performance, but the very next night *Cymon's* gross was only £139.

6. The Duke of York . . . with it] One of the close observers of the duke's theatrical ambitions was Richard Lovell Edgeworth, father of the novelist, who gives a full account in his *Memoirs* (1820); see M. New, "Richard Lovell Edgeworth and Laurence Sterne," *N&Q,* n.s. 51 (December 2004): 417–21. Francis Blake Delaval (1727–1771), who subscribed to *Sermons* in 1760 (his three brothers also subscribed then or subsequently), and his sister, Anne Delaval, Lady Stanhope (1737–1811), were at the center of the dramatic effort. According to Edgeworth, he "was requested by Sir Francis, to fit up a theatre in Petty France, near the gate of the

Park [St. James's; the theater was in James Street, near Downing Street], and no trouble and expense were spared, to render it suitable to the reception of a royal performer. 'The Fair Penitent' was the chosen piece . . ." (1:124). The duke played Lothario, and Lady Stanhope (who was separated from her husband, Sir William Stanhope, at the time; see letters 225 and 226 below) played Calista: "Lothario was as warm, as hasty, and as much in love, as the fair Calista could possibly wish" (1:124). In fact, Edgeworth reports some pages later, "The Duke . . . was in love with Sir Francis Delaval's sister, Lady Stanhope" (1:153). Walpole, *Correspondence,* 22:521, confirms all the details of Edgeworth's account: "He is acting plays with Lady Stanhope, and her family, the Delavals. They have several times played the *Fair Penitent.* His Royal Highness is Lothario, the lady, I am told, an admirable Calista. They have a pretty little theatre in Westminster; but none of the royal family have been audience" (letter dated May 24, 1767).

Walpole seems to believe that the duke's disfavor had more to do with politics than with playacting (22:524). He was sent abroad by the King and died at the palace of the Prince of Monaco the next year; Walpole and Edgeworth both agree that his final illness began with a chill after dancing all night at a ball in Rome (*Correspondence* 22:552ff.; *Memoirs* 1:153–54).

The tragedy, *The Fair Penitent* (1703), by Nicholas Rowe (1674–1718), had its first production at this private theater on April 7 (*Public Advertiser* for April 10, 1767). In addition to the cast already noted, Francis Delaval played Horatio; his brother John Delaval (1728–1808) played Sciolto; and his daughter, Lady Mexborough (*d.* 1821), played Lavinia. All were subscribers to Sterne, which lends a bit more credibility to Curtis's suggestion (296, n. 5) that Sterne possibly attended a performance. Clearly, this was a circle in which he felt quite at home; but see Garrick, *Letters,* 2:567, n. 4, which quotes the theater's designer, Benjamin Wilson, on the exclusivity of the audience allowed.

See also Garrick, *Letters,* 2:559–60, 566–67. In the first letter (March 26, 1767), Garrick responds warmly to John Delaval's request for advice on acting; in the second, to Francis Delaval (April 22, 1767): "We have had Several Accounts here of the excellent doings in James Street . . . . Lady Stanhope is mention'd as a Prodigy." Garrick wrote a prologue for the performance.

7. Lady Catherine] See letters 85, n. 2, and 187, n. 8.

190. *To Thomas Belasyse, Lord Fauconberg*

Text: Curtis

Bond Street [Friday,] Jan: 16. 1767

My Lord

There is a dead stagnation of every thing, & scarse any talk but about the Damages done over the Kingdome by this cruel Storm: it began yesterday morning to thaw gently, and has continued going on so, till now—I hope it will all get away after the same manner—it was so intensely cold on Sunday, that there were few either at the Church or court—but last night, It thaw'd the concert at Soho[1] top full—& was (This is for the Ladies) the best assembly, and the best Concert I ever had the honour to be at—Lady Anne,[2] had the goodness to challenge me, or I had not known her, she was so prudently muffled up— Lord Bellasyse[3]—I never saw him look so well—Lady Bellasyse[4] recovers *a marveille*—& y[r] little neice I believe, grows like flax.—[5]

We had reports yesterday that the York stage coach w[h] 14 people in, & about it were drown'd, by mistaking a bridge—it was contradicted at night.—as are half the morning reports in Town.

The School for Guardians—(wrote by Murphy)[6] could scarse get thro'[a] the 1st night—'tis a most miserable affair—Garrick's Cimon—fills his house brim full every night—

—the Streets are dirtier than in the Town of Coxwould—for they are up to the knees, except on the *Trottoire*[7]

I beg my best comp[s], my Lord, to M[r] Bellasyse[b8]—the Ladies—and to S[r] Bryan Stapleton.[9] & am

with unfeigned Attachm[ts]
Y[r] L[dps] faithful
L. Sterne

MS: Newburgh Priory, now reported "missing."
Pub.: Fitzgerald, *Life* (1864), 2:331; Curtis, no. 179.

[a]Murphy) could scarse get thro'] Murphy) scarse got through *F* [b]M[r] Bellasyse] M[rs] Bellasyse *F*

1. the concert at Soho] Sterne refers to these concerts again in *BJ*, 188 (April 6): "came home to enjoy a more harmonious evening w^{h} my Eliza, than I could expect at Soho Concert." Curtis, 297, n. 1, provides details for these Wednesday evening concerts at Carlisle House, Soho Square, for exclusive subscribers "for whom Theresa Cornelys (1723–97) directed her famous assemblies from 1760 until her failure in 1772. For those who preferred music to cards and dancing she inaugurated in 1765 a series of grand concerts of vocal and instrumental music, which were alternately conducted by Johann Christian Bach and Karl Friedrich Abel." Abel (1725–1787) was a master of Sterne's own instrument, the viol da gamba. *Oxford DNB* adds the additional information that Cornelys was born at Venice, performing in Italy and directing theaters in the Austrian Netherlands before settling in London in 1759, funded in part by one of her many lovers, Casanova. After bankruptcy in 1772 she kept a hotel in Southwark, 1774–76, and ultimately died in the Fleet. *Oxford DNB* quotes from her obituary in *Gentleman's Magazine* (1797): 890: "she was 'a distinguished priestess of fashion,' who 'being of an enterprizing spirit, possessing a good understanding, great knowledge of mankind, and specious manners,' was able to make Carlisle House 'the favourite region of amusement among the nobility and gentry' for more than ten years; she provided such 'diversified amusement' that for many years 'no other public entertainments could pretend to rival' Carlisle House."

Walpole (*Correspondence* 23:271, to Mann, February 22, 1771) is just one of many who commented on Cornelys's brief but blazing career: "This is a singular dame . . . . Her taste and invention in pleasures and decorations is singular. She took Carlisle House . . . enlarged it and established assemblies and balls by subscription. At first they scandalized, but soon drew in both righteous and ungodly. She went on building, and made her house a fairy palace, for balls, concerts and masquerades."

When Sterne returned to London in January 1768, he did not subscribe, but tried hard to find a ticket for the James family (see letters 239 and 240; and Cash, *LY* 262–63, 292). And there is one further Sternean association with Cornelys's concerts, viz., that Catherine Fourmantel's final concert season ended (on February 4, 1763, when Sterne was in Toulouse) at the Dean Street concert rooms, also operated by her; see *LY*, 203.

2. Lady Anne] Lord Fauconberg's youngest daughter had married the Hon. Francis Talbot, brother to the Earl of Shrewsbury, in 1761 (Curtis, 297, n. 2).

3. Lord Bellasyse] Lord Fauconberg's son and heir; see letter 120, n. 8.

4. Lady Bellasyse] Lord Belasyse had married Charlotte Peniston, sister of 1st Viscount Melbourne, on May 29, 1766. A daughter, also named Charlotte, had been born on January 10, 1767 ("as near nine kalendar months as any husband

could in reason have expected" [*TS* 1.5.8]). While *niece* was occasionally still used for granddaughter, its use here is more probably an indication that Sterne has Fauconberg's daughters in mind as the primary recipients of his gossip.

5. grows like flax] Sterne perhaps misremembers a proverbial expression: "At leisure, as flax grows"; see Tilley, L196, and *ODEP*, 455.

6. *The School* . . . Murphy] *The School for Guardians* by Arthur Murphy (1727–1805), after Moliere's *L'École des maris* (1661), opened at Covent Garden on January 12, 1767. Curtis, 297, n. 5, usefully quotes a writer in the *St. James Chronicle* (January 22–24, 1767): 4, on the theatrical season:

> But now have at your Eyes and Ears;
> The high-puff'd *Cymon* next appears:
> Earth, Heav'n and Hell, are all united,
> The Upper Gall'ry, so delighted! . . .
> . . . the *School for Guardians* . . .
> You'd swear, 'twas written by a Lord:
> So fine the *Wit,* so fine the *Plot,*
> You have 'em, and you have 'em not: . . .
> Like Ghosts they're here, and now they're there;
> 'Tis M[urph]y now, and now Moliere.

7. *Trottoire*] *OED's* first illustration is dated 1792: "a paved footway on each side of a street; a pavement." Sterne is perhaps illustrating the effect of his visits to France.

8. Mr Bellasyse] I.e., Rowland Belasyse, Lord Fauconberg's brother; see letter 120, n. 9 (September 30, 1763), in which Sterne sent similar greetings.

9. Sr Bryan Stapleton] Sir Bryan Stapylton (*c.*1712–1772), 5th Baronet of Myton, Yorkshire. He subscribed to *Sermons* (1760).

191. *To Elizabeth (Eliza) Draper*

Text: Cross, *Life*

[London, ?late January 1767][1]

Eliza will receive my books with this—the Sermons came all hot from the heart[2]—I wish that could give em any title, to be offer'd to Y^rs^——the Others came from the head—I'm more indifferent ab^t^ their Reception——

I know not how it comes in—but I'm half in love with You.—I ought to be *wholy so*—for I never valued, (or saw more good Qualities to value,)—or thought more of one of Y^{r} Sex than of You.—

So adieu—

Y^{rs} faithfully if not aff^{tly},
L Sterne[3]

MS: Not located.

Pub.: Yorick to Eliza (1773), 1–2; Cross, *Life* (1929), 431; Curtis, no. 180.

Status: The story of Sterne's affair with Elizabeth Draper (Eliza) is told at length by Cash, *LY,* 268–304; and in the introduction and notes to the Florida edition of *ASJ,* 6:xxi–xxviii, and passim. Curtis, 298, n. 1, offers a succinct account:

> Sometime in Jan. 1767 Sterne had met at the house of Commodore William James [see letter 194] in Gerrard Street, Soho, Elizabeth Sclater (1744–78), daughter of May Sclater, an official of the East India Company. Born at Anjengo on the Malabar Coast [India], 5 Apr. 1744, at four years of age she became an orphan and later found herself miserable in a school in England. In 1757 she returned to Bombay where in July of the next year she married Daniel Draper [see letter 210], a promising official of the Company and a solemn individual of thirty-two. After the birth of her two children, in 1759 and 1761, she and her family returned to England for a visit about the year 1765. Their children put to school, Draper sailed for Bombay and his wife took up her abode with the Jameses, where Sterne came upon her. She was twenty-two; he was fifty-four. . . . Upon Draper's command she sailed for Bombay, 3 Apr. 1767, and finally eloped from her detested husband in 1773. About March 1776 she embarked upon the *Ajax* for England, lived for a short time in London, and died, 3 Aug. 1778 . . . .

We may add that Eliza was buried in Bristol Cathedral, where a memorial plaque is mounted: "Sacred to the memory of Mrs. Eliza Draper, in whom Genius and Benevolence were united." A full—if dated—account of her life is provided in Arnold Wright and William Lutley Sclater, *Sterne's Eliza* (New York: Alfred A. Knopf, 1923).

Sterne's letters to Eliza should be read alongside the *Bramine's Journal,* reprinted with substantial annotative materials, in volume 6 of the Florida *Works;* we have tried not to duplicate the material available therein.

The originals of Sterne's ten letters to Eliza, first published by W. Johnston as *Letters from Yorick to Eliza* (1773) have disappeared. Little is known about William Johnston, of Ludgate Street; he is not the William Johnston that Plomer ranks as "one of the foremost booksellers and publishers in London," but more likely the William Johnston, MA, who authored *A Pronouncing and Spelling Dictionary* (1764), the first and second (1772) editions of which were printed by "W. Johnston, Ludgate Street," as was his *Short Grammar of the English Language* (1772). A "Mr. Johnston" subscribed to *Sermons* (1769); we have tentatively identified him as the same "Mr. William Johnston" who subscribed to Francis Fawkes's *Original Poems and Translations* (1761) and to 25 copies (almost certainly indicating a bookseller) of Fawkes's translation of Theocritus (1767), for which "W. Johnston" appears among the dozen booksellers listed on the title page. There is a telling overlap between Sterne's lists and Fawkes's, but in all likelihood this is the William Johnston listed by Plomer and not the printer of the Yorick to Eliza correspondence in 1773.

The small octavo volume of xviii + 64 pages is dedicated by the anonymous editor (Johnston himself, perhaps?) to Lord Henry Apsley (1714–1794), Lord High Chancellor and son of Lord Bathurst (1684–1775), who offered his famous compliment to Sterne recorded in the third letter to Eliza (see letter 196). In the dedication and the preface that follows there is an elegance of composition that might indeed suggest the author of a grammar book and a dictionary. Acknowledging the bad repute of "dishonest booksellers and profligate scribblers" (i), the editor makes his cogent argument for the authenticity of the ten letters he had received from "the gentleman who had the perusal of the originals, and, with Eliza's permission, faithfully copied them at Bombay . . ." (iv). He is unusually tolerant and open to Sterne, "a man of warm temper and lively imagination" (v); and he does as well as Sterne himself in justifying those moments when the "glowing heat" of his affections might have carried Sterne "beyond the limits of pure platonism" (viii): "it perhaps [is] . . . his fairest encomium, since to cherish the seeds of piety and chastity in a heart which the passions are interested to corrupt, must be allowed to be the noblest effort of a soul, . . . fortified with the justest sentiments of Religion and Virtue" (ix). It is an eloquent plea.

The volume is, however, somewhat carelessly edited. In reprinting the first letter in *Life* (1929; 431), Cross was able to make several emendations based on a copy in Eliza's hand that he had located "in the collection of Lord Basing, at Hoddington"; she had sent a copy of the letter to her cousin Thomas Limbrey Sclater in 1767. The substantive variants agree with the partial version in Wright and Sclater, 47–48, probably based on Eliza's version as well. Curtis, too, used this version. In the absence of cooperation from Hoddington House, we have followed the Cross text, which is identical with that of Curtis.

In his bibliographical description of the 1773 *Letters,* Cross argues that it is evident they were copied from the manuscript letters, showing as they do, "in a marked degree Sterne's peculiarities in style, spelling, abbreviation, and punctuation" (*Life* [1929], 605). But he also calls attention to the numerous errors, and in describing the 1775 edition, suggests that "the letters for this edition were probably set from another copy of the originals, perhaps supplied by Mrs. Draper." He then adds that as many obvious misreadings exist in the 1775 edition as in the 1773 edition, and that "some changes in phrasing were made in the interest of a conventional style" (607).

Curtis decided that because the "text of the first edition is manifestly corrupt," he would base his text for letters 2–10 on the 1775 edition. He goes on to note, however, that both editions were corrupted, that he has made some corrections based on 1773 readings, and that "no satisfactory text of these letters can be had until the original letters are produced" (299). Earlier scholars, including Cross, had assumed that Eliza had returned to London in 1774, and hence, it might be suggested, that she had had a hand in the 1775 production, particularly because it is so often found bound together with the counterfeit *Letters from Eliza to Yorick,* first published in 1775. But Curtis could not have made this mistake because he cites the very document (298, n. 1) that establishes the fact that Eliza did not leave India until the spring of 1776.

This point is made in the very careful analysis of these 1775 publications by J.C.T. Oates, "Notes on the Bibliography of Sterne," *Cambridge Bibliographical Society* 2 (1955): 155–69, who demonstrates that there were no fewer than four printings (A, B, C, D) of *Letters from Yorick to Eliza,* published with the imprint of G. Kearsly and T. Evans, 1775, three of which (B, C, D) have "A New Edition" on their title page. The version (A) without "A New Edition" is established by Oates as the first printing of an unnamed third edition (an unnamed second edition had been published by T. Evans in 1775), the other three being later issues of the same text.

A collation of these editions clearly suggests that the first edition (siglum: *1773*), certainly not as careless or corrupted as Cross and Curtis assumed, should be our copy-text for letters 2–10. The "second" edition (siglum: *Evans*) is a close copy of the first (although one can find evidence of the "correction" of accidentals that will reappear far more extensively in the third edition) and will concern us only occasionally. The third edition (siglum: *1775*)—and its three subsequent issues—contains hundreds of differences from the first, almost all in the accidentals, almost all a result of "normalizing" the text. Thus, Sterne's typical elided past-tense endings have all been altered to "ed" endings, and his indifferent use of the comma and semi-colon has been "corrected," as has his grammar (e.g., "your Pope's and Swift's" becomes "your Popes and

Swifts" [see letter 196]). There is no question in our minds that in accidentals the 1773 version is closer to Sterne's manuscript than the 1775. Even more telling, we cannot discover in the substantive differences any definite evidence for Cross's assertion of another set of manuscripts. To be sure, there are some substantive differences, but in almost every instance they alter an obvious inadvertency or attempt to "polish" Sterne's style, diction, or syntax according to the editor's own predilection. We have recorded all these differences in our collation, including those few we have accepted into our own text.

The first edition does not number the letters, and we have cited them by inclusive page numbers; the second edition also does not number them; only in the third edition is each letter headed with "LETTER" and a roman numeral, very much in imitation of the Medalle format.

One further mystery remains. The second edition (1775) bears the imprint "T. Evans," who reappears as a co-printer with G. Kearsly for the third edition(s). The online *Exeter Working Papers in British Book Trade History* identifies Thomas Evans, near York Buildings, Strand, as a publisher of poets in particular, and a friend of Goldsmith; he seems clearly to be the T. Evans of *Letters,* since his location is exactly the same. Intriguingly, however, another Thomas Evans (1739–1803), dwelling in Paternoster Row, is listed in the same source as having begun his London career in the employ of William Johnston, of Ludgate Street. This is the Thomas Evans that Goldsmith attacked with his cane, to his own detriment. It is probably only a coincidence, but one does wonder if a confusion of biographical detail has occurred and that in some way or another the Thomas Evans who worked for Johnston was given the materials for subsequent reprintings. It might help explain, for example, the fact that the 1773 first edition "was not advertised in the newspapers or given to the magazines for review," leading Cross to suggest that it "appears to have been a semi-private publication" (605).

1. Date] None of the letters from Yorick to Eliza is dated. We have followed the order of the 1773 edition and Curtis's dating.

2. the Sermons . . . heart] Cf. letter 40 (to Catherine Fourmantel): "I beg you will accept of the inclosed Sermon, which I do not make you a present of, merely because it was wrote by myself,—but because there is a beautiful Character in it, of a tender & compassionate Mind . . . ." Sterne often troped, as did the century, on the head-heart dichotomy (see letter 6, n. 15), but he seems particularly to have prided himself on writing sermons that did not come from the "wrong end"—from his head rather than his heart; see Yorick's comments at the Visitation dinner, *TS,* IV.26.376–77. He would seem to be suggesting to Eliza that the *Sermons* would be better reading for her than *Tristram Shandy;* one might suspect that

Sterne's opening gambit was always his sermons, with Shandean bawdy awaiting closer familiarity or encouragement.

3. L Sterne] The brevity of this letter, the fact that we have a record of Eliza's holograph (with its marks of accurate transcription, superscript abbreviations, and varied dash lengths), and the fact that the various texts in the four different states of the 1775 third edition do not differ, makes it a convenient illustration of just how far the printed versions are from the probable Sterne manuscripts. We provide here a complete collation of our present text with the 1773, *Evans* (second edition), and 1775 (third edition) versions:

Florida	*1773*	*Evans*	*1775*(A)
this—the Sermons	this, the summons	this—the summons	this. The sermons
heart—I	heart; I	heart; I	heart: I
that could	that cou'd	that could	that I could
em	them	them	them
title,	title	title	title
offer'd	offered	offered	offered
Y[rs]——the	yours: the	yours; the	yours.—The
Others	others	others	others
head—I'm	head; I am	head—I am	head—I am
ab[t]	about	about	about
Reception——	reception—	reception—	reception.
comes in—but	comes, but	comes, but	comes about, but
I'm	I am	I am	I am
You.—I	you—I	you——I	you—I
wholy so—	wholly so;	wholly so;	wholly so;
valued, (or	valued (or	valued (or	valued (or
Qualities	qualities	qualities	qualities
value,)—or	value) or	value) or	value) or
Y[r] Sex than	your sex, than	your sex than	your sex than
You.—[new line] So adieu—	you—So adieu.	you— | so adieu.	you; so adieu,
Y[rs] faithfully	Yours faithfully,	Yours faithfully,	Yours, faithfully,
aff[tly],	affeionately—	affectionately——	affectionately,
L Sterne	L—S——NE.	L—— S——NE	L. STERNE.

192. *To Elizabeth Draper*

Text: Yorick to Eliza

[London, ?February 1767]

I cannot rest Eliza, tho' I shall call on you at half past twelve, till I know how you do—may thy dear face smile as thou risest, like the sun of this morning! I was much griev'd to hear of your alarming indisposition yesterday; and disappointed too at not being let in—Remember, my dear, "that a friend has the same right as a physician"[1] the etiquettes of this town (you'll say) say otherwise; no matter, delicacy and propriety[a] do not always consist in observing their frigid doctrines—I am going out to breakfast, but shall be at my lodgings by eleven, when I hope to read a single line under thy own hand, that thou art better, and will be glad to see,

Thy
BRAMIN.[2]

Nine o'Clock.

MS: Not located.
Pub.: Yorick to Eliza (1773), 3–4; Curtis, no. 181.

[a]propriety] property *Evans*

1. a friend . . . physician] Proverbial; *ODEP,* 622, with the first example from Chaucer's "Tale of Melibee": "Catoun seith, 'If thou hast nede of help, axe it of thy freendes, for ther nys noon so good a phisicien as thy trewe freend'" (cf. Cato, *De Moribus,* iv.13: "Nec quisquam melior medicus quam fidus amicus"). See also Ecclesiasticus, 6:16: "A faithful friend is the medicine of life." An 1807 edition of *Letters of Yorick and Eliza* (Whittingham) contains a bawdy frontispiece with Yorick feeling the pulse of a recumbent and bare-breasted Eliza, with this very sentence as its legend (see figure 7, p. 532).

2. BRAMIN.] Cf. Curtis, 299, n. 1: "By way of allusion to Sterne's profession and Mrs. Draper's affiliation with India the pair referred to each other as the Bramin and the Bramine." Keymer, in his edition of *ASJ* (Everyman, 1994), 152, points out that Bramins were proverbially wise and austere, as in Pope's "Epistle to Bathurst" (1733), ll. 185–86: "If Cotta liv'd on pulse, it was no more / Than Bramins, Saints, and Sages did before." Sterne's journal to Eliza was headed

Figure 7. "A friend has the same right as a physician," engraving by McKenzie after William Marshall Craig, frontispiece for *Letters of Yorick and Eliza* (1807).

"Continuation of the Bramines Journal," and the Florida editors chose to use that title rather than the title first provided by Cross, "Journal to Eliza."

193. *To Isaac Panchaud*

Text: Ms.

London: [Friday,] Feb. 2<?3>~o~.[1] [1767]

Dear Panchaude—

I paid yesterday (by Becket) a hundred Guineas (*or* pounds)[2] I forget w^{ch}——∧to Mr Selvin∧ But You must remit to Mrs Sterne at Merseilles[3] a hundred Louis. wch she will want before she leaves that place wch will be in 3 Weeks——however let her know she may have the Cash when she draws for it————

Have you got the 9th V. of Shandy?[4]—tis liked the best of all here——

I'm going to publish a *Sentimental Journey* through *France & Italy*—the undertaking is protected & highly encouraged by all our *Noblesse*—& at the rate tis subscribed— | for, will bring me a thousand guineas (au moins)[5]—twil be an Original—in large Quarto—the Subscription half a Guinea[6]—if you can <let me> procure me the honour of a few names of men of Science or Fashon—I shall thank you—<but> they will appear in good Company, as all the Nobility here almost have honourd me wth their Names. my kindest Remembrance to Foley—& to Miss Panchaude—

PS

My daughter has an advantagious offer[7] just now at Merseilles—he has 20,000 Liv^{res} a year—& much at his ease———So I suppose Md^{lle} <will>~w~ith Madame <f>~m~a femme will negociate the Affair

con Effetto—[8]

my best Comp^{s} to B. D'Holbach and all friends ———

[L: Sterne][9]

Address: A Messrs / Messrs Foley & Panchaude / Banquieres. / Rue St Sauveur— / a Paris.

Postmark: 20 FE ES
Endorsed: London 20 feb[r] 1767 / Sterne / Re[çu] le 26e / [Réponse] le 9 Mars / M
MS: Robert H. Taylor Collection, Princeton University Library.
Pub.: Medalle, no. 75 (a partial and garbled version); facsimile in *Autograph Portfolio: A Collection of Fac-simile Letters from Eminent Persons* (1837; lacking second postscript); Curtis, no. 182 (based on facsimile).

1. Date] Medalle dates the letter "February 13" (Cash, *LY* 265, n. 31, is mistaken in thinking she has "February 20"). The second numeral is blotted in the manuscript; Curtis has February 20, while Cash, 352, n. 69, has "25." We have allowed the testimony of the postmark and endorsement to sway us to accept the date of February 20.

2. *or* pounds] There were twenty-one shillings in a guinea, twenty in a pound; the difference of £5 was not an inconsiderable sum in 1767.

3. Merseilles] See letter 186.

4. the 9th V. of Shandy] The single volume was advertised in the *Public Advertiser,* January 29, 1767; 3,500 copies (rather than the usual 4,000) were printed, to be sold for 2 shillings sewed and bound in boards. There is a dedication to William Pitt, now addressed as Lord Chatham, a title he received in 1766; that Sterne had dedicated the second edition of volumes I and II to Pitt in 1760 (as he here gracefully reminds him) may suggest a subtle hint of closure in this new dedication. The reception Sterne boasts of may more truthfully be considered mixed, the usual division between those who were amused and those who were shocked; despite much advice to mine his sentimental vein, volume IX, from Tom's sausage-making venture to the Shandy bull, defiantly continued Sterne's baiting of "Prudes and Tartufs" (*TS* V.1.409).

5. au moins] At least.

6. in large Quarto . . . half a Guinea] Sterne's heady plans did not materialize. *ASJ* was published on February 27, 1768, in the same small octavo format as *TS,* but with a run of only 2,500 copies; another 150 copies on demy (with cut pages measuring approximately 105 x 175 mm.) were printed for subscribers to an "imperial" copy, but the actual size is only slightly larger than the small octavo (95 x 150 mm.). A second edition of another 2,000 copies appeared on March 29, shortly after Sterne's death, and a "New Edition," again of 2,000 copies, toward the end of the summer. The subscribers to the large-paper copies are indicated with an asterisk in the subscription list (134 in the large-paper copies; an additional subscriber, Charles Sloane Cadogan [see letter 189, n. 3], is marked with an asterisk only in the ordinary-paper copies). Each paid a guinea (according to Cross, *Life* [1929], 478, n., but he does not cite a source, perhaps depending on this

letter), while the subscribers to the ordinary-paper copies (some 145 additional subscribers) paid a half guinea, some taking multiple copies. Sterne would not have made much over 180 guineas from subscriptions, well short of the 1,000 guineas he predicts here. See *ASJ*, 6:xxxi–xxxv, lxiii, and appendix 5.

7. My daughter . . . offer] The identity of Lydia's suitor is unknown.

8. *con Effetto*] I.e., *con affetto,* with feeling, with affection, a musical direction; cf. *TS*, VI.11.514–15, where we are told of Yorick's use of similar musical terms to evaluate his sermons.

9. L: Sterne] The signature does not appear in the manuscript; the facsimile edition (1837) does have Sterne's signature directly under "*con Effetto*," and we have included it here, although we are unable to explain why the copyist included the signature while dropping the second postscript or why it is not in the Taylor manuscript.

194. *To Lydia Sterne*

Text: Medalle

Old Bond-street, [Monday,] February 23, 1767.

And so, my Lydia! thy mother and thyself are returning back again from Marseilles to the banks of the Sorgue[1]—and there thou wilt sit and fish for trouts[2]—I envy you the sweet situation.—Petrarch's tomb I should like to pay a sentimental visit to[3]—the Fountain of Vaucluse,[4] by thy description, must be delightful—I am also much pleased with the account you give me of the Abbé de Sade[5]—you find great comfort in such a neighbour—I am glad he is so good as to correct thy translation of my Sermons—dear girl go on, and make me a present of thy work—but why not the House of Mourning?[6] 'tis one of the best. I long to receive the life of Petrarch, and his Laura, by your Abbé, but I am out of all patience with the answer the Marquis[7] made the Abbé—'twas truly coarse, and I wonder he bore it with any christian patience—But to the subject of your letter—I do not wish to know who was the busy fool, who made your mother uneasy about Mrs. ———[8] 'tis true I have a friendship for her, but not to infatuation—I believe I have judgment enough to discern hers, and every woman's faults. I honour thy mother for her answer—"that she wished not to be informed, and begged him to drop the subject."—Why do you say that your mother wants money?—whilst I have a shilling, shall you not both have nine-pence out of it?—I think, if I have my enjoyments, I ought not to grudge you yours.—I shall not begin my Sentimental Journey till I get to Coxwould—I have laid a plan for something new, quite out of the beaten track.—I wish I had you with me—and I would introduce you to one of the most amiable and gentlest of beings, whom I have just been with—not Mrs. ———, but a Mrs. James[a][9] the wife of as worthy a man as I ever met with—I esteem them both. He possesses every manly virtue—honour and bravery are his characteristicks, which have distinguished him nobly in several instances—I shall make you better acquainted with his character, by sending Orme's History,[10] with the books you desired—and it is well worth your reading; for Orme is an elegant writer, and a just one; he pays no man a compliment at the expence of truth.—Mrs. James[a] is kind—and friendly—of a sentimental turn of mind—and so sweet a disposition, that she is too good for the world she lives in—Just God! if all were like her, what a life would this be!—Heaven, my Lydia, for some wise purpose has created different beings—I wish my dear child knew her—thou art worthy of her friendship, and she already loves thee; for I sometimes tell her what I feel for thee.—This is a long letter—write soon, and never let your letters be studied ones—write naturally, and then you will write well.[11]—I hope your mother has got quite well of her ague—I have sent her some of Huxham's tincture of the Bark.[12] I will order you a guittar since the other[13] is broke. Believe me, my Lydia, that I am yours affectionately,

L. Sterne

MS: Not located.
Pub.: Medalle, no. 76; Curtis, no. 183.

[a]James] J. / J—— *M*

1. Sorgue] The river Sorgue, fed by the Fontaine de Vaucluse, runs to Avignon and empties there into the Rhône. See letter 186, n. 3.

2. there thou . . . trouts] Cf. letter 202, to Eliza: "We shall fish upon the banks

of Arno, and lose ourselves in the sweet labyrinths of it's vallies . . . ." As with the Sorgue, the Arno had associations with Petrarch and Laura.

3. Petrarch's tomb . . . visit to] Petrarch was not buried at Vaucluse, but at Arquà in Northern Italy. Cf. Tristram's fruitless pilgrimage to the Tomb of the Two Lovers (*TS* VII.40); and his comments on a gift of prints in *BJ*, 201: "I have a present of the Sculptures upon poor Ovid's Tomb, who died in Exile, tho' he wrote so well upon the Art of Love . . . ." Ovid, too, was missing from *his* tomb, as noted by the Florida editors, *ASJ*, 6:407–8, n. to 201.9–12.

4. the Fountain of Vaucluse] See letter 186, n. 3. From the seventeenth century on, the setting attracted tourists drawn by one of the most powerful springs in the world and its association with Petrarch and Laura. Edward Gibbon, to be sure, was not enthusiastic: "The merits of the lover I am still less qualified to appreciate: nor am I deeply interested in a metaphysical passion for a nymph so shadowy, that her existence has been questioned; for a matron so prolific, that she was delivered of eleven legitimate children, while her amorous swain sighed and sung at the fountain of Vaucluse"; and in a footnote, he adds: "Vaucluse, so familiar to our English travellers, is described from the writings of Petrarch . . . . It was, in truth, the retreat of a hermit; and the moderns are much mistaken if they place Laura and a happy lover in the grotto" (*The History of the Decline and Fall of the Roman Empire* [1776–1788; London: Folio Society, 1990], 8:289–90 [ch. 70]).

5. Abbé de Sade] Jacques-François-Paul-Alphonse de Sade (1705–1778), uncle of the notorious Marquis, whom he helped to educate. He had retired in 1752 to Vaucluse to write his *Mémoires pour la vie de François Pétrarque* (1764–67), in which he attempted to identify Petrarch's Laura with the wife of his forebear Hugues de Sade. Gibbon called it "a copious, original, and entertaining work, a labour of love, composed from the accurate study of Petrarch and his contemporaries; but the hero is too often lost in the general history of the age, and the author too often languishes in the affectation of politeness and gallantry" (*Decline* 8:289n.). And, in a second note, he adds: "The pious grandson of Laura has laboured, and not without success, to vindicate her immaculate chastity against the censures of the grave and the sneers of the profane" (291n.). Sade's identification of Laura (*d.* 1348) has not been universally accepted.

6. House of Mourning] Sterne published "The house of feasting and the house of mourning described" as the second sermon in his first volume of *Sermons* in 1760; its position seems an indication of Sterne's favorable opinion of it. For another translator of this sermon into French, see letter 82, n. 8. No translation by Lydia of any of her father's sermons is known to exist.

7. the Marquis] Curtis, 302, n. 4, offers a possible identification, the notorious Donatien-Alphonse-François de Sade (1740–1814), Marquis de Sade; that the

remark was "coarse" would seem to support this supposition, although we have no further information about the episode that Lydia reported to Sterne.

8. Mrs. ———] Curtis believes this refers to Eliza (Mrs. Draper), which is probably the case, especially given the proximity of her mention to that of the Jameses. Still, it would suggest an extraordinary rapidity of cross-channel rumor-mongering, assuming Sterne first met Eliza only four weeks earlier.

9. Mrs. James] Medalle has her customary initial ("Mrs. J."), but Curtis provides the obvious identification, Anne Goddard James (*d.* 1798), wife of Commodore William James (*c.*1721–1783). James had spent much of his life at sea, and since 1747 had been connected to the East India Company, in which he had made a reputation for military prowess. He had retired to London in 1759, and in 1765 had married Anne, whose father had also been in the Indian service. Shortly after Sterne's death, James became a director of the East India Company, a position he held until his own death. Cash notes that Sterne "seems to have loved them on first sight. Certainly, he treasured their friendship as one of his closest during the few months of life remaining to him" (*LY* 268–69). It was in the house of the Jameses in Gerrard Street, Soho, "the centre of social life for the servants of the East India Company who were in London" (*LY* 269), that Sterne met Eliza. A magnificent portrait of James was painted by Reynolds (1782), but was destroyed in World War II; copies of an engraving survive, as well as a replica (1784), housed in the National Maritime Museum, London.

10. Orme's History] Robert Orme (1728–1801) compliments Commodore James in the first volume of *History of the Military Transactions of the British Nation in Indostan* (1763), 1:404–10.

11. then you will write well] Sterne had given much the same advice to Lydia three years earlier, in letter 129 (May 15, 1764).

12. Huxham's tincture of the Bark] Brookes, *Dispensatory*, 217–18, provides the recipe for *Tinctura Corticis Peruviani* (A Tincture of the Bark), devised by John Huxham (1692–1768), M.D., F.R.S., of Plymouth, the author of *An Essay on Fevers* (1755): "Take of Peruvian Bark in Powder two Ounces; of the yellow Part of *Seville* Orange Peel an Ounce and a half; of Virginian Snake-Root three Drams; of Saffron four Scruples; of *French* Brandy twenty Ounces. Let them stand together in a close Vessel, at least three or four Days, and then strain off the Tincture." Brookes seems to prefer a similar concoction mixed by Dr. John Pringle, but he acknowledges that Huxham gave his "with Success in intermitting and slow nervous Fevers, and in the Decline of putrid, spotted and pestilential Fevers, tho' the Remissions were very obscure." The dose was "a Dram to half an Ounce, every fourth, sixth or eighth Hour."

13. the other] This would be the guitar that Sterne had given Lydia in 1764 (see letter 129), and proudly mentioned in letter 158.

195. *To Isaac Panchaud*

Text: Ms.

London [Friday,] Feb: 27 [1767]

Dear M[r] Panchaude

my daughter begs a present of me—tis a Guittar—it must[a] be strung with cat gut & of 5 Cords—si chiama in Italiano, "La Chitera di cinque corde"[1]—She cannot get such a Thing at Merseilles—at Paris one may have every thing—would you be so good to my Girl as to make her happy in this affaire, by getting some musical Body to buy one, & send it her to Avignon directed to Mons[r] Teste.[2]

I wrote last week to desire you w[d] remit M[rs] Sterne a 100 Louis——twil be all except the Guittar I shall owe you & send me y[r] Acc[t] then, & I will pay it to M[r] Selvin—direct to me at M[r] Beckets—all kind resp[ts] to my friend Foley—and my dear friend Y[r] Sister[b]

Y[rs] cordially—
L. Sterne

Address: a Messrs / Mess[rs] Foley et Panchaude / Banquiers rue S[t] / Sauveur—Paris.
Endorsed: London 27 feb[y] 1767 / L Sterne / Re le 4 mars / le 9[e] / M.
MS: British Library, Addit. MSS. 33964, 381.
Pub.: Medalle, no. 77; Curtis, no. 184.

[a]me—tis a Guittar—it must] me,—and you must know I can deny her nothing—It must *M* [b]and . . . Sister] and your sister *M*

1. cat gut . . . corde] As Sterne's Italian indicates, the "guitar" he requests "is called in Italian, 'La Chitera with five strings,'" rather than the "English" guitar, which at this time had developed as a six-string instrument. The five-string instrument is more difficult to play, so why Lydia would request it is something of a mystery. However, the precise relationship between these two instruments (the guitar and the chitarra) may seem analogous (at least to the uninitiated) to Toby's efforts to distinguish between a half-moon and a ravelin (*TS* II.12.129).

2. Mons[r] Teste] Unidentified; it is possible that Sterne wrote "Feste" instead. Probably a banker in Avignon.

196. *To Eliza Draper*

Text: Yorick to Eliza

[London, March 1767]

I got thy letter last night, Eliza, on my return from Lord Bathurst's,[1] where I din'd; and where I was heard (as I talk'd of thee for an[a] hour without intermission) with so much pleasure and attention, that the good old Lord toasted your health three several[b] times; and tho' he is now[c] in his eighty-fifth year, says he hopes to live long enough to be introduced as a friend, to my fair Indian disciple; and to see her eclipse all other Nabobesses[2] as much in wealth, as she already does[d] in exterior and (what is far better) in interior merit—I hope so too.

This[3] nobleman is an old friend of mine. You know he was always the protector of men of wit and genius, and had[e] those of the last century, Addison, Steele, Pope, Swift, Prior, &c. &c. always at his table.—

The manner in which his notice of me began[f], was singular[g], as it was polite: he came up to me one day, as I was at the Princess of Wales's[4] court—"I want to know you, Mr. Sterne[h]; but it is fit you should also know[i] who it is that wishes this pleasure. You have heard," continued he, "of an old Lord Bathurst, of whom your Pope's and Swift's have sung and spoken so much: I have liv'd my life with genius's of that cast, but have surviv'd them; and despairing ever to find their equals, 'tis some years since I clos'd[j] my accounts, and shut up my books, with thoughts of never opening them again: But you have kindled a desire in me to open[k] them once more before I die, which I now do—so go home and dine with me."

This nobleman, I say, is a prodigy! for at eighty five he has all the wit and promptness of a man of thirty—a disposition to be pleased, and a power to please others, beyond whatever I knew; added to which, a man of learning, courtesy and feeling.—

He heard me talk of thee, Eliza, with uncommon satisfaction, for there was only a third person, and of sensibility, with us—and a most sentimental afternoon, till nine o'clock, have we pass'd! But thou, Eliza, was[l] the star that conducted and enlighten'd[m] the discourse![5] and when I talk'd not of thee, still didst thou fill my mind, and warm[n] ev'ry thought I utter'd! for I am not asham'd to acknowledge, I greatly miss thee—best of all good girls! the sufferings I have sustain'd all night[o] on account of thine, Eliza, are beyond my power of words—assuredly does heaven give strength proportion'd to the weight he[p] lays upon us[6]—Thou hast been bow'd down, my child, with every burthen that sorrow of heart and pain of body cou'd inflict on[q] a poor being—and still thou tell'st me that thou[r] art beginning to get ease, thy fever gone—thy sickness, the pain in thy side vanishing also—

May every evil so vanish, that thwarts Eliza's happiness, or but awakens her[s] fears for a moment—Fear nothing, my dear, hope every thing; and the balm of this passion will shed it's influence on thy health, and make thee enjoy a spring of youth and chearfulness, more than thou hast hardly yet tasted—

And so thou hast fix'd thy Bramin's portrait[7] over thy writing desk, and will consult it in all doubts and difficulties; grateful good[t] girl! Yorick smiles contentedly over all thou dost, his picture does not do justice to his own complacency—

Thy sweet little plan and distribution of thy time, how worthy of thee!

Indeed, Eliza, thou leavest one[u] nothing to direct thee in, thou leavest me nothing to require, nothing to ask, but a continuance[v] of that conduct which won my esteem, and has made me thy friend for ever.

May the roses come quick back to thy cheek[w], and the rubies to thy lips! but trust my declaration, Eliza, that thy husband (if he is the good feeling man I wish him) will press thee to him with more honest warmth and affection, and kiss thy pale poor dejected face with more transport, than he wou'd be able to do in the best bloom of all thy beauty—and so he ought.—I[x] pity him.—He must have strange feelings, if he knows not the value of such a creature as thou art—

I am glad Miss Light[8] goes with you, she may relieve you from many anxious moments.

I am glad too, that your[y] shipmates are friendly beings—you cou'd least dispense with what is contrary to thy[z] own nature, which is soft and gentle, Eliza, it wou'd civilize savages; tho' pity were it, thou should'st be tainted with the office.—

How canst thou make apologies for thy last letter! 'tis most delicious to me, for the very reasons[aa] you excuse it—Write to me, my child, only such, let them speak the easy chearfulness[bb] of a heart that opens itself any how, and every how, to a man you ought to esteem and trust—[9]

Such Eliza, I write to thee, and so I shou'd ever live with thee, most artlessly, most affectionately, if Providence permitted thy residence in the same section of the globe. For I am all that honour and inclination[cc] can make me.

Thy
BRAMIN

MS: Pierpont Morgan Library, New York (a copy, not in Sterne's hand, of the first four paragraphs only, based on the text of the 1775 third edition, is tipped in (fol. 16) the volume containing the Fourmantel letters, MA 849).
Pub.: Yorick to Eliza, 5–13; Curtis, no. 185.

[a]thee for an] thee an *1775* [b]several] different *1775* [c]and tho' he is now] and now he is *1775* [d]already does] does already *1775* [e]and had] and has had *1775* [f]of me began] began of me *1775* [g]was singular] was as singular *1775* [h]Sterne] *1775;* S—ne *1773* [i]should also know] should know, also, *1775* [j]I clos'd] I have closed *1775* [k]to open] of opening *1775* [l]was] wert *1775* [m]enlighten'd] enliven'd *1775* [n]warm] warmed *1775* [o]all night] the whole night *1775* [p]he] it *Evans* [q]on] upon *1775* [r]me that thou] me thou *Evans;* me, thou *1775* [s]her] thy *1775* [t]grateful good] Grateful and good *1775* [u]one] me *Evans, 1775* [v]continuance] continuation *1775* [w]cheek] *Evans;* check *1773;* cheeks *1775* [x]ought.—I] ought, or I *1775* [y]glad too, that your] glad your *1775* [z]thy] your *1775* [aa]reasons] reason *1775* [bb]chearfulness] carelessness *1775* [cc]inclination] affection *1775*

1. Lord Bathurst's] Allen Bathurst (1684–1775), Baron Bathurst (created Earl Bathurst in 1772), was, as Sterne goes on to say, a friend and patron of the Scriblerians, and the dedicatee of one of Pope's finest poems, "Moral Essays: Epistle III: To Bathurst (Of the Use of Riches)." Maynard Mack provides an entertaining portrait that perhaps tells us something about the mutual appeal between Sterne and the baron: "A generous man of large proportions, Bathurst indulged appetites that were equally outsized. He was considerably a womanizer, though the father of seventeen legal offspring . . . . He was also a robust trencherman and tippler who rarely needed to let physicians near him and accordingly lived to be ninety-one" (*Alexander Pope: A Life* [New York: W. W. Norton, 1985], 371).

Bathurst subscribed to *Sermons* in 1760 (and hence we can assume that Sterne's acquaintance with him began at that time) and also to a large-paper copy of *ASJ*. Sterne was clearly proud of Bathurst's recognition, and for at least one critic the meeting between the two has been the starting point for an extended argument linking Sterne to the Scriblerian tradition: "It is a valuable anecdote—one of those fortunately preserved occurrences which make a literary period more than just a convenient textbook label. Pope had been dead for sixteen years, Swift for fifteen—and though the works of Fielding and Johnson had amply filled the literary scene, they were not Augustans; and so, the old Lord Bathurst, seventy-five years old in 1760, wanted to take Sterne home for dinner because he had found another genius of that cast" (New, *Laurence Sterne as Satirist* 1). Sterne's "eighty-fifth year" is a slight miscalculation.

In dedicating *Letters from Yorick to Eliza* to Lord Apsley, Bathurst's son, the editor writes that "he flatters himself a volume of letters, written by such a person as Mr. Sterne, on [*sic*] which your noble father is placed in a light so truly amiable, cannot fail of engaging your Lordship's gracious acceptance and protection" (a2[v]); see also xii–xiii, for the editor's effusive praise of Bathurst's triumph over the "contracted spirit observable in old age." Mack recounts an often repeated story about father and son: "Even at ninety, concluding a long dinner party from which his son . . . had just excused himself, he is reported to have looked about the table with a twinkle and to have said, 'Come, now the Old Gentleman's gone, let's crack another bottle'" (372).

2. Nabobesses] The feminine form of *nabob*, an Anglo-Indian corruption of *nawab*, the Urdu word for governor; *OED* records a second definition, 1.b: "In extended use: . . . *spec.* (now *hist.*) a British person who acquired a large fortune in India during the period of British rule." The first illustration is from Samuel Foote's *The Minor* (1760; see letter 162, n. 3); Sterne's usage here is the first illustration of the feminine form.

3. This, etc.] The third edition does not begin a new paragraph until "He heard me talk . . . ." It also does not have new paragraphs at "May every evil . . ." and "Indeed, Eliza . . ."; and the last four paragraphs of the first edition are printed in the third as one paragraph. This pattern continues throughout the third edition's revision of the first edition; e.g., in letter 197, eleven paragraphs of the first edition become three paragraphs in the third.

4. Princess of Wales's] Augusta (1719–1772), the widow of Frederick Louis (1707–1751), Prince of Wales, reputed mistress of Lord Bute, and mother of George III. Of her, Walpole writes: "The Princess was ardently fond of power and all its appanages of observance, rank and wealth. The deepest secrecy and dissimulation guarded every avenue of her passions . . ." (*Memoirs . . . George III* 1:15).

5. enlighten'd the discourse] The *1775* revision to "enlivened" has a more idiomatic ring, but "enlighten'd" plays off "the star that conducted" and seems to be a splendid metaphorical compliment, missed by an officious editor.

6. heaven . . . lays upon us] At the heart of this rather overworked sentiment is perhaps 1 Corinthians 10:13: "God is faithful, who will not suffer you to be tempted above that ye are able; but will with the temptation also make a way to escape, that ye may be able to bear it"; and 2 Corinthians 12:9: "And he said unto me, My grace is sufficient for thee: for my strength is made perfect in weakness." But perhaps Sterne expressed it most memorably in *ASJ*, 152: "*God tempers the wind* . . . to the shorn lamb" (see n. to 152.19, 6:369).

7. thy Bramin's portrait] As Cash, *LY*, 274, notes, Sterne had "presented her with his picture, probably one of the Fisher mezzotints of the 1760 Reynolds . . . [and] she in turn sat for a miniature portrait for him." See above, letters 53, n. 4, and 141, n. 7.

8. Miss Light] Following the prefatory clues of the *1773* editor, Curtis, 307, n. 6, identifies her as Hester Eleanora Light, who was going out to marry George Stratton, of the Madras branch of the East India Company, and would sail with the East Indiaman, the *Lord Chatham* (erroneously called "the Earl of Chatham" by Sterne in letter 203). The ship sailed for India on April 3, 1767. See also E. A. Greening Lamborn, "Great Tew: A Link with Laurence Sterne," *N&Q* 193 (1948): 512–15.

9. Write to me . . . trust—] Once again Sterne advises his correspondent, whether his daughter or his inamorata, to write from the heart, not the head; see letter 153, n. 10, and passim.

197. *To Eliza Draper*

Text: Yorick to Eliza

[London, March 1767]

I write this Eliza, at Mr. James's, whilst he is dressing, and the dear girl his wife is writing beside me, to thee—

I got your melancholy billet before we sat down to dinner; 'tis melancholy indeed my dear, to hear so piteous an account of thy sickness, thou art encompass'd with evils[a] enow, without that additional weight—I fear it will sink thy poor soul, and body with it, past recovering[b]—Heaven supply thee with fortitude! We have talk'd of nothing but thee, Eliza, and of thy sweet virtues, and endearing conduct, the whole afternoon[c]. —

Mrs. James and thy[d] Bramin have mix'd their tears a hundred times, in speaking of thy hardships, thy goodness, thy graces, 'tis a subject that will never end betwixt[e] us—Oh! she is good and friendly!

The[f] ***[1] by heaven[g] are worthless; I have heard enough to tremble at the articulation of the name—How cou'd you, Eliza leave them (or suffer them to leave you rather) with impressions the least favourable? I have told thee enough to plant disgust against their treachery to thee, to the last hour of thy life—yet still thou told'st Mrs. James at last, that thou believest they affectionately loved[h] thee—Her delicacy to my Eliza, and true regard to her ease of mind, have saved thee from hearing more glaring proofs of their baseness—For God's sake, write not to them, nor foul thy fair character[i] with such polluted hearts—They[j] love thee!—What proof?—Is it their actions which[k] say so? or their zeal for those attachments which do thee honour, and make thee happy? Or their tenderness for thy fame? No, but they weep[l], and say tender things[m]—Adieu to all such for ever.—

Mrs. James's honest heart revolts against the idea of even[n] returning them one visit. I honour her, and honour[o] thee for almost every act of thy life, but this blind partiality to[p] an unworthy being.

Forgive my zeal, dear girl, and allow me a right, which arises only out of that fund of affection I have and shall preserve for thee, to the hour of my death—

Reflect Eliza, what are my motives for perpetually advising thee, think whether I can have any which proceed not from[q] the cause I have mentioned?

I think you a[r] very deserving woman, and that you want nothing but firmness, and a better opinion of yourself, to be the best *female*[s] character[2] I know.—

I wish I cou'd inspire you with a share of that vanity your enemies lay to your charge (tho' to me it has never been visible) because I think, in a well turn'd mind, it will produce good effects—

I probably shall never see you more;[3] yet flatter[t] myself you will[u] sometimes think of me with pleasure; because you must be convinced I love you, and so interest myself in your rectitude, that I had rather hear of any evil befalling you, than your want of reverence for yourself—

I had not power to keep this remonstrance in my breast—tis now out—so adieu! Heaven watch over my Eliza.

Thine
YORICK.

MS: Not located.
Pub.: Yorick to Eliza (1773), 14–19; Curtis, no. 187.

[a]encompass'd with evils] encompassed with evil *Evans;* encountered with evils *1775* [b]recovering] recovery *1775* [c]conduct, the whole afternoon] conduct, all the afternoon *1775* [d]thy] *1775;* the *1773* [e]betwixt] between *Evans* [f]graces, 'tis . . . friendly! ¶ The] graces. | —The *1775* [g]heaven] heavens *1775* [h]loved] love *1775* [i]character] *1775;* characters *1773* [j]They] *They 1775* [k]which] that *1775* [l]weep] *weep 1775* [m]tender things] *tender things 1775* [n]even] ever *1775* [o]and honour] and I honour *1775* [p]to] for *1775* [q]any which proceed not from] any, but what proceed from *1775* [r]you a] you are a *1775* [s]*female*] female *Evans, 1775* [t]yet flatter] yet I flatter *1775* [u]you will] you'll *1775*

1. The ***] The editor of *Letters from Yorick to Eliza* (1773) comments toward the end of his introduction to the collection: "It remains only, to take some little notice of the family marked with asterisks, on whom Mr. Sterne has thought proper to shed the bitterest gall of his pen; it is however evident, even from some passages in the letters themselves, that Mrs. Draper could not be easily prevailed on to see this family in the same odious light in which they appeared to her, perhaps over zealous, friend" (xvii). Curtis, 310, n. 2, and 314, n. 5, identified the family as the Newnhams (as did the *1773* editor on one occasion; see letter 199 and n. 7), a large family of London merchants (bakers and grocers), and politicians, headed by Nathaniel Newnham (*c.*1699–1778), of Newtimber Place, Sussex, MP for Bramber, 1754–1761, and a director of the East India Company intermittently from 1738. He had five sons, two of whom, George Lewis Newnham (*c.*1733–1800) and Nathaniel Newnham (*c.*1741–1809), followed their father into Parliament. Sterne's tone, here and elsewhere in discussing the Newnhams, may suggest he considered them rivals for Eliza's affections; certainly the ages of the brothers suggest a more likely pairing with her than with Sterne. Significantly enough, however, Sterne's hostility did not prevent him from accepting subscriptions: Nathaniel (probably the younger) subscribed as Mr. N. Newnham to two sets of *ASJ,* as did the youngest son, William (*d.* 1781), while yet another, Thomas (*d. c.*1774), subscribed to a large-paper copy, as did both Miss Anne Newnham and Miss Honoria Newnham; Nathaniel senior had only one daughter, but *Honoria* was his mother's name and *Anne* his sister's, so clearly they were family

names. In 1769, by contrast, only one family member subscribed, assuming that "—— Newnham, Esq." represents this Newnham family.

2. *female* character] The *1773* italics (which disappear in subsequent editions) may perhaps signal an allusion to the century's most famous comment on the character of women: "Nothing so true as what you once let fall, / 'Most Women have no Character at all'" (Pope, "Moral Essays: Epistle II: To a Lady," 1–2). Insofar as the poem's main complaint is the unfixedness of a woman's principles, Sterne's suggestion to Eliza that she lacks "nothing but firmness" may also be seen as reflecting the poem, however distantly. Tristram had dismissed the Shandy women by reference to this poem in the very first volume of *TS:* "all the Shandy Family were of an original character throughout;——I mean the males,—the females had no character at all . . ." (I.21.73).

3. I probably . . . you more] Cf. introduction to *ASJ,* 6:xxii–xxiii, commenting on this passage: "Sterne faces a reality he will elide in *Journal* . . . . Written in March 1767, this is a statement we need to grasp in its essential pathos if we are to confront the final year of Sterne's life without being smugly or cynically dismissive."

198. *To Eliza Draper*

Text: Yorick to Eliza

[London, March 1767]

To whom shou'd Eliza apply in her distress, but to the[a] friend that[b] loves her; why then, my dear, do you apologize for employing me?

Yorick wou'd be offended, and with reason, if you ever sent commissions to another, which he cou'd execute—I have been with Zumps[1]—and first[c] your piano-forte must be tun'd from the brass[2] middle string of your guitar, which is C.—I have got you a hammer too, and a pair of pliars to twist your wire with; and may every one of them, my dear, vibrate sweet comfort to thy[d] hopes! I have bought you ten handsome brass screws to hang your necessaries upon: I purchas'd twelve, but stole a couple from you, to put up in my own cabin at Coxwould[3]—I shall never hang or take my hat off one of them, but I shall think of you—I have bought thee, moreover, a couple of iron screws, which are more to be depended on[e] than brass, for the globe[f]—[4]

I have wrote[g] also to Mr. Abraham Walker, pilot at Deal,[5] to acquaint him[h] that I had dispatched these in a packet directed to his care, which I desir'd he wou'd seek after the moment the Deal machine[6] arrives[i]—I have moreover given directions to him, what[j] sort of an arm chair you wou'd want, and have directed him to[k] purchase the best that Deal cou'd afford, and to take[l] it with the parcel in the first boat that went off—Would, I cou'd, Eliza, thus[m] supply all thy wants, and all thy wishes! it would be a state of happiness to me—

The journal[7] is as it should be, all but it's contents—

Poor dear, patient being! I do more than pity you, for I think I lose both firmness and philosophy, as I figure to myself your distresses—

Do not think I spoke last night with too much asperity of ***;[8] there was a cause[n]; and besides, a good heart ought not to love a bad one, and indeed cannot. But adieu to the ungrateful subject—

I have been this morning to see Mrs. James; she loves thee tenderly and unfeignedly; she is alarm'd for thee; she says thou lookedst[o] most ill and melancholy on going away; she pities thee—I shall visit her every Sunday while I am in town—

As this may be my last letter, I earnestly bid thee farewell! may the God of kindness be kind to thee, and approve himself thy protector now thou art defenceless! and for thy daily comfort, bear in thy mind this truth, "That whatever measure of sorrow and distress[p] is thy portion, it will be repaid to thee in a full measure of happiness, by the Being thou hast wisely chosen for thy eternal friend"[9]—Farewell, farewell Eliza, while[q] I live count upon me, as the most disinterested and warm[r] of earthly friends.

YORICK.

MS: Not located.
Pub.: Yorick to Eliza (1773), 20–24; Curtis, no. 188.

[a]the] her *1775* [b]that] who *1775* [c]first] *om. 1775* [d]thy] *1773, 1775 (A);* my *1775 (C, D, E)* [e]on] upon *Evans* [f]globe] globes *1775* [g]wrote] written *1775* [h]to acquaint him] *om. 1775* [i]arrives] arrived *1775* [j]given directions to him, what] given him directions, what *1775* [k]directed him to] *Evans, 1775;* directed to *1773* [l]and to take] and take *1775* [m]thus] so *1775* [n]was a cause] was cause *1775* [o]lookedst] lookest *Evans;* looked'st *1775* [p]distress] dulness *Evans* [q]while] whilst *1775* [r]disinterested and warm] warm and disinterested *1775*

1. Zumps] See *Oxford Companion to Music,* 10th ed. (1970), s.v. *pianoforte:* "The wars of the mid-eighteenth century and especially the Seven Years War (1756–63) drove many German workmen to England. Amongst these was . . . [Johannes] Zumpe, who, on coming to London, at first worked for the great Swiss harpsichord maker Tschudi or Shudi and then set up for himself and became famous all over Britain and France as the inventor and manufacturer of the so-called Square (really oblong) Piano, which he introduced about 1760" (789). Charles Burney's account (quoted from Abraham Rees, *The New Cyclopedia,* 1819) provides additional information: "Zumpé . . . constructed small piano-fortes of the shape and size of the virginals, of which the tone was very sweet, and the touch, with a little use, equal to any degree of rapidity. These, from their low price and the convenience of their form, as well as power of expression, suddenly grew into such favour, that there was scarcely a house in the kingdom . . . but was supplied with one of Zumpé's piano-fortes . . ." (790). Finally, it is noted that the first public performance probably took place at Covent Garden Theatre in 1767, and J. C. Bach performed in 1768 on an instrument for which he paid £50 (795). That Eliza and Sterne were interested in the instrument from its first popularity perhaps attests as much to their stylishness and ready money as it does to their musical accomplishments (on Sterne's lifelong interest in music, see letter 64, n. 10).

2. brass] *Evans* misprints "bass." Sterne's explanation to Eliza is either overly solicitous or an indication that she was a musical novice.

3. Coxwould] That none of the editions spells *Coxwould* correctly indicates that the transcriber (or transcribers) of Sterne's manuscript letters was not very knowledgeable about Sterne or his handwriting: *1773:* Coxwauld; *Evans:* Coywauld; *1775:* Conwould.

4. globe] Based on the *1775* reading "globes," Curtis, 311, n. 2, suggests "the celestial and terrestrial globes, 'elegantly mounted, and neatly coloured,' which George Adams, mathematical instrument maker to George III, was advertising in the papers during March 1767. Sterne had probably added these to the collection of gifts to Mrs. Draper. Their prices ranged from five to twenty-eight guineas." The *1773* "globe" might indicate a less costly gift, perhaps simply a terrestrial globe on which Eliza could chart her progress; on the other hand "a *couple* of iron screws," might indicate an error in *1773,* assuming one were foolish enough to use only one screw to suspend a globe.

5. Abraham Walker, pilot at Deal] Eliza had left London and was now aboard the *Lord Chatham,* which arrived at Deal (just north of Dover), in the Downs, on March 30 (*Public Advertiser,* cited by Cash, *LY* 280); there were now some seventy-five miles between Sterne and Eliza. The ship was awaiting a "fair Wind" before sailing, which happened on April 3. Nothing is known about Abraham Walker except what we gather from this letter—he provided transport service

from the dock at Deal to ships at anchor, ferrying goods as passengers furnished their cabins (see letter 201, where Eliza's "cabin" is called an "apartment") for what—in the case of India—would be nine months at sea.

6. the Deal machine] The mail coach for Deal (*OED,* s.v. *machine,* III.5.b, citing Burke [1772]: "Your very kind letter . . . I received by the machine").

7. journal] Cash's reconstruction of the three parts of *Bramine's Journal,* based largely on hints in the letters from Yorick to Eliza, argues that Sterne started a journal early in his acquaintance with Eliza, and that, by mutual agreement, she was keeping an echoing journal. Curtis, 311, n. 4, and Cash, *LY,* 283–84, agree that this is the journal Sterne is alluding to here, and that he sent it to her while she was at Deal. The very next letter (see letter 199) opens with "I began a new journal this morning," thus validating this scenario. Several weeks later, as he began what survives as *Bramine's Journal,* Sterne tells Eliza that he is sending this second journal; hence *BJ* is the third and final part of Sterne's journal-keeping, the only part that survives. We know that Eliza wrote to Sterne during her voyage, but not whether she kept her side of the bargain; no journal has been located.

Sterne's rather cryptic sentence may simply express his wish that the sorrowful contents of his journal, expressing separation and loss, could have been otherwise.

8. of ***] The Newnham family, one presumes; see letter 197, n. 1.

9. may the God . . . friend] Cf. the introduction to *ASJ,* where this passage is singled out as so intertwining concepts of divine and human love "that we would be foolish to attempt to unravel them." And, the editors continue, "as we read the writings of 1767 [i.e., *ASJ* and *BJ*], it is good to keep in mind that religious declarations of this kind abound in the letters to Eliza [see, e.g., letter 199]" (*ASJ* 6:xxiii).

199. *To Eliza Draper*

Text: Yorick to Eliza

[London, March 1767]

My Dearest Eliza,

I began a new journal this morning: you shall see it, for if I live not till your[a] return to England, I will leave it you as a legacy: tis a sorrowful page, but I will write chearful ones, and could I write letters to thee, they should be chearful ones too, but few (I fear) will reach thee—however, depend upon receiving something of the kind by[b] every post, till thou[c] wavest thy hand, and bidst me write no more—Tell me how

Figure 8. Portrait of Eliza, by Richard Cosway, from *The Shandean* 9 (1997), figure 1.

you are, and what sort of fortitude heaven inspires thee[d] with. How are your accommodations[e] my dear?—is all right?—scribble away any thing and every thing to me. Depend upon seeing me at Deal with the James's, should you be detain'd there by contrary winds. Indeed, Eliza, I should with pleasure fly to you, could I be the means of rendring you any service, or doing you any kindness[f]—

"Gracious and merciful God, consider the anguish of a poor girl, strengthen and preserve her, in all the shocks her frame must be expos'd to, she is now without a protector[g] but thee; save her from all the accidents[h] of a dangerous element, and give her comfort at the last"—[1]

My prayer, Eliza, I hope is heard, for the sky seems to smile upon me as I look up to it—

I am just return'd from our dear Mrs. James's, where I have been talking of thee these[i] three hours—She has got your picture and likes it, but Mariot[2] and some other judges agree, that mine[3] is the better, and expressive of a sweeter character; but what is that to the original? yet I acknowledge her's a picture[j] for the world, and mine only calculated to[k] please a very sincere friend, or sentimental philosopher—[4]

In the one you are dressed in smiles, and with[l] all the advantages of silks, pearls, and ermine, in the other, simple as a vestal, appearing the good girl nature made you; which to me conveys an idea of more unaffected sweetness, than Mrs. Draper[m] habited for conquest in a birth day suit,[5] with her countenance animated and "dimples visible"[n]—[6]

If I remember right, Eliza, you endeavour'd to collect every charm of your person into your face with more than common[o] care, the day you sat for Mrs. James, your colour too brighten'd, and your eyes shone with more than their usual[p] brilliancy—

I then requested you to come simple and unadorn'd when you sat for me, knowing (as I see with unprejudic'd[q] eyes) that you cou'd receive no addition from the silkworm's aid, or jeweller's polish—

Let me now tell you a truth, which I believe I utter'd[r] before—when I first saw you, I beheld you as an object of compassion, and a[s] very plain woman—

The mode of your dress (tho'[t] fashionable) disfigur'd you—but nothing now cou'd render you such, but the being sollicitous to make yourself admir'd as a handsome one—

You are not handsome, Eliza—nor is your's a face that will please the tenth part of your beholders—

But you are[u] something more; for I scruple not to tell you, I never saw so intelligent, so animated, so good a countenance; nor ever was[v] there, nor will there be[w], that man of sense, tenderness, and feeling in your company three hours, that was not, or will not be, your admirer and[x] friend in consequence of it, *i.e.*[y] if you assume or assumed no character foreign to your own, but appear'd the artless being nature design'd you for—a something in your voice and eyes[z], you possess in a degree more persuasive than any woman I ever saw, read, or heard of:

But it is that bewitching sort of nameless excellence, that men of *nice sensibility*[aa] alone can be touch'd with—

Was[bb] your husband in England, I wou'd freely give him £500[cc] (if money cou'd purchase the acquisition) to let you only sit by me two hours in the[dd] day, while I wrote my sentimental journey—I am sure the work wou'd sell so much the better for it, that I should be reimburs'd the sum more than seven times told—

I would not give nine-pence for the picture of you, that the[ee] Newnhams[ff][7] have got executed; it is the resemblance of a concerted[gg],[8] made up coquette—your eyes, and the shape of your face (the latter the most perfect oval I ever saw) which are perfections that must strike the most indifferent judge, because they are equal to any of God's works in a similar way, and finer than any I beheld in all my travels, are manifestly injured[hh] by the affected leer of the one, and strange appearance of the other, owing to the attitude of the head, which is a proof of the artist's, or your friend's false taste—

The ***'s[9] verify[ii] the character I once gave, of teazing and[jj] sticking like pitch or bird lime—

Sent a card that they wou'd wait on Mrs. James[kk] on Friday.

She sent back she was engaged;

Then to meet at Ranelagh to-night; she answer'd she did not go—

She says if she allows the least footing, she never shall get rid of the acquaintance, which she is resolv'd to drop at once—

She knows them; she knows they are not her friends or[ll] yours, and the first use they wou'd make of being with her, would be to sacrifice you to her (if they could) a second time—

Let her not, then, let her not, my dear, be a greater friend to thee than thou art to thyself; she begs I will reiterate my request to you, that you will not write to them—'twill[mm] give her, and thy Bramin too[nn], inexpressible pain—be assur'd, all this is not without reason on her side. I have my reasons too, the first of which is, that I should grieve to excess, if Eliza wanted that fortitude her Yorick has built so high upon—

I said I wou'd never more[oo] mention the[pp] name to thee, and had I not receiv'd it as a kind of charge from a dear woman that loves you, I should not have broke my word—

I will write again to-morrow to thee, thou best, and most endearing of girls: a peaceful night to thee; my spirit will be with thee thro' every watch of it—Adieu.

MS: Not located.
Pub.: Yorick to Eliza (1773), 25–35; Curtis, no. 189.

[a]your] you *Evans* [b]kind by] *1775;* kindly *1773* [c]till thou] till then, thou *1775;* till then, [?when] thou *Curtis* [d]thee] you *1775* [e]your accommodations] you accommodated *1775* [f]you any kindness] you kindness *1775* [g]without a protector] *1775;* without protector *1773* [h]all the accidents] all accidents *1775* [i]these] for *1775* [j]acknowledge her's a picture] acknowledge that hers is a picture *1775* [k]mine only calculated to] mine is calculated only to *1775* [l]smiles, and with] smiles, with *Curtis* [m]Draper] *1775;* Dr—p—r *1773* [n]and "dimples visible"] and her dimples visible *1775* [o]common] *common 1775* [p]than their usual] than usual *1775* [q]unprejudic'd] unpreju- | duc'd *1773;* unprejudiced *Evans; unprejudiced 1775* [r]I utter'd] I have uttered *1775* [s]and a] and as a *1775* [t]tho'] *1775;* the *1773* [u]beholders— ¶ But you are] beholders,—but are *1775* [v]nor ever was] nor was *1775* [w]nor will there be] (nor ever will be) *1775* [x]and] or *1775* [y]*i.e.*] that is *Evans, 1775* [z]your voice and eyes] your eyes, and voice *1775* [aa]*nice sensibility*] nice sensibility *1775* [bb]Was] Were *1775* [cc]£500] five hundred pounds *Evans, 1775* [dd]the] a *1775* [ee]you, that the] you, the *1775* [ff]Newnhams] Newnham's *1773* (state 1), *1775;* ——— *1773* (state 2), *Evans* [gg]concerted] conceited *1775* [hh]'injured]

1775; inspir'd *1773* [ii]*** 's verify] **** 's who verify *1775* [jj]and] or *1775* [kk]James] *Curtis;* *** *1773;* **** *1775* [ll]or] nor *1775* [mm]'twill] It will *1775* [nn]Bramin too,] Bramin, *1775* [oo]I wou'd never more] I never more would *1775* [pp]mention the] *Evans, 1775;* mention | —the *1773*

1. Gracious . . . at the last] Sterne's several impromptu epistolary prayers suggest the naturalness of the gesture for a lifelong parish priest. Their language is steeped in Scripture, the *BCP,* and Sterne's own sermonizing, although the borrowings are almost always echoes rather than quotations. Here, e.g., one can hear echoes of the Litany in the *BCP:* "*We beseech thee to hear us, good Lord.* That it may please thee to strengthen such as do stand, and to comfort and help the weak-hearted . . . That it may please thee to preserve all that travel by land or by water . . ."; and of Sterne's sermon 34 ("Trust in God"): "Without some certain aid within us to bear us up,—so tender a frame as ours, would be but ill fitted to encounter what generally befals it in this rugged journey . . ."; and again, "this tottering, tender frame under many a violent shock and hard justling" (4:322–23). See also *BJ,* 189, and n. to 189.5–6 (6:397–98), where the editors conclude that "the desire to discover and assert a divine presence in all aspects of his relationship with Eliza ought not, perhaps, be dismissed merely as hypocrisy or self-deception."

2. Mariot] Curtis, 314, n. 1, suggests Thomas Marriott (*b. c.*1737), commissioned a major in the marines in 1765; "Major Marriot" subscribed to *Sermons* (1769). Thomas's brother, Randolph (1736–*c.*1790) was also a military man who served under Clive at Plassy (John Burke, *History of the Commoners* 4:583–84); the connection to India might make him a more likely candidate for the James's circle.

3. mine] Sterne mentions on numerous occasions a miniature portrait of Eliza, most publicly in the second paragraph of *ASJ,* 3: "the little picture which I have so long worn, and so often have told thee, Eliza, I would carry with me into my grave"; and in *BJ,* 202 (June 17), when he tells Eliza that he has brought her name "and Picture" into his work. From another allusion in *BJ,* 200 (June 11), "I shall present You [in the pages of his journal] . . . a better Picture of me, than Cusway Could do for You," it has been assumed that Richard Cosway (1742–1821)—deemed by the *Oxford Companion to Art* (1970) "by far the most fashionable miniature painter of his day"—was the artist. Stephen Lloyd, *Richard and Maria Cosway* (Edinburgh: Scottish National Portrait Gallery, 1995), agrees with this, but notes that the miniature remains untraced.

More problematic is the known full-size Cosway portrait of Eliza, which has been taken to be the painting being compared to the miniature in this letter; see, e.g, *ASJ,* 6:232–34, n. to 3.18–19; and Harriet Guest, "Sterne, Elizabeth Draper, and Drapery," *Shandean* 9 (1997): 8–33, in which this discussion of the two portraits is explored at length; and Cash, *LY,* 274, n. 53, where he cautiously notes that in that portrait (reproduced in *Winged Skull,* facing 204, and by Guest, 8) the pearls and ermine mentioned by Sterne are not visible: "But Sterne, who did not have the picture before him when he wrote, must have been speaking loosely." Lloyd, however, dates the painting (beautifully reproduced facing 29) *c.*1775, when Eliza returned to London (32), but cites in evidence only the testimony of Sidney Sabin of Sotheby's "that a letter from Cosway addressed to Mrs. Draper, which mentioned the arrangements for a sitting, once accompanied the picture" (108, n. 21). As noted in the *Status* discussion for letter 191, Eliza seems not to have returned to London until the Spring of 1776, thus contradicting this testimony. In brief, the issue is clouded, but if we were to reconstruct the most probable scenario, we would suggest that Sterne and the Jameses commissioned Cosway to paint both a miniature and a full-size portrait of Eliza, more or less simultaneously (and Cash, *LY,* 275, suggests that the Jameses paid for the miniature), and that Sterne is here praising his miniature at the expense of the full-length portrait, which would have to be redated 1767, one of the earliest of the known Cosway paintings.

All of this is complicated, we might note, by the assertion later in this letter that the Newnhams also had commissioned a painting of Eliza, presumably not by Cosway.

4. sentimental philosopher] Sterne refers to himself as a "philosopher" several times in *ASJ,* although never precisely as a "sentimental" one; e.g., *ASJ,* 43: "[La Fleur] was a faithful, affectionate, simple soul as ever trudged after the heels of a philosopher" and, again, "if I am a piece of a philosopher, which Satan now and then puts it into my head I am." The first use of "sentimental philosopher" we have been able to locate is in the monthly *Sentimental Magazine, Or, General Assemblage of Science, Taste, and Entertainment. Calculated to Amuse the Mind, to Improve the Understanding, and to Amend the Heart,* which, significantly enough, began publication in March 1773, "Printed for the Authors, and sold by G. Kearsley, at No. 46, in Fleet-Street"—i.e., the same publisher who would publish the third edition of *Letters from Yorick to Eliza* in 1775. A group of monthly essays therein, beginning November 1773, is titled "The Sentimental Philosopher," which figure is briefly defined in the heading for the first essay: "The Sentimental Philosopher is in some measure a contrast to the Reasoner [another title for monthly essays]. These two papers are intended to elucidate the principles of our nature, according to the two systems of *Selfishness* and *Benevolence,* which at present divide moralists" (1:441).

5. birth day suit] A dress worn at court for royal birthdays. Mr. B. displays for Pamela "a rich Suit of Cloaths . . . which they call a Birth-day Suit; for he intends to go to *London* against next Birth-day, to see the Court . . ." (Samuel Richardson,

Pamela, ed. Thomas Keymer and Alice Wakely [Oxford: Oxford University Press, 2001], 68).

6. "dimples visible"] The quotation marks, which disappear in *1775,* suggest an allusion, but we found no earlier use of the phrase; the most famous parallel phrase is, of course, Milton's "darkness visible" (*Paradise Lost* I.64).

7. Newnhams] Leaf C8 (pp. 31–32) of *1773* exists in two states; state 1 has the original leaf, reading "Newnham's" on C8[v], l. 2 (p. 32); state 2 contains a cancel leaf (the tip-in is evident in most copies examined) in which the name is replaced with a 3em dash. There are no other differences between the cancellandum and cancellans, suggesting that the use of the name was the sole purpose of the change; perhaps the editor realized he had inadvertently used the name where anonymity was intended (as in the very next paragraph), or perhaps the family or friends had exerted some last-minute pressure to suppress the name. Of twelve copies examined, only two contain the original leaf, the BL and Yale University copies. *Evans* was set from state 2, and hence uses a dash, but *1775* seems to have had state 1 in hand, and "Newnham's" is the reading, although again, as in *1773,* the name is suppressed in the next paragraph.

8. concerted] The *1775* reading, "conceited," is rather harsh, while the *1773* "concerted" makes good contextual sense; see *OED,* s.v. *concerted:* "Arranged by mutual agreement . . . ; planned, contrived; done in concert."

9. The *** 's] We assume this is again the Newnhams, although the syntax makes it just possible that Sterne meant his description was now verified by the Jameses; we have thus allowed the asterisks to stand. The finale of the story Sterne relates is belied in letter 213, where Sterne confesses to having broken off all correspondence between Eliza and the Newnhams "by a falsity," and most specifically mentions that his use of Mrs. James to second his argument "was merely a child of my own brain."

200. *To Eliza Draper*

Text: Yorick to Eliza

[London, March 1767][1]

My dear Eliza,

Oh! I grieve for your cabin, and fresh[a] painting will be enough to destroy every nerve about thee—nothing so pernicious as white lead[2]—take care of yourself, dear girl, and sleep not in it too soon, 'twill[b] be enough to give you a stroke of an epilepsy—[3]

I hope you will have left the ship, and that my letters may meet and greet you, as you get out of your post chaise at Deal—when you have got them all, put them, my dear, into some order—the first eight or nine are number'd, but I wrote the rest without that direction to thee—but thou wilt find them out by the day or hour, which, I hope, I have generally prefix'd to them; when they are got together in chronological order, sew them together under a cover—I trust they will be a perpetual refuge to thee from time to time, and that thou wilt (when weary of fools and uninteresting discourse) retire and converse an hour with them and me—

I have not had power or the heart, to aim at enlivening one[c] of them with a single stroke of wit or humour; but they contain something better, and what you will feel more suited to your situation—a long detail of much advice, truth, and knowledge—

I hope, too, you will perceive loose touches of an honest heart in every one of them, which speak more than the most studied periods, and will give thee more ground of trust and reliance upon Yorick, than all that labour'd eloquence[4] cou'd supply—lean then thy whole weight Eliza, upon them and upon me.

"May poverty, distress, anguish and shame be my portion, if ever I give thee reason to repent the knowledge of me."—

With this asseveration, made in the presence of a just God, I pray to him that so it may speed with me, as I deal candidly and honourably with thee:

I would not mislead thee, Eliza, I would not injure thee in the opinion of a single individual, for the richest crown, the proudest monarch wears—

Remember, that, while I have life and power, whatever is mine you may style, and think yours; tho' sorry should I be, if ever my friendship was put to the test thus, for your own delicacy's sake—

Money and counters are of equal use in my opinion, they both serve to set up with.[5] I hope you will answer me[d] this letter; but if thou art debarr'd by the elements which hurry thee away, I will write one for thee, and knowing it is such an[e] one as thou wouldst have written, I will regard it as my Eliza's—

Honour and happiness, and health and comforts of every kind sail along with thee, thou most worthy of girls! I will live for thee and my Lydia, be rich for ye, dear[f] children of my heart, gain wisdom, gain fame and happiness, to share them with thee[g] and her, in my old age—

Once for all, Adieu! Preserve thy life steadily, pursue[h] the ends we propos'd,[6] and let nothing rob thee of those powers heaven has given thee for thy well being—

What can I add more in the agitation of mind I am in, and within five minutes of the last postman's bell; but recommend thee to heaven, and recommend myself to heaven with thee, in the same fervent ejaculation.

"That we may be happy and meet again, if not in this world, in the next"—

Adieu, I am thine affectionately Eliza[i], and everlastingly.

YORICK.—

MS: Not located.
Pub.: Yorick to Eliza (1773), 36–42; Curtis, no. 191.

[a]cabin, and fresh] cabin.—And the fresh *1775* [b]soon, 'twill] soon. It will *1775* [c]enlivening one] enlivening any one *1775* [d]me] *1775*; in *1773* [e]an] a *1775* [f]for ye, dear] for the dear *Evans, 1775* [g]share them with thee] share with them—with thee *1775* [h]life steadily, pursue] life; steadily pursue *1775* [i]thine affectionately Eliza] thine, Eliza, affectionately *1775*

1. Date] The letters from Yorick to Eliza are all undated; the *1773* and *Evans* editions print this as the seventh letter, while *1775* and Curtis print it as eighth in the sequence, with our letter 201 ahead of it. We can see nothing in either letter that can absolutely determine the priority of one over the other and so have followed the ordering of the first edition; possibly, this letter indicates that the painting of the cabin, advised against in letter 201, has now been undertaken, but the phrasing in both letters remains chronologically indeterminate.

2. white lead] Sterne was not alone in warning against the effects of white lead; cf. Charlotte Brontë, *Shirley* (1849; London: Folio Society, 1991):

> "By-the-bye, do you put your pencil to your lips when you paint?"
> "Sometimes, uncle, when I forget."

"Then it is that which is poisoning you. The paints are deleterious, child: there is white lead and red lead . . . ." (162)

3. stroke of an epilepsy] Possibly Sterne intended what would be a more common phrase, "stroke of an apoplexy."

4. I hope . . . eloquence] Sterne often gives this advice to his correspondents (see letters 153 and n. 10, and 196 and n. 9), and now applies it to his own writing. He had also addressed the distinction in his comments on sermon-writing in *TS*, IV.26.376–77, but it was a commonplace concerning composition throughout the century, marked by a particular reliance on such catch phrases as "studied periods" and "labour'd eloquence." See, e.g., Oliver Goldsmith, *The Bee*, no. 7 (November 17, 1759): "How then are such to be addressed; not by studied periods; . . . not by the labours of the head, but the honest spontaneous dictates of the heart" (*Works* 1:480–82; quoted in *Notes* to *TS*, 3:322–23, n. to 376.23–377.10); and Sarah Fielding, *The Adventures of David Simple* (Oxford: Oxford University Press, 1994), 128: "She returned this Goodness with a Look that expressed more Thankfulness than all the pompous Words of laboured Eloquence could have done" (II.9); and again, 281: "the Wanness of their Looks . . . more strongly pointed out their Thoughts than the most laboured Eloquence could possibly have done" (IV.6). See also Thomas Gray, *Agrippina, a Tragedy*, l. 147: "In gorgeous phrase of labour'd eloquence" (*Poetical Works*, ed. Roger Lonsdale [Oxford: Oxford University Press, 1977], 16).

5. Money and counters . . . set up with] Rather an odd phrase for Sterne to express his disdain for money, perhaps because in reality he had an abiding interest in accumulating it, especially in the last years of his life. *1775* attempts to clarify the sentence by attaching it to the previous paragraph and beginning the new paragraph with "I hope you will answer . . . ."

6. I will . . . propos'd] While the many variants in punctuation between the first and third editions rarely affect the meaning of a sentence, in this passage there are several instances of significant difference. Compare, e.g., *1773:* "I will live for thee and my Lydia, be rich for ye, dear children of my heart . . ." with *1775:* "I will live for thee, and my Lydia—be rich for the dear children of my heart . . . ." And again, *1773:* "Preserve thy life steadily, pursue the ends we propos'd . . ." with *1775:* "Preserve thy life; steadily pursue the ends we proposed . . . ."

201. *To Eliza Draper*

Text: Yorick to Eliza

[London, March 1767]

My dear Eliza,[a]

I think you could act no otherwise than you did with your[b] young soldier,[1] there was no shutting the door against him, either in politeness or humanity—

Thou tell'st me he seems susceptible of tender impressions, and that before Miss Light[c2] has sail'd a fortnight, he will be in love with her—

Now, I think it a thousand times more likely, that he attaches himself to thee, Eliza, because thou art a thousand times more amiable—

Five months with Eliza, and in the same room, and an amorous son of Mars besides, "It no can be Masser[d]."[3]—The sun, if he could avoid it, wou'd not shine upon a dunghill; but his rays are so pure, Eliza, and celestial, I never heard they[e] were polluted by it[4]—Just such will thine be, my dearest[f] child, in this and every such situation as you[g] will be expos'd to, till thou art fix'd for life.—

But, thy discretion, thy wisdom, thy honour, the spirit of thy Yorick, and thy own spirit, which is equal to it, will be thy ablest counsellors—

Surely, by this time, something is doing towards[h] thy accomodation—but why may not clean washing and rubing do, instead of painting your cabin, as it is to be hung[5]—paint is so pernicious both to your nerves and lungs, and will keep you, so much longer too, out of possession[i] of your apartment[j], where I hope you will pass some of your happiest hours—

I fear the best of your shipmates, are only genteel by comparison with the contrasted crew, with which thou must behold them.

So was you know who, from the same fallacy that was put upon the judgment, when—But I will not mortify you—If they are decent and distant, it is enough, and as much as is to be expected; if any of them are more, I rejoice—

Thou wilt want every aid, and 'tis thy due to have them—

Be cautious only, my dear, of intimacies; good hearts are open, and fall naturally into them—heaven inspire thine with fortitude, in this and every other deadly[k] trial!

Best of God's works! Farewell, love me, I beseech thee, and remember for ever, I[l] am, my Eliza, and ever will[m] be in the most comprehensive sense,

Thy Friend—
YORICK—

PS

Probably you will have an opportunity of writing to me by some Dutch or French ship, or from the Cape de Verd Islands,[6] 'twill reach me some how—

MS: Not located.
Pub.: Yorick to Eliza (1773), 43–47; Curtis, no. 190.

[a]My dear Eliza,] *om. 1775* [b]your] the *1775* [c]Miss Light] *1775;* Miss L——t *1773* [d]It no can be Masser] *It can no be masser 1775* [e]heard they] heard that they *1775* [f]be, my dearest] be, dearest *1775* [g]situation as you] situation you *1775* [h]towards] for *1775* [i]of possession] *om. 1775* [j]apartment] apartments *Evans* [k]every other deadly] every deadly *1775* [l]remember for ever, I] remember me for ever! ¶ I *1775* [m]ever will] will ever *1775*

1. soldier] The *Lord Chatham* was partly used for transporting soldiers to India. This "son of Mars" would have been one of their officers.

2. Miss Light] See letter 196, n. 8. The *1773* editor writes about this passage: "Miss Light, now Mrs. Stratton, is on all accounts a very amiable young lady . . . but being mentioned in one of Mrs. Draper's letters to Mr. Sterne, in somewhat of a comparative manner with herself, his partiality for her, as she modestly expressed it, took the alarm, and betrayed him into some expressions, the coarseness of which cannot be excused. Mrs. Draper declares, that this lady was entirely unknown to him, and infinitely superior to his idea of her . . ." (x–xi).

3. It no can be Masser] Cf. *BJ,* 223 (August 1), where Sterne describes the "anguish without end" he finds in Eliza's letters (see n. 6 below): "*it no can be.*" Curtis suggests that Ignatius Sancho may have been behind the phrase; however,

it occurs nowhere in the correspondence we have from Sancho to Sterne. *OED*'s first example of *massa,* as a variant of *master,* is dated 1766, but despite *OED*'s assertion that it is "chiefly . . . U.S. and Caribbean black speech," one suspects that here the pidgin English has more to do with India. The syntax of *1773* makes it clearer than that of *1775* that the meaning is simply "it cannot be, master," perhaps a bit of a private joke between Bramin and Bramine.

4. The sun . . . polluted by it] Proverbial; see Tilley, S982, and *ODEP,* 787, quoting, among others, Lyly's *Euphues* (1579): "The Sun shineth vppon the dungehill and is not corrupted." Sterne elaborates it into a rather charming compliment.

5. to be hung] I.e., with tapestries or other cloth draperies; see *OED,* s.v. *hang,* B.I.5.

6. Cape de Verd Islands] The only landfall of an India-bound ship was Santiago (St. Jago) in the Cape Verde Islands, off the West Coast of Africa, which Eliza reached in early May. She did indeed send letters by means of a passing Dutch ship soon after reembarking on her journey, probably not the packet Sterne received on July 27 but rather a second one that arrived in mid-August; see letter 220. Cash, *LY,* 302, believes Sterne was sadly disappointed in the first packet: "he had not found in her letters what he longed to see, a declaration of her love for him"; the Florida editors agree with this assessment: see *BJ,* 6:xl–xli, and 420, n. to 222.11.

202. *To Eliza Draper*

Text: Yorick to Eliza

[London, March 1767]

I wish to God, Eliza, it was possible to postpone the voyage to India for another year, for I am firmly persuaded within my own breast[a], that thy husband could never limit thee with regard to time—

I fear that Mr. B.[1] has exaggerated matters,—I like not his countenance, it is absolutely killing thee—should[b] evil befall thee, what will he not have[c] to answer for—I know not the being that will be deserving of so much pity, or that I shall hate more; he will be an outcast alien; in which case I will be a father to thy children[2] my good girl, therefore take no thought about them—But, Eliza, if thou art so very ill, still put off all thoughts of returning to India this year—write to your husband—tell him the truth of your case—if he is the generous humane man you describe him to be, he cannot but applaud your conduct—I am credibly[d] informed, that his repugnance to your living in England arises only from the dread which has enter'd his brain, that thou mayest run him in debt, beyond thy appointments, and that he must discharge them—

That such a creature should be sacrificed, for the paultry consideration of a[e] few hundreds, is too, too hard! Oh! my child, that I could with propriety indemnify him for every charge, even to the last mite, that thou hast been of to him! with joy would I give him my whole subsistence, nay, sequester my livings, and trust to the[f] treasures heaven has furnish'd my head with for a future subsistence—

You owe much, I allow, to your husband; you owe something to appearances and the opinions[g] of the world; but, trust me, my dear, you owe much likewise to yourself—Return therefore from Deal if you continue ill: I will prescribe for you gratis. You are not the first woman by many, I have done so for with success—

I will send for my wife and daughter, and they shall carry you in pursuit of health to Montpelier, the wells of Bancer's[h],[3] the Spaw, or whither thou wilt; thou shalt direct them, and make parties of pleasure in what corner of the world fancy points out to you[i]—

We shall fish upon the banks of Arno,[4] and lose ourselves in the sweet labyrinths[j] of it's vallies, and then thou should'st warble to us, as I have once or twice heard thee "I'm lost, I'm lost,"[5] but we would[k] find thee again, my Eliza—

Of a similar nature to this, was your physician's prescription "ease, gentle[l] exercise, the pure southern air of France, or milder Naples, with the society of friendly gentle beings"—

Sensible man, he certainly enter'd into your feelings, he knew the fallacy of medicine to a creature, whose illness has arisen from the affliction of her mind[m]—Time only, my dear, I fear you must trust to, and have your reliance on: may it give you the health so enthusiastic[n] a votary to the charming goddess[6] deserves—

I honour you, Eliza, for keeping secret some things, which if explain'd, had been a panegyric on yourself—There is a dignity in venerable affliction which will not allow it to appeal to the world for pity or redress—Well have you supported that character, my amiable philosophic friend! And, indeed, I begin to think you have as many virtues, as my uncle Toby's widow—[7]

I don't mean to insinuate, hussey, that my[o] opinion is no better founded than his was of Mrs. Wadman[p]; nor do I believe[q] it possible for any Trim[r] to convince me it is equally fallacious; I am sure while I have my reason it is not—

Talking of widows—pray, Eliza, if ever you are such, do not think of giving yourself to some wealthy nabob, because I design to marry you myself—My wife cannot live long—she has sold all the provinces in France already,[8] and I know not the woman I should like so well for her substitute, as yourself—'Tis true, I am ninety five in constitution, and you but twenty-five; rather too great a disparity this! but what I want in youth, I will make up in wit and good humour—Not Swift so lov'd his Stella, Scarron his Maintenon, or Waller his Sacharissa,[9] as I will love and sing thee, my wife elect—all those names, eminent as they were, shall give place to thine, Eliza.

Tell me in answer to this, that you approve and honour the proposal; and that you would (like the Spectator's mistress)[10] have more joy in putting on an old man's slipper, than in associating with the gay, the voluptuous, and the young—Adieu, my Simplicia—[11]

Yours
TRISTRAM.

MS: Not located.
Pub.: Yorick to Eliza (1773), 48–55; Curtis, no. 192.

[a]breast] heart *Evans, 1775* [b]killing thee—should] killing;—should *Evans;* killing.—Should *1775* [c]not have] have not *Evans* [d]credibly] creditably *Evans* [e]consideration of a] *Evans, 1775;* consideration a *1773* [f]trust to the] trust the *1775* [g]opinions] opinion *1775* [h]Bancer's] Bancois *Evans, 1775* [i]you] thee *1775* [j]labyrinths] labyrinth *Evans* [k]would] should *1775* [l]ease, gentle] Use gentle *Evans, 1775* [m]illness . . . mind] ILLNESS HAS ARISEN FROM THE AFFLICTION OF HER MIND *1775* [n]enthusiastic] *Evans, 1775;* enthuastic *1773* [o]my] *my 1775* [p]Wadman] Wadman's *Evans* [q]believe] conceive *1775* [r]Trim] *Trim 1775*

1. Mr. B.] Curtis, 319, n. 2, suggests Charles Boddam, Eliza's brother-in-law, "a merchant of Grenville Street, Holborn, and a former Madras civil servant,

[who] served as a director of the East India Company . . . . If, as is likely, he was a brother of Rawson Hart Boddam (1734–1812), who married Elizabeth Draper's sister, Mary Sclater [1740–1762], he would have been the person to expedite Mrs. Draper's passage to Bombay." We can discover no more likely candidate, although the case for Boddam is merely speculative.

2. thy children] The Drapers had a son (1759–1769) and a daughter, Elizabeth (1761–1824); see Wright and Sclater, *Sterne's Eliza,* 37. Sterne and Eliza may have visited the children at a school in Enfield (just north of London; see *BJ* 217), although, as the Florida editors note, Sterne's geographical references are perhaps ambivalent (*ASJ* 6:410, n. to 206.4).

3. Bancer's] The emendation in *Evans* and *1775* to "Bancois" does not help, there being no place by that name in France. Sterne probably intended Bagnères, but his creative spelling baffled the editor; see above, letters 101, n. 11, 110, n. 2, and 114, n. 6. For Spaw, see letter 170, n. 8.

4. the banks of Arno] Cf. *BJ,* 206 (June 24): "Arno's Vale shall look gay again upon Eliza's Visit.—and the Companion of her Journey, will grow young again as he sits upon her Banks with Eliza seated besides him . . ."; and 211 (July 1): *"I wish I was in Arno's Vale!"* The Florida editors admit to puzzlement: "Sterne may have associated the Arno with Petrarch and Laura [see letter 186, n. 3], but a sexual allusion seems likely as well; it might also have been a private name for a location" Sterne and Eliza frequented on trips to visit the children or otherwise get away from London (see *ASJ* 6:411, n. to 206.13). Certainly Sterne's "sweet labyrinths of it's vallies" does nothing to dispel the notion that a private meaning is intended. See also 6:413, n. to 211.23–24.

5. "I'm lost, I'm lost"] We have not been able to locate an actual song with these words. Possibly, however, we are seeing the germ for the lament of the starling in *ASJ,* "I can't get out—I can't get out" (95).

6. charming goddess] Hygieia, daughter of Asclepius, is the goddess associated with health; Sterne invokes her again in his final letter to Eliza (203).

That the phrase "illness has arisen from the affliction of her mind" is printed in small capitals in *1775* may suggest double underscoring in the manuscript; it is a rare instance in which we are tempted to emend the accidentals of *1773,* since the idea that good spirits could influence one's health seems so essential a part of Sterne's doctrine of "true Shandeism."

7. uncle Toby's widow] Sterne refers specifically to *TS,* IX.31.801ff., where Toby begins to enumerate the "thousand virtues" of widow Wadman, only to be stopped by Corporal Trim, who explains that the widow's interest in Toby's groin is not at all an indication of her "humanity."

8. sold all the provinces in France already] Sterne would seem to indicate that Elizabeth had pursued better health—unsuccessfully—in every corner of France,

but the transcription seems inaccurate; perhaps *told* would make more sense, signifying a numerical reckoning of the spas visited (see *OED*, s.v. *tell*, II.21). In any case, Elizabeth would outlive Sterne by seven years.

9. Not Swift . . . Sacharissa] Swift called Esther Johnson (1681–1728) his "Stella," and addressed his very private *Journal to Stella* to her; John Hawkesworth had published part of it the previous year in his edition of Swift's *Letters*. Paul Scarron (1610–1660) married Françoise d'Aubigné (1635–1719), Marquise de Maintenon, in 1652; after his death she became the mistress and ultimately the wife of Louis XIV. For Scarron's possible influence on Sterne, see letter 42, n. 5. Finally, Lady Dorothy Sidney (1617–1684) was the beloved Sacharissa of the love lyrics of Edmund Waller (1606–1687); he failed in his efforts to marry her, however.

10. the Spectator's mistress] This would appear to refer to *Spectator* 449 (August 5, 1712), although in that essay it is a daughter, Fidelia, who produces the Spectator's admiration for her treatment of her father: "How have I been charmed to see one of the most beauteous Women the Age has produced on her Knees helping on an old Man's Slipper" (ed. Donald Bond [Oxford: Clarendon Press, 1965], 4:79). Sterne's faulty recall of the passage (applying it to a man and his mistress) is rather telling; cf. Yorick's encounter with Maria in *ASJ*, 154, where eroticism and innocence do a dance together, to the music of a scriptural allusion, 2 Samuel 12:3: "she should *not only eat of my bread and drink of my own cup*, but Maria should lay in my bosom, and be unto me as a daughter."

11. Simplicia] The name "Simplicia" does not seem to have been used very often by writers, perhaps because the idea of "simplicity" has too much ambiguity.

203. *To Eliza Draper*

Text: Yorick to Eliza

[London, ?Monday, March 30, 1767][1]

My dear Eliza,

I have been within the verge of the gates of death: I was ill the last time I wrote to you, and apprehensive of what would be the consequence.—My fears were but too well founded, for in ten minutes after I dispatch'd my letter, this poor fine-spun frame of Yorick's gave way, and I broke a vessel in my breast,[2] and could not stop the loss of blood till four this morning—I have fill'd all thy India handkerchiefs[3] with it, it came I think, from the[a] heart—I fell asleep[b] thro' weakness at six, and awoke with[c] the bosom of my shirt steep'd in tears—

I dream'd I was sitting under the canopy of Indolence,[4] and that thou cam'st into the room with a shaul[5] in thy hand, and told me, "my spirit had flown to thee to[d] the Downs with tidings of my fate, and that you was[e] come to administer what consolation filial affection could bestow, and to receive my parting breath and blessings[f]," with that you folded the shaul about my waist, and, kneeling, supplicated my attention.

I awoke, but in what a frame! Oh! my God! but "Thou wilt number[g] my tears, and put them all into thy bottle"[6]—Dear girl, I see thee, thou art for ever present to my fancy, embracing my feeble knees, and raising thy fine eyes to bid me be of comfort—

And when I talk to Lydia, the words of Esau, as utter'd by thee, perpetually ring in my ears.

"Bless me[h] even also, my father."—[7]

Blessings[i] attend thee, thou child of my heart[8]—My bleeding is quite stopp'd, and I feel the principle of life strong within me—so be not alarm'd, Eliza, I know I shall do well—

I have eat my breakfast with hunger, and I write to thee with a pleasure arising from that prophetic impression in my imagination.

"That all will terminate to our hearts content"—Comfort thyself eternally with this persuasion, "That the best of beings[9] (as thou sweetly hast[j] express'd it) could not by a combination of accidents, produce such a chain of events, merely to be the source of misery to the leading person engag'd in them"—

The observation was very applicable, very good, and very elegantly express'd—I wish my memory did justice to the wording of it—

Who taught you the art of writing so sweetly, Eliza? You absolutely have[k] exalted it to a science—When I am in want of ready cash, and ill health will permit my genius to exert itself, I shall print your letters, as *Finish'd Essays*, by an *unfortunate Indian Lady!*[l] The style is new, and would almost be a sufficient recommendation for their selling well, without merit; but their sense, natural ease, and spirit, is not to be equall'd, I believe, in this section of the globe; nor, I'll[m] answer for it, by any of your country women in yours—

I have shew'd your letter to Mrs. B.[10] and to half the literati in town: you shall not be angry with me for it, because I meant to do you honour by it—

You cannot imagine how many admirers your epistolary productions have gain'd you, that never view'd your external merits—

I only wonder where thou couldst acquire thy graces, thy goodness, thy accomplishments! so connected! so educated! Nature has surely study'd to make thee her peculiar care, for thou art (and not in my eyes alone) the best and fairest of all her works—and so this is the last letter thou art to receive from me, because the Earl of Chatham (I read in the papers) is got to the Downs, and the wind (I find) is fair—if so, blessed woman, take my last, last farewell! cherish the remembrance of me, think how I esteem, nay, how affectionately I love thee, and what a price I set upon thee.[11] Adieu, adieu; and with my adieu, let me give thee one short[n] rule of conduct, that thou hast heard from my lips in a thousand forms, but I concenter it in one word,

—Reverence Thyself—[12]

Adieu once more, Eliza, may no anguish of heart plant a wrinkle[13] upon thy face, till I behold it again; may no doubt or misgivings disturb the serenity of thy mind, or awaken a painful thought about thy children, for they are Yorick's, and Yorick is thy friend for ever—

Adieu, adieu, adieu—

PS

Remember that "Hope shortens all journies, by sweetning them;"[14] so sing my little stanza on the subject, with the devotion of an hymn, every morning thou[o] arisest, and thou wilt eat thy breakfast with more comfort for it—Blessings, rest and Hygeia go with thee; may'st thou soon return in peace and affluence to illumine my night. I am, and shall be the last to deplore thy loss, and will be the first to congratulate, and hail thy return—

Fare thee well—

MS: Not located.
Pub.: Yorick to Eliza (1773), 56–64; Curtis, no. 193.

[a]the] my *1775* [b]asleep] *Evans, 1775;* a sleep *1773* [c]weakness at six, and awoke with] weakness. At six I awoke, with *1775* [d]to] in *1775* [e]was] were *1775* [f]blessings] blessing *Evans, 1775* [g]number] *1775;* remember *1773* [h]me] *me 1775* [i]Blessings] Blessing *Evans, 1775* [j]sweetly hast] hast sweetly *1775* [k]absolutely have] have absolutely *1775* [l]*Finish'd Essays,* by an *unfortunate Indian Lady*] finished essays, "by an unfortunate Indian lady" *1775* [m]I'll] I will *1775* [n]short] streight *Evans, 1775* [o]morning thou] morning when thou *1775*

1. Date] This was the last letter that Sterne could expect Eliza to receive before she sailed. We follow Curtis in dating it on the day on which the *Lord Chatham* arrived off Gravesend, as noted in the *Public Advertiser,* Monday, March 30, 1767: "The Lord Chatham East Indiaman, Captain Morris, stationed for Bombay, is arrived in the Downs from Gravesend, and will proceed on her Voyage the first fair Wind." Four days later Sterne would read in *Lloyd's Evening Post* for April 3–6, 1767, under the heading "Port News, Deal, April 3": "Wind N.E. Came down and sailed with his Majesty's ship Tweed, Merlin sloop, and all outward bound, the Lord Chatham East Indiaman; Susannah, Hays, for Cadiz; and Beaver, Hamstrom, for Venice." Sterne would never see Eliza again and received mail from her only twice (see *BJ* 222, and letter 220).

2. broke a vessel in my breast] Sterne uses much the same language again and again to report on his illness; see letters 78 (January 1, 1762), 99 (August 12, 1762), 114 (May 7, 1763), 124 (November 24, 1763), 130 (May 19, 1764), and 151 (May 29, 1765). And cf. *TS,* VIII.6.663, where Tristram reports the same calamity: "thou brakest a vessel in thy lungs, whereby, in two hours, thou lost as many quarts of blood . . . ."

3. India handkerchiefs] Sterne was aware of India handkerchiefs (i.e., from cloth made in India) before meeting Eliza; cf. *TS,* III.2.187: "As my father's *India* handkerchief was in his right coat pocket . . . ."

4. canopy of Indolence] James Thomson's *Castle of Indolence* (1748) attests to the popularity of the theme of indolence in mid-century Britain, but we have found no prior usage of Sterne's faintly exotic "canopy of Indolence."

5. shaul] *OED,* s.v. *shawl,* notes Sterne's variant spelling of this loanword from the Urdu. Imported cashmere shawls were still very much an exotic article of clothing in 1767.

6. Thou wilt . . . bottle] Sterne alludes to the same scriptural passage, Psalm 56:8, twice in the sermons, in sermon 20 ("The prodigal son"), 4:188, and, most significantly, in sermon 34 ("Trust in God"), the lesson of which seems to have been on his mind at this time (see above, letter 199, n. 1). The sermon is one of Sterne's most providential sermons, in which God is said to see "all those conflicts under

which thou labourest,—who knows thy necessities afar off,—and puts all thy tears into his bottle;—who sees every careful thought and pensive look,—and hears every sigh and melancholy groan thou utterest" (4:326). The emendation of *1773*'s "remember" to "number" seems a more accurate rendering of the verse, where "tellest" means "numbering" (see letter 202, n. 8) rather than "narrating" ("Thou tellest my wanderings: put thou my tears into thy bottle: are they not in thy book?"), and ties the passage closely to the most important providential text in Scripture, Matthew 10:30, "But the very hairs of your head are all numbered." Sterne returns to this sermon on several occasions in *TS* (see the headnote and notes, 5:353–64), and again in *ASJ* (see 6:373–74, n. to 155.16–18).

7. words . . . my father] See Genesis 27:38: "And Esau said unto his father, Hast thou but one blessing, my father? bless me, even me also, O my father. And Esau lifted up his voice, and wept."

8. child of my heart] Perhaps a sentimental commonplace; cf. Richardson, *Clarissa* (Harmondsworth: Penguin, 1985), letters 18 and 103; and *Sir Charles Grandison* (London: Oxford University Press, 1972), vol. 3, letter 28, 2:210, and vol. 5, letter 17, 2:541. Significantly enough, in letter 204, Sterne varies it only slightly to address Lydia: "thou child and darling of my heart."

9. best of beings] This passage may be, as Sterne comments, the words of Eliza, but the apostrophe "best of beings" is one Sterne uses in the sermons (see 4:12, 66, and 290) and in *TS*, IV.7.332 (significantly, the very passages in which Sterne leans on sermon 34, "Trust in God"). The first usage in *Sermons* (4:12) is also apropos: "did the Best of Beings send us into the world for this end—to go weeping through it,—to vex and shorten a life short and vexatious enough already" (sermon 2, "The house of feasting and the house of mourning").

10. Mrs. B.] Unidentified, but see letter 202, n. 1; the wife of Charles Boddam seems as likely a guess as any other, although we have been unable to establish that he was, in fact, married.

11. what a price . . . thee] Perhaps an echo, as on April 15, in *BJ*, 172 ("my heart has rated thee at a Price, that all the world is not rich enough to purchase thee from me, at"), of Proverbs 31:10: "Who can find a virtuous woman? for her price is far above rubies."

12. Reverence Thyself] Cf. Edward Young, *Conjectures on Original Composition. In a Letter to the Author of "Sir Charles Grandison"* (1759): "I borrow two golden rules from *Ethics* . . . 1. *Know thyself*; 2dly, *Reverence thyself*."

13. plant a wrinkle] Cf. *ASJ*, 7–8, Yorick's description of the Monk: "He was certainly sixty-five; and the general air of his countenance, notwithstanding something seem'd to have been planting wrinkles in it before their time, agreed with the account."

14. "Hope shortens . . . them"] Sterne would seem to indicate a proverbial expression, but the closest we have discovered is Hesiod, *Works and Days:* "The dawn speeds a man on his journey, and speeds him too in his work" (v. 557).

204. *To Lydia Sterne*

Text: Medalle

Bond Street, [Thursday,] April 9, 1767.[1]

This letter, my dear Lydia, will distress thy good heart, for from the beginning thou wilt perceive no entertaining strokes of humour in it[2]—I cannot be chearful when a thousand melancholy ideas surround me—I have met with a loss of near fifty pounds,[3] which I was taken in for in an extraordinary manner—but what is that loss in comparison of one I may experience?—Friendship is the balm and cordial of life, and without it, 'tis a heavy load not worth sustaining.—I am unhappy—thy mother and thyself at a distance from me, and what can compensate for such a destitution?—For God's sake persuade her to come and fix in England, for life is too short to waste in separation—and whilst she lives in one country, and I in another, many people will suppose it proceeds from choice—besides I want thee near me, thou child and darling of my heart![4]—I am in a melancholy mood, and my Lydia's eyes will smart with weeping when I tell her the cause that now affects me.—I am apprehensive the dear friend I mentioned in my last letter is going into a decline—I was with her two days ago, and I never beheld a being so alter'd—she has a tender frame, and looks like a drooping lily, for the roses are fled from her cheeks—I can never see or talk to this incomparable woman without bursting into tears—I have a thousand obligations to her, and I owe her more than her whole sex, if not all the world put together.—She has a delicacy in her way of thinking that few possess—our conversations are of the most interesting nature, and she talks to me of quitting this world with more composure than others think of living in it.—I have wrote an epitaph,[5] of which I send thee a copy.—'Tis expressive of her modest worth—but may heav'n restore her! and may she live to write mine.

Columns, and labour'd urns but vainly shew,
An idle scene of decorated woe.
The sweet companion, and the friend sincere,
Need no mechanic help to force the tear.
In heart felt numbers, never meant to shine
'Twill flow eternal o'er a hearse like thine;
'Twill flow, whilst gentle goodness has one friend,
Or kindred tempers have a tear to lend.

Say all that is kind of me to thy mother, and believe me my Lydia, that I love thee most truly—So adieu—I am what I ever was, and hope ever shall be, thy

Affectionate Father,

L.S.

As to Mr. ——[6] by your description he is a fat fool. I beg you will not give up your time to such a being—Send me some *batons pour les dents*[7]—there are none good here.

MS: Not located.
Pub.: Medalle, no. 78; Curtis, no. 186.

1. Date] Curtis took the ill "dear friend" in this letter to be Eliza Draper and therefore rejected Medalle's "April 9," redating the letter "?9 March." Cash, *LY*, 283, n. 66, however, follows Rufus Putney, "Alas, Poor Eliza!" *MLR* 41 (1946): 411–13, who "argued convincingly that the woman was Anne James, citing Sterne's letter to the Jameses of 2 August [see letter 218] in which he spoke of Anne's alarming illness during the spring." We have accepted these arguments, agreeing with Putney that "all probabilities point to Mrs. James as the subject of the epitaph" (413). See also letter 194, where Mrs. James is singled out to Lydia for very high praise.

2. strokes of humour in it] Sterne had written in the same vein to Eliza in letter 200: "I have not had power or the heart, to aim at . . . a single stroke of wit or humour."

3. loss of near fifty pounds] Nothing is known about this venture, but one might wonder just how Sterne accounted for the expensive gifts associated with Eliza's departure (see letter 198, esp. nn. 1 and 4).

4. child . . . heart] See letter 203, n. 8.

5. an epitaph] In ignorance of Putney's and Cash's correction of the belief that this epitaph was directed to Eliza, Harriet Guest, "Sterne and Eliza Draper," 11, claimed it for Eliza as late as 1997. Even more puzzling is W. G. Day's account of it in "Sterne's Verse," *Shandean* 14 (2003): 34–35, where, overlooking this letter, he examines Combe's attribution of the poem to Sterne in *OL*, 65, and concludes it was probably written by Combe himself, and "highly unlikely to be by Sterne." The letter published by Combe in which the epitaph appears is almost certainly a forgery, but one built on verses we probably must allow to have been written by Sterne—unless it turns out that this letter, too, is a forgery.

6. Mr. ——] Unidentified, apparently another of Lydia's French suitors.

7. *batons pour les dents*] Toothpicks. Sterne still had most of his teeth, unusual for someone his age in the eighteenth century; see Kenneth Monkman and W. G. Day, "The Skull," *Shandean* 10 (1998): 70–71, figs. 8–9.

205A. *To Anne James*

Text: Ms.

[London, Monday, April 20, 1767][1]

Mr Sterne's kindest & most friendly comp^s^ to Mrs James, with his most sentimental thanks for her obliging enquiry after his health—he fell ill the moment he got to his Lodgings, <illegible> and has been attended by a physician ever Since—he says tis oweing to Mr Sterne's taking James's powder,[2] & venturing out on so cold a day——but Mr Sterne could give a truer Acc^t^—he is almost dead—yet still hopes to glide like a Shadow[3] to Gerard Street in a few days, to thank his good friend for her good will. all Comp^s^ to Mr James—& all Comfort to his good Lady.

Address: To / Mrs James

MS: British Library, Addit. MSS. 54.226, 153–54.

Pub.: Thomas Washbourne Gibbs, *Some Memorials of Laurence Sterne. A Paper Read at the Bath Royal Literary Institution, February 22nd, 1878* (Bath, 1878), 24; *Athenaeum* (March 30, 1878): 413; Curtis, no. 194A.

Status: The dating and status of this manuscript depend to a large extent on the parallel account of Sterne's health in *BJ*. As Curtis points out, and the Florida editors acknowledge, Sterne began the journal on Sunday, April 12, but misdated it April 13. On Tuesday, April 14 (misdated "Munday. Ap: 15"), he reported himself "worn out with fevers," and on Wednesday, April 15, he "took James's Powder" (6:171–72). The next day, April 16, he was well enough to visit the Jameses, and visited again on Saturday, April 18. Then, on Easter Sunday, April 19, he "awoke in the most acute pain" and stayed in all day; the next day, Monday, April 20, he finally, to satisfy his friends, "call'd in a Physician" who took "12 Ounces of blood" (173–75). That evening Mrs. James, "from the forbodings of a good heart, thinking I was ill; sent her Maid to enquire after me . . ." (175).

Curtis, 327, n. 15, suggests, without supporting evidence, that Sterne wrote nothing on Monday, April 20, and resumed the journal on Tuesday, April 21, correctly dated. The Florida editors of *BJ* silently acquiesced to this, but we would now suggest Curtis was in error and that the misdating continued a few more days.

Hence, on Tuesday, April 21 (misdated April 22), he was again visited by his physician and again bled: "my arm broke loose & I half bled to death in bed before I felt it" (176). That afternoon, Mrs. James again sent inquiries. On Wednesday, April 22, Sterne awoke after a poor night, but sat down to write in the journal at 4 p.m., in order to "fulfill my engagement to her [Eliza], 'of letting no day pass over my head without some kind communication with thee'" (176).

But on Thursday, April 23 (misdated "Ap: 24"), he is "So ill, I could not write a word all this morning," and on Friday he starts a new entry, "So—Shall not depart, as I apprehended—being this morning something better" (176). This entry is first dated "Ap: 25" but then is overwritten, and the two morning entries are subsumed under the correct date of April 24—Sterne had finally corrected the dating error begun with the first entry.

If this reconstruction is accurate, Lydia's date of April 21 is correct, and Curtis was in error to alter it to April 22. Sterne indicates he was "bled yesterday, and again to day"—this would be April 20 and 21, not, as Curtis believed, April 21 and 22. Mrs. James made inquiries on the 20th and the 21st; we would suggest that Sterne tried to answer the first inquiry, but it came at night, and he was too weak to do more than scribble letter 205A. In all likelihood, it was never sent; that it was first published by Thomas Washbourne Gibbs, who brought *BJ* to public notice in the same Bath presentation, strongly supports this conjecture. With Mrs. James's second inquiry, however, Sterne gathered his strength and wrote a more formal response (letter 205B), printed by Medalle.

The *Athenaeum* published its detailed summary report—including texts of the letters—of Gibbs's presentation in late March, and almost certainly had Gibbs's own manuscript in hand. We have compared both versions and found no substantive differences, except that Gibbs erroneously dated the letter during Sterne's final illness, February or March 1768; the *Athenaeum* reporter rightly calls attention to its status as a "rough-copy" of letter 205B. We assume the *Athenaeum* version was in print before Gibbs was able to publish his Bath pamphlet.

1. Date] See the discussion under *Status* for our dating of both 205A and 205B.

2. James's powder] A diaphoretic nostrum, invented by Dr. Robert James (1705–1776). At least one contemporary apothecary seems to have attributed Goldsmith's death to its overuse; for a full account, see *BJ*, 6:385, n. to 172.12; and letters 207 and 221.

3. glide like a Shadow] The idea of being reduced to a shadow is a consistent image in Sterne's letters, and appears twice in the opening pages of *BJ*: "poor . . . Yorick! Eliza has made a Shadow of thee" (174), and again, "I am worn down my dear Girl to a Shadow" (176). See also letters 207, 212, 238, and especially 239 (?January 3, 1768), where Sterne repeats to the Jameses the phrasing of this letter, perhaps because he still had the draft in his drawer in Bond Street: "I will glide like a shadow uninvited to Gerrard Street some day this week."

205B. *To Anne and William James*

Text: Medalle

Old Bond-street, [Tuesday,] April 21, 1767.[1]

I am sincerely affected, my dear Mr. and Mrs. James[a] by your friendly enquiry, and the interest you are so good to take in my health. God knows I am not able to give a good account of myself, having passed a bad night in much feverish agitation.—My physician ordered me to bed, and to keep therein 'till some favourable change—I fell ill the moment I got to my lodgings—he says it is owing to my taking James's Powder, and venturing out on so cold a day as Sunday[2]—but he is mistaken, for I am certain whatever bears that name must have efficacy with me[3]—I was bled yesterday, and again to day, and have been almost dead, but this friendly enquiry from Gerrard-street has poured balm[4] into what blood I have left—I hope still (and next to the sense of what I owe my friends) it shall be the last pleasurable sensation I will part with—if I continue mending, it will yet be some time before

I shall have strength enough to get out in a carriage—my first visit will be a visit of true gratitude—I leave my kind friends to guess where—a thousand blessings go along with this, and may heaven preserve you both—Adieu my dear sir, and dear lady.

I am your ever obliged,
L. Sterne

MS: Not located.
Pub.: Medalle, no. 79; Curtis, no. 194B.

[a]James] J.—— *M*

1. Date] See letter 205A, *Status,* for our explanation of why Medalle's dating, rather than Curtis's, seems correct.

2. as Sunday] As Curtis notes, Sterne was home all day on Sunday, April 19, according to *BJ,* 174. He visited the Jameses on Saturday, April 18.

3. but he . . . with me] Sterne's neatly turned witticism makes a strong case against this letter being solely Medalle's rewriting of 204A; Lydia made many editorial changes to the manuscripts, but clever invention does not characterize them.

4. poured balm] Cf. *BJ,* 175: "Alas! alas! the only Physician, & who carries the Balm of my Life along with her,—is Eliza." Behind the image is both Luke 10:34 (the good Samaritan, "pouring in oil and wine") and Jeremiah 8:22 ("Is there no balm in Gilead; is there no physician there?"). See *BJ,* 6:389, n. to 175.4–5.

206. *To Ignatius Sancho*

Text: Medalle

Bond Street, Saturday. [May 16, 1767][1]

I was very sorry, my good Sancho, that I was not at home to return my compliments by you for the great courtesy of the Duke of Montagu's[a] family to me, in honouring my list of subscribers with their names—for which I bear them all thanks.—But you have something to add, Sancho, to what I owe your good will also on this account, and that is to send me the subscription money, which I find a necessity of duning my best friends for before I leave town—to avoid the perplexities of both keeping pecuniary accounts (for which I have very slender talents) and collecting them (for which I have neither strength of body or mind) and so, good Sancho dun the Duke of Montagu[b] the Duchess of Montagu[b] and Lord M.[2] for their subscriptions, and lay the sin, and money with it too, at my door—I wish so good a family every blessing they merit, along with my humblest compliments. You know, Sancho, that I am your friend and well-wisher,

L. Sterne

PS

I leave town on Friday morning—and should on Thursday, but that I stay to dine with Lord and Lady Spencer[c].

MS: Not located.
Pub.: Medalle, no. 86; Curtis, no. 195.

[a]Montagu's] M—g—'s *M* [b]Montagu] M. *M* [c]Spencer] S——— *M*

1. Date] Medalle has only "Saturday." *1780* has "April 25, 1767," but Sterne was not preparing to leave London until the end of May. *BJ*, 189–91, makes it clear that Sterne wrote this letter on May 16, the Saturday before his departure on Friday, May 22; he would dine with the Spencers on Thursday, May 21: "detaind by Lord & Lady Spencer who had made a party to dine & sup on my Acc[t]" (191). See also letter 207.

2. Duke of Montagu . . . Lord M.] For Ignatius Sancho, and his relationship with the Montagu family, see letter 181, n. 1. "Lord M." is identified by Curtis, 340, n. 2, as the son of the Duke and Duchess, John Brudenell-Montagu (1735–1770), created Marquess of Monthermer in 1766. He subscribed to a large-paper copy of *ASJ* (we assume he is intended by the listing "Marquis of Monthidmer"), while the duke and duchess subscribed to both *ASJ* and *Sermons* (1769).

207. *To William Petty, Earl of Shelburne*[1]

Text: Medalle

Old Bond-street, [Thursday,] May [2]1, 1767[2]

My Lord,

I was yesterday taking leave of all the town, with an intention of leaving it this day, but I am detained by the kindness of lord and lady

Spencer[a], who have made a party to dine and sup on my account—I am impatient to set out for my solitude, for there the mind gains strength, and learns to lean upon herself—In the world it seeks or accepts of a few treacherous supports—the feigned compassion of one—the flattery of a second—the civilities of a third—the friendship of a fourth—they all deceive, and bring the mind back to where mine is retreating, to retirement, reflection, and books.[3] My departure is fixed for to-morrow morning, but I could not think of quitting a place where I have received such numberless and unmerited civilities from your lordship, without returning my most grateful thanks, as well as my hearty acknowledgments for your friendly enquiry from Bath. Illness, my lord, has occasioned my silence—Death knocked at my door,[4] but I would not admit him—the call was both unexpected and unpleasant—and I am seriously worn down to a shadow—and still very weak, but weak as I am, I have as whimsical a story[5] to tell you as ever befel one of my family—Shandy's nose, his name, his sash window are fools to it[6]—it will serve at least to amuse you—The injury I did myself last month in catching cold upon James's Powder—fell, you must know, upon the worst part it could—the most painful, and most dangerous of any in the human body. It was on this crisis I called in an able surgeon and with him an able physician (both my friends) to inspect my disaster—'tis a venereal case, cried my two scientific friends—'tis impossible, however, to be that, replied I—for I have had no commerce whatever with the sex, not even with my wife, added I, these fifteen years.—You are, however,[7] my good friend, said the surgeon, or there is no such case in the world—what the devil, said I, without knowing woman?—We will not reason about it, said the physician, but you must undergo a course of mercury—I will lose my life first, said I—and trust to nature, to time, or at the worst to death—so I put an end, with some indignation, to the conference—and determined to bear all the torments I underwent, and ten times more, rather than submit to be treated like a *sinner*, in a point where I had acted like a *saint*.—Now as the father of mischief[8] would have it, who has no pleasure like that of dishonouring the righteous, it so fell out that from the moment I dismissed my doctors, my pains began to rage with a violence not to be expressed, or supported. Every hour became more intolerable.—I was got to bed, cried out, and raved the whole night, and was got up so near dead that my friends insisted upon my sending again for my physician and surgeon. I told them upon the word of a man of honour they were both mistaken, as to my case—but though they had reasoned wrong, they might act right; but that sharp as my sufferings were, I felt them not so sharp as the imputation which a venereal treatment of my case laid me under—They answered that these taints of the blood laid dormant twenty years, but they would not reason with me in a point wherein I was so delicate, but would do all the office for which they were called in, namely to put an end to my torment, which otherwise would put an end to me—and so have I been compelled to surrender myself—and thus, my dear lord, has your poor friend with all his sensibilities been suffering the chastisement of the grossest sensualist.[9]—Was it not as ridiculous an embarrassment as ever Yorick's spirit was involved in?—Nothing but the purest conscience of innocence could have tempted me to write this story to my wife, which by the bye would make no bad anecdote in Tristram Shandy's Life—I have mentioned it in my journal to Mrs. Draper. In[b] some respects there is no difference between my wife and herself—when they fare alike, neither can reasonably complain.—I have just received letters from France, with some hints that Mrs. Sterne and my Lydia are coming to England, to pay me a visit[10]—if your time is not better employed, Yorick flatters himself he shall receive a letter from your lordship, *en attendant*.[11] I am with the greatest regard,

my Lord,
your Lordship's
most faithful humble servant,
L. Sterne

MS: Not located.
Pub.: Medalle, no. 80; Curtis, no. 196.

[a]lady Spencer] lady S— *M* [b]Mrs. Draper. In] Mrs. —— In *M*

1. *Earl of Shelburne*] For Shelburne, see letter 138, n. 3. Medalle has "To the Earl of ———" in the first edition and elaborates it to "Earl of S———" in the second. Cross, *Letters*, 2:149, suggests "without much doubt" Shelburne, and Curtis agrees.

2. Date] Medalle's date of "May 1, 1767" is probably a simple error for May 21, which was almost certainly the actual date; see letter 206, n. 1, for the chronology leading up to Sterne's London departure on Friday, May 22.

3. I am impatient . . . books] Sterne has much the same passage in the entry for May 21, *BJ*, 191: "Impatient to set out for my Solitude—there the Mind, Eliza! gains strength, & learns to lean upon herself,—and seeks refuge in its own Constancy & Virtue—in the world it seeks or accepts of a few treacherous supports—the feign'd Compassion of one—the flattery of a second—the Civilities of a third—the friendship of a fourth—they all decieve—& bring the Mind back to where mine is retreating—that is, Eliza! to itself—to thee (who art my second self) to retirement, reflection & Books." As indicated in the Florida annotation to this passage (6:399, n. to 191.8–16), the two versions indicate "Sterne's capacity entirely to alter the tone—perhaps the sense—of a passage by means primarily of apostrophe." It is also important to note Sterne's penchant for recycling material from one letter to another—this letter in particular exhibits just such a recycling, wherein the same content is made to serve both his intimate journal to Eliza and his cordial letter to a titled acquaintance.

4. Death knocked at my door] As Death does in the opening chapter of *TS*, VII: "when DEATH himself knocked at my door—ye [his spirits] bad him come again; and in so gay a tone of careless indifference, did ye do it, that he doubted of his commission" (576).

5. I have as whimsical a story] Sterne tells the same story, in almost the same words, in *BJ*, 176–78 (April 24). Cash, *LY*, 290, suggests that the doctors were probably incorrect, and that "Sterne suffered from tuberculosis of the fibrocaseous type, as evidenced by the recurrent bleeding of his lungs . . . . Moreover, tuberculosis often attacks other organs besides the lungs, among them the genitals and the vocal cords. In short, one can unify all of Sterne's known symptoms, including his shocking weight loss during his last year, under a diagnosis of tuberculosis."

6. Shandy's nose . . . to it] The problems besetting Tristram Shandy in relation to his nose and his name are first alluded to in the penultimate paragraph of the final chapter of volume II (19.180): "You may raise a system to account for the loss of my nose by marriage articles,——and shew the world how it could happen, that I should have the misfortune to be called TRISTRAM." The incident with the sash window occurs in volume V (17.449–50).

7. You are, however] The surgeon is a little more frank in *BJ*, 177: "You are *****

however," where the asterisks might indicate "clapt" or "poxed." Lydia may have deliberately omitted them.

8. father of mischief] Cf. *TS*, III.2.188, where the "father of mischief" makes it impossible for Walter to remove his handkerchief from his coat pocket without recalling "transverse zig-zaggery" to Toby's mind.

9. the grossest sensualist] Cf. letter 226: "praised be God for my sensibility! Though it has often made me wretched, yet I would not exchange it for all the pleasures the grossest sensualist ever felt."

10. I have just . . . a visit] Cf. *BJ*, 193 (June 2): "This morning surpriz'd with a Letter from my Lydia—that She and her Mama, are coming to pay me a Visit . . . ." What may be indicated here and elsewhere is that Sterne's dating of letters often indicates when he starts rather than when he finishes.

11. *en attendant*] In the meantime.

208. *To John Dillon*[1]

Text: Medalle

Old Bond-street, Friday Morning. [May 22, 1767]

I was going, my dear Dillon[a], to bed before I received your kind enquiry, and now my chaise stands at my door to take and convey this poor body to its legal settlement.[2]—I am ill, very ill—I languish most affectingly—I am sick both soul and body—it is a cordial to me to hear it is different with you—no man interests himself more in your happiness, and I am glad you are in so fair a road to it—enjoy it long, my Dillon[a] whilst I—no matter what—but my feelings are too nice for the world I live in—things will mend.—I dined yesterday with lord and lady Spencer[b] we talked much of you, and your goings on, for every one knows why Sunbury Hill[3] is so pleasant a situation.—You rogue! you have lock'd up my boots—and I go bootless home—and fear I shall go bootless all my life—Adieu, gentlest and best of souls—adieu.

I am yours most affectionately,
L. Sterne

MS: Not located.
Pub.: Medalle, no. 82; Curtis, no. 197.

[a]Dillon] D—n / D. *M* [b]lady Spencer] lady S— *M*

1. *John Dillon*] Medalle has only "To J. D——n, Esq.," identified by Cross in *Letters,* 2:153, as J. Dillon, and in *Life* (1929), 310, as John Talbot Dillon. Who exactly Dillon was remains problematic, since the name was shared by several distant family members, but Curtis, 345, n. 1, in a rather confusing note, seems to argue for the better known John Talbot Dillon (1734–1806), created Baron of the Holy Roman Empire (1767), author of *Travels through Spain* (1780) and *Historical and Critical Memoirs of the General Revolution in France* (1790). We know of no evidence that clearly establishes this identification, as opposed to John Dillon (*c.*1740–1805), Co. Meath, Ireland, also a Baron of the Holy Roman Empire (1782). In the *Oxford DNB,* Katherine Turner attempts to separate their identities, which the earlier *DNB* had confused (along with Curtis); see also William Henry Dillon, *A Narrative of My Professional Adventures (1790–1839),* ed. M. A. Lewis (Navy Records Society, 1953), 1:xiv–xvi.

John Talbot Dillon had a wife who died in childbirth (in 1768 at Liège, according to Curtis, 368, n. 7, citing *Gentleman's Magazine* [June 1768]: 302); John Dillon was married in 1767 to Millicent Drake (*d.* 1788), daughter of George Drake of Fernhill, Berkshire. Insofar as Sterne here, and in letter 213, seems to allude to a courtship and marriage in 1767, both options seem viable—we have been unable to discover an Indian connection for either wife. And, if one is not sufficiently confused, two entries appear among the subscribers to large-paper copies of *ASJ,* one under the other: "Mr. J. Dillon" and "Mr. Dillon."

2. legal settlement] I.e. Coxwold.

3. Sunbury Hill] Sunbury and Sunbury-on-Thames are just south of Windsor and Slough, in the vicinity of "Salt Hill," where Sterne and Eliza visited (see *BJ* 206; and n. to 206.4, 6:410–11). Sunbury Court, in the same area, the vast estate and gardens of George Fermor, 2d Earl of Pomfret (who subscribed to *Sermons* in 1769) and his wife, Anna Maria Delegard, was opened to visitors at about this time. A Sunbury Hill is in Torquay, Devon, but that is very remote from Sterne's allusion, which seems to indicate Dillon's courting someone in the vicinity (see letter 213).

Nor can we explain the remainder of the passage, "lock'd up my boots," etc. If a bawdy undercurrent does exist, perhaps "Sunbury Hill" is related to "Salt Hill" as a euphemism for the female pudendum; see letter 225, n. 4.

Cf. *1 Henry IV,* III.i.65–67, where Glendower brags: "[I] have sent him / Bootless home and weather-beaten back," and Hotspur twits him: "Home without boots, and in foul weather too!"

209. *To John Hall-Stevenson*

Text: Medalle

Newark, Monday ten o'clock in the morn. [May 25, 1767][1]

My dear Cousin,

I have got conveyed thus far like a bale of cadaverous goods consigned to Pluto[2] and company—lying in the bottom of my chaise most of the rout, upon a large pillow which I had the *prevoyance*[3] to purchase before I set out—I am worn out—but press on to Barnby Moor to night, and if possible to York the next.—I know not what is the matter with me—but some *derangement* presses hard upon this machine[4]—still I think it will not be overset this bout.—My love to G.[5]—We shall all meet from the east, and from the south, and (as at the last) be happy together—My kind respects to a few.—I am, dear Hall[a]

truly yours,
L. Sterne

MS: Not located.
Pub.: Medalle, no. 83; Curtis, no. 198.

[a]Hall] H. *M*

1. Date] This letter was written on Sterne's slow journey north, the usual two- or three-day journey stretching out from May 23 to May 28; see *BJ*, 191–92. Newark is on the Great North Road, about 124 miles from London. Sterne reached there on May 24 ("bear my Journey badly—ill—& dispirited all the Way" [*BJ* 191]), and set out again the next day for Barnby Moor, another stage on the Great North Road, 24 miles north of Newark and 12 miles south of Doncaster (see Daniel Paterson, *A New and Accurate Description of All the Direct and Principal Cross Roads in Great Britain* [1772], 111–12). The next day, finding himself too ill to continue on to York, he went only so far as Brodsworth, 5 miles northwest of Doncaster and home of Archbishop Drummond (see letter 78, n. 3): "staid two days on the road at the A-Bishops of Yorks . . . kindly nursed & honourd by both" (*BJ* 192). He departed Brodsworth on May 28 and arrived at his "Thatchd Cottage" [i.e., Shandy Hall] the same day.

In March 1768, Boswell made the trip in the opposite direction, staying at Bluitt's Inn on the 19th and "at the inn on Barnby Moor" on the 20th (*Boswell in Search of a Wife: 1766–1769*, ed. Frank Brady and Frederick A. Pottle [New York: McGraw-Hill, 1956], 136–37); see also letter 226, n. 2.

2. Pluto] One of the sons of Kronos, lord of the lower world. His "company" might include Cerberus, the Harpies, the Eumenides (Furies), and the Parcae (Fates).

3. *prevoyance*] Foresight (properly: *prévoyance*).

4. *derangement* presses hard upon this machine] Disorder, bad state of health (properly: *dérangement*). Sterne refers to his body as a "machine" several times during his final year, including an entry in *BJ*, 178 (April 25): "finding my machine a much less tormenting one to me than before, I become reconciled to my Situation." See also letter 247 (March 1768). But see also *ASJ*, 5, where Yorick expresses contentment: "I felt every vessel in my frame dilate—the arteries beat all chearily together, and every power which sustained life, perform'd it with so little friction, that 'twould have confounded the most *physical precieuse* in France: with all her materialism, she could scarce have called me a machine—." That both in this letter and in *ASJ*, Sterne associates *machine* with something French may indicate a connection in his mind to Julien Offray de La Mettrie's *L'homme machine* (1747), the epitome of mechanistic thinking in the century; see *ASJ*, 6:236, n. to 5.22.

5. G.] Curtis has "G[arland]"—i.e., Nathaniel Garland; see letter 170, n. 13, however, for the difficulty of making a positive identification.

210. *To Daniel Draper*[1]

Text: Ms.

[Coxwold, ?Tuesday, June 2, 1767][2]

Sir

<It is out of th>

<to> I own, it S^{r}, that the writing a Letter to a gentleman I have not the honour to be known to, & <upon (wth Wh>—a Letter likewise upon no ∧kind∧ business (in the Ideas of the world) is ∧a little∧ out of the common Course of Things—but I'm so myself——& the <reason of m> Impulse wch makes me <write> take up my pen——<is all of a piece> is out of <of>~the~ Common Way too—for arises[a] from the honest pain I should feel, in of in[b] <avowing such an> ∧<having

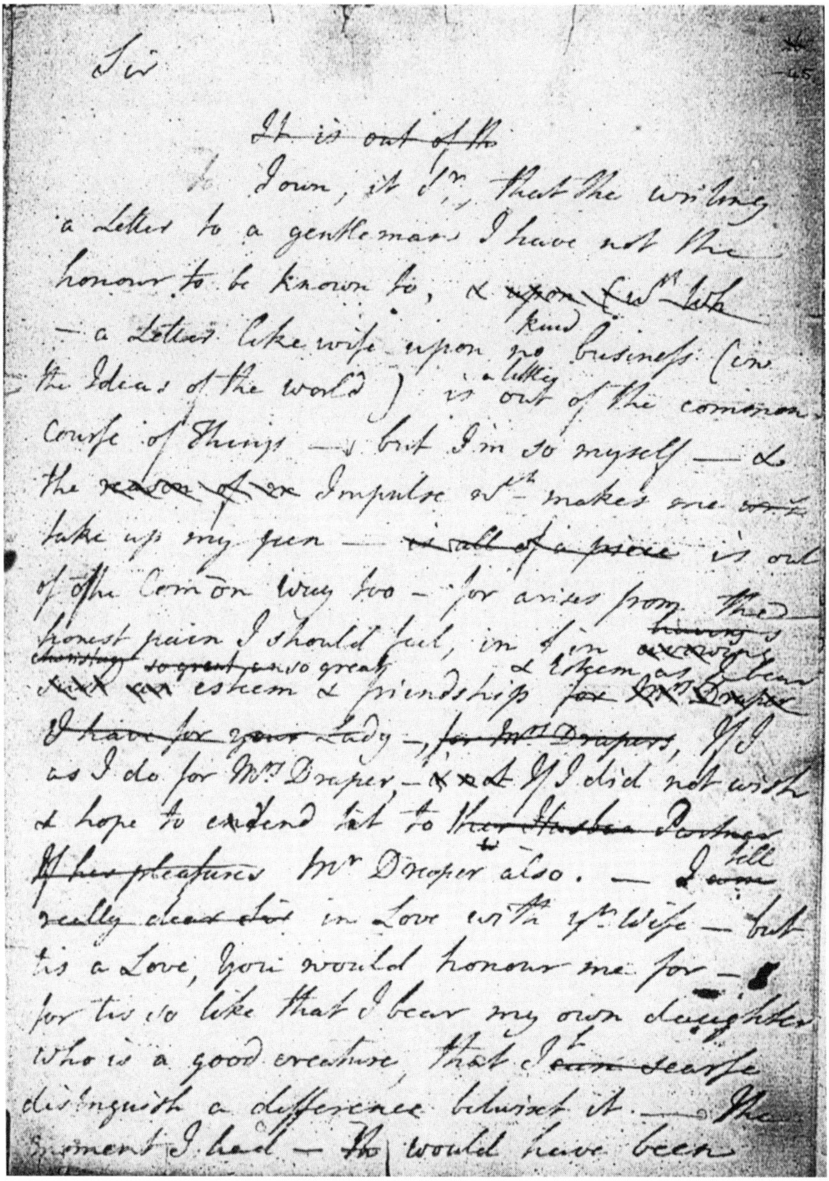

Figure 9. Opening page of letter of June 2, 1767, to Daniel Draper, British Library, Addit. MSS. 34527, 45–61.

& cherishing so great an>∧ ∧so great∧ esteem & friendship <for M[rs] Draper> & Esteem as I bear <I have for your Lady—, for M[rs] Drapers,> If I as I do for M[rs] Draper,—<& not> If I did not wish & hope to end~ext~end but to[c] <[V]t[V]her Husban Partner <I>~of~ her pleasures> M[r] Draper also.—I <am really dear Sir> ∧fell∧ in Love with y[r] Wife—but tis a Love, You would honour me for—<I> for tis so like that I bear my own daughter who is a good creature, that I <can> scarse distinguish a difference betwixt it——The moment I had—<th> would have been ||
<the last, I would>
that Moment would have been the last <of my acq[ce] with my friend (allworthy as she is)>—!

I wish it had been in my power to have been of true use to M[rs] Draper—∧at this Distance from her best Protector——∧I have bestowed a great deal of pains <u>~(~ or rather I sh[d] pleasure[d]) upon her head—her heart needs none—& her *head*[e] as little as ∧any∧ Daughter of Eve's—[3]

—I wish[f] I could make myself of any Service to <her, ∧M[rs] D∧ whilst I, at this distance—> whilst She is in India—& I in the world—<and it would ill answer the purpose & Spirit of this Letter, if,> ||

for wordly affairs, I could be of none—

& indeed less, than any it has been my fate to converse wth for some years,—∧<such as my good fr — God preserve her!—>∧

—I wish[g] you dear Sir, many years happiness <with>

——<I pray> Tis a part of my Litany, to pray <to heaven for> ∧for what I fear she well[4]∧ her health & Life—& <I hope <wi>~G~od.>—She is too good to be lost—& I would out pure zeal to a pilgrimage[h] to Mecca[5] to seek a <specifick> Medcine.

MS: British Library, Addit. MSS. 34527, 45–61.
Pub.: Gibbs, *Some Memorials*, 23; *Athenaeum* (March 30, 1878): 413; facsimile in Cross, *Journal to Eliza and Various Letters* (1904), between 154–55; Curtis, no. 199.

[a]for arises] for [it] arises *C* [b]in of in] in in *C* [c]but to] it to *C* [d]sh[d] pleasure] sh[d] [say] pleasure *C* [e]*head*] head *C* [f]¶—I wish] no ¶ *C* [g]¶—I wish] no ¶ *C* [h]out pure zeal to a pilgrimage] out [of] pure zeal to [take] a pilgrimage *C*

1. *Daniel Draper*] Daniel Draper (1726–1805) held the post of Marine Paymaster at Bombay, a post that "must have brought him into close association with Commodore James," according to Wright and Sclater, 21. They consider him an "assiduous and efficient official" and chronicle his rise in the India Company. In 1768 he was transferred to Tellicherry, as chief of the principal factory of the East India Company on the Malabar Coast, but Wright and Sclater conclude it was the beginning of a downward spiral for the Draper family; by the time the family returned to Bombay in 1772, the marriage seems to have been irrevocably broken. In *BJ*, 173 (April 17), Sterne comments on "an infamous Acc^t of Draper & his detested Character at Bombay—for what a wretch art thou hazarding thy life, my dear friend . . . ." Cash, *LY*, 271–72, tries to offer some substance for the lover's opinion: "Eliza hated her husband. He was thirty-nine years old, exceedingly ugly, as we know from an existing portrait, and a man who knew nothing of the world except the colonial service to which he had been born. . . . Draper was determined to make a great fortune in the service, and to this end was brutally aggressive." Among the opinions of Sterne, Eliza, and unsympathetic biographers, we are probably not likely to have a fully accurate portrait of Daniel Draper.

2. Date] In *BJ*, 194 (June 2), Sterne suggests to Eliza that they pool their "*little Capitals together*" and then asks: "will Mr Draper give us leave?—he may safely—if y^r *Virtue* & Honour are only concernd,—'twould be safe in Yoricks hands, as in a Brothers . . . ." Curtis believes this undated rough draft must have been written at about the same time as the journal entry, a hapless attempt to communicate a proposal for which even his inventive pen could not find adequate language. The *Athenaeum* reporter states the problem with particular acuity: "The very thinness of the social ice-crust upon which he was venturing must have given the task an extra relish to such an adept in unwritable letters as Sterne" (413). As the Florida editors note, "one can only hope Sterne dropped the entire idea" (*ASJ* 6:402, n. to 194.4–5).

3. Daughter of Eve's] See above, letter 144, n. 12.

4. what I fear she well] Here as elsewhere, we have read the manuscript as best we could, without attempting (as Curtis did on occasion) to provide coherence to Sterne's most erratic diction and syntax. Possibly "will" is the word intended rather than "well," or perhaps a word we are unable to decipher; the inserted phrase does not make sense to us.

The opening phrase, "Tis a part of my Litany," is repeated by Sterne in letter 229 to the Jameses (October 3).

5. pilgrimage to Mecca] Sterne had promised a similar "pilgrimage to Mecca" to Ignatius Sancho in letter 181, if it could ease "the burdens which our Brothers & Sisters [in slavery] are *there* carrying."

211. *To A. L——e, Esq.*[1]

Text: Medalle

Coxwould, [Sunday,] June 7, 1767.

Dear L...e,

I had not been many days at this peaceful cottage before your letter greeted me with the seal of friendship, and most cordially do I thank you for so kind a proof of your good will—I was truly anxious to hear of the recovery of my sentimental friend[2]—but I would not write to enquire after her, unless I could have sent her the testimony without the tax, for even how-d'yes[3] to invalids, or those that have lately been so, either call to mind what is past or what may return—at least I find it so.—I am as happy as a prince, at Coxwould[4]——and I wish you could see in how princely a manner I live—'tis a land of plenty. I sit down alone to venison, fish and wild fowl, or a couple of fowls or ducks, with curds, and strawberries, and cream, and all the simple plenty which a rich valley under (Hambleton[a] Hills)[5] can produce—with a clean cloth on my table—and a bottle of wine on my right hand to drink your health. I have a hundred hens and chickens about my yard—and not a parishioner catches a hare, or a rabbet, or a trout, but he brings it as an offering to me. If solitude would cure a love-sick heart, I would give you an invitation—but absence and time lessen no attachment which virtue inspires.—I am in high spirits—care never enters this cottage—I take the air every day in my post chaise, with my two long tail'd horses[6]——they turn out good ones; and as to myself, I think I am better upon the whole for the medicines, and regimen I submitted to in town—May you, dear L——, want neither the one, nor the other.

Yours truly,
L. Sterne

MS: Not located.

Pub.: Medalle, no. 92; Curtis, no. 200.

Status: The recipient of four long letters (see also letters 212, 232, and 235), Medalle's "A. L——e, Esq." remains unidentified. We can surmise that he was acquainted with the Jameses and with Sterne's affair with Eliza, that he was sufficiently young to be still involved in courtship himself, and that he had some health problems. Sterne's subscription lists provide no solution, nor do his biographers (Sterne was probably acquainted in Paris with Arthur Lee [1740–1792], the American patriot, but as Curtis points out, 354, n. 1, Lee was in America at the time of Sterne's correspondence).

The lack of any trace of A. L——e except in Medalle's four letters, and the appearance of substantial echoes from *Bramine's Journal* in three of the four, support the suspicion that the letters are her fabrication, an elaborate "combing" of *BJ* (her access to which she then concealed, along with the journal itself); see, e.g., the extensive borrowing recorded in note 4 below. This suspicion has not been quite as convincing to us, however, as the counterargument that Sterne had few qualms about reusing materials in letters covering the same events of his life, personalizing each version by the slightest of touches—here, e.g., the addition in *BJ* of the parenthetical "as in Bond street."

Letter 213 also has extensive borrowings from *BJ*, again supporting a case for Lydia's fabrication. We would suggest instead—more tentatively, perhaps—that letter 213 was written over the period of a week (as was Sterne's habit), and that Sterne fertilized his journal with his correspondence. There is in the journal a clear waning of energy as Sterne's fantasy begins to weaken, and we suspect he welcomed the hints that his correspondence with others provided; being faithful to his promise to write something every day was proving most difficult, and by the end of the month he skips from July 19 to July 27, and finally ends it at the beginning of August.

Letter 233 does *not* borrow from *BJ;* one would have to accuse Lydia of a good deal of cunning in covering her tracks by varying her use of *BJ* in the four fabricated letters. But while we are reluctant to do so, the borrowings from *BJ* in letter 236, and especially the rather clumsy alterations made to redirect the sentiments from Eliza to Lydia, certainly encourage the speculation that Lydia had access to some or all of *BJ*, and a great deal of cunning indeed (perhaps aided by that practiced forger, William Combe). The alternative possibility, that Sterne himself recycled materials when writing new letters, remains our preferred scenario, although we do feel the full force of the counterargument.

[a]Hambleton] Hamilton *M*

1. *A. L——e*] See *Status.*

2. recovery of my sentimental friend] We assume this refers to the illness of Mrs. James, and is supporting evidence for the assertion that the epitaph in letter 204 was intended for her.

3. how-d'yes] Cf. *TS*, 3:246, n. to 232.27: "Earlier in the century servants called on their master's or mistress's acquaintances to ask, with their compliments, 'How do ye?'"; cf. Swift, "Verses on the Death of Dr. Swift," ll. 123–24: "(When daily Howd'y's come of Course, / And Servants answer; *Worse and Worse*)" (*Poems*, ed. Harold Williams, 2d ed. [Oxford: Clarendon Press, 1958], 2:557).

4. at Coxwould] Sterne recycled his idyllic description of life in Coxwold in his *BJ* entry for July 2: "But I am in the Vale of Coxwould & wish You saw in how princely a manner I live in it—tis a Land of Plenty—I sit down alone to Venison, fish or Wild foul—or a couple of fouls—with Curds, and strawberrys & Cream, and all the simple clean plenty w[ch] a rich Vally can produce,—with a Bottle of wine on my right hand (as in Bond street) to drink y[r] health—I have a hundred hens & chickens ab[t] my yard—and not a parishoner catches a hare a rabbet or a Trout—but he brings it as an Offering—In short tis a golden Vally . . ." (*BJ* 211).

5. Hambleton Hills] Medalle's erroneous "Hamilton" was first corrected by Curtis. The Hambleton Hills, south of Coxwold, lie between the Vale of York and the North Yorkshire Moors.

6. I take . . . horses] See the similar phrasing in letter 222.

212. *To Richard Davenport*[1]

Text: European Magazine

Coxwould, near York [Tuesday,] June 9, 1767.

Dear Sir,

I have this moment received your obliging letter,—and without staying to read it a second time, have thrust aside my *Sentimental Journey*, immediately to acknowledge, and thank you for it and its contents—which by the by, are safer in your pocket than mine, so pray give them room, till I have the pleasure of seeing you in town, or elsewhere. This nasty gout! it's enough to cut away half the comfort of a man's life—I wish it was the portion of splenetic philosophers, and Tartuffe's[2] of all denominations,—at least I should not torment my philanthropy much about them; but when it falls upon an open cheerful hearted man, who would do God honour—I grieve from my soul that such feelings should be thwarted—and would write or fight with more zeal to restore him to himself, than all the *subscriptions* or *subsidies* in the world could kindle in me, in another case; and now I have named subscriptions, I might thank you again (if I chose it) for those you have procured me; however, I should wish to know, if any are upon imperial paper, that it may be so marked[3] in the printed list of their names, who have done me so much honour in this work. I am now seriously set down to it—that is, I began this morning; a five weeks illness, which by the by, *ought* to have killed me—but that I made a point of it, not to break faith with the world,[4] and in short *would* not die, (for in some cases, I hold this affair to be an act of the will). This long illness, which confined me a month to my room, reduced me and my imagination with me, to such mere shadows, that it was not till last night that I felt the least powers or temptations (either ghostly or bodily) within me for what I had undertaken. I have now set to, and shall not take my pen from my paper till I have finished.

By heaven! I think mine is a life of the oddest and most tragicomic incidents in nature; this very morning that I set about writing my Sentimental Journey through France,—have I received a letter from my wife,[5] who is at Marseilles, advertising, that she is going (not to write,—but what is a much better thing) that she is going to make a Sentimental Journey through France, and post it a thousand miles, merely to pay me a visit of three months.—The deuce take all Sentimental Journeys!!—I wish there had never been such a thing thought of by man or woman—tres menses! cum uxore neque leni neque commodâ!—quid faciam?—quo me vertam?[6]—It will quicken my sentiments however. I know not by what authority I go on writing thus to you, without one premeditated thought—but I mean it civilly; for to those I like and esteem, so must I write—or not at all—I wish I could conjure your gout, or rather the causes of it, into the Red Sea, in secula seculorum.[7] But I fear it has too much the nature of original sin in it, or of the obstinacy of that spirit which departeth not,[8] but by much prayer and fasting—if even with that.

Lord God! what weather! till yesterday, nothing but pining[9] penetrating north-east winds—my poor vessel could well have spared this stress, and I fear yours would feel it even before you drew your curtains in the morning. I had once taken up a large folio sheet—you had a narrow escape—for I should have filled it as full as this; God send you well and out of your chamber.

I am, my dear sir, with much esteem,
Your obliged and humble servant,
L. Sterne

Address: To Richard Davenport, Esq. Brereton Green, Cheshire.
MS: Not located.
Pub.: European Magazine, n.s. 1 (October 1825): 194–95; Earl Wasserman, "Letters by Sterne, Hume, and Rousseau," *MLN* 66 (1951): 74–75.

1. *Richard Davenport*] Little is known about Richard Davenport (*c.*1705–1771) except his willingness to provide a residence at Wooton, his estate in Derby, for Jean-Jacques Rousseau during his exile in England between February 1766 and May 1767. See *Letters of David Hume,* ed. J.Y.T. Greig (Oxford: Clarendon Press, 1932), 2:23–24, 27, 29, and 35. Hume variously describes him to different correspondents as "an elderly Man, of a considerable Fortune and a good Character"; "a Gentleman of 5 or 6000 pounds in the North of England, and a Man of great Humanity and of a good Understanding . . . . He has a House, called Wooton, in the Peake of Derby, situated amidst Mountains and Rocks and Streams and Forrests, which pleases the wild Imagination and solitary Humour of Rousseau"; and a few days later: "a worthy man, a man of letters, and sense, and humanity, and of an ample fortune, about 6 or 7000 pounds a year, an elderly man, and a widower." Davenport subscribed to a large-paper copy of *ASJ,* and is likely the "—— Davenport, Esq." who subscribed to *Sermons* (1769).

2. Tartuffe's] Tartuffe is the eponymous sanctimonious hypocrite in Molière's comedy (1664), who uses a mask of religious conviction to conceal his numerous vices, particularly lust and avarice. He appears often in Sterne's writings—e.g., *TS,* V.1.408–9 and VIII.2.657; *ASJ,* 29 and 83; and perhaps most famously in letter 241 to his American admirer, Dr. John Eustace. For a further account of these allusions, see the chapter "Tartuffery," in New, *"Tristram Shandy": A Book for Free Spirits,* 113–34, esp. 118–20.

3. imperial paper . . . marked] In the list of subscribers to *ASJ,* the 134 subscribers to a large-paper copy (as was Davenport himself) are indicated with an asterisk; see *ASJ,* 6:lxiii, n. 31, and letter 193, n. 6.

4. break faith with the world] I.e., he had promised subscribers four volumes of *ASJ;* see letter 180, n. 4, for the "advertisement" inserted into some copies of

ASJ, in which Sterne apologizes for producing only two volumes because of ill health.

5. this very morning . . . wife] Sterne actually received word about this visit in May (see letter 207), although he perhaps was not fully convinced until receiving a letter from Lydia on June 2 (*BJ* 193). The present passage is recycled into an entry in *BJ,* 204–5 (June 20): "I think my dear Bramine—That nature is turn'd upside down—for Wives go to visit Husbands, at greater perils, & take longer journies to pay them this Civility now a days out of ill Will—than good—Mine is flying post a Journey of a thousand Miles—with as many Miles to go back—merely to see how I do . . . ."

6. tres menses . . . vertam?] Cash, *LY,* 295, provides an adequate translation: "three months! with a wife neither pliant nor accommodating!—what am I to do?—where am I to turn?"

7. in secula seculorum] From the *Nunc Dimittis* of Simeon: "Gloria Patri, et Filio: et Spiritui Sancto. Sicut erat in principio, et nunc et semper: et in secula seculorum," translated in the *BCP* (Evening Service) as "Glory be to the Father, and to the Son: and to the Holy Ghost. As it was in the beginning, is now, and ever shall be: world without end."

For the tradition of casting ghosts and spirits into the Red Sea (and their fear of being so cast), see Smollett, *The Life and Adventures of Sir Launcelot Greaves,* ed. Robert Folkenflik and Barbara Laning Fitzpatrick (Athens: University of Georgia Press, 2002), 245, n. 13 (n. to ch. 22, 169–70). While the origins of the notion are obscure, Folkenflik cites Addison's *The Drummer; Or The Haunted House* (1715) as an earlier instance of its usage; we quote from that play, act 1, scene 2: "If the Conjurer be but well paid, he'll take pains upon the Ghost, and lay him, look ye, in the Red-Sea——and then he's laid for ever . . . there must be a power of Spirits in that same Red-Sea——I warrant ye they are as plenty as Fish" (22–23).

8. that spirit which departeth not] Sterne probably is alluding to Luke 9:37ff. (cf. Matthew 17:15 and Mark 9:18 and 22), where Jesus cures a child presented to him by a grieving father: "And, lo, a spirit taketh him, and he suddenly crieth out; and it teareth him that he foameth again, and bruising him hardly departeth from him." Cf. *Sermons,* 4:16 (see 5:72, n. to 16.24–27), where Sterne invokes the story again (sermon 2, "The house of feasting and the house of mourning").

9. pining] Sterne's rather unfamiliar usage is confirmed by *OED,* s.v. *pining, adj.:* "tormenting, afflicting, painful (*obs.*); causing or suffering wasting. Also: languishing, suffering emotional pain"; Gray's "Ode on a Distant Prospect of Eton College (1747)," l. 65, is cited: "Or pineing Love shall waste their youth."

213. *To A. L——e, Esq.*

Text: Medalle

Coxwould, [Tuesday,] June 30, 1767.

I am in still better health, my dear L...e, than when I wrote last to you—owing I believe to my riding out[1] every day with my friend Hall[a] whose castle lies near the sea—and there is a beach as even as a mirrour, of five miles in length before it—where we daily run races in our chaises, with one wheel in the sea, and the other on the land.—Dillon[b2] has obtain'd his fair Indian, and has this post sent a letter of enquiries after Yorick, and his Bramine. He is a good soul and interests himself much in our fate—I cannot forgive you, L...e, for your folly in saying you intend to get introduced to the Newnhams[c3] I despise them, and I shall hold your understanding much cheaper than I now do, if you persist in a resolution so unworthy of you.—I suppose Mrs. James[d] telling you they were sensible, is the ground work you go upon—by—they are not clever; tho' what is commonly call'd wit, may pass for literature on the other side of Temple-bar.[4]—You say Mrs. James[d] thinks them amiable—she judges too favourably; but I have put a stop to her intentions of visiting them.—They are bitter enemies of mine, and I am even with them. La Bramine assured me they used their endeavours with her to break off her friendship with me, for reasons I will not write, but tell you.—I said enough of them before she left England, and tho' she yielded to me in every other point, yet in this she obstinately persisted.—Strange infatuation!—but I think I have effected my purpose by a falsity, which Yorick's friendship to the Bramine can only justify.—I wrote her word that the most amiable of women reiterated my request, that she would not write to them. I said too, she had conceal'd many things for the sake of her peace of mind—when in fact, L——e, this was merely a child of my own brain, made Mrs. James[d]'s by adoption, to enforce the argument I had before urged so strongly.—Do not mention this circumstance to Mrs. James[d], 'twould displease her—and I had no design in it but for the

Bramine to be a friend to herself.—I ought now to be busy from sun rise,[5] to sun set, for I have a book to write—a wife to receive—an estate to sell[6]—a parish to superintend, and what is worst of all, a disquieted heart to reason with—these are continual calls upon me.—I have receiv'd[7] half a dozen letters to press me to join my friends at Scarborough, but I am at present deaf to them all.—I perhaps may pass a few days there something later in the season, not at present—and so dear L...e, adieu.

I am most cordially yours,
L. Sterne

MS: Not located.
Pub.: Medalle, no. 93; Curtis, no. 202.

[a]Hall] H.... *M* [b]Dillon] D... *M* [c]Newnhams] —— *M* [d]James] J—— *M*

1. my riding out, etc.] Cf. *BJ,* 208 (June 28): "I am going to ride myself into better health & better fancies, with Hall—whose Castle lying near the Sea—We have a Beach as even as a mirrour of 5 miles in Length before it, where we dayly run races in our Chaises, with one wheel in the Sea, & the other on the Sand . . . ."

2. Dillon] See letter 208. Cf. *BJ,* 210 (June 30): "Dillon has obtain'd his fair Indian—& has this post wrote a kind Letter of enquiry after Yorick and his Bramine—he is a good Soul—& interests himself much in our fate . . . ." Curtis, 368, n. 7, argues that Eliza certainly knew the bride; "fair Indian" would seem to indicate an English woman from India, but see letter 208, n. 1. Possibly Sterne speaks metaphorically, comparing Dillon's affair with that of "Yorick and his Bramine."

3. the Newnhams] Medalle's usual suppression of the name is echoed by Curtis, 369, but there can be no doubt that Sterne is rehearsing the "story" he had told in letter 199; see esp. nn. 7 and 9.

4. the other side of Temple-bar] The gate separated the Strand from Fleet Street and was erected by Wren, 1670–72; Sterne would seem to be sneering at the business connections of the Newnhams. The remnants of rebel heads from the '45 were still visible at the top of the gate in the 1760s.

5. from sun rise, etc.] Cf. *BJ,* 215–16 (July 7): "I sh[d] write from sun rise to Sun set to thee—But a Book to write—a Wife to receive & make Treaties with—an

estate to sell—a Parish to superintend—and a disquieted heart perpetually to reason with, are eternal calls upon me . . . ."

6. an estate to sell] Cash, *LY,* 294–95, outlines Sterne's financial concerns at this time, including his desire to "sell the Tindal Farm [purchased by Sterne and Elizabeth in 1744] and his other smaller properties and lay out the money in annuities for [Elizabeth and Lydia]." Cf. *BJ,* 193 (June 2): "This unexpected visit, is . . . to pillage What they can from me. In the first place to sell a small estate I have of sixty p[ds] a year—& lay out the purchase money in joint annuitys for them in the french Funds . . . ." Somewhere in Sterne's litany of "things to do" may be heard an echo of Tristram's similar complaint, *TS,* IV.32.400: "I have a thing to name—a thing to lament—a thing to hope—a thing to promise, and a thing to threaten . . . ."

7. I have receiv'd, etc.] Cf. *BJ,* 214–15 (July 5), where Sterne turns a mundane response into a romantic gesture: "tho I've rec[d] half a dozen Letters to press me to join my friends at Scarborough— . . . I've found pretences not to quit You *here*—and sacrifice the many sweet Occasions I have of giving my thoughts up to You—, for Company I cannot rellish *since I have tasted* my dear Girl, the *sweets of thine.*—" For Scarborough, see letter 73, n. 12, and passim. Sterne would accept the invitations by early September, but even before that, on July 19, he went to Harrogate to drink the waters for a week (*BJ* 221).

214. *To Ignatius Sancho*

Text: Ms.

[Tuesday,] June 30 [1767]

I must acknowledge the Courtesy of my good Friend Sancho's Letter, were I ten times busier than I am, & must thank ^him too^ for the many expressions of his good Will, and good Opinion—'tis all affectation to say a man is not gratified with being praised—we only want it to be sincere—and ^then^ it will be taken, Sancho, as kindly as yours. I left Town very poorly & with[a] an Idea I was taking Leave of it for ever[b]—but good air—a quiet retreat; & quiet reflections along with it, with an asse to milk[1] and an other to ride out upon (If I chuse it) all together, do wonders—I shall live this year at least, I hope, be it but to give the world before I quit it, as good impressions of ^me^, as you have Sancho. I would only covenant for just so much health & spirits as are sufficient to carry my pen thro' the Task[2] I have set it this summer—But I am a resign'd Being, Sancho, and take health & Sickness—<just> as I do light and darkness—or the Vicissitudes of Seasons. ˅That | is,˅ just as it pleases God to send them—and accommodate my self to their periodical returns as well as I can—only taking care, whatever befalls me in this silly world—not to lose my temper at it—This I believe Friend Sancho to be the truest philosophy, for this we must be indebted to ourselves, < ?>~but not~ to our fortunes—[3]

farewell—I hope you will not forget y[r] Custome of giving me a Call at my Lodgings next Winter: in the[c] mean time, I am very cordially

my honest friend Sancho, Y[rs]

L. Sterne

MS: Kenneth Monkman Collection, Shandy Hall.

Pub.: Medalle, no. 87; Curtis, no. 203; Peter de Voogd, "The Letters of Laurence Sterne," *Shandean* 4 (1992): 185–86 (facsimile, fig. 54).

[a]poorly & with] poorly [ ] | with *MS* [ms. torn] [b]for ever] for [ ] | *MS* [ms. torn] [c]Winter: in the] Winter: | [ ] the *MS* [ms. torn]

1. asse to milk] Cf. *BJ*, 202 (June 16): "I have bought a milch Asse this Afternoon—& purpose to live by Suction, to save the expences of houskeeping . . . ."

2. the Task] The writing of *ASJ*, which, according to Richard Griffith, he called his "work of redemption" (see letter 229, n. 3).

3. But I . . . fortunes] Sterne paraphrases the conclusion of sermon 15 ("Job's expostulation with his wife"):

> in whatever state we are, we shall find a mixture of good and evil; and therefore the true way to contentment, is to know how to receive these certain vicissitudes of life,—the returns of good and evil, so as neither to be exalted by the one, or overthrown by the other, but to bear ourselves . . . with such ease and indifference of mind, as to hazard as little as may be. . . .
>
> God, for wise reasons, has made our affairs in this world, almost as fickle and capricious as ourselves.----Pain and pleasure, like light and darkness, succeed each other; and he that knows how to accommodate himself to their periodical returns, and can wisely extract the good from the evil,——knows only how to live:——this is true contentment, at least all that is to be had of it in this world,

and for this every man must be indebted not to his fortune but to himself. (*Sermons* 4:148–49)

215. *To Anne and William James*

Text: Medalle

Coxwould, [Monday,] July 6, 1767.

It is with as much true gratitude as ever heart felt, that I sit down to thank my dear friends Mr. and Mrs. James[a] for the continuation of their attention to me; but for this last instance of their humanity and politeness to me, I must ever be their debtor—I never can thank you enough, my dear friends, and yet I thank you from my soul—and for the single day's happiness your goodness would have sent me, I wish I could send you back thousands—I cannot, but they will come of themselves—and so God bless you.—I have had twenty times my pen in my hand since I came down to write one letter to you both in Gerrard-street—but I am a shy kind of a soul at the bottom, and have a jealousy about troubling my friends, especially about myself.—I am now got perfectly well, but was a month after my arrival in the country in but a poor state—my body has got the start, and is at present more at ease than my mind—but this world is a school of trials, and so heaven's will be done!—I hope you have both enjoyed all that I have wanted—and to compleat your joy, that your little lady[1] flourishes like a vine[2] at your table, to which I hope to see her preferred by next winter.—I am now beginning to be truly busy at my Sentimental Journey—the pains and sorrows of this life having retarded its progress—but I shall make up my lee-way, and overtake every body in a very short time.—

What can I send you that Yorkshire produces? tell me—I want to be of use to you, for I am, my dear friends, with the truest value and esteem,

your ever obliged,
L. Sterne

MS: Not located.
Pub.: Medalle, no. 94; Curtis, no. 204.

[a]James] J—— *M*

1. little lady] Curtis, 375, n. 2: "Elizabeth Anne, who was born 2 Aug. 1766, . . . was the sole surviving daughter of [the Jameses]. . . . She died 18 Jan. 1797." The absence of any mention of Eliza in this letter may be the result of Lydia's editorial excisions or of Sterne's waning interest.

2. flourishes like a vine] Cf. Hosea 14:7: "they shall revive as the corn, and grow as the vine."

216. *To Reverend Sir*[1]

Text: Ms.

Coxwould [Saturday,] July 18. 1767[2]

Rev[d] Sir

I am directed by his Grace the Lord Arch Bishop of York to require you to send in a List of the papists or reputed papists within y[r] parish wth all convenient Speed, & that you do it according to the manner pointed out by Order of the house of Lords

I am
Rev[d] S[r]
Y[r] aff[te] Brother
L. Sterne

The List to be sent in to the Dean's Register Office York

MS: York Minster Library.
Pub.: Cash, *LY,* 363.

1. *Reverend Sir*] Cash, *LY*, 363, provides a full account of this hitherto unpublished note:

> This is one of seven nearly identical notes now at the Minster Library. There were originally eight. Sterne intended them to be sent to the clergy of the various parishes which reported to the Peculiar Court of the Dean of York, of which Sterne had been the commissary, or judge, from 1751. On 22 May 1767 the House of Lords had ordered "That an humble Address be presented to his Majesty, 'That He will be Graciously pleased to give Directions to the Archbishops and Bishops, to procure from their Parochial Clergy, and . . . from all Persons invested with Peculiar

Jurisdictions . . . as correct and complete Lists as can be obtained of the Papists or reputed Papists, within the same . . . .'" With each of Sterne's notes is a printed notice of the resolution and of the letter sent to Archbishop Robert Hay Drummond by the Secretary of State, Lord Shelburne. This investigation to determine the numbers of Catholics was quite routine, carried out in the manner of earlier investigations in 1706, 1735 and 1743.

The proposal was introduced by William Bouverie (1725–1776), who had been created Earl of Radnor in 1765; either he or his brother, Edward, subscribed to *Sermons* (1760; "Hon. Mr. Bouverie"); and definitely the latter in 1766 ("Mr. Bouverie"). Cf. Walpole, *Memoirs . . . George III,* 3:143: "the Earl of Radnor proposed that the bishops should give in the numbers of Papists in their several dioceses, which was ordered—and much evaded by the Catholics. In fact there was no singular increase of that sect. Many Jesuits had fled hither on the demolition of their order [1762]; but it was not a moment to make Popery formidable. It was wearing out in England by the loss of their chief patrons the Catholic peers . . . ." Cash, *LY,* 364, n. 2, provides the figures for the diocese, 6,583 Catholics, a substantial increase over the 5,012 reported in 1743; a memorandum explaining the increase as the result of the inadequacies of previous surveys is attached to the document, Cash notes. See also the more extensive discussion of this survey, and Drummond's part in it, in Jago, *Aspects of the Georgian Church,* 183–88.

Sterne's multiple copies have variant readings (e.g., "A. Bishop," "require of you," "in the Order"), but none of any significance.

2. Date] Sterne's date is undoubtedly the date of composition, but subsequent correspondence (see letter 219, and *LY* 364, n. 2) indicates that Sterne did not post the notes until August 7—when it was already too late.

217. *To Isaac Panchaud*

Text: Medalle

York, [Tuesday,] July 28, 1767.[1]

My dear Panchaud[a]

Be so kind as to forward what letters are arrived for Mrs. Sterne[b] at your office by to-day's post, or the next, and she will receive them before she quits Avignon, for England—she wants to lay out a little money in an annuity for her daughter—advise her to get her own life ensured in London, lest my Lydia should die before her.—If there are any packets, send them with the ninth volume of Shandy, which she has failed of getting—she says she has drawn for fifty louis—when she leaves Paris, send by her my account.—Have you got me any French subscriptions, or subscriptions in France?[2]—Present my kindest service to Miss Panchaud[a] I know her politeness and good nature will incline her to give Mrs. James[c] her advice about what she may venture to bring over.[3]——I hope every thing goes on well, though never half so well as I wish.——God prosper you, my dear friend—Believe me most warmly

Yours,
L. Sterne

The sooner you send me the gold snuff box, the better—'tis a present[4] from my best friend.

MS: Not located.
Pub.: Medalle, no. 95; Curtis, no. 205.

[a]Panchaud] P. *M* [b]Sterne] S. *M* [c]James] J. *M*

1. Date] Medalle dates this letter "York, July 20, 1767," but Sterne was then at Harrogate (see *BJ* 221: "July 19. Harrogate Spaws.—drinking the waters here till the 26th"). He returned to York for the Races on July 27 (*BJ* 222). Curtis, 383, assumes, and we agree, that Lydia misread Sterne's "28" as "20."

2. Have you . . . France] Sterne's French friends who had subscribed to *Sermons* (1766)—Diderot, d'Holbach, Voltaire—are not listed for *ASJ,* but Panchaud subscribed himself for twenty copies, suggesting that he had been quite busy soliciting Sterne's friends in France.

3. I know . . . to bring over] We assume, as does Curtis, that Sterne was soliciting advice for the Jameses, who were intending to travel; see letter 218, for what may be the suggestion that a journey to France with Sterne was planned for the winter of 1768—or possibly 1769. Sterne seems to have been urging Mrs. James to repair her health in the south of France.

4. a present] See letter 220 for Sterne's unedited account of this snuffbox. Curtis, 383, n. 2, comments: "This sentence is suspiciously suggestive of Lydia's interference with Sterne's original remarks about the gift of a snuff-box."

218. *To Anne and William James*

Text: Medalle

Coxwould, [Sunday,] August 2, 1767.

My dear friends Mr. and Mrs. James[a] are infinitely kind to me in sending now and then a letter to enquire after me—and to acquaint me how they are.—You cannot conceive, my dear lady, how truly I bear a part in your illness.—I wish Mr. James[a] would carry you to the south of France in pursuit of health—but why need I wish it when I know his affection will make him do that and ten times as much to prevent a return of those symptoms which alarmed him so much in the spring[1]—Your politeness and humanity is always contriving to treat me agreeably, and what you promise next winter, will be perfectly so—but you must get well—and your little dear girl must be of the party with her parents and friends to give it a relish—I am sure you shew no partiality but what is natural and praise-worthy in behalf of your daughter, but I wonder my friends will not find her a play-fellow, and I both hope and advise them not to venture along through this warfare of life without two strings at least to their bow.[2]—I had letters from France by last night's post, by which (by some fatality) I find not one of my letters has reached Mrs. Sterne.[b] This gives me concern, as it wears the aspect of unkindness, which she by no means merits from me.[3]—My wife and dear girl are coming to pay me a visit for a few months; I wish I may prevail with them to tarry longer.—You must permit me, dear Mrs. James[a] to make my Lydia known to you, if I can prevail with my wife to come and spend a little time in London, as she returns to France.—I expect a small parcel[4]—may I trouble you before you write next to send to my lodgings to ask if there is any thing directed to me that you can enclose under cover?—I have but one excuse for this freedom which I am prompted to use from a persuasion that it is doing you pleasure to give you an opportunity of doing an obliging thing—and as to myself I rest satisfied, for 'tis only scoring up another debt of thanks to the millions I owe you both already—Receive a thousand and a thousand thanks, yes and with them ten thousand friendly wishes for all you wish in this world—May my friend Mr.

James[a] continue bless'd with good health, and may his good lady get perfectly well, there being no woman's health or comfort I so ardently pray for.—Adieu my dear friends—believe me most truly and faithfully yours,

L. Sterne

PS

In Eliza's last letter dated from St. Jago[5] she tells me, as she does you, that she is extremely ill—God protect her.—By this time surely she has set foot upon dry land at Madras—I heartily wish her well, and if Yorick was with her, he would tell her so—but he is cut off from this, by bodily absence—I am present with her in spirit however—but what is that you will say?

MS: Not located.
Pub.: Medalle, no. 96; Curtis, no. 206.

[a]James] J— / J. *M* [b]Sterne.] S— *M*

1. those symptoms . . . spring] See letter 204, esp. nn. 1 and 5.

2. two strings . . . bow] Proverbial; see Tilley, S937, and *ODEP,* 852, citing, among others, Smollett, *Humphry Clinker* (1771): "A right Scotchman has always two strings to his bow, and is *in utrumque paratus* [prepared for any alternative]" (ed. Preston, 117). Sterne's usage here, urging the Jameses to have a second child, may suggest residual regret over the loss of his own offspring, excepting Lydia (see Cash, *EMY* 134–35); it is a situation confronted by the Shandys as well, with the death of Bobby.

3. last night's post . . . from me] As Curtis, 386, n. 2, argues, Sterne "is fibbing"; in *BJ,* 214 (July 5), he had reported the same fact in much the same language: "Two Letters from the South of France by this post, by which, by some fatality, I find not one of my Letters have got to them this month—This gives me concern—because it has the Aspect of an unseasonable unkindness in me." At this point, however, the *Journal* and letter diverge, and Sterne is not so generous: "my daughter besides has not deserved ill of me—& tho' her mother has . . . ."

The suggestion by New and Day (*ASJ* 6:415, n. to 214.3–6) that Lydia may have simply misdated the letter is almost certainly not feasible in light of the postscript: Eliza's letter reached Sterne on July 27. It is quite likely that Lydia is guilty of some major manipulation in this letter—rather than that Sterne is again recycling material, having waited to inform the Jameses of the impending visit only when hope of its not happening had been lost.

4. a small parcel] Perhaps the snuffbox mentioned in letter 217.

5. St. Jago] For St. Jago, see letter 201, n. 6. Madras is on the east coast of India; the *Lord Chatham* would then sail around the tip of India, along the Malabar Coast up to Bombay on the west coast. According to Wright and Sclater, 60, Eliza did not arrive at Madras until the middle of October.

219. *To John Clough*[1]

Text: Ms.

Coxwould [Friday,] Aug. 7. 67

Dear Sir

——I have sent 8 Letters to the Clergy of the Dean's Jurisdiction—I know not whether I have wrote a sufficient Number—if not, let me know. & in the mean time direct the Inclosed,[2] & get them sent.

y^rs

L. Sterne

MS: York Minster Library.
Endorsed: Mr Sterne—7th Augst / 1767—and my answer Inclos'd
Pub.: Cash, *LY*, 363–64.

1. *John Clough*] John Clough, registrar of the deanery court and to the dean and chapter of York Minster since 1755; see letter 14, n. 1.

2. the Inclosed] This is, then, the cover letter for letter 216, which the registrar obviously received too late; nor had Sterne written a sufficient number, as Clough's testy answer, dated "York 8th Augt 1767" implies (quoted in Cash, *LY* 364, n. 2):

> The 9th of last Month the AB^p Wrote to the D. & C. requiring them to procure Lists of the papists from their parochial Clergy. . . . The D. & C. ordered me to get the Inclosed printed and the Dean directed me to get the Letter Signed by him printed, and one of each has been sent to the respective Clergy . . . and by this I make no Doubt but his Grace has had returns made confirmable thereto from some of the Clergy—please to let me know what you would have me do with the Let^s you sent me . . . . P.S. You have above double the Number of places within the Deanry

> than you inclosed Lets for—Mr Stables [a York lawyer, commissary of the peculiar court of the dean and chapter] who has hitherto done such business as chanced to be in Court, for you, as the Dean's official lately hinted he wou'd do so no longer. The reason I know not. When you come to York I shall be glad of an opportunity of talking wth you upon the Subject.

It would seem that Sterne was being called to task.

220. *To Anne James*

Text: Ms.

Coxwould [Monday,] Augst 10. 1767[1]

My dear friends.

I but copy your great civility to me—in writing you word, that I have this moment recd another Letter, wrote eighteen days after the date of the last, from St Iago—If Our poor friend could have wrote another Letter to England, You will in course have it[a]—but I fear from the circumstance of great hurry, and bodily disorder when she dispatch'd <this>~it~[b] She might not have time—In Case it has so fallen out—I send you the contents of wtc I have recd—<namely>~and~ that is a melancholly history of herself and sufferings since they left Iago—continual & most violent rhumatism all the time—a fever brought on—with fits—and attended with Delirium: & every terrifying symptome—the recovery from this <left>~has~ left her[d] low—and emaciated to a Skeleton—I give you the pain of this detail with a bleeding heart—knowing how much at the same time it will affect yours—The three or four last days in[e] her journal,[2] leave us with hopes she will do well at last—for she is more chearful, and seems to be getting up her Spirits[f]—& health in course with it[g].—They have cross'd the Line—are much becalm'd—wch with other delays, <I>~——~She fears, they will lose their passage to <Bombay> Madrass—& be some months sooner for it, at Bombay[3]—Heaven protect this worthy creature![h] for She suffers much, & with uncommon fortitude—She writes much to me abt her dear friend Mrs James[i] in her last Packet—in truth, my good Lady, she honours & loves[j] You from her heart—but if She did not—I should not, Love[k] her half so well <half so well> ∧myself∧ as[l] I do. <myself>~———~

adieu my dear friends—you
have very few[m] in the world, more
truely & cordially Yrs
L. Sterne

PS

I have just recd as a present from a right Honble———a[n] most elegant gold Snuff box[o] fabricated for me at Paris[4]—I wish Eliza was here—I would lay it at her feet—however I will enrich my gold Box, with her picture,<?>~——~& if the Donor does not approve of such an acquisition to his pledge of friendship———I will send him his Box again—[5]

May I presume to inclose you the Letter, I write to Mrs Draper—[6]<?> I know you will write yourself—& my Letter may have the honour to chaprone yours to India. Mrs Sterne & my daughter are coming to stay a couple of months with me, as[p] far as from Avignion—& then return—Here's Complaisance for you I went 500 Miles the last Spring, out of my Way, to pay my Wife a weeks <visit> ∧Visit∧—and She is at the expence of coming post a thousand miles to return it<:>~———~ What a happy pair!———however, *en passant,*[7] She takes back sixteen hundred pds into france—∧with her———∧ and will do me the honour, <every thing> ∧likewise∧ to strip me of every thing I have—

—except Eliza's Picture.
Adieu

Address: To / Mrs James in Gerard street / Soho / London / Free / ffauconberg[8]
Postmark: EASINGWOULD 12 AV FREE
MS: British Library, Addit. MSS. 34527, 41–42.
Pub.: Medalle, no. 98; Gibbs, *Some Memorials,* 18–19; *Athenaeum* (March 30, 1878): 412; Curtis, no. 208.

[a]will . . . have it] would . . . have had it *M* [b]disorder when she dispatch'd <this>~it~] disorder in which she was, when she dispatched this *M* [c]contents of wt] contents wh *C* [d]this <left>~has~ left her] this left her *M* [e]in] of *M* [f]up her Spirits] into better spirits *M* [g]health in course with it] health will follow in course *M* [h]protect

this worthy creature!] protect her, *M* [i]James] J—— *M* [j]honours & loves] loves and honours *M* [k]Love] esteem *M* [l]her half so well . . . as] her, or wish her so well as *M* [m]have very few] have few *M* [n]from a right Hon[ble]——a] from a man I shall ever love, a *M* [o]Snuff box] Snuff *MS;* snuff box *M;* snuff [box] *C* [p]months with me, as] month with, as *MS* [ms. torn]

1. Date] Possibly the ms. reading is August "16" rather than "10"; Lydia seems to have noted the difficulty and opted to date the letter between the two possible dates. Of this letter, Curtis, 389, writes: "Lydia's text of this letter contains a glaring example of her habit of correcting or omitting Sterne's phrases. Warm allusions to Mrs. Draper are cooled and uncomplimentary remarks about her mother are cancelled." This is obviously correct, as her version of the postscript attests, but it is interesting to note also how carefully she preserves what she can, despite this constant stylistic tinkering and desire to conceal her father's less attractive moments—in the eyes of a daughter and a wife, and perhaps many readers as well. We have recorded the substantive differences between Medalle and our text in the collation, but see also nn. 5 and 6.

2. The three . . . journal] We can assume, with Wright and Sclater, 60, that "after leaving St. Jago, probably when in the region of the Doldrums," Eliza's ship had encountered another vessel and transferred its mail, including "the second part of Eliza's journal" (the first had arrived on July 27; see above, letter 201, n. 6). Although nothing is known about this packet except what Sterne tells us here, it is worth pointing out that when Eliza wrote to her cousin Thomas Limbrey Sclater, from St. Jago on May 2, she reported that "Health too . . . is once more return'd to her enthusiastic Votary. I am all life and air and spirits" (61). One suspects Eliza's primary ailment was seasickness.

3. at Bombay] See above, letter 218, n. 5. Eliza stayed at Madras for some six weeks before sailing for Bombay, where she arrived in January 1768; see Wright and Sclater, 60ff. Crossing "the Line" is, of course, crossing the Equator.

4. I have just . . . at Paris] Curtis, 389, n. 2, suggests Sir George Macartney; see below, letter 235. This would appear to be the snuffbox Sterne wrote about to Panchaud, letter 217. Cf. *Athenaeum,* 412: "It was quite excusable in the 'sprightly' Lydia, as editor of her father's correspondence, omitting the sarcastic allusion to his wife and daughter's impending visit, or cutting out the dedication of its golden shrine to Eliza's miniature. Yet why the 'Rt. Honble.' should be sentimentalized into 'a man I shall ever love,' one cannot quite discover."

5. I wish Eliza . . . Box again] Lydia had already emended "worthy creature" to "her" and "Love her" to "esteem her," but she now begins her protective rewriting in earnest. This entire passage is deleted and replaced, from the hint of "pledge of

friendship," with a sentence without justification in the manuscript: "'tis not the first pledge I have received of his friendship."

6. May I presume . . . Draper] Medalle: "May I presume to enclose you a letter of chit-chat which I shall write to Eliza?" The entire discussion concerning the impending visit is then erased, and in its place is another invention: "They will neither of them [i.e., the two letters] be the worse received for going together in company, but I fear they will get late in the year to their destined port, as they go first to Bengal."

Sterne had used "chit-chat" ("Prattle; idle prate; idle talk. A word only used in ludicrous conversation," *Johnson's Dictionary)* in *TS,* III.24.246: "opificers of chit chat."

7. *en passant*] In passing, by the way. Sterne may, perhaps, be playing on the idea that her "passing" through Coxwold will greatly enrich her; £1,600 seems, however, an overstatement.

8. Free / ffauconberg] Members of parliament were entitled to "frank" letters that could then be sent free of charge, a perquisite Lord Fauconberg apparently extended to Sterne (see letters 224 and 231). In 1764 the privilege (which had been much abused) was restricted by statute for the first time. Howard Robinson, *The British Post Office: A History* (Princeton: Princeton University Press, 1948), 116–18, has a good discussion of the practice and its abuse. The use of "ff" for capital "F" is quite old-fashioned and perhaps an affectation in 1767, but it would appear to have been Fauconberg's affectation, not Sterne's (see letter 231: *Address).*

221. *To John Hall-Stevenson*

Text: Medalle

Coxwould, [Tuesday,] August 11, 1767.

My dear Hall[a]

I am glad all has passed with so much amity *inter te & filium Marcum tuum,*[1] and that Madame[2] has found grace in thy sight—All is well that ends well—and so much for moralizing upon it. I wish you could, or would, take up your parable, and prophecy as much good concerning me and my affairs.—Not one of my letters have got to Mrs. Sterne[b] since the notification of her intentions, which has a pitiful air on my side, though I have wrote her six or seven.—I imagine she will be here the latter end of September, though I have no date for it, but her impatience, which having suffered by my supposed silence I am persuaded will make her fear the worst—if that is the case she will fly to England—a most natural conclusion.—You did well to discontinue all commerce with James's powder[3]—as you are so well, rejoice therefore, and let your heart be merry—mine ought upon the same score—for I never have been so well since I left college—and should be a marvellous happy man, but for some reflections which bow down my spirits—but if I live but even three or four years, I will acquit myself with honour—and—no matter! we will talk this over when we meet.——If all ends as temperately as with you, and that I find grace, &c. &c. I will come and sing Te Deum,[4] or drink *poculum elevatum*,[5] or do any thing with you in the world.[6]—I should depend upon G—'s critick upon my head, as much as Moliere's old woman upon his comedies[7]—when you do not want her society let it be carried into your bed-chamber to flay her, or clap it upon her bum—to——and give her my blessing as you do it——

My postillion has set me a-ground for a week by one of my pistols bursting in his hand, which he taking for granted to be quite shot off—he instantly fell upon his knees and said (Our Father, which art in Heaven, hallowed be thy Name) at which, like a good Christian, he stopped, not remembering any more of it—the affair was not so bad as he at first thought, for it has only *bursten*[8] two of his fingers (he says).—I long to return to you, but I sit here alone as solitary and sad as a tom cat, which by the bye is all the company I keep[9]—he follows me from the parlour, to the kitchen, into the garden, and every place—I wish I had a dog—my daughter will bring me one—and so God be about you, and strengthen your faith—I am affectionately, dear cousin, yours,

L. S.

My service to the C....[c] though they are from home, and to Panty.[10]

MS: Not located.
Pub.: Medalle, no. 97; Curtis, no. 209.

[a]Hall] H. *M* [b]Sterne] S— *M* [c]C....] C[haloners] *C*

1. *inter te & filium Marcum tuum*] Between you and your son Mark. Hall-Stevenson's second son was named Joseph William (1741–1786), "Mark" being, we assume, Sterne's joking allusion to Hall-Stevenson's nickname, Antony.

2. Madame] As is almost always the case with Sterne's letters to Hall-Stevenson, there is a shorthand allusiveness between friends that defies editorial certainty, especially in the absence of Hall-Stevenson's half of the correspondence. We may guess that Hall-Stevenson had quarreled with his son about his marriage (before 1766) to Anne Forster, of Drumgoon, Co. Fermanagh, and that they had now been reconciled; this seems to have been deduced by Curtis, 390, n. 2, as well. The most apt parable for Hall-Stevenson to have cited would probably be that of the prodigal son.

3. James's powder] See letter 205A, n. 2.

4. Te Deum] *Te deum laudamus* ("We praise thee, O God") are the first words and title of a hymn attributed (probably incorrectly) to St. Ambrose and sung following a victory; Sterne invokes it in *TS*, I.18.55, when the debate over the use of the midwife is settled and "both sides sung *Te Deum*"; cf. *TS*, VIII.28.713. The *BCP* calls for the hymn to be sung during the Morning Service.

5. drink *poculum elevatum*] The slightly blasphemous play on words could be translated: "a wee drink in a raised chalice." The *elevatum*, or raising of the host and chalice during the Eucharist, is a particularly sanctified moment of the ritual.

6. or do any thing . . . world] Cf. *ASJ*, 44, where Yorick affirms that when he is in love, "I am all generosity and good will again; and would do any thing in the world either for, or with any one, if they will but satisfy me there is no sin in it."

7. Moliere's old woman . . . comedies] Molière (like Swift) was in the habit of reading his texts out loud before his old servant, La Foret. Curtis, 391, n. 3, cites Le Gallois de Grimarest, Molière's earliest biographer (*La Vie de Moliere* [Paris, 1710], 1:31), but the practice was chronicled in all biographies of Molière.

Sterne's allusion is not entirely clear, nor for that matter who "G—" is. One candidate is Ralph Griffiths (1720–1803), who, as editor of the *Monthly Review*, had been quite critical of Sterne, but more favorably inclined toward Hall-Stevenson, at least his work in the early sixties: "when Tristram Shandy went to France he certainly left his mantle with his natural brother in jocularity" (cited by Hartley, "Sterne's Eugenius," 436, quoting *MR* [1764]: 415); see, however, letter 179, n. 1, *MR*'s very negative response to the author of an attack on Warburton, perhaps written by Hall-Stevenson. Or, possibly, Sterne was invoking the Bishop of Gloucester himself; Hall-Stevenson certainly remembered him when he wrote a tribute to Sterne in his *Makarony Fables* (1768): "My good Lord Bishop, Mr.

Dean, / You shall get nothing by your spite; / Tristram shall whistle at your spleen, / And put Hypocrisy to flight" (*Works* [1795], 1:202).

8. *bursten*] This form of the past participle of "burst" ("shattered, broken") is considered obsolete by *OED*, which notes, however, that it is "still sometimes used attrib., esp. in poetical or rhetorical language." Steele (1712) and Thomas Carlyle (1843) are among examples cited.

9. tom cat . . . I keep] Cf. *BJ*, 216 (July 8): "as melancholly & sad as a Cat; . . . by the by, I have got one which sits quietly besides me, purring all day to my sorrows—& looking up gravely from time to time in my face, as if she knew my Situation." For Lydia's dog, see next letter.

10. My service . . . Panty] Curtis, 390, suggests the "Chaloners," which seems likely enough; see letters 75, n. 11, and 99, n. 18. "Panty" is, of course, Robert Lascelles; see letter 73, n. 7.

222. *To Lydia Sterne*

Text: Medalle

Coxwould, [Monday,] August 24, 1767.

I am truly surprised, my dear Lydia, that my last letter has not reached thy mother, and thyself—it looks most unkind on my part, after your having wrote me word of your mother's intention of coming to England, that she has not received my letter to welcome you both—and though in that I said I wished you would defer your journey 'till March, for before that time I should have published my sentimental work, and should be in town to receive you—yet I will shew you more real politesses than any you have met with in France, as mine will come warm from the heart.[1]—I am sorry you are not here at the races,[2] but *les fêtes champêtres* of the Marquis de Sade[3] have made you amends.—I know B—— very well, and he is what in France would be called *admirable*[a4]—that would be but so so here—You are right—he studies nature more than any, or rather most of the French comedians—If the Empress of Russia[5] pays him and his wife a pension of twenty thousand livres a year, I think he is very well off.—The folly of staying 'till after twelve for supper—that you two excommunicated beings might have meat![6]—"his conscience would not let it be served before."—

Surely the Marquis thought you both, being English, could not be satisfied without it.—I would have given not my gown and cassock (for I have but one) but my topaz ring[7] to have seen the *petits maitres et maitresses*[8] go to mass, after having spent the night in dancing.—As to my pleasures they are few in compass.—My poor cat sits purring beside me—your lively French dog shall have his place on the other side of my fire—but if he is as devilish as when I last saw him, I must tutor him, for I will not have my cat abused—in short I will have nothing devilish about me—a combustion would spoil a sentimental thought.

Another thing I must desire—do not be alarmed—'tis to throw all your rouge pots into the Sorgue before you set out—I will have no rouge put on in England—and do not bewail them as —— —— did her silver *seringue*[b] or glyster *equipage*[c] which she lost in a certain river[9]—but take a wise resolution of doing without rouge.—I have been three days ago bad again—with a spitting of blood—and that unfeeling brute ******* came and drew my curtains, and with a voice like a trumpet, halloo'd in my ear—zounds[d], what a fine kettle of fish have you brought yourself to, Mr. Sterne[e]![10] In a faint voice, I bad him leave me, for comfort sure was never administered in so rough a manner.—Tell your mother I hope she will purchase what either of you may want at Paris—'tis an occasion not to be lost—so write to me from Paris that I may come and meet you in my post-chaise with my long-tailed horses[11]—and the moment you have both put your feet in it, call it hereafter yours.—Adieu dear Lydia—believe me, what I ever shall be,

Your affectionate father,
L. Sterne

I think I shall not write to Avignon any more, but you will find one for you at Paris—once more adieu.

MS: Not located.
Pub.: Medalle, no. 99; Curtis, no. 210.

[a]*admirable*] admirable *M* [b]*seringue*] seringue *M* [c]*equipage*] equipage *M* [d]zounds] z- - -ds *M* [e]Mr. Sterne] Mr. S—— *M*

1. politesses . . . heart] Cf. letters 97, n. 2, 153, n. 10, and 196, n. 9. It is quite possible that Sterne wrote this letter while writing about Yorick's discussion with the Count de B**** (*ASJ* 118–19), in which the excessive politeness of the French is distinguished from the "*politesse de cœur,* which inclines men more to humane actions, than courteous ones." See also letter 235, where the word is used quite ironically to characterize Elizabeth's visit. And see letter 226 for Sterne's assertion that *ASJ* will prove that his feelings come "from the heart."

2. races] Race Week in York in 1767 was held from Monday, August 17, to Saturday, August 22. For Sterne's deceptive dating in his journal of his attendance there, see *BJ,* 222.8–11, and n. to 222.11 (6:420–21). Curtis, 392, n. 2, garners from the *York Courant* (August 25, 1767) an impressive list of those Sterne would have met there: Lady Bingley, Lady Mary Belasyse, the Cholmleys, the Crofts, the Turners, Francis Delaval, Henry Errington, Hall-Stevenson, the Marquis and Marchioness of Rockingham, the Thornhills, and Dr. Topham, among others.

3. *les fêtes champêtres* of the Marquis de Sade] Rural feasts, probably far more elaborate than the "feast of love" described in *ASJ,* 157–58 ("The Supper"). For the Sternes' acquaintance with the Sades in Avignon, see letter 194, nn. 5 and 7; neither Sterne nor Lydia could possibly have imagined how a "rural feast" with the notorious marquis would strike later generations.

4. *admirable*] As with *seringue* and *equipage* below, Sterne is using a French word, and we have accordingly italicized all three words. Sterne was consistent in suggesting that the French language tended toward hyperbole (see letter 86, n. 3).

5. B—— . . . Empress of Russia] Catherine II (the Great, 1729–1796) became Empress of Russia in 1762; she was an admirer of Sterne (see Maria Lobytsyna, "Sterne and Russian Fictional Memoirs, 1770–1790," *Shandean* 11 [1999]: 98–111) and of English and French culture more generally. In private correspondence Ms. Lobytsyna has concurred with the suggestion of Anne Bandry that B—— may be Beaumarchais (Pierre-Augustin Caron de, 1732–1799), who had strong ties to the empress; his play *Eugénie* had been published earlier in the year, but his best-known—and perhaps most-Shandean—works, *Barber of Seville* and *Marriage of Figaro,* remained in the future. Sterne's B—— seems to have been an actor or playwright, but Catherine's most famous invitation was extended to John Brown, author of *Estimate of the Manners and Principles of the Times* (1757), who committed suicide shortly thereafter (1766), presumably because his doctors would not let him accept the invitation. Walpole, *Memoirs . . . George III,* 2:97, reports this gossip, which would certainly have reached Sterne's ears.

6. might have meat] The marquis had obviously stereotyped his British guests as "beef-eaters," just as Tristram had characterized the French menu as "sallad

and soup—soup and sallad—sallad and soup, *encore*" in *TS*, VII.17.600. The event would have taken place on Friday, when meat was proscribed for Roman Catholics—at midnight, meat could finally be served.

7. not my gown . . . topaz ring] Sterne had bet by his cassock (or cassocks) in letter 177, as had Tristram in III.11.211; see letter 177, n. 3. The topaz ring would be the same worn by Tristram when writing (*TS* IX.13.763). Sterne probably hoped Lydia did not know topaz was recommended as a sexual depressant; see *TS*, VI.36.563, and *Notes* to *TS*, 3:439–40, n. to 563.19–564.3.

8. *petits maitres et maitresses*] Literally: "little masters and mistresses," but pejoratively used for "fine young gentlemen and ladies." Cf. Smollett (*Travels*, letter 7, 1:110): "Of all the coxcombs on the face of the earth, a French *petit maitre* is the most impertinent: and they are all *petit maitres*, from the marquis who glitters in lace and embroidery, to the *garçon barbier* . . . who struts with his hair in a long queue, and his hat under his arm."

9. throw all . . . certain river] Sterne's distaste for cosmetics is evident in letter 199, when he praises his portrait of Eliza over that painted for the Jameses; and in *ASJ*, 23, when Yorick observes the face of Madame de L***: "it was . . . of a clear transparent brown, simply set off without rouge or powder." Many travelers commented on the lavish use of cosmetics in France, including Smollett (*Travels*, letter 7, 1:104): "As for the *fard*, or *white*, with which their necks and shoulders are plaistered, it may be in some measure excusable, as their skins are naturally brown, or sallow; but the *rouge*, which is daubed on their faces, from the chin up to the eyes, without the least art or dexterity, . . . conveys nothing but ideas of disgust and aversion"; see Lynn Festa, "Cosmetic Differences: The Changing Faces of England and France," *SECC* 34 (2004): 25–54.

Sterne's allusion to the woman who bewailed her loss has eluded us. The lost *equipage* would be for administering clysters, the common treatment for bowel disorders, but also as a douche after intercourse. That Sterne uses French might indicate either an incident he and Lydia observed in France or an episode in a French novel they had both read.

10. that unfeeling brute . . . Mr. Sterne] We have been unable to identify Sterne's visitor, perhaps his doctor. The scene recalls Eugenius's much more kindly visit to Yorick's deathbed: "Upon his drawing *Yorick*'s curtain, and asking how he felt . . ." (*TS* I.12.33).

Zounds, the Elizabethan version of the oath "God's wounds," was famously sworn by Phutatorius in *TS*, IV.27.377; "fine kettle of fish" is proverbial (*ODEP* 420), the first illustration being Fielding, *Joseph Andrews*, ed. Martin Battestin (Middletown, Conn.: Wesleyan University Press, 1967), I.12.57: "Here's a pretty Kettle of Fish . . . you have brought upon us!"

11. long-tailed horses] Sterne echoes the phrase in letter 211.

223. *To Thomas Becket*

Text: Ms.

Coxwould. [Thursday,] Sept. 3/ 67

Dear Sir

I shall take it as a favour if you will send a porter with the Inclosed to the Direction, when[a] it comes to y^{r} hand.

I don't See when I shall have any Occasion for money, so it may lay safe where it is, till I do——But I sh^{d} be obliged to you, if You will settle the little Acc^{t} betwixt us from the time the last was ballanced[b]—& I will draw for that Summ, to leave all straight betwixt us, to the 300 p^{ds}—W^{ch} I hope I shall want not much of till Winter.—my Sentimental Journey goes on well—and some Geniuses[c] <f> in the North declare it an <?> Original work, and likely to take in all Kinds of Readers——the proof of the pudding is in the eating.[1]

I am faithfully Y^{rs},
L. Sterne

Do not forget to send the Letter to day.

Address: To / Mr Becket / Bookseller in the Strand / London
MS: Robert H. Taylor Collection, Princeton University Library.
Pub.: Edward Foss, *N&Q*, 2d ser. 4 (August 1857): 126; Curtis, no. 211.

[a]when] whe *MS* [b]ballanced] ?ballaned *MS* [c]Geniuses] Geniuss *MS*

1. proof . . . the eating] Proverbial; see Tilley, P608 (first listing, *c.*1300), and *ODEP,* 650.

224. *To Hannah*[1]

Text: Ms./Medalle

Coxwould, [Saturday, September][2] 12, 1767.

Ever since my dear Hannah[a] wrote me word she was mine, more than ever woman was, I have been racking my memory to inform me where it was that you and I had that affair together.—People think that I have had many, some in body, some in mind, but as I told you before, you have had me more than any woman—therefore you must have had me, Hannah[a], both in mind, and in body.——Now I cannot recollect where it was, nor exactly when—it could not be the lady in Bond-street, or Grosvenor-street, or ——— Square, or Pall-mall.—We shall make it out, Hannah[a] when we meet—I impatiently long for it——

Tis no matter, Hannah! I[b] cannot stand[c] writing to you to day—Ill make it up next post—for Dinner is upon the Table[d]—& if I make stay Ld Fauconberg[3] wont[e] frank this—how do you do?—which parts of Tristram do you like best?[4]—

god bless you.
Y^{rs} aff
L. Sterne

[on the verso][5]

Mrs Liegh	15: 0: 0
Molly	1: 1: 0
Sally Sparks	0: 3: 6
Water	0: 1: 6
Decr ye 24 ?Buy	2: 15: 6
Frid^{y}	0: 3: 9
B^{k} Loer	0: 7: 6
Paid Bid:	0: 3: 10
Paid Lovisay	0: 2: 7½

MS: Houghton Library, Harvard University, Autograph File (last paragraph and verso only).
Pub.: Medalle, no. 88; Curtis, no. 212.

[a]Hannah] H. / H—— *M* [b]¶Tis no matter, Hannah! I] no ¶ 'tis no matter—I *M* [c]cannot stand] cannot now stand *M* [d]upon the Table] upon | table *M* [e]make stay Ld Fauconberg wont] make Lord F—— stay, he will not *M*

1. *Hannah*] Unidentified. She lived in London, probably (see letter 231) in St. James's Street, had a sister named Fanny (see letter 232), and apparently visited Sterne in his London lodgings on March 16, 1768, shortly before his death (*LY*

327). That Medalle printed this letter suggests that her protective attitude toward her father did have its limits.

2. Date] Medalle has "October 12" but in letter 225, dated September 19, Sterne almost certainly alludes to this very letter, unless several women were writing to him saying they were his "more than ever woman was." We have followed Curtis in dating the letter a month earlier—that is, September 12.

3. Ld Fauconberg] See letter 220, n. 8.

4. which parts . . . best?] The innuendo is hard to avoid, given the many plays on "parts" in eighteenth-century literature, including Fielding's in *Shamela,* when, during the attempted rape scene, Shamela begins to "scratch very liberally . . . without any great Regard to the Parts I attacked" (*Joseph Andrews and Shamela,* ed. D. Brooks-Davies, rev. Thomas Keymer [Oxford: Oxford University Press, 1999], 318); Pope's *Epistle to Dr. Arbuthnot,* l. 333: "Beauty that shocks you, Parts that none will trust"; and, of course, Sterne's "It had ever been the custom of the family . . . that the eldest son of it should have free ingress, egress, and regress into foreign parts before marriage,—not only for the sake of bettering his own private parts, etc." (*TS* V.31.396).

5. verso] On the verso of the ms. is this list of cryptic names (unidentified except that Sterne did have a servant named "Molly") and other entries, deleted with typical Sternean loopings; we have drawn only blanks trying to decipher what is underneath.

225. *To Sir W.*[1]

Text: Medalle

[Coxwold, Saturday,] September 19, 1767.

My dear Sir,

You are perhaps the drollest being in the universe—Why do you banter me so about what I wrote to you?—Tho' I told you, every morning I jump'd into Venus's lap[2] (meaning thereby the sea) was you to infer from that, that I leap'd into the ladies beds afterwards?—The body guides you—the mind me.—I have wrote the most whimsical letter to a lady[3] that was ever read, and talk'd of body and soul too—I said she had made me vain, by saying she was mine more than ever woman was—but she is not the lady of Bond-street nor ——— square, nor the lady who supp'd with me in Bond-street on scollop'd oysters, and other such things—nor did she ever go *tete-a-tete* with me to Salt

Hill.[4]——Enough of such nonsense—The past is over—and I can justify myself unto myself[5]—can you do as much?—No faith!—"You can feel!" Aye so can my cat, when he hears a female caterwauling on the house top—but caterwauling disgusts me. I had rather raise a gentle flame, than have a different one raised in me.[6]—Now, I take heav'n to witness, after all this *badinage*[7] my heart is innocent—and the sporting of my pen is equal, just equal, to what I did in my boyish days, when I got astride of a stick, and gallop'd away—The truth is this—that my pen governs me——not me my pen.[8]—You are much to blame if you dig for marle,[9] unless you are sure of it.—I was once such a puppy myself, as to pare, and burn, and had my labour for my pains,[10] and two hundred pounds out of pocket.—Curse on farming (said I) I will try if the pen will not succeed better than the spade.—The following up of that affair (I mean farming) made me lose my temper, and a cart load of turneps was (I thought) very dear at two hundred pounds.—

In all your operations may your own good sense guide you—bought experience is the devil.[11]—Adieu, adieu!—Believe me

Yours most truly,
L. Sterne

MS: Not located.
Pub.: Medalle, no. 100; Curtis, no. 213.

1. *Sir W.*] Medalle has only "To Sir W."; Cross, *Life* (1909), 439, seems to have been the first to suggest Sir William Stanhope (1702–1772), of Eythrope, Buckinghamshire, the wealthy younger brother of the famous 4th Earl of Chesterfield (1694–1773). Curtis accepts the identification, as does Cash, *LY,* 309–10. Since Stanhope subscribed to *Sermons* in both 1760 and 1769, Sterne may have known him before their paths crossed in Naples in 1766 (see letter 169). He represented Buckinghamshire from 1727 to 1741, and again from 1747 to 1768, was a friend of Wilkes (see Cash, *John Wilkes* 23, 28, 184, 189), and is characterized by Namier and Brooke as a wit, a man of taste, and a collector of art. He had married three times, his last wife being Anne Delaval, for whom, see letter 189; by 1767, they had been separated for four years.

Precisely because Sterne may have been a close friend of Anne Delaval and her circle (see letter 189, n. 6) in the winter of 1767, Sir William Stanhope might not be the most reasonable guess as to the identity of Sir W., and indeed there are a dozen subscribers on Sterne's lists who might also be addressed in that manner. The most likely alternative, we believe, is Sir William Boothby (see letter 189, n. 3). Boothby subscribed to *Sermons* in both 1760 and 1766, and to a large-paper copy of *ASJ* (and is listed, in fact, as Sir W. Boothby). In that Sterne's second letter to Sir W. very particularly mentions the *Journey,* it seems odd that the addressee would not have subscribed (as is the case with Stanhope). Also, although equally circumstantial, Sterne's letters to Sir W. seem to be directed toward a younger man; Stanhope was 65 in 1767 (with "a crazy, battered constitution, and deaf into the bargain" [Cash, *John Wilkes* 184]); Boothby was 46.

2. Venus's lap] Cash, *LY,* 309–10, rather misreads the tone of this letter, suggesting that "Stanhope had made some coarse comment about Sterne's past, to which Sterne responded" defensively. But the letter throughout is quite bawdy, and Sterne seems to us as playful in his (mock) reformation as in this opening gambit, where clearly his implications are neither innocent nor suggestive of reformation: Venus can, indeed, be associated with the sea from which she was born, but the mons veneris is certainly and intentionally hovering over the exchange.

3. a lady] The mysterious Hannah, we assume (see letter 224).

4. Bond-street . . . Salt Hill] Again, the passage is bawdy: Bond-street is, of course, Sterne's London address; Eliza visited him there on occasion (she had her own chair), and whether she actually dined on "scollop'd oysters" (oysters baked in a scallop shell or scallop-shaped dish "with bread crumbs, cream, butter, and condiments" [*OED,* s.v. *scallop,* v.2.]) or not, we cannot help but recall the joke Eugenius is telling Tristram, about a "nun who fancied herself a shell-fish, and of a monk damn'd for eating a muscle," when Death interrupts him (*TS* VII.1.576); see the note to the passage, 3:445–46, n. to 576.9–10. For "Salt Hill" and its possibly bawdy implications, see *BJ,* n. to 206.4 (6:410–11); a *tête-à-tête* (face to face) at "Salt Hill" might be innocent in a Richardson novel, but not in Sterne's hands.

5. justify myself unto myself] Job 9:20 comes to mind, most appropriately: "If I justify myself, mine own mouth shall condemn me: if I say, I am perfect, it shall also prove me perverse." Sterne had quoted the verse in sermon 6 ("Pharisee and publican in the temple") as an example of false religious pride: "the best of us fall seven times a day, and thereby add some degree of unprofitableness to the character of those who do all that is commanded them—was I perfect therefore, says Job, I would not know my soul, I would be silent, I would be ignorant of my own righteousness, for should I say I was perfect, it would prove me to be perverse" (*Sermons* 4:61).

6. rather raise . . . in me] Almost certainly Sterne is alluding to the "heat" of venereal infection, as in the term *fire-ship* for a prostitute (*OED,* seventeenth–

eighteenth century), as he had done in *TS*, IV.28.386: "can you tell me, *Gastripheres,* what is best to take out the fire?"; see *Notes* to *TS*, 3:326, n. to 386.5–8.

7. *badinage*] Raillery (see letter 81, n. 2).

8. the sporting . . . my pen] Cf. *TS*, VI.6.500: "Ask my pen,—it governs me,—I govern not it." The image of a boy astride a stick is one of several possible forms of the "hobby-horse," and Sterne is here striking Tristram's most characteristic hobby-horsical posture.

9. You are . . . marle] Lydia's penchant for ignoring paragraph indications in the manuscript is never more annoying than in this instance; the opening play of sexual innuendo now turns to quite practical matters, and a new paragraph would have been helpful. Sir W. obviously was about to embark on the "farming" of *marl,* "a kind of soil consisting principally of clay mixed with carbonate of lime . . . , valuable as a fertilizer" (*OED*); again, this clue points away from the aged Stanhope, who spent his last years on the continent.

10. I was once . . . pains] On Sterne's farming see letter 19, n. 2. "To have nothing but one's labour for one's pains" is proverbial; see Tilley, L1, and *ODEP*, 438.

11. bought experience is the devil] Sterne's variant on a proverbial expression; see Tilly, W546 ("Bought wit is dear"), and *ODEP*, 78; as Tilley and *ODEP* both chronicle, the opposite observation is also proverbial: "Bought wit is best."

226. *To Sir W.*

Text: Medalle

Coxwould, [Sunday,] Sept. 27, 1767.

Dear Sir,

You are arrived at Scarborough, when all the world has left it—but you are an unaccountable being, and so there is nothing more to be said on the matter—You wish me to come to Scarborough, and join you to read a work that is not yet finish'd—besides I have other things in my head.—My wife will be here in three or four days, and I must not be found straying in the wilderness[1]—but I have been there.—As for meeting you at Bluit's,[2] with all my heart—I will laugh, and drink my barley water[3] with you—As soon as I have greeted my wife and daughter, and hired them a house at York, I shall go to London where you generally are in spring—and then my Sentimental Journey will, I dare say, convince you that my feelings are from the heart, and that that heart is not of the worst of molds—praised be God for my sensibility! Though it has often made me wretched, yet I would not exchange it for all the pleasures the grossest sensualist ever felt.[4]—Write to me the day you will be at York—'tis ten to one but I may introduce you to my wife and daughter. Believe me,

My good Sir,
Ever yours,
L. Sterne

MS: Not located.
Pub.: Medalle, no. 101; Curtis, no. 214.

1. in the wilderness] A biblical commonplace, but perhaps most apropos is Psalm 95:8: "Harden not your heart, as in the provocation, and as in the day of temptation in the wilderness"; the psalm ("Venite, exultemus Domino") is part of the morning service in the *BCP.*

2. Bluit's] An inn near the Assembly Rooms in York, from which coaches departed for London (see letters 47, n. 1, and 209, n. 1). Curtis, 396, n. 2, quotes Boswell's opinion: "I never saw a better inn. The waiters had all one livery: brown coats and scarlet vests" (*Boswell in Search of a Wife,* 136 [Saturday, March 19, 1768]). Thus Boswell was entertaining himself in York the day after Sterne died in London.

3. barley water] We hope Sterne meant a glass of ale (*strong* barley water) rather than the medicinal concoction (*aqua hordeata*) prescribed for a variety of ailments.

4. praised be . . . ever felt] Cf. Sterne's account to Eliza of having to undergo treatment for a venereal disorder: "& thus Eliza is your Yorick . . . with all his sensibilities, suffering the Chastisement of the grossest Sensualist" (*BJ* 177–78, April 24, 1767); and letter 207, where Sterne tells the same story, in very similar language, to the Earl of Shelburne.

227. *To Isaac Panchaud*

Text: Medalle

York, [Thursday,] October 1, 1767.

Dear Sir,

I have order'd my friend Becket to advance for two months your account which my wife this day deliver'd—she is in raptures with all your civilities.—This is to give you notice to draw upon your correspondent—and Becket will deduct out of my publication.—Tomorrow morning I repair with her to Coxwould, and my Lydia seems transported with the sight of me.—Nature, dear Panchaud[a], breathes in all her composition; and except a little vivacity—which is a fault in the world we live in—I am fully content with her mother's care of her.—Pardon this digression from business—but 'tis natural to speak of those we love.—As to the subscriptions which your friendship has procured me, I must have them to incorporate with my lists[1] which are to be prefix'd to the first volume.—My wife and daughter join in millions of thanks—they will leave me the 1st of December.—Adieu, adieu—believe me,

Your's most truly,
L. Sterne

MS: Not located.
Pub.: Medalle, no. 102; Curtis, no. 215.

[a]Panchaud] P—— *M*

1. As to . . . my lists] For Panchaud's efforts to add to the subscription list of *ASJ*, see letters 193, n. 6, and 217, n. 2.

228. *To Mrs. F——*[1]

Text: Medalle

Coxwould, Friday. [?October 2, 1767][2]

Dear Madam,

I return you a thousand thanks for your obliging enquiry after me—I got down last summer very much worn out—and much worse at the end of my journey—I was forced to call at his Grace's house (the Archbishop of York) to refresh myself a couple of days upon the road near Doncaster[3]—Since I got home to quietness, and temperance, and good books, and good hours, I have mended—and am now very stout—and in a fortnight's time shall perhaps be as well as you yourself could wish me.—I have the pleasure to acquaint you that my wife and daughter are arrived from France.—I shall be in town to greet my friends by the first of January.—Adieu dear madam—believe me

Yours sincerely,
L. Sterne

MS: Not located.
Pub.: Medalle, no. 104; Curtis, no. 216.

1. *Mrs. F——*] For Sterne's correspondence with various women labeled Mrs. F——, see letter 148, n. 1 (and letters 41 and 63). Of these letters, this is certainly the coolest and most formal, perhaps a warning to Mrs. F—— that Sterne's days of dalliance were numbered, at least until he could return to London, and that receiving letters from her in Coxwold was no longer possible. One might read "as well as you yourself could wish me" as a sly innuendo, but the letter does seem to have had a quite thorough cleansing—whether by Sterne himself or by Lydia, we will never know, unless the ms. resurfaces.

2. Date] Medalle gives only "Friday"; Curtis suggests October 2, 1767, which seems probable enough based on the letter's content, although possibly it could have been written on a Friday later in the month—but not earlier, since Elizabeth and Lydia had arrived at York at the very end of September (see letter 227).

3. Doncaster] See letter 209.

229. *To Anne and William James*

Text: Medalle

Coxwould, [Saturday,] October 3, 1767.

I have suffered under a strong desire for above this fortnight, to send a letter of enquiries after the health and the well-being of my dear friends, Mr. and Mrs. James[a], and I do assure you both, 'twas merely owing to a little modesty in my temper not to make my good-will troublesome, where I have so much, and to those I never think of, but with ideas of sensibility and obligation, that I have refrain'd.—Good God! to think I could be in town, and not go the first step I made to Gerrard Street!—My mind and body must be at sad variance with each other, should it ever fall out that it is not both the first and last place also where I shall betake myself, were it only to say, "God bless you."—May you have every blessing he can send you! 'tis a part of my litany, where you will always have a place whilst I have a tongue to repeat it.—And so you heard I had left Scarborough, which you would no more credit, than the reasons assign'd for it—I thank you for it kindly—tho' you have not told me what they were, being a shrewd divine,[1] I think I can guess.—I was ten days at Scarborough in September, and was hospitably entertained by one of the best of our Bishops;[2] who, as he kept house there, press'd me to be with him——and his houshold consisted of a gentleman,[3] and two ladies[4]—which, with the good Bishop, and myself, made so good a party that we kept much to ourselves.—I made in this time a connection of great friendship with my mitred host, who would gladly have taken me with him back to Ireland.—However we all left Scarborough together, and lay fifteen miles off, where we kindly parted——Now it was supposed (and have since heard) that I e'en went on with the party to London, and this I suppose was the reason assign'd for my being there.—I dare say charity would add a little to the account, and give out that 'twas on the score of one, and perhaps both of the ladies—and I will excuse charity on that head, for a heart disengaged could not well have done better.—I have been hard writing ever since—and hope by Christmas I shall be able to give a gentle rap at your door—and tell you how happy I am to see my two good friends.—I assure you I spur on my Pegasus more violently upon that account, and am now determined not to draw bit,[5] till I have finish'd this Sentimental Journey——which I hope to lay at your feet, as a small (but a very honest) testimony of the constant truth, with which I am,

My dear friends,
Your ever obliged
And grateful,
L. Sterne

PS

My wife and daughter arrived here last night from France.—My girl has return'd an elegant accomplish'd little slut[6]—my wife——but I hate to praise my wife[7]—'tis as much as decency will allow to praise my daughter.—I suppose they will return next summer to France.——They leave me in a month to reside at York for the winter—and I stay at Coxwould till the first of January.

MS: Not located.
Pub.: Medalle, no. 103; Curtis, no. 217.

[a]James] J—— *M*

1. shrewd divine] "*Dennis* the critick could not detest and abhor a pun, or the insinuation of a pun, more cordially than my father" (*TS* II.12.128).

2. one of . . . our Bishops] Cf. *BJ*, 223–24 (August 2): "The Bishop of Cork & Ross has made me great Offers in Ireland . . . . He is the best of feeling tender hearted men—knows our Story—sends You his Blessing . . . but more of this good Man, and his attachments to me—hereafter. and of a couple of Ladies in the family &c. &c."

See Cash, *LY*, 302, n. 85, for the argument that this journal entry was probably written during York Race Week (August 16–23), and hence that, as Curtis had surmised, Sterne met Dr. Jemmett Browne (*c.*1703–1782), during the York races. After serving twenty-seven years (1745–72) as Bishop of Cork and Ross, he was successively, Bishop of Elphin (1772–75) and Archbishop of Tuam (1775–*d.*). Curtis, 384, n. 2, quotes Elizabeth Carter on his character: "Never surely . . . was there so perfectly anti-sublime a dignitary!" (*A Series of Letters between Mrs. Elizabeth*

Carter and Miss Catherine Talbot [1809], 3:320). The bishop subscribed to a large-paper copy of *ASJ.*

3. gentleman] J.M.S. Tompkins, "Triglyph and Tristram," *TLS* (July 11, 1929): 558, first identified this gentleman as Richard Griffith (*c.*1704–1788); for Sterne's acquaintance with his wife in Paris, see above, letter 86, n. 8. Curtis, 398, n. 3, quotes from their joint enterprise, *A Series of Genuine Letters between Henry and Frances* (volume 5, 1770), in which Richard gives some account of his fellowship with Sterne at Scarborough: "Now we talk of Philosophy, the modern Democritus, Tristram Shandy, is here. The Bishop has invited him, and introduced us to each other. He mentioned my Strictures on his Writings to me [i.e., in *The Triumvirate* (1764), 1:xiii–xviii], and said that they had hurt him a little at first, notwithstanding the fine Qualifications I had thrown in, in Compliment to his moral Character. . . . He has communicated a Manuscript to us, that he means soon to publish. It is stiled a *Sentimental Journey through Europe,* by Yoric. . . . He promises to spin the Idea through several Volumes, in the same chaste Way, and calls it his *Work of Redemption;* for he has but little Superstition to appropriated Expressions" (5:83; quoted from Howes, *Critical Heritage* 185). And again, several days later: "*Tristram* and *Triglyph* have entered into a League, offensive and defensive, together, against all Opponents in Literature. We have, at the same Time, agreed never to write any more *Tristrams* or *Triglyphs.* I am to stick to *Andrews,* and he to Yoric" (5:86; Howes 186).

A "Mr. Griffith" subscribed to *ASJ,* and we assume it was Richard. For excerpts from *The Triumvirate* relating to Sterne, see Howes, 142–43; Griffith attacked the "obscenity" of *Tristram,* but praised the *Sermons* (1760), and gave Sterne some accolades: "This then, may seem to have been the design of that anomalous, heteroclite genius . . . whose principal end, I hope and believe, was to inculcate that great *Magna Charta* of mankind, humanity and benevolence" (Howes 142). After Sterne's death, Griffith published *The Posthumous Works of a Late Celebrated Genius (The Koran)* in 1770, often taken for Sterne's own work throughout much of the nineteenth century and certainly one of the better imitations of Sterne. He also delivered one of the most memorable sentences on Sterne's affair with Eliza: "The World that knew of their Correspondence, knew the worst of it, which was merely a simple Folly. Any other Idea of the Matter would be more than the most abandoned Vice could render probable. To intrigue with a Vampire! To sink into the Arms of *Death alive!*" (5:199–200; quoted in Howes 187).

4. two ladies] As Cash, *LY,* 307, n. 5, points out, Tompkins, in "Triglyph and Tristram," 558, had identified one of the women as Lady Anne Dawson (1733–1769), daughter of the 1st Earl of Pomfret, who had married Elizabeth Vesey's cousin Thomas Dawson in 1754. Tompkins also established that although

Vesey (see letter 177, n. 1) had been in Scarborough with Lady Anne, she had departed before Sterne's arrival. Cross, *Life* (1929), 452, and Curtis, 399, n. 4, fail to notice Tompkins's argument about Vesey and claim that she was the second woman, but Cash seems correct in maintaining that the second woman remains unidentified. Lady Anne's brother, George Fermor (1722–1785), 2d Earl of Pomfret, subscribed to Sterne's *Sermons* (1769); see letter 208, n. 3.

5. Pegasus . . . draw bit] See *OED, bit,* II.8.d.: "*to draw bit:* to stop one's horse by pulling at the reins; hence *fig.*, to stop, slacken speed." Sterne nicely combines the literal and the figurative by reference to Pegasus, the winged horse of poetry.

6. slut] See letter 38, n. 1.

7. I hate to praise my wife] Sterne contradicts the advice of Proverbs 31:28, concerning the good wife: "Her children arise up, and call her blessed; her husband also, and he praiseth her."

230. *To Anne James*[1]

Text: Medalle

Coxwould, [Thursday,] November 12, 1767.

Forgive me, dear Mrs. James[a], if I am troublesome in writing something betwixt a letter and a card, to enquire after you and my good friend Mr. James[a], whom 'tis an age since I have heard a syllable of.——I think so however, and never more felt the want of a house I esteem so much, as I do now when I can hear tidings of it so seldom—and have nothing to recompence my desires of seeing its kind possessors, but the hopes before me of doing it by Christmas.—I long sadly to see you—and my friend Mr. James[a]. I am still at Coxwould—my wife and girl here.[2]—She is a dear good creature—affectionate, and most elegant in body, and mind—she is all heaven could give me in a daughter—but like other blessings, not given, but lent; for her mother loves France—and this dear part of me must be torn from my arms, to follow her mother, who seems inclined to establish her in France where she has had many advantageous offers.—Do not smile at my weakness, when I say I don't wonder at it, for she is as accomplish'd a slut as France can produce.—You shall excuse all this—if you won't, I desire Mr. James[a] to be my advocate—but I know I don't want one.—

With what pleasure shall I embrace your dear little pledge[3]—who I hope to see every hour encreasing in stature, and in favour, both with God and man![4]—I kiss all your hands with a most devout and friendly heart.——No man can wish you more good than your meager friend does—few so much, for I am with infinite cordiality, gratitude and honest affection,

My dear Mrs. James[a],
Your ever faithful,
L. Sterne

PS

My Sentimental Journey will please Mrs. James[a], and my Lydia—I can answer for those two. It is a subject which works well, and suits the frame of mind I have been in for some time past—I told you my design in it was to teach us to love the world and our fellow creatures better than we do[5]—so it runs most upon those gentler passions and affections, which aid so much to it.—Adieu, and may you and my worthy friend Mr. James[a] continue examples of the doctrine I teach.

MS: Not located.
Pub.: Medalle, no. 105; Curtis, no. 218.

[a]James] J—— *M*

1. *To Anne James*] Medalle has "To Mr. and Mrs. J——" but we follow Curtis, 400, in indicating the addressee as Mrs. James, which seems obviously the case.

2. wife and girl here] Medalle has an asterisk after "girl" and a note at the bottom of the page: "Mrs. Medalle thinks an apology may be necessary for publishing this letter—the best she can offer is—that it was written by a fond parent (whose commendations she is proud of) to a very sincere friend." One hopes Lydia did not write the passage herself; that Sterne was an affectionate father seems apparent throughout the letters.

3. little pledge] I.e., their daughter (see letter 215, n. 1).

4. encreasing . . . God and man] Cf. Luke 2:52, on Jesus visiting Jerusalem in his twelfth year: "And Jesus increased in wisdom and stature, and in favour with God and man."

5. love the world . . . we do] Sterne has Yorick utter the same sentiment to the Count de B**** in *ASJ*, 111, about his own journey: "'tis a quiet journey of the heart

in pursuit of NATURE, and those affections which rise out of her, which make us love each other—and the world, better than we do." As the Florida editors note, Sterne's pointing to his recent "frame of mind" appears covertly to allude to his relationship with Eliza, and hence we may draw yet another link between that affair and the writing of *ASJ*.

231. *To Hannah*

Text: Ms.

[Coxwold, ?November 1767][1]

Hanah!

If you don't[a] give these Letters as inclosed Ill never speak another word to You as long as I live.

I am
Y[rs]
L. Sterne

Address: [in the hand of Lord Fauconberg] [?St. James]'s Street[2] / London / Free[3] / ffauconberg

MS: Kenneth Monkman Collection, Shandy Hall.

Pub.: Kenneth Monkman, "Two More Unpublished Sterne Letters," *Shandean* 2 (1990): 149–51 (facsimile, 150).

[a]don't] d[on't] *MS* [ms. torn by seal]

1. Date] The note is undated. Monkman has "[?1767]," but on the basis of letter 232, we have added November—October might, of course, also be possible; see letter 224.

2. [?St. James]'s Street] Monkman has "[?Gt James']s street," based on the two descenders left on the torn manuscript ("Unfortunately a former owner has cut away the blank half of the page, thinking it not worth keeping, so robbing the verso of the name of the addressee and the revealing portion of her address" [Monkman 149]). Great James Street is the continuation northward of Bedford Row, Holburn (*London Past and Present* 2:273); Bedford Row was an elegant neighborhood; Warburton had lived there until 1757. However, St. James Street, between Pall Mall and Piccadilly, is in the very area where many of Sterne's friends lived or lodged (see letters 70, n. 3, and 189, n. 6), and we believe that is the proper reading of the torn manuscript.

3. Free] See letter 220, n. 8. As Monkman, 151, n. 3, notes, "Sterne had obviously been taking advantage [of Lord Fauconberg's franking privileges] to enclose several letters under one 'Free' cover which Hannah . . . might then deliver in town by hand." See also letter 232.

232. *To Hannah*

Text: Curtis

[Coxwold, Sunday, November 15, 1767][1]

Now be a good dear girl, Hannah![a] and give these to Fanny[2]—& Fanny will give that wh belongs to her sister, herself—and[b] when I see you I'll give you a kiss—there's for you!

—but I have something else for you, which I am fabricating at a great rate, & that is my Journey[c], which shall make you cry as much as ever it made me laugh[d]—or I'll give up the Business of sentimental writing—& write to the Body

—that is Hannah![e] what I am doing in writing to you—but you are a *good Body,* & that's worth half a Score *mean Souls*

Upon mine[f]
I am yrs
L. Sterne[g]

MS: Present whereabouts unknown.
Pub.: Medalle, no. 89; Curtis, no. 219.

[a]girl, Hannah!] woman my H———, *M* [b]and give . . . herself—and] and execute these commissions well—and *M* [c]my Journey] my Sentimental Journey *M* [d]as much . . . laugh] as much as it has affected me *M* [e]Hannah!] H. *M* [f]Upon mine] *om. M* [g]L. Sterne] L. Shandy. *M*

1. Date] The date is Medalle's. Curtis, who had access to the manuscript, writes: "First published with foolish alterations by Medalle . . . . Since [the] MS. is without date, I print Lydia's date for what it is worth" (401). Given letters 224 and 232, it seems Curtis is probably right to have done so. We have indicated in the collation Lydia's substantive alterations, including the rather culpable emendation of "which shall make you cry as much as ever it made me laugh" to the bland "as much as it has affected me"; whatever else we might think of *ASJ,* Sterne's

characterization of his own response certainly strikes a sympathetic chord, while Lydia's version, typically enough, is tone deaf.

It is also worth noting that Medalle prints Sterne's three paragraphs as one paragraph, her usual habit.

2. Now be . . . Fanny] Cf. letter 231, n. 3.

233. *To A. L——e, Esq.*

Text: Medalle

Coxwould, [Thursday,] November 19, 1767.

You make yourself unhappy, dear L——e, by imaginary ills—which you might shun, instead of putting yourself in the way of.—Would not any man in his senses fly from the object he adores, and not waste his time and his health in increasing his misery by so vain a pursuit?—The idol of your heart is one of ten thousand.—The duke of ——[1] has long sighed in vain—and can you suppose a woman will listen to you, that is proof against titles, stars, and red ribbands?[2]—Her heart (believe me, L——e) will not be taken in by fine men, or fine speeches—if it should ever feel a preference, it will chuse an object for itself, and it must be a singular character that can make an impression on such a being—she has a platonic way of thinking, and knows love only by name—the natural reserve of her character, which you complain of, proceeds not from pride, but from a superiority of understanding, which makes her despise every man that turns himself into a fool—Take my advice, and pay your addresses to Miss ——— she esteems you, and time will wear off an attachment which has taken so deep a root in your heart.——I pity you from my soul—but we are all born with passions which ebb and flow[3] (else they would play the devil with us)[4] to different objects—and the best advice I can give you, L——e, is to turn the tide of yours another way.—I know not whether I shall write again while I stay at Coxwould.—I am in earnest at my sentimental work—and intend being in town soon after Christmas—in the mean time adieu.—Let me hear from you, and believe me, dear L.

Yours, &c.

L. Sterne

MS: Not located.
Pub.: Medalle, no. 106; Curtis, no. 220.

1. duke of ——] The recipient and the parties alluded to are all unidentified, which makes this a particularly frustrating letter.

2. titles, stars, and red ribbands] Red ribbons would indicate a Knight of the Bath, who would also wear an ornamented star, but Sterne may just be generalizing about the emblems of rank.

3. passions . . . flow] A commonplace in Sterne's writings, as in *TS,* II.17.164 ("the ebbs and flows of his own passions"), or *Sermons,* 4:37 ("the various ebbs and flows of their passions"); for additional examples, see *Notes* to *TS,* 3:187, n. to 164.19–20.

4. play the devil with us] Another favorite expression with Sterne; see *TS,* III.4.190, VIII.19.686, and VIII.26.709, where we are told that Walter in love would "pish, and huff, and bounce, and kick, and play the Devil . . . ." The presence of "favorite" expressions is as often an indication of imitation as of authenticity—this passage in particular seems suspicious.

234. *To the Earl of ——*[1]

Text: Medalle

Coxwould, [Saturday,] November 28, 1767.

My Lord,

'Tis with the greatest pleasure I take my pen to thank your Lordship for your letter of enquiry about Yorick—he has worn out both his spirits and body with the Sentimental Journey—'tis true that an author must feel himself, or his reader will not[2]—but I have torn my whole frame into pieces by my feelings—I believe the brain stands as much in need of recruiting as the body—therefore I shall set out for town the twentieth of next month, after having recruited myself a week at York.—I might indeed solace myself with my wife,[3] (who is come from France) but in fact I have long been a sentimental being—whatever your Lordship may think to the contrary.—The world has imagined, because I wrote Tristram Shandy, that I was myself more Shandean than I really ever was—'tis a good-natured world we live in, and we are often painted in divers colours according to the ideas each one frames in his head.———A very agreeable lady[4] arrived three years ago at York, in her road to Scarborough—I had the honour of being acquainted with her, and was her *chaperon*—all the females were very inquisitive to know who she was—"Do not tell, ladies, 'tis a mistress my wife has recommended to me—nay moreover has sent her from France."——

I hope my book will please you, my Lord, and then my labour will not be totally in vain. If it is not thought a chaste book, mercy on them that read it, for they must have warm imaginations indeed!—Can your Lordship forgive my not making this a longer epistle?—In short I can but add this, which you already know—that I am with gratitude and friendship,

My Lord,
Your obedient faithful,
L. Sterne

If your Lordship is in town in Spring, I should be happy if you became acquainted with my friends in Gerrard-street[5]—you would esteem the husband, and honour the wife—she is the reverse of most her sex—they have various pursuits—she but one—that of pleasing her husband.—

MS: Not located.
Pub.: Medalle, no. 107; Curtis, no. 221.

1. *Earl of*——] The recipient has never been identified. There is some similarity of tone and content to letter 207, also addressed by Medalle to "the Earl of——" and subsequently presumed to be the Earl of Shelburne (see letters 207 and 138, n. 3), though without anything approaching certainty. Sterne's identification of himself as "Yorick" and the play between being a sensualist or a man of sensibility occur in both letters. But in the subscription lists alone we can count more than fifty earls, so we have—as did Curtis—left the recipient of this letter unidentified (as, perhaps, should also be the case with letter 207).

2. 'tis true . . . will not] A critical commonplace, usually traced to Horace, *Art of Poetry,* ll. 102–3 (458–59): "si vis me flere, dolendum est / primum ipsi tibi" (If you would have me weep, you must first feel grief yourself).

3. solace myself with my wife] By no means an innocent expression; see *TS,*

III.35.266: "when my father got home, he solaced himself with *Bruscambille* after the manner, in which, 'tis ten to one, your worship solaced yourself with your first mistress . . . ."

4. A very agreeable lady] Unidentified; the story may well be apocryphal, helping Sterne to make his point about gossip, a subject he glances at in *TS*, both in Slawkenbergius's Tale in volume IV and again when "all the world, as usual," credits the rumors concerning Tristram's encounter with the window-sash (VI.14.521).

5. friends in Gerrard-street] I.e., the Jameses. It might be argued that since the recipient of letter 207 knew about Eliza, this recipient, who has never met the Jameses, cannot be the same person. However, Sterne's penchant for sharing his amours with his acquaintances makes it possible that a person could have learned about Eliza from Sterne without ever meeting her or the Jameses.

235. *To Sir George Macartney*[1]

Text: Medalle[2]

To his Excellency Sir G.M.

Coxwould, [Thursday,] December 3, 1767.

My dear Friend,

For tho' you are his Excellency, and I still but parson Yorick—I still must call you so—and were you to be next Emperor of Russia, I could not write to you, or speak of you, under any other relation—I felicitate you, I don't say how much, because I can't—I always had something like a kind of revelation within me, which pointed out this track for you, in which you are so happily advanced—it was not only my wishes for you, which were ever ardent enough to impose upon a visionary brain, but I thought I actually saw you just where you now are—and that is just, my dear Macartney, where you should be.—I should long, long ago have acknowledged the kindness of a letter of yours from Petersbourg; but hearing daily accounts you was leaving it[3]—this is the first time I knew well *where* my thanks would find you—how they will find you, I know well—that is—the same I ever knew you. In three weeks I shall kiss your hand—and sooner, if I can finish my Sentimental Journey.—The duce take all sentiments! I wish there was not one in the world!—My wife is come to pay me a sentimental visit as far as from Avignon—and the *politesses*[4] arising from such a proof of her urbanity, has robb'd me of a month's writing, or I had been in town now.—I am going to ly-in;[5] being at Christmas at my full reckoning—and unless what I shall bring forth is not *press'd* to death by these devils of printers, I shall have the honour of presenting to you a *couple of as clean brats* as ever chaste brain conceiv'd—they are frolicksome too, *mais cela n'empeche pas*[6]—I put your name down with many wrong and right *honourables,* knowing you would take it not well if I did not make myself happy with it.

Adieu my dear friend,

Believe me yours, &c.
L. Sterne.

PS

If you see Mr. Crauford,[7] tell him I greet him kindly.

MS: Duke University, James Iredell Papers (not in Sterne's hand).
Pub.: Medalle, no. 90; Curtis, no. 223.

1. *Sir George Macartney*] George Macartney (1737–1806) had met Sterne in 1762 in Paris, where he was serving as a tutor and bear-leader for Charles James Fox. In 1764 he had been appointed envoy extraordinary to the court of Catherine the Great of Russia, from which post he had just returned (Curtis, 405, n. 1). Walpole, *Memoirs . . . George III,* 4:37, offers his usual tart assessment: "Sir George Macartney, who was returned from Russia and had married Lord Bute's second daughter [in 1768], spoke [in Parliament] for the first time, and with very bad success, though his parts had been much cried up. He was a young and handsome Irishman, attached to Lord Holland [i.e., Henry Fox], with whose eldest son he had travelled as a kind of governor. He was an amiable man, with various knowledge and singular memory, but no other extraordinary talents." Macartney subscribed to *Sermons* (1766) and to five large-paper copies of *ASJ.* See also Cash, *LY,* 125.

2. *Text:* Medalle] A manuscript of this letter exists, an attempt to mimic Sterne's handwriting, but in a dubious hand, possibly Lydia's. Based on the nearly total coincidence of her text and the manuscript, which occurs in no other instance where such a comparison can be made, we believe the manuscript was copied from Medalle rather than being her source—unless it is indeed her handwriting, in which case we might suggest that she copied the original, and

type was set accurately from that copy. There are, in fact, only two instances of variance, "My wife" in Medalle, where the manuscript has "My Wife"; and the spelling of "Crauford" in the postscript, where Medalle has "Crawfurd." Curtis did not have access to the manuscript and follows Medalle; "Crauford" is clearly the manuscript reading, and we have altered Medalle in this one instance; see n. 7.

3. but hearing . . . leaving it] For the London intrigues that threatened Macartney's ambassadorship in Russia, see Walpole, *Memoirs . . . George III*, 4:64–65, 107.

4. *politesses*] See letter 222, n. 1.

5. going to ly-in] See letter 186, n. 4. Sterne's puns are obvious, including "devils of printers," which he had played with in *TS*, IV.28.387; the errand-boys in printing offices, often covered with ink, were called devils according to *OED*, s.v. *Devil*, 5a.

6. *mais cela n'empeche pas*] But that doesn't matter (properly: *n'empêche*). Cf. *ASJ*, 92: "Poo! said I, the king of France is a good natured soul—he'll hurt no body.—*Cela n'empeche pas*, said he—you will certainly be sent to the Bastile to-morrow morning."

7. Crauford] Presumably "Fish" Craufurd (see letter 164, n. 6). In the subscription lists, his name is spelled "Crawford"; if it is indeed true that his experience inspired the final chapter of *ASJ* ("The Case of Delicacy"), it is no accident that he would be on Sterne's mind at this time.

236. *To A. L——e, Esq.*

Text: Medalle

Coxwould, [Monday,] December 7, 1767.

Dear L.

I said I would not perhaps write any more, but it would be unkind not to reply to so interesting a letter as yours—I am certain you may depend upon Lord ——'s promises[1]—he will take care of you in the best manner he can, and your knowledge of the world, and of languages in particular, will make you useful in any department—If his Lordship's scheme does not succeed, leave the kingdom—go to the east, or the west, for travelling would be of infinite service to both your body and mind—But more of this when we meet—now to my own affairs.——I have had an offer of exchanging two pieces of preferment I hold here, for a living of three hundred and fifty pounds a year, in Surry, about thirty miles from London, and retaining Coxwould, and my prebendaryship—the country also is sweet[2]—but I will not, cannot come to any determination, till I have consulted with you, and my other friends.—I have great offers too in Ireland[3]—the bishop of Cork and Ross is my friend[a]—but I have rejected every proposal, unless Mrs. Sterne[b], and my Lydia could accompany me thither—I live for the sake of my girl, and with her sweet light burthen in my arms, I could get up fast the hill of preferment, if I chose it—but without my Lydia, if a mitre was offered me, it would sit uneasy upon my brow.[4]—Mrs. Sterne[b]'s health is insupportable in England.—She must return to France, and justice and humanity forbid me to oppose it.—I will allow her enough to live comfortably, until she can rejoin me.—My heart bleeds, L—e, when I think of parting with my child——'twill be like the separation of soul and body—and equal to nothing but what passes at that tremendous moment; and like it in one respect, for she will be in one kingdom, whilst I am in another.[5]—You will laugh at my weakness—but I cannot help it—for she is a dear, disinterested girl—As a proof of it—when she left Coxwould, and I bad her adieu, I pulled out my purse and offered her ten guineas for her private pleasures—her answer was pretty, and affected me too much. "No, my dear papa, our expences of coming from France may have straiten'd you—I would rather put an hundred guineas in your pocket than take ten out of it"—I burst into tears—but why do I practice on your feelings—by dwelling on a subject that will touch your heart?—It is too much melted already by its own sufferings, L—e, for me to add a pang, or cause a single sigh.—God bless you—I shall hope to greet you by New-years-day in perfect health—Adieu my dear friend—I am most truly and cordially yours,

L. Sterne

MS: Not located.

Pub.: Medalle, no. 108; Curtis, no. 224.

[a]bishop of Cork and Ross is my friend] bishops of C——, and R——, are both my friends *M* [b]Mrs. Sterne] Mrs. S—— *M*

1. Lord ——'s promises] Unidentified, as is the entire context for understanding Sterne's advice to A. L——e in this letter.

2. I have . . . sweet] Cf. *BJ,* 224 (dated August 3, but almost certainly written in late September): "I have had an offer of exchanging two pieces of preferment I hold here (but sweet Cordelia's Parish is not one of 'em) for a living of 350 p^{ds} a year in Surry ab^{t} 30 miles from London—& retaining Coxwould & my Prebendaryship—wch are half as much more—the Country also is sweet . . . ."

3. I have . . . Ireland] Cf. *BJ,* 223 (dated August 2, but almost certainly written in late September): "The Bishop of Cork & Ross has made me great Offers in Ireland." See also letter 229 and n. 2. The error in Medalle could not have been Sterne's, so we must assume that Lydia, unaware of the see, thought that two persons must be intended; we have corrected the sentence accordingly (see collation).

4. I live . . . brow] Again, the passage occurs in the August 3 entry in *BJ,* 224: "I cannot take any step unless I had thee my Eliza for whose sake I live, to consult with—& till the road is open for me as my heart wishes to advance—with thy sweet light Burden in my Arms, I could get up fast the hill of preferment, if I chose it—but without thee I feel Lifeless—and if a Mitre was offer'd me, I would not have it, till I could have thee too, to make it sit easy upon my brow . . . ."

5. 'twill be like . . . another] This repeats an earlier passage in *BJ,* 215 (July 6), once again substituting Lydia for Eliza: "How oft have I smarted at the Idea, of that last longing Look by wch thou badest adieu . . . twas the Separation of Soul & Body—& equal to nothing but what passes on that tremendous Moment.—& like it in one Consequence, that thou art in another World; where I w^{d} give a world, to follow thee . . . ." For a discussion of these parallel passages, see letter 211, *Status.*

237. *For Elizabeth Sterne*[1]

Text: Letter Book

[Coxwold, end of December 1767][2]

Fothergil, I know has some good ones—Garrick some—<Hall, I fear not tho he has rec^{d} hundreds, they have been wrote most of 'em in too careless a way. besides he's careless.>—Berenger has one or two—

Govr Littletons Lady (Miss Macartney) numbers—Countesse of Edgecomb—Mrs Moore of Bath—Mrs Fenton[3] London—cum multis aliis[4]— These all if collected with the large number of mine & friends in my possession would print & sell to good Acc^t - - - -

☞Hall has by him a great number wth those in this book & in my Bureau—& those above w^d make 4 Vo^ls the size of Shandy——they would sell well—& produce 800 p^ds at the least—

J Hall as—
J Hall has—
try him a
great Number[5]

MS: Letter Book, Pierpont Morgan Library, New York.
Pub.: Cross, *Life* (1925), 2:231 (facsimile, facing 228); Curtis, no. 225.

1. *For Elizabeth Sterne*] Cross's summary of this memorandum raises more questions than it answers: "This is the surviving part of the wrapper which contained the letters in the *Letter Book.* It is a memorandum which Sterne evidently wrote down and left at Coxwold for his wife and daughter just before he set out on his last trip to London" (*Life* [1925], 2:230). For a full discussion of the *Letter Book,* see introduction, lii–liv.

2. Date] If Cross is correct, Sterne wrote this just before departing for London at the very end of December; see letters 238 and 239.

3. Fothergil . . . Fenton] Sterne's list is a depressing reminder of how few of his letters survived; we have none of all those "good ones" to Marmaduke Fothergill (see letter 17, n. 5); one letter to Richard Berenger (see letter 48, and n. 1); one letter to Mary Macartney (see letter 62, and n. 1); none or possibly one to the archbishop's daughter, Emma Gilbert, Baroness Edgcumbe (see letters 68, n. 2, and 150, n. 1); none to Mrs. Moore, perhaps the "charming widow *Moor*" of letter 152; and, finally, Mrs. Fenton of London may be Jane Fenton, for whom see letters 63, 127, and 148.

4. cum multis aliis] With many others.

5. J Hall . . . Number] This appears to be in a different hand, using different ink, perhaps Lydia's reminder to talk to Hall-Stevenson.

238. *To Anne or William James*

Text: Ms.

York [Monday,] Dec. 28—1767

I was afraid that either my friend Mr James, or Mrs James[a], or their little Blossome was drooping, or that some of You were ill by not <hear>~hav~ing the pleasure of a line from You, & was thinking of writing again to enquire after you all—when I was cast down myself with a fever, & bleeding at my lungs, which ha<s>~d~ confine<me>~d~ me to my Room three weeks[b], when I had the[c] favour of Yrs which till to day I had[d] not been able to thank you both kindly for, as I most cordially now do,——as well as for all yr proofs & professions[e] of good will to me—I will not say, I have not ballanced Accts with You in this—all I know, is, That I honour and value you more than I ^do^ any good creature[f] upon earth—& that I could ^not^ wish yr happiness and the Successe of whatever[g] conduces to it, more than I do, was I your Brother——but good god! are we not all brothers and Sisters,[1] who are friendly & virtuous & good?—

Surely my dear friends,[2] <I am>~My~ Illness has been a sort of sympathy for yr Afflictions upon the Score of yr dear little one—and I make no doubt when I see Eliza's Journal, I shall find She has ^been^ ill herself at that time—I am rent to pieces with Uncertainty abt this dear friend of ours—I think too much—& intereste myself <too> ^so^ deeply by My friendship for her,—that I am worn down to a Shadow[3]——to this I owe my decay of health—but I can't help it————

As my fever has left me, I set off the latter end of the week[h] with my friend ˅Mr˅ Hall for Town—I need not tell my friends in Gerard Street, <it will> I shall do myself the Honour to visit them before either Lord Shelburn or Lord Spencer[i] &c—&c————

I thank you my dear friend, for What You say so kindly abt my Daughter—it shews yr good heart, as[j] She is a Stranger—<but I ?kn> 'tis a free Gift in You—but When She is known to you—She shall win it *fairly*[k]—but Alas! when this event is to happen, is in the clouds—

M[rs] Sterne[l] <wished>~has~ hired a house ready furnish'd[m] at York, till She returns to france & my Lydia must not leave her———

What a sad Scratch of a Letter—but I am weak my dear friends, both in body & mind—so god bless you—Youl see Me enter like a Ghost—so I tell you before hand, not to be frighten'd

I am, my dear friend[s]
with truest attachment & esteem[n]
Y[rs][o]
L. Sterne.

Address: To / M[r] or M[rs] James / Gerrard Street / Soho / London—
Postmark: YORK 30 DE
MS: British Library, Addit. MSS. 34527, 43–44.
Pub.: Medalle, no. 109; Curtis, no. 226.

[a]either my friend . . . James] either Mr. or Mrs. —— *M* [b]three weeks] near three weeks *M* [c]the] th[ ] [ms. torn] [d]had] ha[ ] [ms. torn]; have *M* [e]proofs & professions] professions and proofs *M* [f]creature] creatures *M* [g]whatever] what | ver *MS* [h]of the week] of next week *M* [i]Lord Shelburn or Lord Spencer] Lord ——— or Lord ——— *M* [j]heart, as] heart, for as *M* [k]*fairly*] fairly *M* [l]M[rs] Sterne] M[ ] Sterne [ms. torn]; Mrs. S— *M* [m]furnish'd] f[ ] [ms. worn] [n]& esteem] & end estemn *MS* [o]Y[rs]] ever yours *M*

1. are we not . . . Sisters] Cf. the similar sentiments expressed to Ignatius Sancho in letter 181.

2. Surely my dear friends, etc.] As with other letters printed by Medalle, an extant manuscript makes clear the freedoms she assumed as an editor. Here, for example, she very carefully excised all mentions of Eliza in this paragraph, and rendered it thus: "Surely, my dear friends, my illness has been a sort of sympathy for your afflictions upon the score of your dear little one.—I am worn down to a shadow—but as my fever has left me . . . ." We have recorded other substantive changes in the collation.

3. worn down to a Shadow] On this persistent image to describe himself, see letter 205A and n. 3. See also *BJ*, 173 (April 19): "poor Sick-headed, sick hearted Yorick! Eliza has made a Shadow of thee." Cf. n. to 173.29–30 (6:388) for other examples scattered throughout his last letters, including also the image of "gliding" like a shadow or a ghost to the Jameses (see next letter).

239. *To Anne and William James*

Text: Medalle

Old Bond Street [Sunday, ?January 3, 1768][1]

Not knowing whether the moisture of the weather will permit me to give my kind friends in Gerrard Street a call this morning for five minutes—I beg leave to send them all the good wishes, compliments, and respects I owe them.—I continue to mend, and doubt not but this, with all other evils and uncertainties of life, will end for the best. I send all compliments to your fire sides this Sunday night—Miss Ascough[2] the wise, Miss Pigot[3] the witty, your daughter the pretty, and so on.—If Lord Ossory[a4] is with you, I beg my dear Mrs. James[b] will present the enclosed to him——'twill add to the millions of obligations I already owe you.—I am sorry that I am no subscriber to Soho[5] this season—it deprives me of a pleasure worth twice the subscription——but I am just going to send about this quarter of the town, to see if it is not too late to procure a ticket, undisposed of, from some of my Soho friends, and if I can succeed, I will either send or wait upon you with it by half an hour after three to-morrow—if not, my friend will do me the justice to believe me truly miserable.—I am half engaged, or more, for dinner on Sunday next, but will try to get disengaged in order to be with my friends.—If I cannot, I will glide like a shadow uninvited to Gerrard Street some day this week, that we may eat our bread and meat in love and peace together.[6]—God bless you both!—I am with the most sincere regard,

Your ever obliged,
L. Sterne

MS: Not located.
Pub.: Medalle, no. 111; Curtis, no. 227.

[a]Lord Ossory] Lord O—— *M* [b]James] J—— *M*

1. Date] Medalle has "January 1," but Sterne had not left York before December 30 or 31, and probably arrived at his lodgings in Old Bond Street on January 2 or 3. See Cash, *LY,* 320–21.

2. Miss Ascough] A "Miss Ayscough" subscribed to *Sermons* (1769), but nothing else is known about her. George Edward Ayscough (*d.* 1779), a military man, dramatist, friend of Wilkes, and author of the Smollett-like *Letters . . . Containing Some Account of France and Italy* (1778), might have been someone attracted to Sterne, but he did not have a sister—perhaps she was a more distant member of his family.

3. Miss Pigot] Possibly Sophia Pigot, a natural daughter of George Pigot (1719–1777), Baron Pigot, Governor of Madras 1755–63, 1775–*d.* He subscribed to *Sermons* (1766, 1769), so Sterne may have known him before he met the Jameses.

4. Lord Ossory] Curtis provides the probable identification. Cf. letters 164, n. 4, and 242, where Sterne spends an hour with Lord "O——." Lord Ossory subscribed to *Sermons* (1766) and to a large-paper copy of *ASJ*, but the identification remains only a probability.

5. subscriber to Soho] See letter 190, n. 1. The Jameses would appear to have been seeking tickets for the opening night, Thursday, January 7.

6. eat our bread . . . together] Cf. *ASJ*, 157–59 ("The Supper." and "The Grace."), where Sterne describes a peasant meal that several critics have identified with the "feast of love" in the early church (see notes to *ASJ* 158.2–3 and 159.15–27; 6:377–80).

240. *To Anne and William James*

Text: Medalle

Old Bond Street, Monday. [January 4, 1768]

My dear Friends,

I have never been a moment at rest since I wrote yesterday about this Soho ticket—I have been at a Secretary of State[1] to get one—have been upon one knee to my friends Sir George Macartney[a],[2] Mr. Lascelles[3]—and Mr. Fitzmaurice[4]——without mentioning five more——I believe I could as soon get you a place at court, for every body is going—but I will go out and try a new circle—and if you do not hear from me by a quarter after three, you may conclude I have been unfortunate in my supplications.—I send you this state of the affair, lest my silence should make you think I had neglected what I promised—but no—Mrs. James[b] knows me better, and would never suppose it would be out of the head of one who is with so much truth

Her faithful friend,
L. Sterne

MS: Not located.
Pub.: Medalle, no. 112; Curtis, no. 228.

[a]George Macartney] G—— M——— *M* [b]James] J—— *M*

1. Secretary of State] Lord Shelburne had been named a Secretary of State in 1766; see letters 138, n. 3, and 207.

2. Sir George Macartney] Curtis makes the identification; see above, letter 235, n. 1.

3. Lascelles] Probably Edward Lascelles (1740–1820), of Stapleton, Yorkshire, husband of Anne Chaloner, a neighbor of Sterne in New Bond Street (an extension northward of Old Bond Street), and a subscriber to *ASJ;* see letter 75, n. 11, and Curtis, 410, n. 2.

4. Fitzmaurice] Curtis, 410, n. 3, identifies him as Thomas Fitzmaurice (1742–1793), brother of the Earl of Shelburne, "and the intimate of Johnson and Garrick." He subscribed to *Sermons* (1766), and to a large-paper copy of *ASJ.*

241. *To Dr. John Eustace*[1]

Text: Life and Correspondence of James Iredell

London, [Tuesday,] Feb. 9, 1768.

Sir,—

I this moment received your obliging letter, and Shandean[2] piece of sculpture[3] along with it; of both which testimonies of your regard I have the justest sense, and return you, dear Sir, my best thanks and acknowledgments[a]. Your walking stick is in no sense more Shandaic than in that of its having more handles than one—The parallel breaks only in this, that in using the stick, every one will take the handle which[b] suits his convenience. In Tristram Shandy, the handle is taken which suits their[c] passions, their ignorance or sensibility[d]. There[e] is so little true feeling in the herd of the world, that I wish I could have got an act of parliament, when the books first appear'd, "that none but wise men should look into them." It[f] is too much to write books and find heads to understand them. The world, however, seems to come into a better[g] temper about them, the people of genius here being, to a man, on its side, and the reception it has met with in France, Italy and Germany, hath[h] engag'd one part of the world to give it a second reading, and the other part of it, in[i] order to be on the strongest side, have[j] at length agreed to speak well of it too. A few Hypocrites and Tartufe's[k],[4] whose approbation could do it nothing but dishonour, remain unconverted.

I am very proud, Sir, to have had a[l] man, like you, on my side from the beginning; but it is not in the power of any[m] one[5] to taste humour, however he may wish it—'tis[n] the gift of God—and besides, a true feeler always brings half the entertainment along with him.[6] His own ideas are only call'd forth by what he reads, and the vibrations within, so entirely[o] correspond with those excited, 'tis like reading himself and not the book.

In a week's time, I shall be deliver'd of two volumes of the Sentimental travels[p] of Mr. Yorick through France and Italy; but, alas! the ship sails three days too soon, and I have only[q] to lament it deprives me of the pleasure of sending[r] them to you, being, dear[s] Sir, with great thanks for the honour you have done me, and with[t] true esteem,

Your oblig'd and humble[u] servant,
Lau. Sterne.

MS: Not located.

Pub.: Court Miscellany; or New Ladies Magazine 6 (November 1770): 509; *Sterne's Letters to His Friends on Various Occasions* (1775), no. 3; *Massachusetts Magazine* 2 (1790): 238–39; Griffith J. McRee, *Life and Correspondence of James Iredell* (New York: D. Appleton, 1857), 1:27–28; Curtis, no. 229.

Status: The original manuscript is lost. The letter was published in three versions before 1800, first in the *Court Miscellany* (*CM,* 1770), a second time in *Various Occasions* (*VO,* 1775), and a third time in *Massachusetts Magazine* (*MM,* 1790). Lodwick Hartley, "The Eustace–Sterne Correspondence: A Note on Sterne's Reputation in America," *ELN* 5 (1968): 176–83, and Arthur S. Marks, "Connections: Sterne, Shandy and North Carolina," *Shandean* 10 (1998): 32–33, examine these versions and agree that the *CM* text was probably derived from a copy and not from the actual letter sent across the Atlantic to Eustace. The version in *VO* is derived, with a few accidental variants, from the *CM* copy; and the version in *Collected Works* (1780) is derived from the *VO* text. The version in *MM* was based on a text submitted by "C."—who has never been identified. Obviously the person had some knowledge of Eustace, and, as Hartley notes, "was not merely following the standard practice of reprinting from an English magazine" (179). Thus, he provides his version with a headnote informing readers that the letter was "*transcribed from the original copy . . . in possession of Mrs. Eustace, the Doctor's widow.*" Marks takes this as sufficient evidence of access to the actual manuscript and in his essay reprints the *MM* version as authoritative.

Curtis was aware of the *CM* printing, but not of the *MM* (at least he gives no indication of being so). His own copy-text, however, was a version in Griffith J. McRee, *Life and Correspondence of James Iredell* (New York: D. Appleton, 1857), 1:27–28. Iredell, a Supreme Court justice, was another Sterne enthusiast in North Carolina (see letter 235, a transcription of which is found in the Iredell Papers, Duke University). Curtis mistakenly believed McRee consulted the holograph, but in fact it was Iredell who makes that claim; McRee's text is based, at best, on a transcription of the original. Marks goes further, suggesting that Iredell himself saw only a transcription, and not the original manuscripts of the Eustace–Sterne exchange because of C.'s claim to have transcribed the *MM* version from the "*original.*" Hence, Marks concludes: "the differences in text, whether in punctuation, word choice and order or in the use of emphases were not Sterne's but Iredell's or [McRee's]. . . . Curtis unaccountably chose to give prominence and authority to the Iredell versions [i.e., Eustace's letter and Sterne's response] and it is these which are consistently cited in Sterne studies" (33).

There are problems with this argument, most obviously that Iredell could well have purchased the letters from C. sometime between 1790 and his death in 1799. And, in defense of Curtis, it may well be argued that the Iredell–McRee version does seem closer to Sterne's manuscript than any earlier version, primarily because those versions were altered for house style, most apparent in the "correction" of elided past tense endings, the conversion of "'tis" to "it is," and the correction of a typical Sterne manuscript error, "Tartufe's," where the apostrophe represents the plural rather than possession. On the other hand, Marks is correct in singling out the heavy use of emphases (actually small capitals) in Iredell–McRee, reproduced as italics in Curtis, which does indeed seem atypical of Sterne; and we may add to this, Iredell–McRee's probable failure to recognize Sterne's capital "S," and their American spellings of "honour" and "humour." The fact is that every version we have is probably printed from an unreliable transcription, each corrupting the original in its own manner. Thus Hartley finally chooses *CM* as his copy-text, providing alternative readings from Iredell–McRee in brackets and *MM* in parentheses, not a very convenient—nor very accurate—rendition. Our own version returns to Curtis's choice, and is based on Iredell–McRee, but with the small capitals rendered in lower case, capital "S" restored where we believe it appropriate, and British spellings restored. The collation list indicates every substantive variant between our text and *CM, VO,* and *MM.* As Hartley astutely observes, "the large measure of similarity between the three versions may be more surprising than their differences" (180). Indeed, despite the headnote to *MM,* it is quite possible that C. also examined—as, probably, did Iredell and McRee—earlier print versions, particularly the version (based on the *CM* and *VO* texts) in the often reprinted *1780*.

[a]acknowledgments] acknowledgement *VO* [b]which] that *MM* [c]their] the *VO* [d]or sensibility] or their sensibility *CM, VO* [e]There] ¶ There *Marks* [in error] [f]appear'd, "that . . . them." It] appeared, that . . . them. It *CM, VO;* appeared, that . . . them; it *MM* [g]into a better] into better *MM* [h]hath] has *CM, VO;* have *MM* [i]reading, and the other part of it, in] reading. The other, in *CM, VO* [j]have] has *VO* [k]Tartufe's] Tartufes *CM;* tartuffes *VO, MM* [l]have had a] have a *MM* [m]any] every *CM, VO, MM* [n]it—'tis] it; it is *VO, MM* [o]within, so entirely] within him, intirely *CM, VO;* within him so entirely *MM* [p]travels] Travels *VO;* Journey *MM* [q]only] but *CM, VO;* this *MM* [r]sending] presenting *CM, VO, MM* [s]you, being, dear] you. ¶Believe me, dear *CM, VO;* you. ¶I am, dear *MM* [t]me, and with] me, with *CM, VO* [u]oblig'd and humble] obliged humble *CM, VO*

1. *Dr. John Eustace*] For Dr. John Eustace (*d.* 1769), a physician in Wilmington, North Carolina, see the account by Hartley, repeated with a few additional comments by Marks. For Eustace's letter to Sterne, see appendix, letter xxii. Although little is known of Eustace, Hartley, 178, notes that "tradition in the area has it that there were both a Shandy Hall and a Toby Hall on Masonboro Sound"; that area, on the outskirts of Wilmington, continues to this day to have streets and lanes named "Shandy." That Sterne's popularity in America was hardly confined to North Carolina is indicated by the *Massachusetts Magazine,* which, according to Herbert R. Brown, "paid homage" to Sterne in every issue: "no author, sacred or profane, is mentioned so frequently and worshiped so fervently as Sterne" ("Richardson and Sterne in the *Massachusetts Magazine,*" *New England Quarterly* 5 [1932]: 76).

2. Shandean] As noted in *Status,* several words and phrases are printed in small capitals in Iredell–McRee, altered to italics in Curtis. We have silently altered them, instead, to lower case, capitalizing "s" where it seems appropriate to Sterne's usual practice, as in this instance.

3. piece of sculpture] As Eustace's letter indicates, he presented Sterne with what he called "a piece of Shandean statuary" (or "true Shandean statuary" [*VO*]; or "truly Shandean sculpture" [*MM*]). This was a curiously formed walking stick with several handles, originally the property of Arthur Dobbs (1689–1765), the governor of North Carolina, whose widow, Justina, gave it to Eustace. For a possible description, see Marks, 35.

4. Tartufe's] See above, letter 212, n. 2. New, *Book for Free Spirits,* 130–31, discusses this passage at some length, noting the popularity among modernists and postmodernists of the concept of multiple handles to a literary work, but also cautioning that Sterne seems to have had little sympathy with those who grasped the *wrong* handle, the "herd of the world" that failed to "understand" him.

5. any one] The reading of *VO* and *MM* ("every") seems indicative of an editorial hand working to "correct" Sterne's less than felicitous phrasing. Sterne would seem to mean "of *just* any one"; the phrase seems clear enough, and, to our minds, an indication that Iredell–McRee were less prone to tamper than were these other editors. The collation list tends to support the same conclusion.

6. brings half . . . with him] See letter 143, n. 4.

242. *To Laurence Sulivan*[1]

Text: Medalle

Old Bond Street, Wednesday. [February 17, 1768][2]

Dear Sir,

Your commendations are very flattering. I know no one whose judgement I think more highly of, but your partiality for me is the only instance in which I can call it in question.—Thanks, my good sir, for the prints—I am much your debtor for them—if I recover from my ill state of health, and live to revisit Coxwould this summer, I will decorate my study with them, along with six beautiful pictures I have already of the sculptures on poor Ovid's tomb, which were executed on marble at Rome.—It grieves one to think such a man should have dy'd in exile, who wrote so well on the art of love.[3]—Do not think me encroaching if I sollicit a favour—'tis either to borrow, or beg (to beg if you please) some of those touched with chalk which you brought from Italy—I believe you have three sets, and if you can spare the imperfect one of cattle on colour'd paper, 'twill answer my purpose, which is namely this, to give a friend of ours.[4]—You may be ignorant she has a genius for drawing, and whatever she excells in, she conceals, and her humility adds lustre to her accomplishments—I presented her last year with colours, and an apparatus for painting, and gave her several lessons before I left town.—I wish her to follow this art, to be a compleat mistress of it—and it is singular enough, but not more singular than true, that she does not know how to make a cow or a sheep, tho' she draws figures and landscapes perfectly well; which makes me wish her to copy from good prints.——If you come to town next week, and dine where I am engaged[5] next Sunday, call upon me and take me with you—I breakfast with Mr. Beauclerc,[6] and am engaged for an hour afterwards with Lord Ossory[a] so let our meeting be either at your house or my lodgings—do not be late, for we will go half an hour before dinner, to see a picture executed by West,[7] most admirably—he has caught the character of our friend—such goodness is painted in that face, that when one looks at it, let the soul be ever so much un-harmonized, it is impossible it should remain so.——I will send you a set of my books—they will take with the generality—the women will read this book in the parlour, and Tristram in the bed-chamber.[8]—Good night, dear sir—I am going to take my whey,[9] and then to bed. Believe me,

Yours most truly,
L. Sterne

MS: Not located.
Pub.: Medalle, no. 114; Curtis, no. 230.

[a]Lord Ossory] Lord O—— *M*

1. *Laurence Sulivan*] Medalle has "L. S. Esq." in 1775, but her second edition (1776) extends this to "L. S——n, Esq." Curtis, 413, n. 1, narrows the possibilities,

using Sterne's subscription lists, to two subscribers (both to *Sermons* in 1769), Luke Scrafton (1732–1770) or Laurence Sulivan (*c.*1713–1786). Both were connected to the East India Company (and hence with the Jameses), but Curtis suggests that since Scrafton died before 1780, the editor of *Works* would no longer have concealed his name, and hence that Sulivan is more probable. He was a director of the East India Company for many years. An additional bit of support for the identification may be Walpole's opinion that Sulivan "was the creature of Lord Shelburne" (*Memoirs . . . George III* 2:37); see letters 138, n. 3, and 207 for Sterne's acquaintance with Shelburne and his circle.

2. Date] Where Medalle merely has "Wednesday" for this letter and "Thursday" for letter 243, Curtis supplies the date for both, based on the anticipated publication of *ASJ* in the following week.

3. six . . . art of love] Cf. *BJ*, 201 (June 13): "I have a present of the Sculptures upon poor Ovid's Tomb, who died in Exile, tho' he wrote so well upon the Art of Love—These are in six beautiful Pictures executed on Marble at Rome." See n. to 201.9–12 (6:407–8). Ovid, author of *Ars amatoria,* was actually buried in Tomi, on the Black Sea, and not in the family tomb in Rome; the designs of that richly illuminated family sepulcher were engraved by Pietro Sante Bartoli (*c.*1635–1700) and became part of the neoclassical canon.

4. a friend of ours] I.e., Anne James. Sterne had referred to his gift in *BJ,* April 17: "with my friend M[rs] James in Gerard Street, with a present of Colours & apparatus for painting . . ." (173). The "apparatus" may have been a so-called Claude glass, named after the French landscape painter Claude Lorraine (1600–1682), "a small black convex glass used for reflecting landscapes in miniature" (*Oxford Companion to Art,* s.v.). It was often used by amateur painters in search of the picturesque, as were other "instruments," including the pantograph and the camera obscura, both of which Sterne mentions in *TS,* I.23.85.

5. where I am engaged] Gerrard Street, at the Jameses, where he was to view the West portrait; see below, n. 7.

6. Mr. Beauclerc] Curtis, 413, n. 5, suggests Topham Beauclerk (1739–1780), the great-grandson of Charles II and Nell Gwynne, who married Lady Diana Spencer in 1768. Given his association with Boswell and the Literary Club (some dozen or more members of which subscribed to Sterne), it seems a likely guess. Lord Ossory (see letter 239, n. 4) was also a member of the Literary Club. We also assume it was Topham Beauclerk who subscribed to *Sermons* in 1766 ("Beauclerk, —— Esq."), and to a large-paper copy of *ASJ* ("Mr. Beauclerc").

7. West] Benjamin West (1738–1820), the American painter, settled in London in 1763, became historical painter to George III, and was to succeed Reynolds as president of the Royal Academy in 1792. He designed the frontispiece portrait for Medalle's edition of the *Letters,* and between 1772–80 illustrated "The Captive"

and "The Dead Ass" from *ASJ*. We have been unable to locate his portrait of Mrs. James.

8. the women . . . bed-chamber] Cf. *TS*, VII.20.605, where Tristram is tempted to tell his readers the two French words that can move a post-horse, but if he does, "though their reverences may laugh at it in the bed-chamber—full well I wot, they will abuse it in the parlour." The notion had been in Sterne's mind since the first pages of volume I: "in the end, [his work will] prove the very thing which *Montaigne* dreaded his essays should turn out, that is, a book for a parlour-window . . ." (I.4.5). See notes to both passages, 3:470, n. to 605.16–18, and 3:49, n. to 5.10–11. The passage underlying all these instances is from Montaigne, "Upon Some Verses of Virgil" (*Essays,* trans. Charles Cotton, 5th ed. [1738], III.5.71): "I am vexed that my *Essays* only serve the Ladies for a common moveable, a Book to lie in the Parlour Window; this Chapter shall prefer me to the Closet . . . ."

9. whey] Cf. *TS*, VII.29.624, where Tristram responds to his sexual failure with Jenny, with his own medication: "I'll go into Wales for six weeks, and drink goat's-whey—and I'll gain seven years longer life for the accident." The note to the passage (3:480, n. to 624.17–18) indicates that throughout the century "whey" was thought to have medicinal properties.

243. *To Anne and William James*

Text: Medalle

Thursday, Old Bond Street. [February 18, 1768]

A thousand thanks, and as many excuses, my dear friends, for the trouble my blunder has given you. By a second note I am astonish'd I could read Saturday for Sunday, or make any mistake in a card wrote by Mrs. James[a], in which my friend is as unrival'd, as in a hundred greater excellencies.

I am now tyed down neck and heels[1] (twice over) by engagements[2] every day this week, or most joyfully would have trod the old pleasing road from Bond to Gerrard Street.—My books will be to be had on Thursday, but possibly on Wednesday in the afternoon.[3]—I am quite well, but exhausted with a room full of company every morning till dinner—How do I lament I cannot eat my morsel (which is always sweet)[4] with such kind friends!—The Sunday following I will assuredly wait upon you both—and will come a quarter before four, that I may have both a little time, and a little day light, to see Mrs. James's[a] picture.—I beg leave to assure my friends of my gratitude for all their favours, with my sentimental thanks[5] for every token of their good will.—Adieu, my dear friends—

I am truly yours,
L. Sterne

MS: Not located.
Pub.: Medalle, no. 113; Curtis, no. 231.

[a]James] J———s / J———'s *M*

1. tyed down neck and heels] *OED,* s.v. *neck,* II.6.b, equates the phrase *neck and heels* with *neck and crop,* meaning "completely, altogether" and considered dialect; eighteenth-century examples are offered from 1734 and 1778 (Burney, *Evelina*). See also *neck,* II.7: "*To tie . . . neck and heels,* to confine or bind securely" (seventeenth century); see letter 184, n. 8.

2. engagements] Cash, *LY,* 321, notes that Sterne had appointments with Sir Joshua Reynolds on February 23 at 9 a.m. and March 1 at 4 p.m. (Reynolds, "Appointment Book," Burlington House) and suggests that these would have been social (and dining) occasions rather than sittings. A third appointment for March 9 is erased; Sterne had, by then, entered his final illness. See also Curtis, 414, n. 2. Had we the social calendars of other Londoners, we might find Sterne's name again and again; he did not seem to enjoy dining alone.

3. Wednesday in the afternoon] *ASJ* was in fact published on Saturday, February 27, 1768 (*Public Advertiser* for that date); see *ASJ,* 6:461ff. (appendix 5), for full bibliographical details of this edition and the second edition, published on March 29, 1768, eleven days after Sterne's death.

4. morsel (which is always sweet)] Sterne would seem to be referring to something specific, but the gist has eluded us. In *2 Henry IV,* II.iv.367–68, Falstaff speaks of the coming of "the sweetest morsel of the night, and we must hence and leave it unpick'd." Cf. the often-quoted phrase of Matthew Henry (1662–1714), in his commentary on Psalm 36: "He rolls it under his tongue as a sweet morsel" (*Bartlett's Familiar Quotations,* rev. and enl. ed. [Boston: Little Brown, 1980], 319).

5. sentimental thanks] Sterne uses this phrase earlier to Mrs. James in letter 205A. With all the other possible—and intricate—meanings of *sentimental* in Sterne's usage, we are here reminded that at times the word quite simply meant for him something equivalent to "heartfelt."

244. *To Elizabeth Montagu*

Text: Curtis

[London, ?February 1768][1]

Thanks, thanks—my dear and kind Cosin, for the domestick supply[2]—it is all I wanted—and this bottle alone will be enough to restore to me what I have lost—w^h^ is a little strength—which I usually regain in as short time, as I lost it; I am absolutely this morning free from every bodily distemper that is to be read of in the catalogue of human infirmities and I know I shall not be able to delay paying you my thanks in person, longer than till to-morrow noon; if you are *visible*[3] as the French say:

I follow no regimen, but that of strict Temperance, and so am with all sense of y^r^ goodness, Dr Madame

Your affec^te^ cosin,
L. Sterne

MS: Not located.

Pub.: Lewis Melville, *Life and Letters of Laurence Sterne* (London: Stanley Paul and Co., 1911), 2:310; Curtis, no. 232.

1. Date] The letter is undated; the prevalent assumption, that it was written during Sterne's final illness, is probably based on the two following letters, also to Montagu and more datable; we see no reason to question that assumption.

2. domestick supply] Sterne probably refers to a medicinal preparation she had sent, and hence his "Dr Madame" in closing (of course, he may simply be abbreviating "Dear" but he does so nowhere else).

3. *visible*] In French, "être visible" means that one can be visited, rather like the English expression, "the doctor will see you now"; see n. above.

245. *To Elizabeth Montagu*

Text: Ms.

[London, ?February 1768][1]

Upon my Soul, I know not whether my Cosin Montague subscribed to my sentimental Travels or no——if She did not—She ought—but I think She did[2]—be that as it may<,>~—~as I have[a] been able to procure a set upon Imp[l] Paper before the publication, I mean it civilly, to <?>~Lay~ it at her feet, w[ch] I sh[d] have done in person had not it been too late ∧in the day∧ before I could get them from the Press.

M[r] Sterne presents his comp[s] to M[r] Montague,[3] & is with a just sense of all favours, Dear Mad[m]

Y[r] faithful & obliged.
L Sterne

Address: M[rs] Montague / Hill Street
MS: Henry E. Huntington Library, San Marino, Calif., MO 5090.
Pub.: Blunt, *Mrs. Montagu* (1923), 1:191; Curtis, no. 233.

[a]—as I have] —I have *Blunt*

1. Date] Clearly Sterne is writing shortly before the publication of *ASJ* on February 27, but Curtis's assumption that Sterne "is writing on the eve of the publication" (415) is unjustifiably specific; large-paper copies, probably printed first, may have been available days before the actual publication date.

2. I think She did] Her name appears as "Mrs. Mountague," a subscription for an ordinary copy only; cf. the same misspelling in letter 247. Mrs. Montagu had subscribed to *Sermons* in 1760 and 1766.

3. M[r] Montague] Edward Montagu (1692–1775), of Allerthorpe, Yorkshire, MP for Huntingdon, 1734–68, married Elizabeth Robinson in 1742. He was the grandson of the Earl of Sandwich and a distinguished mathematician. Blunt provides an account: "Mr. Montagu was nearly thirty years older than his bride . . . and was a man of sound judgement, retiring, sober, and rather indolent habit, and of ample means, derived largely from collieries and farms near Newcastle and in Yorkshire. The marriage can scarcely be called a love match . . . but it proved as satisfactory a union of tolerant contentment as could be expected; and it was only towards the close of his life, when he was over eighty, that the peevish tantrums

of an invalid strained wifely devotion . . . . For the most part the pair pursued their somewhat divergent paths—he with his microscope and his instruments in studied seclusion, she with her coteries of literary friends . . . in mutual tranquillity and esteem" (*Mrs. Montagu* 1:2–3). Montagu subscribed separately from his wife to *Sermons* in 1760, 1766, and 1769—but not to *ASJ*.

246. *To Lydia Sterne*

Text: Medalle

Old Bond Street. [March 1768][1]

My dearest Lydia,

My Sentimental Journey, you say, is admired in York[2] by every one—and 'tis not vanity in me to tell you that it is no less admired here—but what is the gratification of my feelings on this occasion?—the want of health bows me down, and vanity harbours not in thy father's breast—this vile influenza—be not alarm'd, I think I shall get the better of it——and shall be with you both the first of May, and if I escape 'twill not be for a long period, my child——unless a quiet retreat and peace of mind can restore me.—The subject of thy letter has astonish'd me.—She could but know little of my feelings, to tell thee, that under the supposition I should survive thy mother, I should bequeath thee as a legacy to Mrs. Draper[a].[3] No, my Lydia! 'tis a lady, whose virtues I wish thee to imitate, that I shall entrust my girl to—I mean that friend whom I have so often talk'd and wrote about—from her you will learn to be an affectionate wife, a tender mother, and a sincere friend—and you cannot be intimate with her, without her pouring some part of the milk of human kindness[4] into your breast, which will serve to check the heat of your own temper, which you partake in a small degree of.—Nor will that amiable woman put my Lydia under the painful necessity to fly to India for protection, whilst it is in her power to grant her a more powerful one in England.—But I think, my Lydia, that thy mother will survive me—do not deject her spirits with thy apprehensions on my account.—I have sent you a necklace, buckles, and the same to your mother.—My girl cannot form a wish that is in the power of her father, that he will not gratify her in—and I cannot in justice be less kind to thy mother.—I am never alone——The kindness of my friends is ever the same—I wish tho' I had thee to nurse me—but I am deny'd that.—Write to me twice a week, at least.—God bless thee, my child, and believe me ever, ever thy

Affectionate father,

L. S.

MS: Not located.
Pub.: Medalle, no. 115; Curtis, no. 235.

[a]to Mrs. Draper] to —— *M*

1. Date] Medalle has "February 20"; Curtis, 417, emends this to "March 1768" and explains: "Since Sterne has heard of the kind reception at York given to the *Sentimental Journey,* the letter was written not on 20 Feb. . . . but during the first week of March." Cf. Cash, *LY,* 325, n. 26, who argues the same point, and then adds that this letter was written before letter 247 (to Mrs. Montagu), because Sterne seems to be writing it "under a threat of death"; Curtis had placed it after. In letter 248, Sterne describes this letter as having been written "a fortnight ago," but, as Cash points out, Sterne may not have been counting accurately. It seems impossible, in fact, to assign definitive dates to the final three letters, although it seems likely that this letter was written at the earliest toward the end of the first week in March, and the next two letters probably at the end of the second week or beginning of the third—Sterne would die on Friday, March 18.

2. admired in York] *ASJ* reached York on Tuesday, March 1, 1768 (*York Courant* of that date).

3. Mrs. Draper] We follow Curtis, 417, in repairing Medalle's usual blank. It seems obvious from the context here and corroborative comments in letter 248 that Elizabeth Sterne had warned Lydia that Eliza was to be her "new" mother if she predeceased Sterne; Sterne hastens to assure his daughter that Anne James would fulfill that role if necessary. It proved unnecessary, of course, Elizabeth outliving Sterne by five years, dying at Albi, in the south of France, on July 11, 1773. See also appendix, letter li.

4. milk of human kindness] The famous phrase from *Macbeth,* I.v.16–18, spoken by Lady Macbeth in disapproval of her husband's character: "Yet do I fear thy nature, / It is too full o' th' milk of human kindness / To catch the nearest way."

247. *To Elizabeth Montagu*

Text: Ms.

[London, March 1768]

The seasonable benignity of dear Mrs Mountague's<,> Billet, has extorted, what neither Sickness or Affliction have ever had force to do, from me—need I <need> tell you,—that this was a couple of tears, which I found necessary to wipe away, before I could see, to tell her—I <h>~a~m more thankful & have a deeper sense of it, than if <you>~She~ had sent me a conveyance of <Y^{r}>~h~er Estate—<&>~—~ ∨&∨ What I prize more than that, of <y^{r}> ∧her∧ Wit & Talents along with ∧it—∧—a kind word or look, in my situation (or indeed in any) conquers me (if I was not conquer'd[a] before) for ∧ever—∧——But I brave evils.—et quand Je serai mort, on mettra mon nom dans le liste de ces Heros, qui sont Morts en plaisantant.[1]

The Account, dear Lady, which has interested You so humanely, is a point I cannot contest or deny—tho' I ever make a mystery of these evils—I am ill—very ill—Yet I feel my Existence strongly, and something like revelation along with it, which tells, I shall not dye—but live——& yet any other man w^{d} set his house in order——[2]

O! I envy Scarron—tho' I lye most abominably—for <th>~w~hen y^{r} kind Billet came in—I was writing a Romance, in truth, & which, as it is most comic—if my Sickness continues but 7 days—I shall finish——tell me the reason, why Cervantes could write so fine and humourous a Satyre, in the melancholly regions of a damp prison—or why Scarron in bodily pain[3]——or why the Author of the Moyen de parvenir (a vile,—but Witty book)—under the bondage of a poor *Canonical*[4]

——but that *Word,* girds me too close— there is either an Obliquity in Nature or some unknown Spring only sufferd to act within us, when, ∧we are thus∧ in the house of Bondage[5]————

—excuse a weak brain for all this—and to strengthen this poor Machine, send me, gently[6] Lady, at Y^{r} Leisure a <few> very few Jellies—the people ab^{t} me oppress me but with their attention—I hope in 2 or

3 days, to say my Matins to You—& believe Madame, there is no one ^worshiper^ can approach y[r] Altar with a more unblemished Offering

than Y[r] most obliged & most
humble Servant
L Sterne

Address: To / M[rs] Montagu
MS: Henry E. Huntington Library, San Marino, Calif., MO 5091.
Pub.: Blunt, *Mrs. Montagu* (1923), 1:192–93; Curtis, no. 234.

[a]conquer'd] conqur'd *MS*

1. et quand . . . plaisantant] And when I've died, they'll place my name in the list of those heroes who have died in a jest. Cf. *TS,* V.3.425: "For this reason, continued my father, 'tis worthy to recollect, how little alteration in great men, the approaches of death have made.—*Vespasian* died in a jest upon his close stool . . . ." Sterne would seem to allude to *Réflections sur les grands hommes qui sont morts en plaisantant* (1712) by Andre-François Boureau-Deslandes, translated into English in 1713 and 1745.

2. not dye . . . in order] Sterne used the same scriptural passages, 2 Kings 20:1 and Psalm 118:17, some four years earlier in making the exact same protestation against the possibility of dying; see letter 126 (January 5, 1764), and n. 7.

3. I envy Scarron . . . pain] See letter 42 (December 14, 1759), where Sterne makes almost the exact same observation about Scarron and Cervantes and writing humor under adversity. These evidences (see n. 2 above) of Sterne's consistency of thought in his penultimate surviving letter are both touching and significant. The "Romance" Sterne mentions has never been found.

4. the Author . . . *Canonical*] François Béroalde de Verville (1558–1612) was canon of St. Gratien de Tours when he wrote *Le Moyen de parvenir* (1610). Cf. introduction to *Notes* to *TS,* 3:20–21: "There has been a persistent myth about Sterne's reading, begun by [John] Ferriar, and reflecting his own interest in French imitators of Rabelais, that Sterne was heavily indebted to such authors as François Béroalde, Guillaume Bouchet, Gilles Ménage, and Bruscambille. Cross is particularly enthusiastic on the subject of this debt, without offering any concrete evidence, and he has been often echoed by later critics, despite the fine 1931 doctoral dissertation of C. F. Jones, 'The French Sources of Sterne' [University of London], which concluded that Sterne was probably not familiar with these

authors in any significant way. Our own view is similar." Curtis, 417, n. 5, calls attention to Ferriar's discussion of Sterne's supposed debt in *Illustrations of Sterne,* 2d ed. (1812), 1:49–53, including a note on p. 53, where he reports seeing a copy of *Le Moyen* (characterized by Ferriar, 50, as "a book disgusting by its grossness, but extremely curious") with a blank leaf containing "Sterne's Autograph, *L. Sterne, a Paris,* 8 *livres.*" The book, we are also told, "bears evident marks of its having been frequently turned over." Nevertheless, the Florida editors were unable to discover a single borrowing in *TS* or *ASJ* from Béroalde, and there the case seems, thus far, to rest.

5. some unknown . . . Bondage] The idea of a secret or unknown spring that guides our actions is a favorite with Sterne, often appearing in his fictions (see, esp., *TS,* IV.8.333–34, and n. to 333.17–334.9; 3:304–5); and sermons (see, esp., sermon 34, "Trust in God," and the notes to it in *Sermons* 5:353–64). "House of Bondage" is a biblical commonplace for Egypt; Sterne's usage would seem to be figurative for both ill health and, more generally, physical suffering.

6. poor Machine . . . gently] Sterne may have intended "gentle." For the body as "Machine," see letter 209, n. 4.

248. *To Anne James*

Text: Medalle

[London,] Tuesday [March 15, 1768][1]

Your poor friend is scarce able to write—he has been at death's door this week with a pleurisy—I was bled three times on Thursday, and blister'd on Friday—The physician says I am better—God knows, for I feel myself sadly wrong, and shall, if I recover, be a long while of gaining strength.—Before I have gone thro' half this letter, I must stop to rest my weak hand above a dozen times.—Mr. James[a] was so good to call upon me yesterday. I felt emotions not to be described at the sight of him, and he overjoy'd me by talking a great deal of you.—Do, dear Mrs. James[a], entreat him to come to-morrow, or next day, for perhaps I have not many days, or hours, to live—I want to ask a favour of him, if I find myself worse—that I shall beg of you, if in this wrestling I come off conqueror[2]—my spirits are fled—'tis a bad omen—do not weep my dear Lady—your tears are too precious to shed for me—bottle them up, and may the cork never be drawn.[3]—Dearest, kindest, gentlest, and best of women! may health, peace, and happiness prove your handmaids.—If I die, cherish the remembrance of me, and forget the follies which you so often condemn'd—which my heart, not my head betray'd me into. Should my child, my Lydia want a mother, may I hope you will (if she is left parentless) take her to your bosom?—You are the only woman on earth I can depend upon for such a benevolent action.—I wrote to her a fortnight ago, and told her what I trust she will find in you.—Mr. James[a] will be a father to her—he will protect her from every insult, for he wears a sword which he has served his country with, and which he would know how to draw out of the scabbard in defence of innocence—Commend me to him—as I now commend you to that Being who takes under his care the good and kind part of the world.——Adieu——all grateful thanks to you and Mr. James[a].

Your poor affectionate friend,
L. Sterne[4]

MS: Not located.
Pub.: Medalle, no. 116; Curtis, no. 236.

[a]James] J——— *M*

1. Date] Medalle has "Tuesday" without a date; *1780* assigned Sterne's last known letter to March 8; Cross, *Letters* (1904), 2:222, followed by Curtis, has the more likely "March 15."

2. that I shall . . . conqueror] Sterne's syntax (or Medalle's editing) is confusing, but he seems to be saying that he will ask the favor of Mr. James if necessary, but if he regains his health, he will ask it of Mrs. James; since he goes on to detail the probable favor he has in mind (serving as guardian for Lydia), he is perhaps indicating the importance of asking for a favor in person if the situation allows.

3. your tears . . . drawn] Sterne plays a variation on one of his favorite scriptural passages, Psalm 56:8: "put thou my tears into thy bottle"; see letter 203, n. 6.

4. L. Sterne] Death finally came for Sterne in his lodgings in Old Bond Street on Friday, March 18, 1768, at four o'clock in the afternoon. Cash, *LY,* 327–29, provides an anecdotal account and a possible diagnosis: "In all probability it was a painless death: his disintegrated lungs had filled with fluid, bringing oxygen starvation, often a euphoric condition, and finally heart failure."

APPENDIX

Letters Pertaining to Sterne and His Family

i. *Laurence Sterne to Elizabeth Lumley*

Text: Medalle

[?1740][1]

You bid me tell you, my dear L. how I bore your departure for Staffordshire[a], and whether the valley where D'Estella[2] stands retains still its looks—or, if I think the roses or jessamines smell as sweet, as when you left it—Alas! every thing has now lost its relish, and look! The hour you left D'Estella I took to my bed.—I was worn out with fevers of all kinds, but most by that fever of the heart with which thou knowest well I have been wasting these two years—and shall continue wasting 'till you quit Staffordshire[a].[3] The good Miss S——, from the forebodings of the best of hearts, thinking I was ill, insisted upon my going to her.[4]—What can be the cause, my dear L. that I never have been able to see the face of this mutual friend, but I feel myself rent to pieces? She made me stay an hour with her, and in that short space I burst into tears a dozen different times—and in such affectionate gusts of passion that she was constrained to leave the room, and sympathize in her dressing room—I have been weeping for you both, said she, in a tone of the sweetest pity—for poor L's heart I have long known it—her anguish is as sharp as yours—her heart as tender—her constancy as great—her virtues as heroic—Heaven brought you not together to be tormented. I could only answer her with a kind look, and a heavy sigh[5]—and return'd home to your lodgings (which I have hired 'till your return) to resign myself to misery—Fanny had prepared me a supper—she is all attention to me—but I sat over it with tears; a bitter sauce, my L. but I could eat it with no other—for the moment she began to spread my little table, my heart fainted within me.—One solitary plate, one knife, one fork, one glass!—I gave a thousand pensive, penetrating looks at the chair thou hadst so often graced, in those quiet, and sentimental repasts—then laid down my knife, and fork, and took out my handkerchief, and clapped it across my face, and wept like a child.[6]—I do so this very moment, my L. for as I take up my pen my poor pulse quickens, my pale face glows, and tears are trickling down upon the paper, as I trace the word L——. O thou! blessed in thyself, and in thy virtues—blessed to all that know thee—to me most so, because more do I know of thee than all thy sex.—This is the philtre, my L. by which thou hast charmed me, and by which thou wilt hold me thine whilst virtue and faith hold this world together.—This, my friend, is the plain and simple magick by which I told Miss —— I have won a place in that heart of thine, on which I depend so satisfied, that time, or distance, or change of every thing which might alarm the hearts of little men, create no uneasy suspence in mine—Wast thou to stay in Staffordshire[a] these seven years, thy friend, though he would grieve, scorns to doubt, or to be doubted—'tis the only exception where security is not the parent of danger.[7]—I told you poor Fanny was all attention to me since your departure—contrives every day bringing in the name of L. She told me last night (upon giving me some hartshorn)[8] she had observed my illness began the very day of your departure for Staffordshire[a]; that I had never held up my head, had seldom, or scarce ever smiled, had fled from all society—that she verily believed I was broken-hearted, for she had never entered the room, or passed by the door, but she heard me sigh heavily—that I neither eat, or slept, or took pleasure in any thing as before;[9]—judge then, my L. can the valley look so well—or the roses and jessamines smell so sweet as heretofore? Ah me!—But adieu—the vesper bell calls me from thee to my God!

L. Sterne

MS: Not located.

Pub.: Medalle, no. 2; Curtis, no. 1.

Status: Medalle published four letters from Sterne to Elizabeth Lumley (see above, letter 2, *Status*). This is the second letter in her collection, but Curtis prints it as the first in his edition, although only to highlight his strong conviction that it is largely Lydia's fabrication based on access to *BJ.* By printing the letter alongside relevant portions of the *Journal,* he certainly makes clear that almost the entire text, excepting only the images of D'Estella's valley of roses and jessamines at the opening and closing, is duplicated in journal entries for April 15, 21, 19, 16, 25, and 26, in that order.

The question can be put directly: Did Sterne in this instance, as we know he did on other occasions, recycle epistolary materials for different correspondents? Or did Lydia, with access to *BJ,* create this letter with an eye toward her father's reputation and her family's honor? While we have tended to lean toward the recycling theory in almost every previous instance, this letter seems to us very strong evidence for the alternative view, and we have accordingly relegated it to this appendix.

Curtis's lengthy account, 12–15, is still worth consulting, although it too remains largely inconclusive (see, e.g., Duke Maskell's detailed—but equally inconclusive—rebuttal of Curtis in "The Authenticity of Sterne's First Recorded Letter," *N&Q,* n.s. 17 [1970]: 303–7). We do suggest that Curtis's moralistic argument against Sterne's recycling ("one is asked to believe that after eleven days his passions were so withered that he was obliged to interpolate material from an old letter which he may not have had with him in London" [14]) might be countered with a more psychological view that Sterne's affairs, including that with Eliza, were all efforts to recapture his younger days, and thus were structured by him in such a manner that what he had written in 1740 was indeed applicable in 1767. On the other hand, we can certainly accept Curtis's other moralistic argument, that "Sterne's daughter, inheriting a wayward unscrupulousness from her father, was neither above nor below the necessary thefts . . ." (15). And one final alternative explanation may be suggested—namely, that Lydia had access not to the *Journal* itself, but to a letter addressed to Eliza that Sterne constructed from his own entries. Hence, by just suppressing her name and altering a minimum number of details, Lydia could readdress a love letter meant for Eliza to one directed to her mother.

[a]Staffordshire] S—— *M*

1. Date] Cf. Curtis, 12: "The conventional date of this letter is the winter of 1740/1. In that year it is believed Elizabeth Lumley visited her sister Lydia . . . [in

Staffordshire]. But since Sterne speaks of Miss Lumley's return to York when 'she fell into a consumption,' and of his marriage to her in 1741 after 'it pleased God that she recovered' [citing Sterne's *Memoirs* 19–20], this letter together with three that follow may well belong to the year 1739–40" (see letter 2 above).

2. D'Estella] Perhaps, as Curtis, 15, n. 2, suggests, a pious reference to Diego de Estella (*c.*1524–1578), whose *Contempt of the World, and the Vanities Thereof*, a popular devotional tract often reprinted during the seventeenth century, was in the York Minster Library. On the other hand, Sterne invoked the same "curate of *d'Estella*" in his bawdy "Chapter on Whiskers" (*TS* V.1.414; see *Notes* to *TS*, 3:343, n. to 414.13–14). A third suggestion is hinted at by David A. Brewer, "Scholia to *Tristram Shandy*," *Scriblerian* 30.2 (Spring 1998): 91—namely, that Sterne was already playing with the relationship between his name and "star" ("starn" or "starling"), as he would do in presenting his coat of arms in *ASJ*, 100; see 6:332–33, n. to 100.13.

3. I was worn . . . Staffordshire] Cf. *BJ*, 171 (April 15): "worn out with fevers of all kinds but most, by that fever of the heart with w[ch] I'm eternally wasting, & shall waste till I see Eliza again . . . ." It is sad enough to observe that this chronicle of his illness might have been as apropos in 1740 as in 1767—and in every intervening year as well.

4. The good Miss S—— . . . her] Cf. *BJ*, 175 (April 21): "our dear friend M[rs] James, from the forbodings of a good heart, thinking I was ill; sent her Maid to enquire after me . . . ." As Curtis, 14, points out, Mrs. James did indeed send to inquire about Sterne (see letters 205A and 205B), which would argue, of course, for the letter having been copied from the *Journal*. We have not been able to identify "Miss S——."

5. What can be . . . heavy sigh] Cf. *BJ*, 174 (April 19): "What is the Cause, that I can never talk ab[t] my Eliza to her, but I am rent in pieces—I burst into tears a dozen different times after dinner, & such affectionate gusts of passion, That She was ready to leave the room,—& sympathize in private for us——I weep for You both, said she (in a whisper,) for Elizas Anguish is as sharp as yours—her heart as tender—her constancy as great—heaven join Your hands I'm sure together!" Curtis, 14, notes that the phrase "sympathize in her dressing room" is deleted in *BJ* (Sterne substituted "& sympathize in private for us") and confesses that this works against his basic argument: "Lydia Sterne with more cunning than was hers would hardly have rejected her father's correction for a passage half-buried under ink." This is, however, the sole example of Lydia's adopting a canceled phrase, every other reading being that of the emendation. We might note that one sentence in this passage does not appear in *BJ*, "Heaven brought you not together to be tormented"; cf., however, letter 203 (March 30, 1767), to Eliza: "That the best of beings (as thou sweetly hast express'd it) could not by a combination

of accidents, produce such a chain of events, merely to be the source of misery to the leading person engag'd in them."

6. Fanny . . . child] Cf. *BJ*, 172 (April 16), where except that Molly replaces Fanny as the maid, the repast is precisely the same. Curtis, 14–15, calls attention to the word "sentimental" in the letter, since it would predate by nine years Lady Bradshaigh's famous inquiry to Richardson concerning this unknown word so "much in vogue among the polite," usually taken to be the first known usage of the word. Sterne, he argues, "an obscure country parson in Yorkshire, can hardly have used it nine years before." This may be a specious argument, however, given that the inquiry was prompted precisely by the popularity of the word—Lady Bradshaigh's London circle may well have been more provincial in this regard than young Cambridge scholars (and recent graduates) looking for women to woo and wive. Research into the lexical history of "sentimental" should begin with Erik Erämetsä's *A Study of the Word "Sentimental" and of Other Linguistic Characteristics of Eighteenth-Century Sentimentalism in England* (Helsinki, 1951).

7. this very moment . . . danger] Cf. *BJ*, 179–80 (April 25): "this moment—when upon taking up my pen, my poor pulse quickend——my pale face glowed—and tears stood ready in my Eyes to fall upon the paper, as I traced the word Eliza. O Eliza! Eliza! ever best & blessed of all thy Sex! blessed in thyself and in thy Virtues—& blessed and endearing to all who know thee—to Me, Eliza, most so; because I *know more* of thee than any other—This is the true philtre by which Thou hast charm'd me & wilt for ever charm & hold me thine, whilst Virtue & faith hold this world together; tis the simple Magick, by which I trust, I have won a place in that heart of thine on w[ch] I depend so satisfied, That Time & distance, or change of every thing w[ch] might allarm the little hearts of little men, create no uneasy suspence in mine—It scorns to doubt—& scorns to be doubted—tis the only exception—When Security is not the parent of Danger." We quote at length if only to emphasize how much more like a young man's letter to a young woman (and potential wife) this seems than an address to Eliza, whom he had known for perhaps a month, and whom, he realized in his more rational moments, he would never see again; to be sure, the *Bramine's Journal* is not a very rational document.

Sterne's last phrase plays on the proverbial "danger is next neighbour to security" (*ODEP* 167).

8. hartshorn] Brookes, 335–36, provides the recipe for "*Spirit, Salt and Oil of Hartshorn*" (*cornu cervi*), noting its virtue as "a most penetrating Medicine . . . excellent to rouse the Spirits when Nature is sinking at the Decline of Fevers. It is good in nervous Cases, the Vertigo, the Epilepsy, Palsy, Lethargy, Jaundice, Swooning, the Trembling of the Heart, and the Pleurisy." No wonder Sterne dosed himself with it.

9. she had observed . . . as before] Cf. *BJ*, 181 (April 26), where it is Molly and Mrs. James who "had observed, I had never held up my head, since the Day you last dined with me—That I had seldome laughd or smiled—had gone to no Diversions—but twice or thrice at the most, dined out—That they thought I was broken hearted, for She never enterd the room or passd by the door, but she heard me sigh heavily—That I neither eat or slept or took pleasure in any Thing as before, except writing." Sterne's one possible witticism, perhaps already suggestive of a distancing himself from Eliza, is omitted in the letter—i.e., the two or three times he had dined out despite his "misery."

ii. *Jaques Sterne to Francis Blackburne*[1]

Text: Ms.

[York, Thursday,] Decem: 6: 1750

Good M[r] Archdeacon,

I wil beg Leave to rely upon Your Pardon for taking the Liberty I do with you in relation to your Turns of preaching in the Minster. What occasions it is, M[r] Hildyard's employing the last time the Only person unacceptable to me in the whole Church, an ungrateful & unworthy nephew of my Own, the Vicar of Sutton; and I shoud be much obligd to you, if you woud please either to appoint any person Yourself, or leave it to Your Register to appoint One when you are not here. If any of my turns woud Suit you better than Your Own, I woud change with you.

I cannot write to so good a Protestant without taking Occasion to let you know how my Causes, with the Popish Nunnery here, go on. We have had an Hearing at D[rs] Commons, & D[r] Lee[2] opend it in a facetious, & I think not a very becoming manner—He said he was sorry the Clergy of York had occasion to have recourse to such rough methods of making Converts of the Ladies—that the Laws for establishing the Reformation were now grown obsolete & out of date, & the present age too polite & refind to mind or submit to such old unfashionable proceedings—But I hope the Judges in this Commission of Delegates are not such fine Gentlemen; but that they wil treat the Laws of their Country with more reverence, and Consider the Tendency of the appeal: It may be ludicrously said, why shou'd the

Public be in Danger of being put into a flame upon the account of two or three old women, but the Serious way of putting it is, whether ^there^ shal be a Popish Seminary set up, for poisoning the minds of the King's Subjects & drawing them from their Allegiance, in every Town in the Kingdom. I doubt not but to be able to support the Decree in the Court of York, which was a very mild one, and I liked it the better for being so. Their Collusive Conviction at the Sessions I hope wil not avail them, for there was Certainly a new offence created upon the Statute of the 23d of Eliz: by a twelve-month's absence, which was not satisfied by the 12 pence a Sunday;[3] and the Ordinary had doubtless sufficient Evidence before him to justify him in taking care of their future Behaviour by a Monition, tho' Dr Lee was pleasd to treat ^it^ as an old Stale Ecclesiastical trick. I hope I shal soon have it in my power to prove these innocent Ladies (as some have represented them) guilty of a most treasonable Correspondence, during the late Rebellion, with a Seminary of Jesuits in Scotland & with a Seminary Abroad, in which the Head of the Nunnery here stild herself Abbess, tho' a noble Lord[4] in Your Archdeaconry laid his hand upon his Heart, & assurd me, upon his Honour, that it was no Religious House. When I am come at the Proof, I wil let you know it.

Dr Topham Acquainted me with the handsome & kind mention you made of me in Your Charge, and I beg leave to thank you for your good Opinion. But Believe me, I had infinitely more ^Pleasure^ in hearing of Other parts of Your Charge to the Clergy.

I am, Dear Sr
Your most obedient
& obligd Servant
Jaques Sterne

York Dec. 6th 1750—

My Causes with the Nunnery are to come on at Sergeants In<?>~n~ in Hilary Term.[5]

Endorsed: Mr Jaques Sterne reprobation of his nephew Yorrick.—& mention of the Popish nunnery at York.——

MS: British Library, Egerton MS. 2325, 3–4v.

Pub.: Fitzgerald, "Sterne at Home," 489 (first paragraph only); Curtis, no. viii.

1. *Jaques Sterne to Francis Blackburne*] See letter 6 for Sterne's side of the quarrel with his uncle, and for details on the persons mentioned—i.e., Blackburne, n. 1, Hildyard, n. 4, and Jaques Sterne, n. 5; for the "Popish Nunnery," see Forrester, "Uncle Jaques Sterne," 217–21.

2. D[r] Lee] Cash, *EMY,* 240, in his account of this letter, identifies him as "Dr George Lee, a celebrated lawyer and judge of the Prerogative Court of Canterbury." Since he first became a judge in December 1751, at the time of this letter he was an advocate in the Court; see *The Political Journal of George Bubb Dodington*, ed. John Carswell and Lewis Arnold Dralle (Oxford: Clarendon, 1965), xx and passim, for a further account of Lee (1700–1758), an admiralty lawyer and the Prince of Wales's "closest adviser"; as Cash notes, his criticism "must have had a special cutting edge, coming from . . . an active member of the Leicester House faction to which Jaques aspired" (*EMY* 241). Lee's religious tolerance is worth noting, given that Sterne would not reach the same position until *ASJ.*

Doctors Commons was an area near St. Paul's Cathedral, where ecclesiastical courts (including the Prerogative Court of Canterbury) heard civil cases.

3. the Statute . . . a Sunday] Forrester, 217–18, calls attention to Jaques's similar legalistic arguments in his 1747 pamphlet, "The Danger Arising to Our Civil and Religious Liberty from the Great Increase of Papists . . . ," where particular attention was paid to "public schools and seminaries for the teaching of youth in the pernicious tenets and principles of popery." In the first year of Elizabeth's reign, absence from public worship brought a twelve-penny fine, but by 23 Eliz. c. 1, s. 5 (1581), a forfeiture of £20 a month was levied, directed almost solely at Roman Catholics; see Richard Burn, *Ecclesiastical Law,* 4 vols., 3d ed. (1775), 3:106ff., 216ff. (entries under "Popery" and "Publick Worship"). Such laws had not been enforced for many years, and despite some strong anti-Catholic sentiment associated with the '45, Jaques's invocation of them suggests his fanaticism.

4. a noble Lord] Curtis, 428, n. 1, identifies him as Charles Gregory Fairfax, Viscount Fairfax of Emley, for whom see letter 187, n. 2. Forrester accepts the identification.

5. Sergeants Inn . . . Hilary Term] Sterne would preach to the assembled congregation of jurists at Sergeants Inn, Chancery Lane, in May 1760; see letter 58, n. 8. Hilary Term, when the courts sat, usually began on January 11 and ended the Wednesday before Easter; it is named after St. Hilary, whose day is January 13. Jaques, however, dropped his case in the next year, perhaps when he realized that Dr. Lee had been named a judge. As Forrester, 221, notes, "it would seem there were more Dr Lees around than he had bargained for."

iii. *Elizabeth Sterne to Theophilus Garencieres*

Text: Ms.

[Sutton, 1751]

Mr Garancier's[1]

I am Subject to great Heats, am Costive, have the Piles, & can't Swallow Lenitive Electuary;[2] Cassia in the Canes I have known some people make use of; send me some, & let me know how, & in what quantity I may take it. let me likewise have 1 Ounce of Syrup of Violets 1 Ounce of Oil of Almonds. let them be sent to the Angel in Godram Gate.[3]

E Sterne

Address: To / Mr Garanc[ieres][4]
MS: Robert H. Taylor Collection, Princeton University Library.
Pub.: Curtis, 45, n. 2.

1. Mr Garancier's] The apothecary Theophilus Garencieres (see letter 9; we assume this letter was written during the same illness, sometime in 1751).

2. Lenitive Electuary] Elizabeth's self-prescriptions are all laxatives; Brookes, 79–83, provides several recipes for "lenitive electaries" (medicines in which the operative ingredients are blended with conserves, honey, or syrup), including several in which the primary ingredient is the pulp of cassia (*cassia fistularis,* the pudding pipe tree or "Cassia in the Canes"); see Brookes, 16–17. Several recipes are given for "Syrup of Violets" (239), although its specific use is not mentioned; and "Oil of Almonds" seems to be a universal panacea: "useful to sheath the Acrimony of the Humours, to soften and relax the crisp and indurated Fibres in Inflammations, in Heat and Suppression of Urine, Colic and nephritic Pains, Coughs, and to promote Expectoration; as also to promote Urine, loosen the Belly, and to ease Pain" (296).

3. the Angel in Godram Gate] A public house in York; Goodramgate runs just east of the Minster and led to roads north, including the road to Sutton-on-the-Forest.

4. Mr Garanc[ieres]] Ms. defective.

iv. *Elizabeth Sterne to Elizabeth Montagu*[1]

Text: Ms.

Sutton [Friday,] March ye 9th [1753][2]

Dear Mad^m^

I return you my Sincere & hearty Thanks[3] for the Favour of your most welcome Letter; which had I received in a more happy Hour, wou'd have made me almost Frantick with Joy; For being thus Cruelly Seperated from all my Friends, the least mark of their kindness towards me, or Remembrance of me, gives me unspeakable Delight; But the Dismal Account I receiv'd at the same time of my poor Sister, has render'd my Heart Incapable of Joy, nor can I even know Comfort, till I hear of Her Recovery.

Believe me Dear Mad^m^ You were never more mistaken, than when You imagine that Time, & Absence can remove you from my Remembrance, I do assure you I do not so easily part with what affords me so great Delight; on the Contrary, I spare no pains to improve every little Accident that recalls you to my Remembrance, as the only amends which can be made me for[4] those Unhappinesses my Situation deprives me of[a]. As a proof of this, I must inform you, that about three weeks ago, I took a long Ride Thro' very bad weather, & worse Roads, merely for the Satisfaction of enjoying a Conversation with a Gentleman who though unknown to You, had conceiv'd the highest Opinion of you from the perusal of several of your Letters, for which he was Indebted to Mrs Clayton:[5] Had this Gentleman had nothing else to Recommend him, it Certainly wou'd have been Sufficient to have made me desirous of his Acquaintance, But he is both a Man of Sense, & Good-Breeding, so that I am not a little pleas'd with my new Acquaintance.

Your Supposition of my Sister's having Boasted to me of her Children, is doubtless extreamly Natural, I wish it had been as just; But I can in three words inform you of all I know about 'em; to wit, their Number, & their Names, for which I am indebted to Johnny. Had my Lydia been so obliging as to have made them the Subject of her Letters, I shou'd by this time have had a tolerable Idea of them by Considering what she said with some abatement; But as it is, I no more know whether they are Black, Brown, or Fair, Wise, or Otherwise, Gentle, or Froward, than the Man in the Moon:[6] Pray is this strange Silence on so Interesting a Subject Owing to her profound Wisdom, or her abundant Politeness? But be it to which[b] it will, as soon as she recovers her Health, I shall insist on all the satisfaction she can give me on this head. In the mean time I rejoice to find they have your Approbation, & am truly Thankful that Nature has done her part, which indeed is the most Material, though I frankly Own I shall not be the first to Forgive any Slights that Dame Fortune may be dispos'd to shew them.

Your God-Daughter as in Duty bound sends her best Respects to you, I will hope that she may enjoy what her poor Mother in Vain Laments, the want of a more intimate Acquaintance with her Kindred.

Be so good as to make M[r] Stern's & my Compliments to M[r] Montagu &

Believe me Dear Mad[m]
Your most Affectionate Cousin
& Oblig'd Humble Servant
E Sterne

MS: Henry E. Huntington Library, San Marino, Calif., MO 5087.
Pub.: Emily J. Climenson, *Elizabeth Montagu* (1906), 2:27–28 (much altered); Curtis, xi.

[a]of] off *MS, C* [b]it to which] it which *C*

1. *Elizabeth Montagu*] See letter 66, n. 1.

2. Date] Elizabeth's sister, Lydia Lumley, died on March 22, 1753, leaving her husband, Rev. John Botham, the "Johnny," we assume, of the third paragraph, a widower with five children. For Botham, see letter 3, n. 6. We date the letter, as did Curtis, on the basis of this event.

3. hearty Thanks] Here and elsewhere in this letter, Elizabeth draws a line after a word, when she feels she is too close to the right margin to begin another word—hence, "hearty— | Thanks." Curtis treats these as Shandean dashes, but we have omitted them precisely because they should not be confused with Sterne's hallmark.

4. made me for] Curtis emends to "made for me" in a vain effort to repair the syntax of this sentence; its meaning is clear enough, the phrase "deprives me of" creating its confusion. Too often Elizabeth is victimized by a compound sentence; see below, the sentence beginning "Your God-Daughter . . ." for a particularly mangled effort.

5. Mrs Clayton] Wife of Robert Clayton (1695–1758), Bishop of Killala, afterwards of Clogher; he was the author of *A Dissertation on Prophecy* (1749), a distinctly Arian treatise. Her sister, Anne Donellan, was a member of at least two circles, one around Swift, the other around Mrs. Montagu, and the two sisters are mentioned together on several occasions in Climenson (1906). The gentleman for whom Elizabeth Sterne braved the bad roads has not been identified.

6. Man in the Moon] Elizabeth's commonplace dullness here again suggests her distance from her husband; when Burney uses the phrase in *Evelina* (1778), vol. 2, ch. 9, she assigns it to one of her most ignorant and distasteful creations, Madame Duval: "he'd no more right to our money than the man in the moon" (ed. Margaret Anne Doody [London: Penguin, 1994], 186).

v. *Laurence Sterne to Stephen Croft*[1]

Text: Ms.

[Sutton, Friday,] May. 13. 1757

Rc^d of Stephen Croft Esqre: Two pounds ten shillings for Tyth. and eighteen Shillings for Glebe Land inclosed, due at last Lady Day[2]

Laurence Sterne

Rc^d at the same Time two pounds five Shillings being the half years Payment of a Contract made of the Glebe &c &c of North Skew[3]

2:10:0
0:18:0
2:05:0
———
5:13:0

L. Sterne

MS: Robert H. Taylor Collection, Princeton University Library.

1. *Stephen Croft*] Stephen Croft, Stillington's lord of the manor (see letter 37, n. 3).

2. Lady Day] One of the quarter-days, the Feast of the Annunciation, March 25.

3. North Skew] Northskeugh, the northern portion of Stillington (see letter 65, n. 4).

vi. *Elizabeth Sterne to John Blake*[1]

Text: Ms.

[Sutton, Saturday Night, 1758]

My most worthy Friend

A Thousand Blessings on your Heart for your kindness to me; You sent my Husband home to me in a disposition which promises me better Days, therefore not one word of ^our^ Conversation to T—r,[2] or any one Soul, for that might Blast all my hopes. I likewise find he has not told Mr T.r the worst of his Circumstances,[3] but as he has Comply'd with all that can reasonably be expected to mend 'em, I cou'd wish he might not be further press'd. therefore if you have told Mr Taylor give him a little Caution lest 'tis suspected from whence the Intelligence came. I trust I shall e'er long tell you by word of mouth how truely Thankfull I am to you, had I opportunity at present I cou'd not my head & Heart are so disturb'd by the extravagance of his Repentance. Farewell Believe me,

Your's most truely
Eliza: Sterne

Sutton Saturday Night

The Gravity of your Countenance was remark'd wch I attributed to ye plague of your own affairs[4] Remember[a] your promise or I may yet be no gainer.

Address: To / The Revd Mr Blake
MS: Kenneth Monkman Collection, Shandy Hall.
Pub.: Shandean 3 (1991): 179–82 (facsimile, fig. 54).

[a]Remember] Rebember *MS*

1. *John Blake*] See letter 16, and subsequent letters to Blake, for the context of this letter; it belongs, almost certainly, to the same period as Sterne's own surviving letters to Blake, and has been dated accordingly.

2. T—r] Elizabeth reveals the name "Taylor" in the course of the letter. As Monkman suggests, 182, n. 3, this is almost certainly John Taylor of Fulford, for whom see letter 22, n. 3.

3. his Circumstances] Perhaps the same mysterious "Bristol Affair" discussed in letter 16 (see, esp., n. 2), but whether that had to do with clerical advancement, financial dealings, or sexual matters (perhaps the Sturdy affair—see letter 15) has not been determined.

4. your own affairs] This would refer to Blake's contracted (and failed) courtship of Miss Margaret Ash.

vii. *William Warburton to David Garrick*[1]

Text: Private Correspondence of Garrick

Grosvenor-square; March 7, 1760.

My dear Sir,

You told me no news when you mentioned a circumstance of zeal for your friends; but you gave me much pleasure by it and the inclosed, to have an impertinent story confuted the first moment I heard of it; for I cannot but be pleased to find I have no reason to change my opinion of so agreeable and so original a writer as Mr. Sterne; I mean my opinion of his moral character, of which I had received from several of my acquaintance so very advantageous an account.[2] And I cannot see how I could have held it, had the lying tale been true, that he intended to injure one personally and entirely unknown to him. I own it would have grieved me, (and so, I believe, it would him too, when he had known me and my enemies a little better,) to have found himself in company with a crew of the most egregious blockheads that ever abused the blessing of pen and ink.

However, I pride myself in having warmly recommended "Tristram Shandy" to all the best company in town, except that at Arthur's.[3] I was charged in a very grave assembly, as Dr. Newton[4] can tell him, for a particular patronizer of the work; and how I acquitted myself of the imputation, the said Doctor can tell him. I say all this to show how ready I was to *do justice* to a stranger. This is all I expect from a stranger. From my friends, indeed, I expect, because I stand in need of, much *indulgence*. To them, (being without reserve,) I show my weaknesses. To strangers I have the discretion not to show them; at least, those *writing* strangers, I mentioned before, have not yet had the wit to find them out.

If Mr. Sterne will take me with all my infirmities,[5] I shall be glad of the honour of being better known to him; and he has the additional recommendation of being your friend.

I am, dear Sir,
Your most affectionate and faithful humble servant,
W. Gloucester

MS: Not located.

Pub.: Private Correspondence of David Garrick, 2 vols., ed. James Boaden (London: Henry Colburn and Richard Bentley, 1831), 1:115–16; Cross, *Letters* (1904), 1:160–61; Curtis, 94, n. 4.

1. *William Warburton to David Garrick*] For the context of this letter (and letters xii, xiii, and xiv), see letter 46 and notes. It was letter 46 that Garrick had enclosed and to which Warburton is here responding. Much of Warburton's personality can be deduced from his characterization of his enemies at the end of the first paragraph: "a crew of the most egregious blockheads . . . ."

2. I mean . . . account] Boaden, 115, provides a footnote: "It is melancholy to find the good Bishop subsequently compelled to change this opinion. Sterne had distinguished the *Divine Legation* in his 'Shandy,' and Warburton was amused by his pleasantry, originality, and power of embodying character; but he at length opened his eyes to the indecency of Sterne's Life, and in a letter to Hurd, dated Dec. 27, 1761, writes thus:—'Sterne has published his fifth and sixth volumes . . . . The fellow himself is an irrecoverable scoundrel.'" Boaden is inaccurate in assuming that Sterne had spoken well of *Divine Legation* anywhere in *TS;* he would eventually pair it ironically with Swift's *Tale of a Tub* in his only direct mention, IX.8.754.

3. I pride . . . at Arthur's] Horace Walpole wrote to Sir David Dalrymple on April 4, 1760, that "Bishop Warburton . . . recommended the book to the bench of bishops and told them Mr Sterne, the author, was the English Rabelais—they had never heard of such a writer" (*Correspondence* 15:66–67). Since Arthur's, in

St. James's Street, had become a rather notorious gambling club, it would be an unlikely place for the bishop to appear, much less with *Tristram Shandy* in his hands.

4. Dr. Newton] Thomas Newton (1704–1782), the precentor of York, who was made bishop of Bristol the next year; see letter 46, n. 1. He had written to an acquaintance on March 4, 1760: "Many people are pleased even with the oddness and wildness of [*Tristram Shandy*], and no body more than the new Bishop of Gloucester, who says that it is wrote, in the very spirit of Rabelais, and has spoke to me highly of it several times . . ." (see Curtis, "New Light on Sterne," 501; New, "Sterne, Warburton," 249–51).

5. with all my infirmities] The editor of Shakespeare (1747) may have been recalling *Julius Caesar,* IV.iii.86: "A friend should bear his friend's infirmities."

viii. *Laurence Sterne and James Dodsley* [1]

Text: Ms.

[March 8, 1760]

It is hereby agreed between Mr Dodsly & Mr Sterne, that Mr Sterne sells the Copy Right of the first & 2^{d} Vol^{s} of Tristram Shandy, for the Summ of two hundred & fifty Pounds—fifty p^{ds} to be paid in hand—& that the remainder at the end of six Months—Mem^{dm} the Profits of the Books already printed to be all Mr Sternes—the Receipt of which fifty pounds I hereby acknowledge. and it is further agreed that the 3^{d} & 4th Volumes, are to be sold & bought for the Summ of <four hundred Guineas.> three hundred & eighty <G>~P~ounds.—

L. Sterne
Ja^{s} Dodsley

Mar. 8. 1760
Witness
Richd Berenger[2]

MS: The Berg Collection, New York Public Library.
Pub.: Curtis, 98, n. 3.

1. *James Dodsley*] For the context of this letter, see letters 36, n. 8, and 47, nn. 1 and 4. The agreement is in Sterne's hand.

2. Richd Berenger] See letter 48, n. 1.

ix. *Laurence Sterne to Richard Berenger*

Text: Letter Book[1]

[London, Saturday, March 8, 1760]

my dear Berenger.

You bid me tell you all my wants——what the duce can the man want now? what would I not give to have but ten strokes of Howgarth's witty chissel at the front of my next Edition of Tristram Shandy (the Vanity of a pretty woman in the hey-day of her Triumphs, is a fool to the vanity of a successful author——*Orna me,* sigh'd Swift to Pope,—unite[2] something of yours to mine to <?bind> wind us together in one sheet down to posterity—I will, ˅I | will;˅ said Pope—but you don't do it enough said Swift———

Now the loosest Sketch in nature of Trim's reading the sermon to my father & my uncle Toby[3] will content me———

I would hold out my lank purse,——I would shut my eyes,—& you should put your hand into it, & take out what you liked[a] for it——Blockhead! This gift is not bought with money—perish thee, & thy gold with thee.

What shall we do? I would not propose a disagreeable thing to one I so much admire, for the whole world:—You are a hard faced, impudent honest dog—prithee step, & *sans menagement*[b],[4] begin thus.

"Mr Hogarth, my friend Shandy"——but go on your own way——as I shall do mine, all my Life.

So adieu.

MS: Letter Book, Pierpont Morgan Library, New York.
Pub.: Cross, *Life* (1925), 2:233–34; Curtis, no. 50B.

[a]what you liked] what liked *MS* [b]*menagement*] *menage-* | ment *MS*

1. *Text: Letter Book*] As Curtis, 101, notes, "This letter is a draft [that] . . . never passed through the post" of letter 48; see the notes to that version, above.

2. unite] See letter 48, n. 8.

3. my father & my uncle Toby] Sterne altered this to "my Father &c.," a slight change that perhaps was responsible for giving us Hogarth's wonderful rendition of Dr. Slop's "sesquipedality" along with the Shandy brothers.

4. *sans menagement*] Correctly: ménagement. Bluntly; without ceremony.

x. *Thomas Belasyse, Lord Fauconberg, to John Gilbert, Archbishop of York*[1]

Text: Ms.

[London, Friday, March 28, 1760]

To his Grace John by divine Providence Lord Arch-Bishop of York.

May it please your Grace—

The Curacy of Coxwold in the Arch-Deaconry of Cleveland & Diocese of York being vacant by the Death of the late Curate The Revd Mr Richard Wilkison,[2] And the Right of Nomination to the said Curacy being in me, I do hereby nominate the Revd Mr Laurence Sterne Master of Arts, & Prebendary of York, to your Grace for that Curacy; and I do desire your Grace would be pleased to admit the said Mr Sterne to the same.

witness my hand & Seal this twenty & eighth Day of March, one Thousand seven hundred & sixty.

ffauconberg

MS: British Library, Addit. Ch., 16166.
Pub.: Facsimile in Curtis, facing 102.

1. *Thomas Belasyse . . . York*] See letters 15, n. 4, and 50, n. 1; the nomination letter was written by Sterne and signed by Fauconberg.

2. Richard Wilkison] Richard Wilkinson died on March 12, 1760. See Cash, *EMY*, 257, and letters 8, n. 13, and 58, n. 7.

xi. *Anonymous Letter*[1]

Text: Cross, *Letters*

[Tuesday,] April 15th, 1760.

Indeed, my dear Sir, your Letter was quite a Surprise to me; I had heard that Mr. Shandy had engaged the Attention of the gay Part of the World, but when a Gentleman of your active and useful Turn can find Time for so many Enquiries about him, I see it is not only by the Idle and the Gay that he is read and admired, but by the Busy and the Serious: Nay, Common-Fame says, but Common-Fame is a great Liar, that it is not only a Duke and an Earl and a new made Bishop,[2] who are contending for the Honour of being Godfather to his dear Child Tristram, but that Men and Women too, of all Ranks and Denominations, are caressing the Father, and providing Slavering-Bibs for the Bantling.

In Answer to your Enquiries, I have sate down to write a longer Letter than usual, to tell you all I know about him and the Design of his Book. I think it was some Time in June last that he showed me his Papers, more than would make four such Volumes as those two he has published, and we sate up a whole Night together reading them. I thought I discovered a Vein of Humour, which must take with Readers of Taste, but I took the Liberty to point out some gross Allusions which I apprehended would be Matter of just Offense, and especially when coming from a Clergyman, as they would betray a Forgetfulness of his Character. He observed, that an Attention to his Character would damp his Fire and check the Flow of his Humour, and that if he went on, and hoped to be read, he must not look at his Band or his Cassock. I told him, that an over Attention to his Character might perhaps have that Effect, but that there was no Occasion for him to think all the Time he was writing his Book, that he was writing Sermons.—That it was no difficult Matter to avoid the Dirtiness of Swift on the one Hand, and the Looseness of Rabelais on the other—and that if he steered in that middle Course, he might make it not only a very entertaining, but a very instructive and useful Book;

and on that Plan I said all I could to encourage him to come out with a Volume or two in the Winter.[3]

At this Time he was haunted with Doubts and Fears of its not taking. He did not, however, think fit to follow my Advice, yet when the two Volumes came out, I wrote a Paper or two by the Way of recommending them, and particularly pointed to Yorick, Trim reading the Sermon, and such Parts as I was most pleased with myself.

If any Apology can be made for his gross Allusions and *double Entendres,* it is, that his Design is to take in all Ranks and Professions, and to laugh them out of their Absurdities. If you should ask him, why he begins his Hero nine Months before he is born, his Answer would be, that he might exhibit some Character inimitably ridiculous, without going out of his Way, and which he could not introduce with Propriety, had he begun him later. But as he intends to produce him somewhere in the 3d or 4th Volume, we will hope, if he does not keep him too long in the Nursery, his future Scenes will be less offensive. Old Women indeed there are of both Sexes, whom even Uncle Toby can neither entertain nor instruct, and yet we all have Hobby-Horses of our own. The Misfortune is we are not content to ride them quietly ourselves, but are forcing every Body that comes in our Way to get up behind.[4] Is not Intolerance the worst Part of Popery? what Pity it is, that many a zealous Protestant should be a staunch Papist without knowing it!

The Design, as I have said, is to take in all Ranks and Professions. A System of Education is to be exhibited, and thoroughly discussed; for forming his future Hero, I have recommended a private Tutor, and named no less a Person than the great and learned Dr. Warburton: Polemical Divines[5] are to come in for a Slap. An Allegory has been run up on the Writers on the Book of Job. The Doctor is the Devil who smote him from Head to Foot, and Grey, Peters and Chappelow[6] his miserable Comforters. A Groupe of mighty Champions in Literature is convened at Shandy-Hall. Uncle Toby and the Corporal are Thorns in the private Tutor's Side, and operate upon him as they did on Dr. Slop at reading the Sermon. All this for poor Job's Sake, whilst an Irish Bishop,[7] a quondum Acquaintance of Sterne's, who has written on the same Subject, and loves dearly to be in a Crowd, is to come uninvited and introduce himself.

So much for the Book, now for the Man. I have some Reason to think that he meant to sketch out his own Character in that of Yorick, and indeed in some Parts of it I think there is a striking Likeness, but I do not know so much of him as to be able to say, how far it is kept up. The Gentlemen in and about York will not allow of any Likeness at all in the best Parts of it; whether his Jokes and his Jibes[8] may not be felt by many of his Neighbours, and make them unwilling to acknowledge a Likeness, would be hard to say; certain, however, it is, that he has never, as far as I can find, been very acceptable to the Grave and Serious. It is probable too he might give Offense to a very numerous Party, when he was a Curate and just setting out, for he told me, that he wrote a weekly Paper[9] in support of the Whigs during the long Canvas for the great contested Election for this County, and that he owed his Preferment to that Paper—so acceptable was it to the then Archbishop.[10]

From that Time, he says, he has hardly written any Thing till about two Years ago; when a Squabble breaking out at York, about opening a Patent and putting in a new Life, he sided with the Dean and his Friends, and tryed to throw the Laugh on the other Party, by writing the History of an old Watchcoat; but the Affair being compromised he was desired not to publish it. About 500 Copies were printed off, and all committed to the Flames, but three or four, he said, one of which I read, and, having some little Knowledge of his *Dramatis Personæ,* was highly entertained by seeing them in the Light he had put them.[11] This was a real Disappointment to him, he felt it, and it was to this Disappointment that the World is indebted for Tristram Shandy. For[a] till he had finished his Watchcoat, he says, he hardly knew that he could write at all, much less with Humour, so as to make his Reader laugh. But it is my own Opinion, that he is yet a Stranger to his own Genius, or at least that he mistakes his Fort. He is ambitious of appearing in his Fool's Coat, but he is more himself, and his Powers are much stronger, I think, in describing the tender Passions, as in Yorick, Uncle Toby, and the Fly, and in making up the Quarrel between old Mr. Shandy and Uncle Toby.[12]

I can say nothing to the Report you have heard about Mrs. Sterne; the few Times I have seen her she was all Life and Spirits, too much so, I thought. He told me, in a Letter last Christmas, that his Wife had lost her Senses by a Stroke of the Palsy; that the Sight of the Mother in that Condition had thrown his poor Child into a fever; and that in the Midst of these Afflictions, it was a strange Incident that his ludicrous Book should be printed off; but that there was a stranger still behind, which was, that every Sentence of it had been conceived and written under the greatest Heaviness of Heart, arising from some Hints the poor Creature had dropped of her Apprehensions; and that in her Illness he had found in her Pocket-Book

"Jan. 1st, Le dernier de ma vie, helas!"[13]

Thus, my dear Sir, I have been as particular as I well can, and have given you as ample an Account both of the Man and the Design of his Book as you can reasonably expect from a Person, who, bating a few Letters, has not conversed more than three or four Days with this very eccentrick Genius.

Your's, &c.

MS: Not located.

Pub.: St. James Chronicle (April 22–24, 1788): 2; *European Magazine* 21 (March 1792): 169–70; Cross, *Letters* (1904), 1:25–32; Howes, *Critical Heritage,* 57–60.

[a]For] *EM;* So *Cross*

1. *Anonymous Letter*] The author has never been identified. The letter was sent to the *St. James Chronicle* by "G.E.G." with a headnote: "The following Letter was written to a Friend of mine by one of his Acquaintance, in Answer to some Queries proposed by the former, concerning Mr. Sterne. . . . The Gentleman did not then choose to put his Name to it, and my Friend not having taken any Memorandum of it, does not recollect who his Correspondent was" (quoted from Cross, *Letters* 1:24). Cross reprinted this version, and we have taken our text from his, having been unsuccessful in locating a copy of the *St. James Chronicle* for 1788. In 1792 the letter was reprinted in *European Magazine* by "H.H."; the

author includes it in a communication that also identifies a passage in "Abuses of conscience" as possibly derived from a sermon by Richard Bentley (see *Notes* to *TS* 3:183–84, n. to 160.3ff.). The *EM* version, reprinted by Howes, seems to have been altered to conform to house style—e.g., the capitalized nouns have been lowercased.

For an extended discussion of this letter, see New, "Sterne, Warburton," 247–49, and Cash, *EMY*, 279–80.

2. new made Bishop] Warburton had been consecrated Bishop of Gloucester some three months before, on January 20, 1760.

3. I took the Liberty . . . Winter] The tenor of this exchange closely parallels that chronicled by Sterne himself in letter 35A (B, C). And see also letter 46.

4. The Misfortune . . . behind] The letter closely shadows Sterne's own language about the hobby-horse in *TS*, I.7.12: "so long as a man rides his HOBBY HORSE peaceably and quietly along the King's highway, and neither compels you or me to get up behind him,——pray, Sir, what have either you or I to do with it?"

5. Polemical Divines] Sterne's primary attack on polemical divinity appears in *TS*, V.28–29.462–64, where Yorick reads out of Rabelais, I.35.295–98, the description of Gymnast's antics on his horse, by way of defining a "polemic divine" for Uncle Toby; see *Notes*, 3:376–78, nn. to 462.17, 462.19, and 463.1ff. It is no accident, perhaps, that in 1763 Warburton delivered a stinging defense of polemical divinity in the closing pages of *Doctrine of Grace*, singling out "small-dealers in second-hand Ridicule" for his particular scorn.

That Sterne probably did have "impractical" theological speculation as a target from the very beginning is suggested by his "Rabelaisian Fragment," usually considered his first effort at what would develop into *TS*; see New, "Sterne's Rabelaisian Fragment," 1083–92, and Cash, *EMY*, 280–81.

6. Grey, Peters and Chappelow] The identification of the figures represented by the original initials (in both the *St. James Chronicle* and *European Magazine* versions) was made by "A. B." in the *European Magazine* for October 1792, 255–56. Warburton had argued in his monumental *Divine Legation of Moses* (1737–41) that the book of Job was written after the patriarchs (by Ezra), and was an *allegory* of the Captivity. This notion was fiercely attacked by a host of clerics, among them Richard Grey (1694–1771), prebendary of St. Paul's and commissary of the archdeacon of Leicester, who published an *Answer to Mr. Warburton's "Remarks on Several Occasional Reflections"* (1744); Charles Peters (1695–1760), a Hebrew scholar, Exeter College, Oxford, who published his *Critical Dissertation on the Book of Job* in 1751; and Leonard Chappelow (1683–1768), professor of Arabic at Cambridge, author of a *Commentary on the Book of Job* (1752).

For an extensive discussion of the controversy and Sterne's take on it, see Jonathan Lamb, "The Job Controversy, Sterne, and the Question of Allegory,"

ECS 24 (1990): 1–19, which supplements his earlier discussion in *Sterne's Fiction and the Double Principle* (Cambridge: Cambridge University Press, 1989), 20–21, 90–91, and 145, and is in turn supplemented by his *The Rhetoric of Suffering: Reading the Book of Job in the Eighteenth Century* (Oxford: Oxford University Press, 1995).

7. an Irish Bishop] John Garnett (1709–1782), a fellow of Sidney Sussex College, Cambridge, when Sterne was at Jesus College, and Bishop of Clogher since 1758; his *Dissertation on the Book of Job* was published in 1749. Garnett subscribed to *Sermons* (1760).

8. his Jokes and his Jibes] Cf. *Hamlet,* V.i.189–91: "Where be your gibes now, your gambols, your songs, your flashes of merriment"; and *TS,* I.11.29: "he had but too many temptations in life, of scattering his wit and his humour,—his gibes and his jests about him . . . ."

9. a weekly Paper] For Sterne's early political writings on behalf of Jaques Sterne and the Whig cause in the election of 1741–42, see Curtis, *Politicks of Laurence Sterne;* Cash, *EMY,* ch. 5; and Monkman, "More of Sterne's *Politicks* 1741–1742," 53–108. Much of this writing appeared in the *York Gazetteer.*

10. the then Archbishop] Lancelot Blackburn (1658–1743); see Cash's brief account of this colorful—and licentious—cleric, *EMY,* 93–94.

11. when a Squabble . . . put them] For a full account of Sterne's *A Political Romance,* see Cash, *EMY,* ch. 13; and *TS,* 2:815–17 ("Introduction to the Text"). Sterne appears to have dropped the title "History of a Good Warm Watch-Coat," but it was revived in *1780* and thereafter. Six copies have been located.

12. Uncle Toby . . . Uncle Toby] Both incidents take place in *TS,* II.12.

13. *Jan. 1st, Le . . . helas!*] "The last [year] of my life, alas!"

xii. *William Warburton to Laurence Sterne*

Text: Medalle[1]

Prior-Park, [Sunday,] June 15, 1760.

Reverend Sir,

I have your favour of the 9th Instant,[2] and am glad to understand, you are got safe home, and employ'd again in your proper studies and amusements. You have it in your power to make that, which is an amusement to yourself and others, useful to both: at least, you should above all things, beware of its becoming hurtful to either, by any violations of decency and good manners; but I have already taken such repeated liberties of advising you on that head, that to say more would be needless, or perhaps unacceptable.

Whoever is, in any way, well received by the public, is sure to be annoy'd by that pest of the public, *profligate scribblers.* This is the common lot of successful adventurers; but such have often a worse evil to struggle with, I mean the over-officiousness of their indiscreet friends. There are two Odes,[3] as they are call'd, printed by Dodsley. Whoever was the author, he appears to be a monster of impiety and lewdness—yet such is the malignity of the scribblers, some have given them to your friend Hall; and others, which is still more impossible, to yourself; tho' the first Ode has the insolence to place you both in a mean and a ridiculous light. But this might arise from a tale equally groundless and malignant[a], that you had shewn them to your acquaintances[b] in *M.S.* before they were given to the public. Nor was their being printed by Dodsley the likeliest means of discrediting the calumny.

About this time, another, under the mask of friendship, pretended to draw your character, which was since[c] published in a *Female Magazine,*[4] (for dulness, who often has as great a hand as the devil, in deforming God's works of the creation, has *made them,* it seems, *male* and *female*) and from thence it was transformed[d] into a *Chronicle.* Pray have you read it, or do you know its author?

But of all these things, I dare say Mr. Garrick, whose prudence is equal to his honesty or his talents, has remonstrated to you with the freedom of a friend. He knows the inconstancy of what is called the Public, towards all, even the best intentioned, of those who contribute to its pleasure, or amusement. He (as every man of honour and discretion would) has availed himself of the public favour, to regulate the taste, and, in his proper station, to reform the manners of the fashionable world; while by a well judged œconomy, he has provided against the temptations[e] of a mean and servile dependency, on the follies and vices of the great.

In a word, be assured, there is no one more sincerely wishes your welfare and happiness, than,

Reverend Sir,
W. G.

MS: Not located.
Pub.: Medalle, no. 14; Kilvert, *A Selection from Unpublished Papers of . . . William Warburton,* (1841), 240–42; John Selby Watson, *Life of William Warburton* (London: Longman, Green, 1863), 503–4; Curtis, no. 62.

[a]malignant] maglignant *M* [b]acquaintances] acquaintance *Kilvert, Watson* [c]since] first *Kilvert, Watson* [d]transformed] transferred *Kilvert, Watson* [e]temptations] temptation *Kilvert, Watson*

1. *Text:* Medalle] Kilvert's text seems derived from Medalle's rather than from any "unpublished papers" as his title promises; he then exercised an editorial hand, evident in emending several elided past-tense endings and erratic punctuations, and in dropping one sentence (see n. 4 below). Watson followed his text. Curtis follows Medalle, and we are happy to acknowledge at least this instance where her text appears to be closer to the original than the other alternatives.

2. your favour of the 9th Instant] See letter 3, n. 1; Sterne may have had Warburton's letter in mind when he wrote to a female admirer a few days later (see letter 62, to Mary Macartney, June 1760): "I could easily mend it, by saying with the dull phlegm of an unfeeling John Trot . . . '*That Y*[rs] *of the 8*[th] *Inst*[t] *came safe to hand.*'"

3. two Odes] I.e., Hall-Stevenson's *Two Lyric Epistles* (see letters 59 and 60). They were printed by R. and J. Dodsley; clearly Warburton believed the gossip of collusion between Sterne, Hall, and the Dodsleys was neither groundless nor malignant. Letter 60 is Sterne's direct—if not very convincing—response to Warburton's complaints in this letter.

4. About this time . . . *Magazine*] On Dr. John Hill and his account of Sterne, see letters 58 and 59. Warburton's clumsy parenthetical play on "dulness" seems unworthy of Pope's editor and defender, and indeed is omitted by Kilvert.

xiii. *William Warburton to David Garrick*

Text: Private Correspondence of David Garrick

Prior Park, [Monday,] June 16, 1760.

Dear Sir,

I must not forget to thank you for the hints I received from you by Mr. Berenger, concerning our heteroclite Parson.[1] I heard enough of his conduct in town since I left it, to make me think he would soon lose the fruits of all the advantage he had gained by a successful effort, and would disable me from appearing as his friend or well-wisher.

Since he got back to York, I had the inclosed letter[2] from him, which afforded me an opportunity I was not sorry for, to tell him my mind with all frankness, as you will see by the copy of what I wrote to him.[3] If it have the effect I wish, it will be well for him; if it have not, it will be at least well for me, in the satisfaction I shall receive by the attempt to do him service. I am, dear Sir,

Your very affectionate friend and faithful humble servant,

W. Gloucester

MS: Not located.

Pub.: Boaden, *Private Correspondence of David Garrick* (1831), 1:117; Curtis, 114, n. 5.

1. our heteroclite Parson] Warburton lifts the phrase from Sterne's portrait of Parson Yorick: "he was . . . as mercurial and sublimated a composition,----as heteroclite a creature in all his declensions;-----with as much life and whim, and *gaité de cœur* about him, as the kindliest climate could have engendered and put together" (*TS* I.11.27).

2. the inclosed letter] I.e., letter 59.

3. what I wrote to him] I.e., letter xii. For Warburton's increasing hostility toward Sterne and later volumes of *TS,* and what the conflict may have meant to Sterne, see New, "Warburton, Sterne," 252–54.

xiv. *William Warburton to Laurence Sterne*

Text: Unpublished Papers of William Warburton

P.[rior] P.[ark, Thursday], June 26, 1760.

Rev. Sir,

I have the favour of your obliging Letter of the 19th.[1] It gives me real pleasure (and I could not but trouble you with these two or three lines to tell you so) that you are resolved to do justice to your genius, and to borrow no aids to support it, but what are of the party of honour, virtue, and religion.

You say you will continue to laugh aloud. In good time. But one who was no more than even a man of spirit would choose[a] to laugh in good company; where priests and virgins may be present. . . .[2]

Do not expect your friends to pity you for the trash and ribaldry[3] scribbled against you; they will be apter to congratulate you upon it.

Notwithstanding all your wishes for your former obscurity, which your present chagrin excites, yet a wise man cannot but choose the sunshine before the shade; indeed he would not wish to dwell in the malignant heat of the dog-days, not for the teasing and momentary annoyance of the numberless tribes of insects abroad at that time, but for the more fatal aspect of the superior bodies.

I would recommend a maxim[4] to you which Bishop Sherlock formerly told me Dr. Bentley recommended to him, that a man was never writ out of the reputation he had once fairly won, but by himself.

I am, &c.,
W. G.

MS: Not located.
Pub.: Kilvert, *A Selection from Unpublished Papers of . . . William Warburton* (1841), 245–46; Watson, *Life of William Warburton* (1863), 506–7; Curtis, no. 65.

[a]choose] wish *Watson, C*

1. your obliging . . . 19th] I.e., letter 60. Warburton passed Sterne's letter to Garrick, with a note:

> I trouble you with the inclosed, because I was willing you should see the whole of our correspondence.
>
> I have done my best to prevent his playing the fool in a worse sense than, I have the charity to think, he intends. I have discharged my part to him. I esteemed him as a man of genius, and am desirous he would enable me to esteem him as a clergyman. (June 26, 1760; Boaden, 117–18)

2. where priests . . . present. . . .] The four stops at the end of the paragraph appear in all versions and may be Warburton's rather than an editorial indication of an omission. As first noted by Michael O. Houlahan, "William Warburton and 'Tristram Shandy': An Ironic Source," *N&Q*, n.s. 19 (1972): 378–79, Sterne parodies Warburton's advice in *TS*, V.20.453, when Trim tells the story of Tristram's "circumcision" in a manner "so that priests and virgins might have listened to it." Warburton had made no secret of his advice, as Bishop Hurd's letter to William Mason, March 30, 1761, makes evident: "And he [Sterne] does not seem capable

of following the advice which one gave him—*of laughing in such a manner, as that Virgins and Priests might laugh with him*" (*Correspondence of Richard Hurd and William Mason,* ed. E. H. Pearce and L. Whibley [Cambridge: Cambridge University Press, 1932], 53); Sterne's allusion, we may surmise, was perhaps not as private as Warburton might have desired.

3. trash and ribaldry] One of the first pamphlets written to profit from the popularity of *TS* was *The Clockmakers Outcry* (1760), the dedication of which is to the "Most Humble of Christian Prelates," the author "of MOSES' *Divine Legation,*" who is accused of having begged the friendship of the author "of SHANDY'*s Obscene Legation*" (ed. Anne Bandry and Geoffrey Day [Winchester: Winchester College Printing Society, 1991], xi). For an argument—not persuasive—that Sterne wrote this pamphlet himself, see the comments by Bandry and Day, 45–57.

4. a maxim] Curtis, 119, n. 3, notes that Warburton had told the same anecdote in a note in his edition of Pope's *Works* (1751), 4:159n. Bishop Thomas Sherlock (1678–1761) urged Bentley (1662–1742) not to be disheartened during the Phalaris controversy (1697–99) by the raillery of his enemies. "To which the other replied, 'Indeed, Dr. S[herlock], I am in no pain about the matter. For I hold it as certain, that no man was ever written out of reputation, but by himself.'" Sherlock, bishop of London (1748–*d.*), is best remembered today for his pamphlet on the 1750 London earthquakes espousing God's hand, prompting sharp responses from Voltaire and others; see Sterne, *Sermons,* 5:451, n. to 422.22–423.9. The scholar Bentley is known today primarily as a target in *The Dunciad.* Warburton did not weigh very carefully the authorities he cited in order to change Sterne's mind.

XV. *Robert Brown to John Hall-Stevenson*[1]

Text: Letter Book

From Mr Brown to J. Hall Esqre

Geneva. <Sept.> [Friday,] July 25. 1760

——Tristram Shandy has at last made his way here. never did I read any thing with more delectation. What a comical Fellow the author must be! & I may add also what a Connoisseur <of> in Mankind! Perhaps if the Book has any fault at all, it is, that some of his touches are too refined to be perceived in their full force & extent by every Reader. We have been told here he is a Brother of the cloath; pray is it really so? or in what part of the Vineyard does he labour? I'd ride fifty miles to smoak a pipe with him,[2] for I could lay any wager that so much humour has not been hatch'd <n>or concocted in his pericrainium without the genial fumes of celestial Tobacco: but perhaps like one of the same Trade, tho' his Letters be strong and powerful, his speech is mean and his bodily presence contemptible——Yet I can hardly think it. He must be a queer dog, if not sooner, at least after supper; I would lay too, that he is no stranger to Montaigne;[3] nay that he is full as well acquainted with him, as with the book of common prayer, or the Bishop of London's pastoral Letters;[4] tho at the same time I would be far from insinuating, either on one hand, that his Reverence is not as good a Tradesman in his way as any of his neighbours,—or on the other, That this celebrated Performance of his, is not perfectly an Original. The Character of Uncle Toby, his conversations with his Brother, who is also a very drole and excellent personage, & I protest such Characters I have known—his Acc^{ts} of the Campaign &c &c are inimitable. I have been much diverted wth some people here who have read it. they torture their brains to find out some hidden meaning in it, & will per force have all the Starts—Digressions—& Ecarts[5] which the Author runs ∧out∧ into, & which are surely the Excellencies of ∧his∧ Piece, to be the constituent Members of a close connected Story. is it not provoking to meet with such wise acres who, tho' there be no trace of any consistent plan in the whole of their insipid Life, & tho their Conversation if continued for half a quarter of an hour has neither head or tail, yet will pretend to seek for connection in a Work of this Nature.

adieu. Dear Sir
&c &c—

MS: Letter Book, Pierpont Morgan Library, New York.
Pub.: Cross, *Life* (1925), 2:236–37; Curtis, no. xiv.

1. *Robert Brown to John Hall-Stevenson*] For Rev. Robert Brown, see letter 64, n. 1. Sterne responded on September 9, which accounts for his misstep in first dating his copy of the letter as "Sept." Clearly Sterne was pleased with Brown's

response and copied the letter himself, now in the *Letter Book*. The original, probably returned to Hall-Stevenson, is lost.

2. I'd ride . . . with him] See letter 64, n. 6, for Sterne's earlier and subsequent use of this metaphor.

3. Montaigne] See letter 64, n. 5, for Sterne's response to this suggestion.

4. Bishop of London's pastoral Letters] Probably a reference to Edmund Gibson (1669–1748), bishop of London, whose *Pastoral Letters* (1732) went through a good number of reprintings, including one in 1760, the year of this letter. The subtitle of that work is significant: "In defence of the gospel revelation, and by way of preservative against the late writings in favour of infidelity." It is also possible that Brown refers instead to Gibson's successor, Bishop Sherlock, for whom see letter xiv, n. 4; the publications of bishops to their congregations are generically labeled "pastoral letters," and Brown's connection to writers like Voltaire and Rousseau (see letter 64, n. 1) at least raises the possibility that he wanted to recruit Sterne for their side in this important debate.

5. Ecarts] "Deviations" (properly: "écarts"). Brown's astute observation stands up very well indeed after some 250 years of critical commentary on Sterne.

xvi. *Elizabeth Sterne to Elizabeth Montagu*

Text: Ms.

[Sutton-on-the-Forest, November 1760][1]

Cou'd Mrs Montagu think this the way to make a bad Husband better. she might indeed have found a better, which I have often Urgd, though to little purpose. namely, shewing some little mark ^of^ kindness or regard to me as a Kindswoman, I meant not such as would have cost her money but indeed this neither she or any one of the Robinsons[2] vouchsafed to do though they have seen Mr Sterne frequently these two last winters & will the next. so that surely never poor Girl who had done no one thing to merit such neglect <e> was ever so cast off by her Relations as I have been.

I writ 3 posts ago to inform Mrs Montagu of the sorrow her indiferition[3] had brought upon me, & beg'd she wou'd do all that was in her power to undo the mischeif, though I can't for my soul see which way & must expect to the last hour of my Life to be reproach'd ^by Mr Sterne^ as the blaster of his fortunes

I Learn from Mr Sterne that there was both Letters & Conversations pass'd betwixt them ^last winter^ on this subject. & though I was an utter stranger to that, & every other part of this affair, 'till 10 days ago when the Chancellor[4] wrote his 1st Letter, wch Mr Sterne communicated to me, Yet in several he wrote to me from London, he talk'd much of the honours & civillities Mrs Montagu shew'd him, wch I was well pleas'd to hear as the contrary behaviour must have wrought me sorrow. I only wish'd that amongst them ^she had mixt some^ to her Cousin. but that I heard not one Syllable of.

I beg you will give me one gleam of Comfort by answering this directly. Mr Sterne is on the wing for London, & ^we^ remove ^to York^ at the same time so that I fear thy Letter will not arrive before me. Direct to Newton[5]

Mine & Lydias Love thine most truely & Affectionately

E Sterne

MS: Henry E. Huntington Library, San Marino, Calif., MO 5088.
Pub.: Climenson, *Elizabeth Montagu* (1906), 2:176–77; Curtis, 136–37, n. 7.

1. Date] On the dating and context of this letter, see letter 66, n. 2; Curtis's "November 1761" is almost certainly incorrect; see also Cash, *LY,* 77–79.

2. Robinsons] Elizabeth Montagu was one of the twelve children of Matthew Robinson (1694–1778) of West Layton Hall, Yorkshire, and Elizabeth Morris (*d.* 1745). See letter 66, n. 1.

3. indiferition] Climenson tries to help with "indifferation," but neither is recorded by *OED*. One assumes Elizabeth meant "indifference."

4. the Chancellor] I.e., William Herring; for Sterne's quarrel with him, alluded to here, see letter 66, and Cash, *LY,* 77–79.

5. Newton] Probably Rev. Thomas Newton (*b.* 1732), curate of Husthwaite and master of the grammar school in Coxwold. See letter 132, n. 3, and letter 88.

xvii. *"Jenny Shandy" to Laurence Sterne*

Text: Letter Book

[Bath, ?April 1765][1]

Sir

Poor M[r] Shandy's Sister Jenny[a] going down into the cellar (tho' I am not very sure with which foot she took the first step, but believe it was the left[2]) to draw beer, surrounded with a cloud of philosophical thoughts, observed the beer run in a constant stream into the black utensil—the noise immediatly calling to her remembrance that which she ^had heard^ so often, she naturally look'd down, but saw no water———

The Shandy-family desire this may be the 2[d] chapter of y[r] next book, and that this original Letter be preserved with the same care, & in the same Cabinet with the Bishop of Glocester's Letter.

from Sir
y[r] humble Servant
Jenny Shandy

Bath

MS: Letter Book, Pierpont Morgan Library, New York.
Pub.: Cross, *Life* (1925), 2:245; Curtis, 241–42, n. 2.

[a]Jenny] Jennny *MS*

1. Date] Curtis, 241, n. 2, assigns the letter this date, based on its Bath address and—one assumes—its tone, because Sterne had received another letter, probably in April 1765, from Bath, whence he had recently returned to London (see letter 148). That the author is invoking Sterne's use of the Lockean "association of ideas" in *TS* is probable, but hardly indicates, as Curtis argues, specific allusions to VII.13 and VIII.5; the most famous "association" in *TS* remains in the opening scene of volume I, and the allusion to Warburton may well indicate a correspondent familiar with the 1760 exchange with the bishop of Gloucester. Sterne thought the joke funny enough to copy, but we cannot know when he received it; it never was used.

2. the first step . . . the left] Crossing a threshold (or doorsill) with the left foot was deemed unlucky from classical—and biblical—times.

xviii. *John Hall-Stevenson to Laurence Sterne*[1]

Text: Letter Book

Crasy Castle [Sunday,] July 13. 1766

From J. Hall Esq[re]

You see, my dear Cosin, the Reviewers have had a stroke at me, and in good truth not without cause—and so I am very contrite for my bestiality with the Bishop of Gloucester[a] but there is no help for it; so lend me some assistance to set me well again with myself. it was against my own feelings—but for the sake of a Joke many a wiser man has done as beastly a thing.

Adio.
Antonio.

MS: Letter Book, Pierpont Morgan Library, New York.
Pub.: Cross, *Life* (1925), 2:246–47; Curtis, no. 166.

[a]Gloucester] G—— *MS*

1. *John Hall-Stevenson to Laurence Sterne*] This is a fair copy made by Sterne of a letter now lost. Sterne responds to it in letter 179; see esp. n. 1 for the context of Hall-Stevenson's joke and contrition.

xix(a). *Ignatius Sancho to Laurence Sterne*[1]

Text: Letters of the Late Ignatius Sancho

[London, Monday, July 21, 1766]

Reverend Sir,

It would be an insult on your humanity (or perhaps look like it) to apologize for the liberty I am taking.—I am one of those people whom the vulgar and illiberal call *"Negurs."*[a]—The first part of my life was rather unlucky, as I was placed in a family who judged ignorance the best and only security for obedience.[2]—A little reading and writing I got by unwearied application.—The latter part of my life has been—thro' God's blessing, truly fortunate, having spent it in the service of one of the best families[b] in the kingdom.[3]—My chief pleasure has been books.—Philanthropy I adore.—How very much, good Sir, am I (amongst millions) indebted to you for the character of your amiable uncle Toby!—I declare, I would walk ten miles in the dog-days, to shake hands with the honest corporal.—Your Sermons have touch'd me to the heart, and I hope have amended it, which brings me to the point.—In your tenth discourse, page seventy-eight, in the second volume—is this very affecting passage[4]—"Consider how great a part of our species—in all ages down to this—have been trod under the feet of cruel and capricious tyrants, who would neither hear their cries, nor pity their distresses.—Consider slavery—what it is—how bitter a draught—and how many millions are made to drink of it[c]!"—Of all my favorite authors, not one has drawn a tear in favour of my miserable black brethren—excepting yourself, and the humane author of Sir George Ellison.[5]—I think you will forgive me;—I am sure you will applaud me for beseeching you to give one half-hour's attention to slavery, as it is at this day practised in our West Indies.[6]—That subject, handled in your striking manner, would ease the yoke (perhaps) of many—but if only of one—Gracious God!—what a feast to a benevolent heart!—and, sure I am, you are an epicurean[7] in acts of charity.—You, who are universally read, and as universally admired—you could not fail—Dear Sir, think in me you behold the uplifted hands of thousands of my brother Moors.—Grief (you pathetically observe) is eloquent;[8]—figure to yourself their attitudes;—hear their supplicating addresses!—alas!—you cannot refuse.—Humanity must comply—in which hope I beg permission to subscribe myself,

Reverend, Sir, &c.

I. Sancho[d]

MS: Not located.

Pub.: Letters of the Late Ignatius Sancho (1782), no. 35; Medalle, no. 84; *Letters of Ignatius Sancho,* ed. Paul Edwards and Polly Rewt (Edinburgh: Edinburgh University Press, 1994); *Letters of the Late Ignatius Sancho,* ed. Vincent Carretta (Harmondsworth: Penguin, 1998), 73–74.

[a] "*Negurs.*"] negroes *M* [b]best families] best and greatest families *M* [c]drink of it] drink it *Sancho* (1782) [d]I. Sancho] I.S. *M*

1. *Ignatius Sancho to Laurence Sterne*] For Ignatius Sancho, and Sterne's reply to this letter, see letter 181. We have used here the text published by Frances Crewe in her collection of Sancho's *Letters* (1782), rather than the version in Medalle, no. 84, because the many differences in accidentals between the two versions suggest Lydia's usual editorial habits; while Crewe also probably "corrected" her available text, we believe precedence accrues in this instance to Sancho's editor rather than to Sterne's. Sterne's version, now in the *Letter Book,* is presented below, letter xix(b); the supposition that it was altered because Sterne was thinking of publishing it seems credible. The dating "July 21" is provided from the *Letter Book* version; Crewe had wildly misdated it "July, 1776."

2. I am one . . . obedience] Joseph Jekyll (1754–1837) used the closing phrase in his "Life of Ignatius Sancho" prefacing the edition of Sancho's *Letters:* "At little more than two years old, his master brought him to England, and gave him to three maiden sisters, resident at Greenwich; whose prejudices had unhappily taught them, that African ignorance was the only security for his obedience" (ed. Carretta 5). Medalle's "negroes" for Sancho's "*Negurs*" (and Sterne's "Nee-gur"; see next letter) raises the question, not to be answered here, whether Sancho's usage is neutral or a predating of the *OED*'s earliest illustration of the abusive use of "nigger" (1775); Robert Folkenflik has suggested to us that it would be a "striking cultural moment" if this letter was indeed the first recognition of such negative usage.

3. one of the best families in the kingdom] That of John Montagu, 2d Duke of Montagu; see letter 181, n. 1. Since "and greatest" appears in neither Crewe's version nor Sterne's copy, we may assume it was Lydia's addition, perhaps with the hope of further ingratiating herself with a family that had subscribed to both *ASJ* and *Sermons* (1769).

4. In your tenth discourse . . . passage] See letter 181, n. 4. The passage is quoted, not quite accurately, from sermon 10, "Job's account of the shortness and troubles of life, considered." Sancho was looking at the second or a later edition (the 7th ed. appeared in 1765), where the passage does indeed occur on page 78 (p. 98 in the first ed.).

5. author of Sir George Ellison] Sarah Robinson Scott (1723–1795), Elizabeth Montagu's sister, whose *A Man of Sensibility, or the History of Sir George Ellison* had appeared in two volumes in 1766. Its protagonist is a reasonably enlightened slave owner in Jamaica who, however, "rejects emancipation as impolitic" (Carretta 278, n. 4). Sterne had met Scott in Bath in 1765; see Cash's account, *LY,* 206–7.

6. our West Indies] See letter 181, n. 1. Sancho had been born on a slave ship bound for the West Indies and was taken from there by his owner when he was two years old.

7. epicurean] A rather odd usage, but suggesting, by transference, a relish for or delight in benevolent actions.

8. Grief . . . is eloquent] Sancho seems to refer to the opening paragraph of sermon 10, where Sterne, with echoes of Wisdom 10:21 and other scriptural passages, praises Job 14:1–2, as a "specimen of eloquence . . . owing in some measure, to the pathetic nature of the subject . . ." (*Sermons* 4:91; see 5:141–42, nn. to 91.8–12 and 91.16–19).

xix(b). *Ignatius Sancho to Laurence Sterne*

Text: Letter Book

[London, Monday, July 21, 1766]

Reverend Sir—

It would be an insult, (or perhaps look like one), on your Humanity, to apologise for the Liberty of this address—*unknowing* and *unknown*.[1] I am one of those people whom the illiberal and vulgar call a Nee—gur—: the early part of my Life was rather unlucky; as I was placed in a family who judged that Ignorance was the best Security for obedience: a little Reading and writing, I got by unwearied application—the latter part of my life has been more fortunate; having spent it in the honourable service of one of the best families in the kingdome; my chief pleasure has been books; philanthropy I adore——how much do I owe you good Sir, for that soul pleasing[2] Character of your amiable uncle Toby! I declare I would walk ten miles in the dog days, to shake hands with the honest Corporal—Your Sermons good Sir, are a cordial:[3] but to the point, the reason of this address. in your 10th Discourse. p. 78 Vol. 2^{d} is this truely affecting passage. "Consider how great a part of our species in all ages down to this, have been trod under the feet of cruel and capricious Tyrants who would neither hear their cries, nor pity their distresses—Consider Slavery—what it is,—how bitter a draught! and how many millions have been made to drink of it——"

of all my favourite writers, not <an>~on~e do I remember, that has had a tear to spare[4] for the distresses of my poor moorish brethren, Yourself, and the truely humane author of Sr George Ellison excepted: I think Sir, you will forgive, perhaps applaud me for zealously intreating you[5] to give half an hours attention to slavery (as it is at this day undergone in the West Indies); that subject handled in your own manner, would ease the Yoke of many, perhaps occasion a reformation throughout our Islands[6]——But should only *one* be the better for it—<good> ∧gracious∧ God! what a feast! very sure I am, that Yorick is an Epicurean in Charity—universally read & universally admired—you could not fail. dear Sir think in me, you behold the uplifted hands of Millions[7] of my moorish brethren—Grief (you pathetically observe) is eloquent—figure to yourselves their attitudes—hear their supplicatory address—humanity must comply

in which humble hope permit me to subscribe myself Revd Sir, your most humble and Obedient Servant[8]

Ignatius Sancho

Jury 21. 1766
(Lord Cadogan's White hall)[9]—

MS: Letter Book, Pierpont Morgan Library, New York.
Pub.: Cross, *Life* (1925), 2:248–49; Curtis, no. 168; Carretta, *Letters of . . . Sancho,* 331–32.

1. *unknowing* and *unknown*] Sterne's addition. We have called attention only to the more interesting changes; the annotations for xix(a) are, of course, relevant to this version as well.

2. soul pleasing] Sterne's addition.

3. are a cordial] Sancho had written "have touch'd me to the heart and I hope have amended it," which Sterne may have found stale.

4. writers, not one . . . to spare] Sterne alters Sancho's "authors, not one has drawn a tear" and then emends "black brethren" to "moorish brethren."

5. perhaps . . . intreating you] Sterne flattens out "I am sure you will applaud me for beseeching you . . . ." At some point one begins not only to disagree with Curtis's notion that Sterne made "effective alterations," but even to have a suspicion that Lydia's editorial itch was in her genes.

6. perhaps occasion . . . Islands] Sterne's addition.

7. Millions] Sterne stretches Sancho's "thousands." He had, indeed, written of the "many millions" who had been made to suffer slavery (*Sermons* 4:99) in the passage cited by Sancho.

8. your most . . . Servant] Not in Sancho, although he did sign off other letters with this typical phrasing.

9. Lord Cadogan's White hall] See Curtis, 284, n. 7: "Sancho had probably written 'Lord Cardigan's.' He was at this time in the service of George Brudenell-Montagu (1712–90), fourth Earl of Cardigan . . . ." See letter 181, n. 1. Whitehall was one of the London residences of the Cardigan family, just a block away from Charles Street, where Sancho would set up separate residence in the 1770s.

Sterne's confusion may have been aided by his acquaintance with Hon. Charles Sloane Cadogan (1728–1807), treasurer to the Duke of York and subscriber to *Sermons* (1766) and to a large-paper *ASJ*.

xx. *Laurence Sterne to Ignatius Sancho*[1]

Text: Letter Book

Coxwould [Sunday,] July 27. 1766

There is a strange coincidence, Sancho, in the little events, as well as the great ones of this world; for I had been writing a tender tale of the sorrows of a <distressd> friendless poor negro girl, and my eyes had scarse done smarting, When your Letter of recommendation in behalf of so many of her brethren and Sisters came to me——but[a] why, *her brethren?*—or yours? Sancho,—any more than mine: it is by the finest tints and most insensible gradations that nature <?> descends from the fairest face about S[t] James's, to the sootyest complexion in Africa: at which tint of these, is it, Sancho, that the ties of blood & nature[2] cease? and how many tones[3] must we descend lower still in the scale, 'ere Mercy is to vanish with them? but tis no uncommon thing my good Sancho, for one half of the world to use the other half of it like brutes, and then endeavour to make 'em so.

for[4] my own part, I never look westward, (when I am in a pensive mood at least) but I think of the burdens which our brethren[5] are there carrying; and could I take one ounce from the Shoulders of a few of 'em who are the heaviest loaden'd,[6] I would go a Pilgrimage to Mecca[7] for their Sakes—which by the by, exceeds your Walk, Sancho, of ten miles to see the honest Corporal,[8] in about the same proportion that a Visit of Humanity should one, of mere form—if you meant the Corporal more he is your Debtor.[9]

If I can weave the Tale I have wrote, into what I am about, tis at the service of the <unfortunate> afflicted; and a much greater matter: for in honest[10] truth, it casts a great Shade[11] upon the world, that so great a part of it, are, and have been so long bound down in chains of darkness & ^in^ chains of misery; and I cannot but both honour[12] and felicitate you, That by so much laudable diligence you have free'd yourself from one——and that, by falling into the hands of so good & merciful a family, Providence has rescued you from the other———and[13] so, good hearted Sancho, adieu! & be assured[14] I will not forget y^r^ Letter.

L. Sterne——

MS: Letter Book, Pierpont Morgan Library, New York.
Pub.: Cross, *Life* (1925), 2:250–51; Curtis, no. 170B.

[a]but] by *MS*

1. *Laurence Sterne to Ignatius Sancho*] Curtis, 287, suggests this is an altered version of letter 181, "with perhaps an eye to publication." Rather, it would appear to us an earlier draft of the letter he polished and sent to Sancho. We have noted the primary differences in the notes below; see also the notes to letter 181.

2. ties of blood & nature] Letter 181: "ties of blood."

3. tones] Letter 181: "shades."

4. ¶ for] Letter 181: no ¶.

5. brethren] Letter 181: "Brothers and Sisters."

6. could I . . . loaden'd] Letter 181: "could I ease their shoulders from <an> one ounce of 'em." See letter 130, n. 6, for "loaden'd."

7. go a Pilgrimage to Mecca] Letter 181: "set out this hour upon a pilgrimage to Mecca."

8. to see the honest Corporal] Letter 181: *om.*

9. if you meant . . . Debtor] Sterne wrestles with this in his rewriting but to no avail. Sancho had clearly indicated he would walk ten miles to "shake hands" with Trim, and Sterne still cannot turn his own analogy, which seems to belittle that "walk," into a compliment, "if you meant <the Corporal> my uncle Toby, more—he is y^r^ Debter."

10. honest] Letter 181: "serious."

11. great Shade] Letter 181: "<melancholy> sad Shade." Sterne clearly had difficulty finding the right adjective.

12. honour] Letter 181: "respect."
13. other———and] Letter 181: "other. ¶ and."
14. be assured] Letter 181: "believe me."

xxi. *Laurence Sterne to Thomas Becket*

Text: Ms.

Rec[d] January 21[1]—1767 of T Becket & Co two Hundred five pounds 17[s] being in full ballance of all Accounts to this day as paid. deliverd me
£205:17:0

L. Sterne

MS: Houghton Library, Harvard University, Autograph File.
Pub.: Curtis, 300, n. 1.

1. January 21] This is eight days before the publication of volume IX of *TS*.

xxii. *John Eustace to Laurence Sterne*[1]

Text: Life and Correspondence of James Iredell

[Wilmington, North Carolina, ?November 1767]

Sir,

When I assure you, that I am a very great[a] admirer of Tristram Shandy, and have been, ever since his introduction to the world, one[b] of his most zealous defenders against the repeated assaults[c] of prejudice and misapprehension, I hope you will not treat my[d] unexpected appearance in his company as an intrusion. You[e] know it is an observation as remarkable for its truth as its[f] antiquity, that a similitude of sentiments is the general parent of friendship.[2] It cannot be wondered at, that I should conceive an esteem for a person whom nature had[g] most indulgently enabled to frisk and curvet[3] with ease through all the[h] intricacies of sentiment[i], which, from irresistible propensity, she had compelled[j] me to trudge through without merit or distinction.

The only reason that gave rise to this address to you, is my accidentally having met with a piece of truly Shandean statuary[k]—I mean, according to the vulgar[l] opinion; for, to such judges, both appear equally destitute of regularity or design. It was made by a very ingenious gentleman of this province, and presented to the late Governour Dobbs;[4] after his death, Mrs. Dobbs[m] gave it to me[n]. Its singularity made many very desirous[o] of procuring it, but I had resolved, at first, not to part with it, till,[p] upon reflection, I thought it would be a very proper, and probably not an unacceptable compliment to my favourite author, and, in his hands might prove as ample a field for meditation as a buttonhole or a broomstick.[5]

I am, &c.
John Eustace[q]

MS: Not located.

Pub.: Court Miscellany; or New Ladies Magazine 6 (November 1770): 509; *Sterne's Letters to His Friends on Various Occasions* (1775), no. 2; *Massachusetts Magazine* 2 (1790): 238–39; Griffith J. McRee, *Life and Correspondence of James Iredell* (New York: D. Appleton, 1857), 1:27–28; Curtis, no. 222.

[a]a very great] a great *CM, VO* [b]and have . . . world, one] and have, ever since his introduction into the world, been one *CM, VO;* and have ever been, since his introduction to the world, one *MM* [c]assaults] assults *MM* [d]my] this *CM, VO* [e]intrusion. You] intrusion. ¶You *CM* [f]as its] as for its *CM, VO* [g]had] has *MM* [h]the] these *CM, VO* [i]sentiment] sentiments *CM, VO* [j]had compelled] had impelled *CM, VO;* has impelled *MM* [k]of truly Shandean statuary] *CM;* of true Shandean statuary *VO;* of truly Shandean sculpture *MM;* of Shandean statuary *McRee* [l]to the vulgar] to vulgar *CM, VO* [m]Mrs. Dobbs] Mrs. D. *VO* [n]it to me] it me *VO* [o]many very desirous] many desirious *CM, VO, MM* [p]till,] until *MM* [q]I am, &c. / John Eustace] I have the honour to be, &c. &c. [no name] *CM, VO; om. MM*

1. *John Eustace to Laurence Sterne*] See Sterne's response to Eustace, letter 241. The account of that text can serve as a parallel to this, in that the publication of letter 241 was always accompanied by Eustace's initial letter of praise and compliment. We have again selected the Iredell–McRee version as copy-text, silently emending its small capitals and American spellings. The relationship between the various texts suggests that each copier and editor it passed through altered an original text with a very free hand. Eustace's letter is undated in all versions; our

date is based on Sterne's reply date of February 9, 1768, allowing sufficient time for the cross-Atlantic posting.

2. an observation . . . friendship] Curtis, 404, n. 2, identifies the source as Sallust (Gaius Sallustius Crispus, [86–*c.* 35 B.C.], in *The War with Catiline* 20.4 [34–35]): "nam idem velle atque idem nolle, ea demum firma amicitia est" ("for agreement in likes and dislikes—this, and this only, is what constitutes true friendship").

3. frisk and curvet] Eustace recalls *TS,* IV.20.356: "What a rate have I gone on at, curvetting and frisking it away, two up and two down for four volumes together . . . ."

4. Governour Dobbs] See letter 241, n. 3, for details about the governor and his walking stick.

5. buttonhole or a broomstick] Sterne does indeed promise us a chapter on "buttonholes" (IV.14.345, IV.32.401, and V.8.434), but not on "broomsticks"; Eustace probably had in mind Swift's *Meditation upon a Broom-stick* (1710), published in volume 2 of *Miscellanies in Prose and Verse* (1727), 265–67.

xxiii. *Robert Hay Drummond, Archbishop of York, to Elizabeth Montagu*

Text: Ms.

Dartmouth, SW., [Saturday,] Mar. 26. 1768.

Madam

I have just rec^d the honor of your letter; & I can only blame you for making any apology for giving me an opportunity to obey your commands. The Widow & daughter of Mr Sterne are most distressed objects, & have a Scene of unhappiness opened to them, wch it will be difficult for the best-intentioned to prevent.—There may be some application for a small pension of £6 or £8 for the Widow f^m the Corporation ^of Clergymens Widows here in London^. But that will be a trifle. What seems to lye heavy, is the repair of the Parsonage house;[1] ab^t wch I rec^d a letter from Miss Sterne. I have properly nothing to do wth it; but the Successor[2] has a right to claim it to be done by Mr Sterne's Executors. I hope it may be so far accomodated, that the expence, wch he neglected to lay out upon a plan wch he mentioned to me, may be lessened[a]: & in that case I can advise the Successor to compromise the affair. He is bound to build a house; & I am bound in duty to call upon him & oblige its being done. but the compassion due to the Widow & orphan will probably operate, as it should.

I am very glad to find that M[rs] Montagu is recovered; & M[rs] Drummond will be very glad soon to fix a day, when I hope to have the pleasure of meeting you

I am wth the best regard
Madam Your most obd[t]
& most humble Serv[t]
R. Ebor.

MS: Henry E. Huntington Library, San Marino, Calif., MO 879.
Pub.: Blunt, *Montagu* (1923), 1:195; Curtis, no. xv (first paragraph only).

[a]lessened] lessoned *Blunt, C*

1. the repair of the Parsonage house] See letter 158, and n. 10, for the fire that had destroyed the Sutton parsonage house in 1765; Sterne seems not to have made any move toward rebuilding it during the two years before his death, although it was his responsibility to do so. For the general tenor of this letter, cf. Cash, *LY,* 335–36: "The women were in a panic about money. The only regular income they could foresee was about £80 per annum .... No doubt Elizabeth and Lydia thought they had a right to live as gentlewomen, and the archbishop quite misconceived their situation at first when he pondered applying to the Corporation of Clergymen's Widows for a pension of £8."

2. the Successor] Curtis, 433, n. 1: "The Rev. Andrew Cheap was collated and instituted to the vicarage of Sutton, 25 March 1768 (*Institutions of the Diocese of York 1755–1768,* 415). He was the son of George Cheap, of Prestonpans, and matriculated from Balliol College at Oxford, 1 Dec. 1750, aged 16. He received the degrees of B.A. in 1754 and M.A. in 1757." Curtis is citing Foster's *Alumni Oxonienses.* See letters xxvi and xxvii, and Cash, *LY,* 336–37, for further discussion about the settlement of Cheap's suit.

xxiv. *Elizabeth Montagu to Sarah Scott*[1]

Text: Ms.

[London, April 1768]

. . . I went last night to the archBishop of Yorks to whom I wrote in behalf of Mr Sternes family. Mr Sternes Parsonage was burnt down, ye new incumbent has a right to require it sh^d^ be new built, but as the archbishop presents, his good interposition w^d^ mitigate the expence, he answerd my letter in the most obliging & friendly manner, enters with great humanity into their situation, & will do as much in their favour as is consistent with justice, he talkd a great deal on ye subject, & will get ye Widow a little pension of £8 a year if it be necessary. The only thing for these people w^d^ be to board in a cheap place, but my good Cousin is si tracassiere[2] she puts every Town into a combustion in a month. I shall not mention it till they have settled a saving plan, & then I will offer them £20 a year, & my Bro^r^ Morris[3] will do something for them. I w^d^ do more but alas I have more Cousins, who I fear may soon want assistance. Mr Botham seems in a poor state of health. . . .

Address: To / Mrs Scott / In Miles Court / Bath
MS: Henry E Huntington Library, San Marino, Calif., MO 5881.
Pub.: Blunt, *Montagu* (1923), 1:195–96; Curtis, no. xvi.

1. *Sarah Scott*] See letter 148, n. 1. We have excerpted from a longer letter those sections relevant to Sterne.

2. si tracassiere] So troublesome. Cf. letter xxx.

3. Morris] Morris Robinson (1715–1777), a solicitor in Chancery; he subscribed to *Sermons* (1760, 1769).

XXV. *Lydia Sterne to Elizabeth Montagu*

Text: Ms.

Tuesday. evening [York, April 5, 1768][1]

Dear Madam

I did myself the pleasure to write to you this morning, but I wrote in such a hurry that I omitted several very material things which I ought to have mention'd but I do not doubt but you will make some allowances for the circumstances we are in which scarce leave us time to think of every thing we have to say. but first let me return to Mr Botham.[2] mama answer'd the letter that he wrote to me, in which he complains that I write in a dictating manner & . . . I am sure I need not tell Mrs Montagù that when a person writes on business, there is much less occasion for compts than for directions. however I meant not to offend any-one much less my uncle whom I much esteem—not one of these directions has Mr Botham follow'd. they were first to sell all Mr Sterne's wearing apparel, & trinkets to the best advantage, to present Mr Hall: my Father's Gold snuff-box which he desired to purchase.<——>~(~indeed many of his friends would have been glad to have purchased his trinkets at even more than their value only because they once belong'd to Mr Sterne) to send down all his papers & give us an account for what he sold his effects for instead of doing this he has <in> read every paper of my poor Father's & has burnt what he did not think proper to communicate to us.—it was not mama's intention that any one shou'd read my Father's papers. well knowing that there was some amongst them which ought not to have been seen no not even by his Daughter nor shd I have wish'd to see one of them! mama is very much chagrin'd at this for notwithstanding she can perhaps rely on Mr Botham's secrecy yet it grieves that ever[a] he should be so well accquainted with certain anecdotes. but to burn any paper was very wrong I hope he will cease so doing, & leave that care to mama.—Mr Botham refuses to send mama either the Cash he has sold Mr Sterne's effects for or his *papers,* unless somebody gives a sufficient Bond for the value of the effects or that mama takes administration.[3]—now as mama finds that Mr Sterne's personel estate will pay all his debts (except the mortgage to which her estate is *liable* <)> to) she risks nothing in taking it and it would be a great[b] satisfaction to her to leave no debt unpaid || if she does not take administration the principal Creditor will. & that would be to our disadvantage we shall have £1500 secure when all his debts are paid. but mama desires you will give us y^{r} kind advice in this as well as in every other matter.—I spoke to you my dear Cousin in my last <?> of the many friends it has pleased God to raise us up in this part of the world, & that they had proposed a *Collection*[4] for us in the race week.—a judicious sensible gentleman, & one of our sincerest friends has made that collection appear to us in a very different light from what it did before | But this is only *a supposition that such a thing takes place.*

Begun by the Marquiss of Rockingam & continued by the principal gentlemen of the County & nothing less than 5 Guineas to be recieved is putting it upon such a footing that it is an *honour* to Mr Sterne's memory & no small one to us & cannot lessen us in the eyes of the world. would to God it may succeed. if *you approove of it.* and in case you do my dear madam may we hope that you will second our ‸friends‸ endeavours in the south as they will do ‸yours‸ in the North?

do my dear cousin give us y^{r} friendly advice for we can think of taking no step without it

I am somewhat indisposed & therefore must conclude my mama is really wore down.

I am my dear Madam
y^{r} obliged & affectionate God Daughter
Lydia Sterne

mama joins in most affectionate compliments

Address: To / Mrs Montagu / Hill street / London
Postmark: York 5 AP
MS: Henry E. Huntington Library, San Marino, Calif., MO 1513.
Pub.: Blunt, *Montagu* (1923), 1:198–200; Curtis, no. xvii.

[a]ever] even *C* [ms. unclear] [b]be a great] be great *C* [ms. "a" is blotted]

1. Date] The postmark and Lydia's providing the day of the week allows us to date this letter with some certainty.

2. M[r] Botham] Rev. John Botham (1710–1773), husband of Elizabeth Sterne's sister, Lydia Lumley, and rector of Albury, Surrey. For his destruction of Sterne's writings (which Blunt, 1:200, aptly labels "Johnny Botham's pious holocaust"), see Cash, *LY,* 334–36. He subscribed to *Sermons* (1769), even though he obstructed their being printed (see letter xxxv below).

3. takes administration] On June 4, 1768, Elizabeth Sterne appeared before Francis Topham (see letter 32, n. 3) in the Exchequer and Prerogative Court of the Archbishop of York and was granted the necessary letters of administration. Arthur Ricard (see letter 8, n. 15) and his son, also Arthur, acted as sureties. She had to post bond for the considerable sum of £500. Before this event, on April 14, "Sterne's personal effects were put up for auction at Coxwold, including his furniture, hand-painted china and a cow near calving. His gigantic chaise and long-tailed horses [see letter 211] sold for £60, his books for £80" (Cash, *LY* 337, citing *York Courant,* April 12 and August 16, 1768; see also letter xxviii below).

4. proposed a *Collection*] As Lydia notes, Lord Rockingham (see letter 42, n. 1; Lydia misspells his name) took the lead in raising a subscription during Race Week in York and contributed £50 himself. The total raised was £800; see Cash, *LY,* 338. After this effort, additional collections on behalf of the widow and her daughter brought in, by Cash's estimate, an additional £1,000. Lydia's suggestion that Montagu join in raising funds "in the south" seems worthy of the daughter of Sterne, at least in his subscription-seeking persona.

xxvi. *Robert Hay Drummond, Archbishop of York, to Elizabeth Montagu*

Text: Ms.

Brodsworth. [Monday,] June 6. 1768.

As I had not the good fortune to see you before I came out of town, I sh[d] be obliged to you if you w[d] let me know whether M[rs] Sterne agrees to the compromise wth M[r] Cheap for dilapidations:[1] ^that is to^ pay him one hundred Guineas & be quit of all demands from him as Successor to M[r] Sterne at Sutton upon the acc[t] of dilapidations.

I was at Bishopthorpe last week but heard nothing particular of the mother or daughter; & I go there for the summer on the 12th of July. I may probably see Mrs Sterne & Mr Cheap: & I sh^{d} wish to know what she has wrote to you, that I may finish the affair, if possible.[2] . . .

MS: Henry E. Huntington Library, San Marino, Calif., MO 880.
Pub.: Blunt, *Montagu* (1923), 1:200; Curtis, no. xviii.

1. dilapidations] See letter xxvii, n. 1.
2. finish the affair, if possible.] For the outcome of the archbishop's efforts, see letters xxvii and xxviii. This letter continues about matters unrelated to Sterne.

xxvii. *Robert Hay Drummond, Archbishop of York, to Elizabeth Montagu*

Text: Ms.

Brodsworth. [Friday,] June 17. 1768.

Madam

I was honoured wth your letter yesterday, & am not surprised at the absurdity of Mrs Sterne wth regard to the dilapidations at Sutton; considering the different bubbles of Vanity & levity wch have upheld her for sometime, & the silly cunning of that crooked-headed Attorney,[1] into whose hands she hath unluckily fallen. Perhaps I may see her when I go to Bishopthorpe, but the plain sincerity of real friendship wch I w^{d} wish to show her, will be of no account wth her. I shall at present let Mr Cheap know her answer, & he will probably enter into suit directly: & every thing, that they have mentioned to you ‸will when known,‸ make agst them. The Inclosure was no merit of Sterne's, but it was a profit to him:[2] the materials were much hurt by the fire, but they were all removed & used upon his own Estate etc—However, after all, I have a suspicion, ‸not from very bad authority, for it came from Ld Fauconbridge's Steward[3],‸ that there will be a better surplus than they give out: for her Estate (w^{ch}, by being settled after marriage, is liable to Creditors) will pay all the debts & dilapidations. There is generally falshood mixed wth little cunning; & as it is designed to have a subscription for them opened at York, they think it their interest to depreciate their estate.——I think they depreciate themselves, to think of a collection, wthout making it appear by a fair acc^{t} how far they may want it: & I am sure, you w^{d} rather assist them, when they are returned to a sober sense of their circumstances & their character; than let your name be mentioned in the roll of ostensible benefactors; wch will only increase their vanity, & can tend to no good in the way that it is meant to carry on such a collection.—If your name is mentioned either by them or by any person, I shall very plainly declare, that you are desirous to shew your friendship ^to them^ but without ostentation; at a proper time, when you saw upon what footing their affairs were. I think I may venture to enter so far into your Ideas, as to answer for you in that way, if occasion requires.[4] . . .

MS: Henry E. Huntington Library, San Marino, Calif., MO 881.
Pub.: Blunt, *Montagu* (1923), 1:201; Curtis, no. xix.

1. Attorney] Tentatively identified by Curtis, 437, n. 1, and 455, n. 1, as John Graves, attorney-at-law in Petergate, York, who acted as Elizabeth Sterne's agent (see also letter xlviii below). As Cash, *LY,* 336–37, notes, Cheap did file suit, but Elizabeth and her attorney seem to have triumphed in court, and Cheap received only £60 rather than the £100 he had sought. "Dilapidations" was the legal term for the costs charged to the former incumbent (or his heirs) to repair any damages or destruction of church property. Cheap's version of the quarrel survives in the Parish Register of Sutton: "In the year 1764 [*sic*], during the Incumbency of Mr. Lawrence Sterne, the Vicarage House was burnt down. Tho' frequently admonished and required to rebuild the Vicarage House, he found means to evade the performance of it. He continued Vicar till he died, in March, 1768. Andrew Cheap was appointed his successor, and was advised to accept a composition for Dilapidations from the Widow. A Suit was instituted for Dilapidations, but after a time (the Widow being in indigent circumstances) sixty pounds were accepted" (reprinted in Alfred Gatty, "Sterne at Sutton on the Forest," *N&Q* 5 [May 1852]: 410; and Curtis, 437, n. 2). Cheap then adds that the new construction took place from April 1770 to April 1771, and that the suit and new vicarage together cost him £577.

2. Inclosure . . . to him] Cf. Cash, *EMY,* 259–61: "Sterne's business affairs took a turn for the better with the Sutton Enclosure Act of 1756. This enclosure of 3,000 acres was the largest in Yorkshire during the eighteenth century . . . . Sterne did

not get legal possession of his portion until 7 December 1762, long after he had moved away from Sutton." But, Cash continues, he probably did begin to fence and improve the allotment before then, two fields of 30 acres each, and smaller parcels next to the church and vicarage. We may surmise that Elizabeth is trying to deduct those improvements from the dilapidations, an argument that fails to convince the archbishop.

3. L[d] Fauconbridge's Steward] For Richard Chapman, see letter 15, n. 5. Both his observation and Drummond's suggestion of a purposeful underestimation by the Sterne women seem to have truth on their side. The archbishop's misspelling of Fauconberg's name would not have pleased the peer, but, as Sterne notes, it happens to "the best surnames in the kingdom" (*TS* I.11.25).

4. requires.] The letter continues about other matters. Drummond would again write to Montagu about the Sternes (among other subjects) on July 3: " . . . The Family is at present dispersed; but we shall re-unite in the course of this week & go to B[p]thorpe for the Summer. If anything occurs ab[t] M[rs] Sterne, I will communicate it to you, & I shall wish to be of service to them in the most friendly way, w[ch] is to bring them down f[m] those flights of pride & vanity; that will certainly expose them to ridicule, if not to worse dangers. . . ." (Huntington Library, MO 882; cf. Blunt, *Montagu* [1923], 1:201–2, and Curtis, letter xx).

xxviii. *Lydia Sterne to Elizabeth Montagu*

Text: Ms.

York. Wed.—[August 31, 1768][1]

I promised to give my dear Cousin an account of the Collection.[2] I think I cannot take a better method than to send her a list of the Subscribers which I do.—how gracious, how merciful is God to us! what comfort has he sent us what friends has he rais'd us up! O may we ever retain a just sense of his mercy, and the most grateful remembrance of what we owe to our friends. indeed Madam I scarce can write for Tears when I think how peculiarly kind providence has been towards us. what reason had we to expect such benefits as these—none indeed—but I hope we shall never be undeserving of the kindness that has been shewn us. I am sure we never can forget it.——it was some time before the Arch-Bishop subscribed his Grace thought that it was from obstinacy that my mother refused to answer for the Dilapidations.[3]

upon hearing this my mother sent by a friend the Recorder's opinion in writing (after having ask'd his leave) which he freely gave, & wrote underneath the opinion his reasons &cc &c—this was but right. and his Grace seem'd satisfied, & subscribed ten Guineas—the Arch-Bishop my dear Cousin speaking of you said you was unacquainted with our affairs.—I could not tell Mrs Montagu 'till we knew ourselves but my Fathers debts the Curates included amounted to near a £1000 his personels have rais'd very little after his funeral & debts were paid in London the ballance <was> ∧in∧ my Mother's favour was but £22: his furniture a Cow, & some hay included £56 his Chaise, & horses 60. his Books 80.[4]—my mother has paid every farthing she has rec^{d} & is now advertising her estate to be sold as soon as possible to pay off[a] every Shilling. & lives herself upon borrow'd money. but we have had[b] hopes of the sale of this estate which was let for £40 a Year 'till this Year my Father let it for 50 but upon account of some tyths which he let the Tenant have too cheap[5] but the rent will be diminish'd after this year as the Tyths are now in Mr Cheap's disposal. but to convince you how hard it will be for us to learn all Mr Sterne's debts I must tell my Cousin that notwithstanding our advertising (which we did four months ago) last night we rec^{d} a Bill from a person in York. for wine the summ £25. and the other day we rec^{d} a Bill for Shoes from London.—we went up into a Garret this race week in order to let our Landlord have the benefit of the races. if we had not we must have paid five Guineas for the week which suited not our present circumstances. and twenty pounds a Year which is what we pay is even too much for us.—my mother purposes to settle this Collection money upon me which is very kind considering the many debts she has to pay out of her estate.—We hope Mr Montagu enjoys a better state of health, and that my Cousin is as well as we wish her. we are both very ill. I am scarce able to write! let us have the pleasure of hearing from my Cousin you do not know with what pleasure I communicate this success to you—I think our friends have done wonders.—there is scarce any subscribers but of this County apropos—the Anonymus underneath Sr George Saville's name is himself[6] he would not give more than Ld Scarborough[7] but sent it afterwards.—we have no occasion for the List[8] I send you.——adieu my dear Cousin believe me your most affectionate obedient

humble servant & Cousin

Lydia Sterne

my mama joins in most affectionate comp[ts] & wishes for your happiness.——

MS: Henry E. Huntington Library, San Marino, Calif., MO 1514.
Pub.: Blunt, *Montagu* (1923), 1:204–5; Curtis, no. xxi.

[a]off] of *MS* [b]had] *C;* bad *?MS, Blunt*

1. Date] Curtis, 439: "Lydia writes, it seems, on Wednesday, 31 Aug. 1768, one week following the sale of her father's library." See n. 4 below.

2. Collection] See letter xxv, n. 4.

3. Arch-Bishop . . . Dilapidations] See letter xxvii, n. 1, for Drummond's active hand in trying (unsuccessfully) to resolve the dispute between the Sternes and Andrew Cheap.

4. his furniture . . . his Books 80] See letter xxv, n. 3. Curtis, 439, n. 1, provides the text advertising the auction of Sterne's estate, which took place at Shandy Hall, April 14, 1768: "To be SOLD On Thursday . . . All the Household Goods and Furniture of the late Mr. STERNE, deceased, at Coxwold, with a Cow near calving, and a Parcel of Hay; also a handsome Post-Chaise, with a Pair of exceeding good Horses; and a complete Set of coloured Table China. The Chaise and Horses may be seen at Mr. Bluitt's in Lendale, and the China at Mrs. Reynoldson's.—And all Persons who have any Claim upon the Estate and Effects of the said Mr. Sterne, are desired immediately to send in an Account of their Demands to Mr. Ricard, Attorney in York. Likewise all Persons who stood indebted to the said Mr. Sterne, at the Time of his Decease, are desired immediately to pay the same to the said Mr. Ricard." Curtis adds that he purchased, in 1927, "a china cow, said to have belonged to Sterne. This garland-decked ornament of Delft workmanship may have been included in the sale." After Curtis's death, the china was returned to Shandy Hall and now stands displayed in the dining room.

A *Catalogue Of a Curious and Valuable Collection of Books, Among which are included The Entire Library Of the late Reverend and Learned Laurence Sterne* was published by J. Todd and H. Sotheran, the successors to Hildyard and Hinxman (see letters 6, n. 4, and 34, n. 2), for the sale that began on August 23, in the very house where Sterne had quarreled with Hildyard. For the necessary caution required when consulting this catalogue, see letter 73, n. 11.

5. too cheap] Cash, *LY*, 336, n. 18, comments: "Lydia may have reduced the actual figure, or the lands may have been managed better after Sterne's death," citing Curtis, 455, n. 1, who discovered in the papers of Elizabeth's attorney, John Graves (see letter xxvii, n. 1), evidences of remittances of £76 in 1772 and £94 in 1773; these papers have since been lost.

6. S[r] George . . . himself] Sir George Savile (see letter 150, n. 4) gave £35 in his own name and another £15 anonymously (and not "half" of £50, as Cash, *LY*, 338, has it; see letter xxix). He had subscribed to *Sermons* (1760), but not thereafter.

7. L[d] Scarborough] This is Savile's brother-in-law, Richard Lumley-Saunderson (1725–1782), 4th Earl of Scarborough. He, too, subscribed to *Sermons* (1760), but not thereafter.

8. the List] The subscribers' list has, unfortunately, vanished. Lord Rockingham's initiative during York Race Week yielded almost £800 (Cash, *LY* 338).

xxix. *Elizabeth Montagu to Sarah Scott*

Text: Ms.

[Sandleford, Sunday,] September 4 [1768].

. . . I had a letter from Miss A. Moritt[1] of York on sunday, telling me, she had collected ^upwards of^ £700 for Miss Sterne, that she had promised y[e] subscribers it shd be converted into an annuity[2] for the girl for she added, Mrs Sterne was so little loved or esteemed there w[d] not have been a single guinea given if that condition had not been made. I had heard Miss Moritt extreamly well spoken of, & by her manner of acting by the Sternes, & from her letters, I imagine she has an uncommon share of goodness & of sense. She begs of me to advise Miss Sterne not to affect witt, a desire of being distinguishd that way she says has ruined the whole family. I shall now tell Miss Sterne I will allow her £20 p[r] ann: & I hope that will give my advice more weight; she writes with y[e] highest sense of the blessing of this collection, & is now grateful to God & her benefactors, but how far the pride of her Mothers precepts & the levities of her Father may have renderd her incapable of deep impression on that head I cannot tell. L[d] Rockingham subscribed 50 guineas, as in fact did S[r] G: Savile tho he gave 15 of them without his name, because he w[d] not seem to give more than L[d] Scarborough, how delicate & how generous![3] . . .

Address: To / Mrs Scott at Dr Domeniceti,[4] / at Chelsea
MS: Henry E. Huntington Library, San Marino, Calif., MO 5898.
Pub.: Blunt, *Montagu* (1923), 1:202; Curtis, no. xxii.

1. Miss A. Moritt] Curtis, 440, n. 1, identifies her as Anne Eliza Morritt (*c.*1724–1795), a daughter of Bacon Morritt, of York and Cawood, a neighbor of Jaques Sterne. She subscribed to *Sermons* (1760, 1766). Croft, *Whitefoord Papers,* 231, mentions her initiative, and overstates the result as "above 1000£."

2. an annuity] Elizabeth Sterne gave a bond to Stephen Croft on March 17, 1769, securing £200 to Lydia, the Ricards (father and son) acting as witnesses (Curtis, 440, n. 3).

3. Ld Scarborough ... generous!] Curtis fails to indicate that this is a fragment from a longer letter, and stops at "Scarborough."

4. Dr Domeniceti] Mrs. Scott suffered from perpetual headaches, and often went to the famous Venetian quack doctor, Bartholomew Dominicetti, who provided baths and fumigatories; see Blunt, *Montagu* (1923), 1:175; and *Life of Johnson,* 420: "Dominicetti being mentioned, he would not allow him any merit. 'There is nothing in all this boasted system. No, Sir; medicated baths can be no better than warm water ....'"

XXX. *Elizabeth Montagu to Leonard Smelt*[1]

Text: Ms.

Sandleford near Newburg Berks [?September] 1768

Dear Sir,

Our amiable friend Mrs Ash,[2] would give you such an account of the state of Mr Montagus health, as would in some manner make my excuse to you for my long omission of correspondence. I wrote to Miss Morrit upon the subject of my unfortunate Cousins, it will be very happy for them if they will be advised by so judicious & so kind a friend. Mrs Sterne is a woman of great integrity & has many virtues, but they stand like quills upon the fretfull porcupine,[3] ready to go forth in sharp arrows on ye least supposed offence; she w^d not do a wrong thing, but she does right things in a very unpleasing manner, & the only way to avoid a quarrel with her is to keep a due distance: I have not seen Mrs Sterne since I was a girl in hanging sleeves,[4] but I know her character well. Miss Sterne I never saw,[5] but by her letters I judge she is very sensible, lively & clever; if these qualities are softend with virgin modesty, tinctured with that maiden blush of the mind which so adorns, so sanctifies female excellence, she must be a charming creature, & like ye fairies of the Leases, & the nymphs of Fenham.[6] Miss Morrits ^good^ opinion & regard does Miss Sterne great honour. Poor Tristram Shandy had an appearance of philanthropy that pleased one, & made one forgive in some degree his errors. However as I think, there is but one way of a mans proving his philanthropy to be real & genuine, & that is by making every part of his conduct of good example to mankind in general, & of good effect towards those with whom he is connected. If Tristram gave an ill example to the clergy, if he renderd his Wife & Daughter unhappy, we must mistake good humour for good nature.[7] By many humble addresses, he forced me to take some kind of civil notice of him. I assure you his witt never attoned with me for the indecency of his writings, nor could the quintessence of all the witt extracted from all the most celebrated beaux esprits that ever existed, make amends for one obscene[a] period. There are but two kinds of people that I think myself at liberty to hate & despise, the first is of the class of soi disant philosophers, who by sophistry w^{d} cheat the less acute out of their principles of religion, the only firm basis of moral virtue; the second are witts who ridicule whatsoever things are lovely, what soever things are of good report.[8] The lowest animal in society is a Buffoon. He willingly degrades himself in the rank of rational Being, assumes a voluntary inferiority of soul, defaces the Divine image in his mind to put on the monkey & the ape & is guilty of spiritual bestiality. Poor Tristrams last performance was the best, his Sentimental journey w^{d} not have misbecome a young Ensign. I cannot say it was suitable to his serious profession. I used to talk in this severe manner to him, & he w^{d} shed penitent tears, which seem'd to shew he erred from levity not malice, & the great who encourage such writings are most to blame, for they seduce the frail witt to be guilty of these offenses, but we are now a Nation of Sybarites who promise rewards only to such as invent some new pleasure.[9] . . .

MS: Henry E. Huntington Library, San Marino, Calif., MO 4999.
Pub.: Blunt, *Montagu* (1923), 1:196–97; Curtis, no. xxiii (neither Blunt nor Curtis prints the opening two sentences).

[a]obscene] obscure *Blunt, C*

1. *Leonard Smelt*] Leonard Smelt (*c.*1719–1800) was a Yorkshire military engineer and courtier. According to Burney, King George III considered Smelt "perhaps the man in the world most to his taste of any person outside his own family" (*Diary and Letters,* quoted in *Oxford DNB);* indeed, he became sub-governor to the royal princes in 1771. He was also an acquaintance of Johnson, Reynolds, and Mary Delany.

2. M[rs] Ash] Unidentified.

3. they stand . . . porcupine] For her cruel if probably astute characterization of Elizabeth Sterne, Montagu probably misrecalls *Hamlet,* I.v.20: "Like quills upon the fearful porpentine."

4. in hanging sleeves] A loose-sleeved child's garment; cf. *Pamela,* vol. IV, letter 49: "when I was a girl . . . in hanging sleeves" ([London: Everyman, 1963], 362).

5. Miss Sterne I never saw] This comment, along with her assertion that she had not seen Elizabeth Sterne since she was a child, is a useful reminder for biographers to weigh their evidence with care; the number of letters still extant between the Sterne women and Mrs. Montagu would seem to suggest a much closer acquaintance than probably was the case.

6. fairies . . . Fenham] Leases was Smelt's ancestral home; he had returned to it on his father's death in 1755; Fenham is in Newcastle-upon-Tyne, where Montagu's husband had inherited large holdings in 1758. On her first trip to the property, Elizabeth Montagu visited Lord and Lady Spencer, soon to be Sterne's ardent patrons, at Althorpe, and also Lumley Castle, the ancestral home of Elizabeth Sterne's father (see Climenson, *Elizabeth Montagu,* 2:129–40).

7. we must . . . good nature] Montagu's intent is clear enough, but her phrasing is obscure; perhaps the negative makes more sense: "we must *not* mistake good humour for good nature." Her criticism of Sterne's "sentimentalism" is noteworthy and was shared by others in her circle, including Elizabeth Carter, who wrote to Elizabeth Vesey some weeks after Sterne's death:

> I thought the tone of one paragraph in your Letter did not seem your own, even before you gave me an intimation that it belonged to the Sentimental Traveller, whom I neither have read nor probably ever shall; for indeed there is something shocking in whatever I have heard either of the author, or of his writings. It is the fashion, I find, to extol him for his benevolence, a word so wretchedly misapplied,

> and so often put as a substitute for virtue, that one is quite sick of hearing it repeated either by those who have no ideas at all, or by those who have none but such as confound all differences of right and wrong. Merely to be struck by a sudden impulse of compassion at the view of an object of distress, is no more benevolence than it is a fit of the gout .... Real benevolence would never suffer a husband and a father to neglect and injure those whom the ties of nature ... have entitled to his first regards. Yet this unhappy man, by his carelessness and extravagance, has left a wife and child to starve, or to subsist on the precarious bounty of others. (*A Series of Letters Between Mrs. Elizabeth Carter and Miss Catherine Talbot* [1809], 3:334–35)

In a footnote, the editor waxes even more indignant: "It were to be wished that these observations of Mrs. Carter were bound up with every edition of his works as a proper antidote to their poison. Few writers have done so much mischief to the world ..." (335); this wish is now fulfilled, but whether to Sterne's or Carter's discredit, the reader must decide.

8. things are of good report] See Philippians 4:8.

9. pleasure.] The letter, signed "EMontagu" continues about other matters.

xxxi. *Lydia Sterne to Thomas Becket*

Text: Curtis

York. *Wednesday* [?September 1768][1]

Dear S^r^

My Mother sends up a Bill of 58 pounds, six shillings which together with what you have in your hands you will be so good as to pay into Mr Selwin's for the use of Mr Panchaud.—the account I believe stands thus that is supposing my uncle Mr Botham has paid into your hands the ten Guineas he rec^d^ for my Fathers picture, & six more for a Bass viol. but to make all sure I will write to him & desire him if he has not to do it immediately.

first the	17:12:6 in your hands.
then the Bill we sent before	36:13:10
then what Mr Edmonds paid you——	22:13:6
from Mr Botham—	16:16:6
	93:15:10
the Bill I now send.	58:6
	£152:1:10[2]

the 150 is to be paid into Mr Selwin's the rest to the Bookseller who valued the Books. be so good as to take a proper reciept in full from Mr Selwin—as the Bill is drawn we cannot get it chang'd. for the Bill you sent us for shoes but if you will be so good as to pay him we will take care to remit it you.——I write by this post to Mr Botham.—my Mother joins in comp^ts^

I am dear S^r^ y^r^ sincere friend
& Obliged humble ser^vt^
Lydia Sterne

Endorsed: York Sept: 1768 / Mrs. Stern / amt. paid / 150£ to M^r^ S[elwin].
MS: Not located.
Pub.: Curtis, no. xxiv.

1. Date] Curtis dates the letter from the endorsement, and suggests it may have been written on September 7, two weeks after the sale of Sterne's library at York.
2. [Account] We have reformatted the account for the sake of clarity.

xxxii. *Lydia Sterne to Thomas Becket*

Text: Curtis

York [Thursday,] oct^r^ 6th 1768—

Dear S^r^

I enclose you a letter to a gentleman whose direction I have quite forgot—but 'tis of the greatest consequence that he should recieve this letter but I entreat you find him out by the discription I shall give of him you cannot fail, & send it by a careful person—his name is *Oswald*[1] he is a Scotch gentleman. & was Commissary to the troops in Germany during the last war—he has a gentleman that lives with [him] & who did part of his business for him whose name is *Mills*[2] they were both extreamly intimate with my poor Father—I beg you will let me know when you have found him out & I beseech you lose no time—I wrote to you some time ago but have rec^d^ no answer—

Mama joins in best comp^{ts} our kind love to Mrs Becket—as well as to the pretty little Lady[3]—

I am dear S^{r}
y^{r} obliged friend
L Sterne

MS: Not located.
Pub.: Curtis, no. xxv.

1. *Oswald*] See letters 105 and 107. Cf. Curtis, 205, n. 6: "In 1768 Lydia Sterne, then arduously collecting funds for her maintenance, was eager to seek out both Mill and Oswald, perhaps with the intention of borrowing from them as her father had done before her." Or, more likely perhaps, she wanted to solicit a subscription, in which event she was quite successful: Richard Oswald subscribed to five sets of *Sermons* (1769).
2. *Mills*] See letter 105.
3. little Lady] Curtis, 442, n. 2, suggests Becket's daughter Peggy (*c.*1766–1813).

xxxiii. *John Hall-Stevenson to Lydia Sterne*

Text: Curtis

Skelton, [Friday,] Nov. 18, 1768.

Dear Madam,

I will write this post, to Lord Irwin.[1] I received the favour of your List, the reason of my desiring one was only to see whether all had subscribed that I expected, and except Lord Irwin, I think they have. The Sermon you sent, is already printed. I got his printed Sermons, and have compared them, tho' not sufficiently to prevent your doing it yourself. I find several passages in some of these amongst his printed Sermons, which has given me some trouble to patch and botch differently. There are Eighteen Sermons divided into three vols of six Sermons each. I think you judge rightly to fix the price at three half crowns, then make a bargain to clear your subscription, and sell the Copy.[2] Mr Becket, to whom I would advise you to give the preference, because your father had a regard for him; was certainly mistaken when he told me, your father had assured him, that he had nothing but the Sweepings of his study, in the Sermon way.[3] Outre que ce n'etoit pas son usage de mipriser ses Ouvrages.[4] I can aver upon my honour, and could I dare say, have the evidence of twenty people, who must have heard your Father, as well as myself, declare a hundred times, that all the Sermons which he had, were in a bag, and in order to make up the Volumes printed, he had no other method, than to put his hand into the bag, and take out what came first,[5] therefore you have no reason to set a less value upon these, than your father did upon his other; and if Mr Becket offers to treat differently with you, I make no doubt but you may meet with booksellers enough who will be glad to act in a more generous way.

I am, with respects to your Mama,
Dear Madam,
Your most obed^t humble Servant,
J Hall Stevenson

Address: To Miss Sterne, in Blake Street, York.
MS: Not located; Curtis derived his text from a nineteenth-century copy in his own possession.
Pub.: Curtis, no. xxvi.

1. Lord Irwin] Charles Ingram (1727–1778), 9th Viscount Irvine, of Temple Newsam, near Leeds. He appears on none of Sterne's subscription lists, but his sister, Elizabeth, subscribed to *ASJ* ("Hon. Miss Ingram").

2. There are . . . the Copy] For a full account of the posthumous publication of the final three volumes of Sterne's sermons, see *Sermons,* 5:5–7 and 479–83. They appeared on June 3, 1769, price *7s.6d.* for the set, with a subscribers' list of more than 700 names. A second edition was required before the end of the year.

3. nothing but . . . Sermon way] When Sterne published two volumes of sermons in 1766, he offered an "Advertisement" with the final sermon ("Abuses of conscience"), apologizing for reprinting a sermon that had "already appeared in the body of a moral work, more read than understood [i.e., *Tristram Shandy*]," and suggesting that the two volumes in hand were "probably the last (except the sweepings of the Author's study after his death) that will be published" (*Sermons* 4:255).

4. Outre ... Ouvrages] Except that it was not his habit to undervalue [properly: mépriser] his own works.

5. he had no ... came first] If the account is reliable, it portrays Sterne striking his typical authorial posture of nonchalance and carelessness, which must always be taken *cum grano salis*. See letter 44, n. 3, and Lydia's own astute reading of this passage in the letter following (xxxiv).

xxxiv. *Lydia Sterne to Thomas Becket*

Text: Ms.

[November 1768][1]

D^{r} S^{r}

I rec^{d} the favour of y^{rs}—as we are not accquainted with matters of that nature I mean with regard to the sermons we must be guided & advised by Mr Hall or some one who understands these affairs better than ourselves.—I have wrote to Mr Hall.—at present I send you the *advertisement* but I suppose my mother w^{d} not print any more at least very few more than she may have subscribers for & that you know cannot yet be determined | —as Mr Hall does not go to London I believe 'till Spring he cannot correct ye press.—who can we get think you?—in short 'tis a troublesome business for us—yet I hope we shall get thro' it.—I imagine we must get the sermons copied, & the *originals* must go up with them for y^{r} satisfaction. as to what Mr Botham may have said of their not being his own, he is under a great mistake[2] | my Father would not sit down, & copy other peoples sermons. he wanted no powers himself.—as to vouching them to be my Father's that I am sure <you> ^we^ can.—Mrs Montagu has promised to patronize the sermons.—much is in her power. Mrs James also does all she can. so will Mr Botham Mr Edmonds[3]—Mr Garrick &cc &cc!!—had Mr Sterne been alive, ^he^ would have corrected these sermons himself. & would then have made I dare say the same bargain as usual.—for what signifies the thing he says ab^{t} ye sweepings of his Study. has he not to every one said he kept all his sermons in a bag, & shaked it up, & took the first that came. which is nothing but the truth.—but you must easily imagine that what he has said ab^{t} the sweepings &c. has been little regarded & twas a Shandeism. like many others.—and consider my d^{r} S^{r} that my father as an author was much admired, & his last works will assuredly sell well—I think Mr Becket would have be<i>~e~n at no loss to have settled this with Mr Sterne why sh^{d} he then with us?——*the sermons are his*——'upon my word.—'till I hear from Mr Hall I cannot answer w^{t} you say ab^{t} the Copy right—but this I am persuaded he thinks we sh^{d} make ye same bargain Mr Sterne did—

I am dear S^{r}
y^{r} obliged friend
LS

in ^a^ short time will be publish'd by subscription three vol^{s} of sermons by the late Mr Sterne which he intended for the press for the Benefit of his Widow and Daughter.—

VOL. 1[4]

1 Temporal advantages of Religion
2 our Conversation in heav'n
3 description of the world
4 St Peter's character
5 30th of January
6 as you like it

VOL. 2

7 Trust in God
8 on murder
9 sanctity of the apostles
10 Penances
11 Enthusiasm
12 eternal advantages of Religion

VOL. 3

13 Asa Religious and Political moral and Historical
14 follow peace

15 search the Scriptures
16 upon all saints
17 The ways of Providence justify'd to Man
18 The ingratitude of Israel

Subscriptions to be paid in at Mr Becket's Bookseller in the Strand, & Mr Edmonds Stationer in the Poultry <London> <———price 7^{s} 6^{d}> if the price is to be added you must put 7^{s} 6^{d} but the sermon call'd as you like it I would have Mrs Montagu's opinion whether it is proper | I enclose you a letter to her. & she will tell you if she approoves of it, & do not advertise 'till you have seen her.

Y^{rs}
LS

pray give Mrs Montagu some little Books
She lives in Hill street

MS: Houghton Library, Harvard, Autograph File: Murdock MS, 55.

1. Date] Cash, *LY,* 340, n. 34, assigns November and December 1768 for the probable dates of this letter and the next, based on Lydia's ongoing correspondence with both Becket and Hall-Stevenson. His account is, however, a bit muddled, in that he believes this letter accompanied Hall's letter (above, letter xxxiii), although it is in the subsequent letter (letter xxxv) that Lydia encloses Hall-Stevenson's correspondence. A more likely chronology might suggest that Becket had raised some objections to the project in a letter now lost. In response, Hall-Stevenson sent Lydia his advice in letter xxxiii (November 18), and she wrote to Becket shortly thereafter, repeating Hall-Stevenson's observations as her own (this present letter). Becket remained lukewarm at best, perhaps offended by Lydia's somewhat belligerent tone. At this point, probably now into December, Lydia tried again, but Becket failed to respond. And so she writes yet again (letter xxxv), perhaps sending Hall-Stevenson's letter of November 18, but more likely a new letter in which Hall-Stevenson responded directly to Becket's objections.

2. Mr Botham . . . great mistake] In the words of Cash, *LY,* 340, "John Botham was making trouble again: he had told Becket that not all the sermons were Sterne's, and Becket was uncertain whether to take them." On the vexed question

of Sterne's borrowings from other sermon writers, see *Sermons,* 5:xv–xvii, 21–27, and passim.

3. M[r] Edmonds] Sterne's London stationer; see above, letter 89, n. 16.

4. Vol. 1, etc.] The three posthumous volumes contain the sermons as Lydia lists them. Montagu obviously approved of "as you like it," which appears untitled (the *Florida Edition* entitles it "God's forbearance of sin"). Lydia's title came from the opening sentence, commenting on the texts, Romans 2:4 and Ecclesiastes 8:11: "Take either as you like it, you will get nothing by the bargain" (sermon 33, 4:313). Cf. the comment in the sermon's headnote, 5:343: "Except for the opening turn on the text (similar to that in sermons 2, 18, and 27), the sermon is in no way objectionable, as perhaps Lydia's advisors pointed out. The subject of the sermon, God's forbearance of sin, or the unequal distribution of rewards and punishments in this world, is one of the most traditional of all sermon topics in the eighteenth century."

The sermon on murder also was untitled in the first edition; the *Florida Edition* labels it "The sin of murder" (sermon 35). As the headnote indicates, much of the sermon is derived from Samuel Clarke's sermon "Of the heinousness of the sin of wilful murder" (5:365); it is the sort of extensive borrowing that Botham may have had in mind. The sermon on Asa is retitled "Asa: a thanksgiving sermon" (sermon 40), and "Upon all saints," which appeared untitled, is titled "Efficacy of prayer" (sermon 43) in the *Florida Edition;* it is a sermon for All Saints' Day, but is primarily about the usefulness of public prayer.

We have emended the list by removing some of Lydia's superfluous punctuation.

xxxv. *Lydia Sterne to Thomas Becket*

Text: Ms.

York Monday [December 1768][1]

Dear S[r]

I enclose you a letter I recieved from M[r] Hall—you see he wishes us to give you the preference in regard to M[r] Sterne's sermons which we are much inclined to do—you will consider of it my dear S[r]—your answer I wish as soon as possible to my last letter as also this—you cannot but think we sh[d] wish to treat with you as a person my father had a regard for—and as a person who has behaved in so friendly a manner towards us——M[r] Hall has corrected them & we shold take his opinion in every thing that relates to them | you will tell us your intentions which we must communicate to Mr Hall——

I am dear S^r yours sincerely
Lydia Sterne

MS: Houghton Library, Harvard University, Autograph File: Murdock MS, 56.

1. Date] See letter xxxiv, n. 1.

xxxvi. *Lydia Sterne to Thomas Becket*

Text: Ms.

York Tuesday. [?December 1768][1]

Dear S^r

I wonder I do not hear from you I have wrote you two or 3 letters lately which were of consequence—I enclosed you a letter to Mr Oswald pray did you send it?[2]——I told you my good friend we sh^d have occasion for some of the Sentimental Travels to send to fort St George.[3] I enclose you a list of ye subscribers. please to put each subscribers name upon every different parcel. to prevent any mistake[a]. & they must be put into a Box a deal one. directed to Mr George Stratton[4] at Fort St George. Commodore James will send some one to inform you when a Ship sails so that they may be put on board. and I believe will get them put on board. only have them ready when call'd for.—I dare say we shall have occasion for more || I sh^d take it as a favour if you would let me hear from you. as soon as possible. mama joins in all kind compliments

I am dear S^r
y^r obliged friend, &
humble serv^t
L Sterne

PS

I do not know what they mean by Quarto's[5] I thought there was none—if I am right you must send such as there is with a line to Mr Stratton intimating there was none

---

Endorsed: Books Sent in a / Box to the Care of Cap[t] / Waddle at the [illegible] / & order of M[rs] James / . . . Jan[y] 17/1767
MS: Hyde Collection, Harvard University.
Pub.: Curtis, no. xxvii (from a transcription).

[a]prevent any mistake] prevent mistake *C*

1. Date] Curtis was certainly correct in assigning this letter to Lydia, one more in the flurry of correspondence with Becket in the winter of 1768, despite not having access to the manuscript (which is indeed in Lydia's hand), and despite Cross's belief (*Life* [1929], 631) that the letter was Sterne's. However, although Cross could not have read the letter carefully ("mama joins in all kind compliments"), his dating of it as probably "December, 1767" is based on his *accurate* reading of the endorsement, which clearly has "1767" and not, as in Curtis, "1769" (444, n. 2); we assume this is a scribal error. The letter itself is a confusing one, not helped by Lydia's syntax and punctuation. She seems to be sending copies of *ASJ* to India, but using a different subscription list from that published in 1768. Possibly, the Jameses had received a belated list from Eliza—it would, at any rate, be nice to think that Eliza had organized this last tribute to the Bramin's memory.

2. I enclosed . . . send it?] See letter xxxii, and n. 1.

3. fort S[t] George] In Madras, the present Chennai. Built by the East India Company in 1639, the fort was one of the first bastions of British power in India. Today it is used by the state legislative assembly and as the secretarial offices of the Tamil Nadu government.

4. George Stratton] See letter 196, n. 8.

5. Quarto's] Almost certainly, the large-paper copies of *ASJ*.

xxxvii. *Lydia Sterne to Elizabeth Montagu*

Text: Ms.

York [Thursday,] Dec[r] 15th 1768.

my dear Cousin

I beg you to forgive my troubling you so often, but as I know you will rejoice with us when you have read my letter I will make no further apologies. you will see my ^dear^ M[rs] Montagu that I have not always bad news to tell you.—this letter we rec[d] from Lady Spencer.[1] I only send the copy. "Madam I can plead no other merit in the following transaction than that it occurred to me, that I should be to blame if I did not tell Mr Crawfurd[2] of the subscription that was making to assist you while I was at York as I thought from the sincere regard he had for Mr Sterne that it would give him pleasure to be of any service to his familly for his sake.—he has accordingly sent me the money mention'd in the following list, & I beg I may have your directions what to do with it, & into whose hands you would have it paid

I am Madam y^{r} faithful
humble servant
G: Spencer

I hope you rec^{d} a trifle from Ld Spencer by ye hands of Mr Croft"

Mr Crawfurd	10:10:0
Mr Fox	10:10:0
Ld Ossory	10:10:0
Duke of Roxburghe	10:10:0
Ld Shellburne	10:10:0
Mr James	10:10:0
Mr Meynell	10:10:0
Mr Crewe	10:10:0
Mr Fitzpatrick	5: 5:0
Mr Boothby	5: 5:0
Mr Upton	5: 5:0
Mr Southwell	5: 5:0
Mr Hume the Historian	5: 5:0
	£108:15:0[3]

judge my dearest Cousin what pleasure this kind letter, & *agreeable* news gave us!—how kind is providence to us!—we thought rather improper to send Becket or Mr Edmonds to Lady Spencer and could by no means desire Mr Botham to do it as poor soul he was unfortunately guilty of a sad mistake relating to Ld Spencer which had <b> near proved very unfortunate to us as his Lordship was extreamly displeased with us thinking us the author's of the story and insisted upon seeing the letter which we were forced to send my Lord to clear ourselves. but this I will explain when I have the happiness to see you.—I took the liberty to make use of M[rs] Montagu's name only saying "that M[rs] Montagu would I am sure receive the money."—so I dare say Lady Spencer will pay it into my dear Cousin's hands, who I doubt not will receive it with pleasure.——my Mother since my last has been much indisposed.[a] I have wrote to M[r] Crawfurd to thank him for his great goodness.—I have been writing since seven and my hand is cramp'd—my Mother joins in most affectionate comp[ts]

believe me my dear
M[rs] Montagu most truly
most affectionately Yours
L S.

Address: To / M[rs] Montagu / Hill street / London
Postmark: YORK 17 Db
MS: Henry E. Huntington Library, San Marino, Calif., MO 1516.
Pub.: Blunt, *Montagu* (1923), 1:202–3; Curtis, no. xxviii.

[a]indisposed.] indis [ms. torn]

1. Lady Spencer] Margaret Georgiana Poyntz. See letter 69, n. 8.
2. M[r] Crawfurd] John Craufurd. See letter 164, n. 6.
3. £108:15:0] Blunt's editorial "*sic*" alerts us to the fact, possibly overlooked by Curtis, that Lydia's sum is wrong; the total should be £110:5:0.

This list is worth comparing with Sterne's subscription lists. "Crawfurd," James, and Hume are obvious enough. Fox may be Stephen Fox (1745–1774), Lord Holland's eldest son, brother to Charles James Fox. He was in the circle Sterne frequented in Paris in 1764, and subscribed to *Sermons* (1766); see letter 123, n. 3. Lord Ossory is probably John Fitzpatrick, 2d Earl of Upper Ossory (see letter 164, n. 4), who subscribed to *Sermons* (1766) and a large-paper copy of *ASJ*. Mr. Fitzpatrick would perhaps be his brother, Richard Fitzpatrick (1748–1813), who subscribed to *Sermons* (1769). John Ker, 3d Duke of Roxburghe (1740–1804), a celebrated book collector, subscribed to *Sermons* (1766) and to a large-paper copy of *ASJ*, as did William Petty, 2d Earl of Shelburne (see letter 138, n. 3). Mr. Meynell might be Hugo Meynell (1735–1808), MP for Lichfield, 1762–68, known for his gambling, foxhunting, and horseracing interests, an identification made a bit more likely if Mr. Crewe is John Crewe (1742–1829), MP for Stafford, 1765–68, Cheshire, 1768–1802, and Meynell's good friend. Meynell subscribed to

Sermons in 1760, Crewe, in 1766 and 1769. Meynell was related by marriage to the Boothby-Skrymsher family, several of whom appear on the subscription lists, including Sir William Boothby (1721–1787), an army officer (to *Sermons* in 1760 and 1766, and a large-paper *ASJ),* and Charles Skrymsher Boothby (to *Sermons* in 1760). John Upton (*b.* 1718), of Ingmire Hall, Yorkshire, represented Westmoreland, 1761–68, and subscribed to *Sermons* (1760); a C. Upton subscribed in 1766. Finally, Mr. Southwell does not appear in any subscription list, but the prevalence of MPs on Lydia's list might suggest Edward Southwell (1738–1777), who represented Gloucestershire, 1763–76 (much of the information for these identifications is garnered from Namier and Brooke). Even if not all the identifications are correct, the most obvious fact about these contributors is the youthfulness of most of them; as in his travels, Sterne sought the company of young men and was admired by them.

xxxviii. *Lydia Sterne to Elizabeth Montagu*

Text: Ms.

York Saturday [?January 1769]

Dear Madam.

I waited 'till I rec[d] your second letter before I would answer the particulars of your first. after once more returning my dear Cousin our best, our most grateful thanks for her kindness towards us I will proceed. but think not that we over-value your generosity | no my dear M[rs] Montagu that is impossible words cannot express what we feel & thanks are too poor upon such an occasion.—the manner of doing a generous action is even more than the thing it-self, and my Cousin has confer'd this obligation in the most engaging manner, truly great, and worthy of herself—M[rs] Montagu's praises flatter me much as she is the person in the world whose approbation, & good opinion I most value—but my dear Cousin over rates my talents—I have had more advantages than fall to most peoples share particularly that of seeing good company, but what I esteem one of the greatest is that of having spent my days with my mother who has taken great pains to form both my head, & heart, the latter indeed she most consider'd—the few accomplishments I am mistress of I owe them partly to my own industry—for my mother, and myself have calculated has not cost eighteen pounds—yet I look'd upon those little accomplishments as rather a misfortune than otherwise, at least those were my reflections when I lost my father for at that time I had a very melancholly prospect before me.—as to inheriting my fathers wit I have not the least grain in my composition | we both thought it an unhappy turn in my father——I look upon satire with detestation and I must own when we returned from france we were much hurt with the satirical things we heard in every company we went into. having lived six Years amongst people who know not what it is to be satirical—and <indeed> ∧instead∧ of attacking any-body endeavour to make every one in the company happy and *never speak ill of the absent* I am so far from being a diseuse de bons mots[1] I think I never was guilty of one in my life. I am when in company extreamly diffident seldom give my opinion but upon the most trivial things—I am "often check'd for silence but never tax'd for speech"[2]—I have always follow'd Polonius's advice to his son in this for I give every one my ear but few my voice[3] | excuse these two miserable quotations but they came so pat to my purpose (as Sancho says)[4] that I could not let them pass.—now my dear Mrs Montagu may safely tell any one who speaks of me as a wit, that I am no such thing—in short I am I hope what Mrs Montagu will ever approve—but no babillárde[5] | I return my Cousin a thousand thanks for her kind advice 'tis the greatest proof of her regard, & be assured I will ever follow it—Mrs Montagu may depend upon it that the sermons we shall publish *are my Father's own* & the gentlemen who have look'd them over say that they are very good ones—there will be *three vol^{s}*. & as the subscription was 5^{s} for the two vol^{s} the subscription now will be fix'd at three half crowns—they will come out when the Parl^{t} meets[6]—my dear Cousin was so kind as to say she would push the subscription for us—we cannot push it ourselves and we cannot expect any subscribers here[7]—we thought we should have done with debts | no such matter—a Country man brought a note of hand of Mr Sterne's & told us of another which we should hear of soon—I must tell you what the honest soul said—I would not have made this demand had not I heard that your affairs have turn'd out better for had you been left destitute the money would have been much at your service.—if it is inconvenient defer the payment—I have that dependance on you Madam that if you do not pay these two years I shall not be uneasy—he would take no interest.—we are glad your arm is got better. we wish Mrs Montagu all possible happiness and Mr Montagu a better state of health—Mama joins in most affectionate comp^{ts}.—

I am dear Madam
your ever grateful
& affectionate <comp^{ts}>
God Daughter.
Lydia Sterne[8]

MS: Henry E. Huntington Library, San Marino, Calif., MO 1515.
Pub.: Blunt, *Montagu* (1923), 1:205–7; Curtis, no. xxix.

1. diseuse de bons mots] Someone who utters witticisms. Sterne compares French *politesse* with British "originality" in *ASJ*, 119; see the note to the passage, 6:349 (n. to 119.5), where this letter is quoted as a reflection of what Sterne may have found objectionable in French society—blandness.

2. often . . . speech] Cf. *All's Well That Ends Well*, I.i. 67–68, where the Countess of Rossillion advises her son Bertram, in the manner of Polonius: "Be check'd for silence, / But never tax'd for speech."

3. Polonius's advice . . . voice] In *Hamlet*, I.iii.58–80, Polonius gives Laertes "a few precepts," including "Give every man thy ear, but few thy voice" (l. 68).

4. Sancho says] I.e., *Don Quixote*'s Sancho Panza, who several times defends his flood of proverbs with this excuse.

5. babillárde] Chatterbox.

6. when the Parl^{t} meets] In fact, volumes V–VII of *Sermons by the Late Rev. Mr. Sterne* were published on June 3, 1769; see *Sermons*, 5:479–83, for the bibliographical details.

7. we cannot . . . here] As Curtis suggests, 447, n. 1, Lydia is probably alluding to the recent collection made during York Race Week. There is, however, as Curtis also notes, a strong York presence in the 1769 subscription list.

8. God Daughter. Lydia Sterne] Cf. Blunt, *Montagu* (1923), 1:207: "An odd thing about this letter is that Mrs. Sterne writes [these last four words] in her large handwriting . . . . Probably she read the letter over and then indicated her approval in this way, Mrs. Montagu knowing her calligraphy."

xxxix. *Lydia Sterne to William Strahan*[1]

Text: Ms.

[?March 1769]

... I enclose you Mr Beckett's proposal—when he last offer'd £400 for the copyrights he insisted on no such terms as these—this affair of not offering them to anyone else must be managed with the greatest caution—for you see he says that he will not take them if offer'd elsewhere. He will be judge of the quantity and quality—& insists on a year's credit. All these points my mother and myself most earnestly desire you to consider—unless you could be pretty sure of getting us more than £400 the offering them might perhaps come to Beckett's knowledge—yet believe me, Sr we had rather anyone had them than Becket—he is a *dirty fellow*....

MS: The Beinecke Rare Book and Manuscript Library, Yale University, James Marshall and Marie-Louise Osborn Collection.

Pub.: Catalogue of Autograph Letters of William Wright, Sotheby, (June 1899), 79; Curtis, no. xxx. (Only this fragment survives.)

1. *William Strahan*] William Strahan (1715–1785), printer and bookseller. He was a partner of the publishing house of Thomas Cadell (1742–1802). The posthumous sermons (vols. V–VII) were jointly published by Strahan, Cadell, and Becket, on June 3, 1769. Perhaps Curtis overstates matters when he calls this letter proof of Lydia's "double-crossing" of Becket (447–48); after all, Becket and Strahan had collaborated before, with Strahan printing *TS,* V–IX, and vol. I of *ASJ,* and it is clear from Strahan's ledgers, now in the British Library, that he was very much involved in the project from the beginning (see Cash, *LY* 340–41, and n. 37). Still, Lydia was probably trying to out-maneuver Becket in their negotiations, not realizing his ties to Strahan; if so, the letter may have bemused both of these veterans of the book trade.

xl. *Elizabeth and Lydia Sterne to John Wilkes*

Text: Ms.

[London, ?May 1769][1]

M[rs] & Miss Sterne's compliments wait on M[r] Wilkes—they intend doing themselves the pleasure of calling upon him if not disagreable <to him> & would be obliged to him if he would appoint an hour when he will not be *better engaged* they would not intrude yet should be happy to see a person whom they *honour* & M[r] Sterne *justly admired*—they will (when they see <him)> M[r] Wilkes) entreat him to ask some of his friends to subscribe to 3 Vol[s] of M[r] Sterne's sermons which they are now publishing not to have a melancholly story to tell M[r] Wilkes when they meet Miss Sterne begs leave to tell it now in a few words. my Father dy'd & left his unhappy Widow & Daughter in the most distress'd circumstances his debts amounted to eleven[a] hundred pounds——his effects when sold did not raise above four hundred—my mother nobly, <&> engaged to pay the rest out of a little estate of £40 per an which was all she had in the world—she could not bear the thoughts of leaving his debts unpaid & I honour her for it—this was or rather <is> ^would have been^ a scanty provision at least to us who have seen better days!—heav'n raised us up friends who both saw, & pitied our distress & gave a most convincing proof of it by making a collection in our behalf in the race week at York which amounted to £800. We are now publishing these sermons in hopes of raising something for our future comfort—we have sold the copy right for a trifle—our greatest hopes are that we may have a good many subscribers—several of our friends have used their interest in our behalf—the simple story of our situation will I doubt not engage Mr Wilkes to do what he can in getting us some subscriptions[2] & we should be glad to know by a line what day what hour will be most à propos for <them> us to wait on him———if defering that pleasure a few days will be *better* or more convenient they leave him to determine.

& beg leave to assure Mr Wilkes
that they are his sincere

well-wishers & humble serv[ts]
L Sterne

at M[r] Williams paper merch[t]
Gerrard street soho—
Tuesday—

Address: To / John Wilk's Esq[r] / King Bench Prison[3] / London
MS: British Library, Addit. MSS. 30877, 74–75.
Pub.: J. Almon, *Correspondence of the Late John Wilkes* (1805), 5:7–9; Curtis, no. xxxi.

[a]eleven] *Almon;* <l>elven *MS;* el[e]ven *C*

1. Date] Curtis, 449: "it is probable that this letter was written sometime in May, shortly after the Sternes' arrival in London." It is the first of four letters in Almon's "Letters from Mrs. and Miss Sterne, to Mr. Wilkes," the others being our letters xliii, xliv, and xlv. While the Almon version is essentially faithful to the substance, an editorial hand is everywhere evident as it attempts to bring some order to Lydia's eccentric grammar and punctuation; with one exception, we have not listed the many resulting variants.

2. some subscriptions] It is impossible to know just how much support Wilkes provided, but he is not on the 1769 subscription list (he did subscribe to *Sermons* in 1760). The Miss Wilkes who subscribed in 1769 might well be his daughter Mary (1750–1802); she had almost certainly met Sterne when she lived with her father in Paris between 1763 and 1767 (and see next letter). Among those supporters of Wilkes who subscribed in 1769 and not earlier, we might note Sir Robert Bernard, Welbore Ellis, Evan Evans, James Eyre, John Horne (later Tooke), Evan Lloyd, Sir Joseph and Lady Mawbey, Richard Oliver, and James Townsend. Others, such as Frederick Bull, John Lee, and Sir William Stanhope, all subscribed in 1760 and 1769. Finally, perhaps the "Mrs. Gardener" who subscribed in 1769 was Wilkes's mistress, known only as Mrs. Gardiner (Cash, *John Wilkes* 300).

3. King Bench Prison] See Curtis, 449, n. 1: "Wilkes, who had been committed to the King's Bench Prison in Apr. 1768 because of the outlawry proclaimed upon him, was still serving his sentence of twenty-two months."

xli. *Elizabeth and Lydia Sterne to John and Mary Wilkes*[1]

Text: Ms.

[London, ?May 1769]

M[rs] & Miss Sterne present their best comp[ts] to M[r], and Miss Wilkes we're engaged this day to dine with M[rs] Montagu their relation—they went out just when Miss Sterne dispatch'd the note & at their return found his obliging card which has mortified them greatly they cannot express the concern this has given them but hope this will be a sufficient excuse, & also ^they^ entreat M[r] Wilkes to appoint any other day when they may do themselves the pleasure of waiting on him & Miss Wilkes any day except Thursday & Saturday they will be at liberty——
Tuesday evening[a]

MS: British Library, Addit. MSS. 30877, 76.
Pub.: Curtis, no. xxxii.

[a]evening] eving *MS, C*

1. *Mary Wilkes*] See letter xl, n. 2.

xlii. *Lydia Sterne to David Garrick*

Text: Ms.

[?June 1769]

S[r]

after returning you our most grateful thanks for the favours you have confer'd upon us, I must beg leave to tell you that S[r] Tho[s] Robinson[1] has (by some *mistake* or other) made us appear in a very ridiculous light.—I should not I declare to you have troubled M[r] Garrick with this letter had not S[r] Thomas told a friend of ours (M[rs] *James*) that he would tell M[r] Garrick what a letter Miss Sterne had wrote him | *I hope he will shew it.* S[r] Thomas sent us a very great and noble list of subscribers | as he had not collected the money I wrote him a card to beg he would give us his advice as to what method we should use for getting it as names alone was not all we wanted.—no answer to this note. we met him at Ranelagh on wednesday and he seem'd much displeased that I had taken such a liberty—& beg'd leave to tell us that it was our affair not his that he was not a Collector of money &cc. &cc & left us very abruptly.—<not> the only step left for us to take (not to make a confusion with the Booksellers as his subscribers were the only ones who had not paid) was to deliver the Books ourselves.—two or three of the people sent us word they knew nothing at all of the matter. but as <?w> they kept the Books we hope they will send the money. the Earl and Lady Chesterfield[2] after having made us wait a quarter of an hour sent us word that they never had subscribed & were very much astonish'd we should bring them Books that Sr Thos Robinson had never ask'd them—& begd us to take back the Books!——we could not after that deliver any more. we were shock'd & truly unhappy.—this morning Lord and Lady Beachamp[3] sent back their Books & bid us tell Sr Thos they never did ∨subscribe∨ || I really believe we shall have a good many returnd in this manner!—but our vexation arises from our having sent Sr Thos Robinson's list to the Printer's <?where> names are printed when the people themselves have never subscribed.—however we cannot bear the blame for the following card was deliver'd with each set of Books "Mrs and Miss Sterne's most respectful compts and thanks wait on ______ they have brought the Books themselves that ______ were so kind as to subscribe to, to Sr Thos *Robinson* & request the subscription may be paid either to Mrs S. Gerrard 12 soho[4] or Becket Bookseller in the strand"—I wrote Sr Thos word <how> ∧what∧ <w>~L~ord Chesterfield had said—&cc &cc—and at the same time represented to him that it was not the most agreable light for us to appear in that we wish'd he had recd the money. that Mrs Montagu Mrs James Lady Carlisle[5] &cc had thought it no dishonour to *collect* it for us—this letter has offended him—*tant pis pour lui*[6]—let him shew it to Mr Garrick he cannot blame me.—

I am Sr your most obliged
faithful humble servant
L Sterne

my mother joins in best comp^{ts}—
PS

I thought it better to tell you the affair myself as Sr Thos might misrepresent things—and there is no one I would wish <to> more to stand well in the opinion of than Mr Garrick—

Address: To / David Garrick, Esq.
Endorsed: Miss Lydia Sterne
MS: Pusey Library, Harvard Theatre Collection, TS937.3 (5:115).

1. Sr Thos Robinson] Thomas Robinson, first baronet (1702/3–1777), of Rokeby, in Yorkshire, a cousin of Elizabeth Montagu, called "Long Sir Thomas" to distinguish him from "Short Sir Thomas" Robinson, later first Baron Grantham (1695–1770), of Newby. An amateur architect, he was one of the owners of Ranelagh, and built in 1764–65 Prospect Place, a very large residence adjoining the Gardens. While his enemies "considered him something of a bore and numerous caustic comments survive," the *Oxford DNB*'s entry suggests primarily a longtime patron of literature and the arts, and an active member of the Royal Society of the Arts.

A "Sir Thomas Robinson, Bt." subscribed to *Sermons* in both 1760 and 1766, but which Sir Thomas this was cannot be determined; Sterne would definitely have known both. The absence of the name in 1769 may suggest Lydia's complaint was not totally unjustified, although her version of events is probably not without bias. Cash suggests that because of Robinson's "irresponsible behaviour, one ought to reduce the number of subscribers in the list from 770 to, say, 720 or 730" (*LY* 342–43).

2. Earl and Lady Chesterfield] See letter 49, n. 2.

3. Lord and Lady Beachamp] I.e., Beauchamp; see letter 130, n. 15.

4. Gerrard 12 soho] I.e., 12 Gerrard Street, where the Sterne women took residence; see letter xl. It was, of course, the street on which the Jameses lived, where Sterne had spent so many hours during his final months, and where he had met Eliza. Possibly, the text reads "Gerrard in soho," but providing the house number was common.

5. Lady Carlisle] Isabella, Dowager Countess of Carlisle (*d.* 1795); see letter 22, n. 4.

6. *tant pis pour lui*] Too bad for him. Lydia gives life to Sterne's comment in *ASJ*, 39: "I cannot take a fitter opportunity to observe once for all, that *tant pis* and *tant mieux* being two of the great hinges in French conversation, a stranger would do well to set himself right in the use of them, before he gets to Paris."

xliii. *Lydia Sterne to John Wilkes*

Text: Ms.

angouleme. [Saturday,] july 22 1769.

Dear S^r

'tis with the greatest pleasure I take my pen to fulfil the promise I made you the last time I had the pleasure of seeing you. I mean that of writing to you; & to give you an account of us, and of our situation—a correspondent like Mr Wilks gives your humble servant more vanity than I thought I was capable of—I am an inch taller to day than I was yesterday: I wish the french may not find a difference in my behaviour—ce sera bien pire[1] when I receive a letter from you. they will certainly say "peste que cette fille est aujourd'ui dans ses grands airs decampons au plus vite."[2]—this is supposing you will favour me with an answer else I have done wrong to stile you "correspondent." but I know you are polite, & never want what the French call égards pour les femmes.—encore moins je m'imagine vis à vis les filles.[3]—you expected an english letter, and not a pot-pourri—I will not write one word more of French. I know not why I do for I am no very great admirer of the language—'tis better calculated for nonsense than my own and consequently suits me better to write, tho' not Mr Wilks to read——thank my stars you promised me not to shew my letters to any one. not even to your Confessor. remember that.——now as to our journey nothing either agreeable in it or diverting I promise you. a journey thro' France (that is to say the posting part of it), I am sure cannot be a sentimental one; for it is one continual squabble with Innkeepers, & postillions.—yet not like Smellfungus[4] who never kept his temper, but we kept ours and laugh'd whilst we scolded.—how much the French have the advantage over us—they give themselves ease by swearing (which you know is <?> talking Bawdy)[5] we english women do not know how to set about it—yet as Arch-Bishops in France swear as well as their neighbours (for I have heard them to my edification) I cannot see why we women may not follow their example. the french women however do it sans façon[6]—again! scratch out the word sans façon yourself and put an english one in the place which I will hereafter adopt.—Angouleme[7] is a pretty town, the country most delightful; and from the principal walk there is a very fine prospect: a serpentine River which joins the Garonne at Bordeaux has a very good effect: trees in the middle of it which form little Islands where the inhabitants go and take the fresco—in short 'tis a most pleasing prospect—and I know no greater pleasure than sitting by the side of the River reading Milton or Shakespear to my mother—sometimes I take my Guitarr and sing to her.—thus do the hours slide away imperceptibly, with reading, writing drawing and musick.

"Thus wisely careless, innocently gay
We play the trifle life away."[8]

yet dear S[r] often do we wish ourselves in England. necessity sent us hither, may fortune bring us back! We receive much civility from the people here we had letters of recommendation which I would advise every english person to procure where ever he goes in France.—we have visitors even more than we wish as we ever found the French in general very insipid—I would rather chuse a converse with people much superiour to me in understanding—(that I grant I can easily do so you need not smile.) with the one I can have no improvement but with people of sense I am sure of learning something every hour. as being intimate with a person of an excellent heart, & sensible feelings mends sometimes ones own. 'tis now time to remind M[r] Wilks of his kind promise to exhort him to fulfill it[9]—if you knew dear S[r] how much we are straiten'd as to our income you would not neglect it—We shall be truly happy to be so much obliged to you that we may join to our admiration of M[r] Wilks in his publick character, tears of gratitude when ever we hear his name mention'd for the peculiar service he has render'd us——much shall we owe to M[r] Hall for that and many other favours—but to you do we owe the kind intention which we beg you to put in practice.—as I know M[r] Hall is somewhat lazy as you was the promoter write to himself yourself he will be more attentive to what you say—in regard to the frontispieces which you wish me to draw tho' I am not very capable of it yet if you think it will be of use (that is to say enhance the price of the work.) I will get (not an Aid de camp) but a drawing master to assist me—Becket purposes to put the 9 vols. into 6[10] you know there is already two done to my hands, do tell me. if you think they will do. with four others—the first you know represents Trims reading the sermon with the figures of Dr Slop Mr Shandy & uncle Toby.——the 2^{d} is the Baptism of Tristram. now as to the four others, do my dear S^{r} give me hints of what you think will be most suitable.—what think you of Maria. & the goat with my Father besides her?—the sick Bed of poor Le Fever for another with uncle Toby Trim by his bed side and Le Fever's son with the picture of his mother in his hand—the Cushion by the Bed side on which he had just pray'd—chuse me yourself the rest—do not do not dear S^{r} neglect it 'twill be an act of kindness—if you should see Becket speak as if you thought he ought to pay handsomely for the life of Mr Sterne wrote by two men of such genius as Mr Wilks & Mr Hall it will sell extreamly well—if he is cool upon the subject (which by the bye I am sure he will not) say that the life will be printed with the original letters of Mr Sterne & sold to another. but entre nous[11] we neither of us wish to publish those letters but if we cannot do otherwise we will & prefix the life to them.

I fear I have wore out your patience forgive me 'twas a pleasing <subject.> occupation to write to you——I know not whether it is impertinent to ask you if your affairs go on equal to the wishes of your friends that they may believe me is the sincere wish

of dear S^{r} your most faithful
obliged friend.
L Sterne

PS

We flatter ourselves you are well.———my mother joins in most cordial wishes for your welfare & happiness.—may every thing you wish be granted you as I am sure you will grant us ours. nay you even *prevented it.* once more adieu.

our best comp^{ts} wait on Miss Wilks—

A Mad^{lle}
Mad^{lle} Sterne demoiselle angloise
chez Monsieur Bologne, ruë Cordeliers a Angouleme
France.

Address: To / John Wilks Esqr / Kings Bench Prison / in the Borough / London / Angleterre / single sheet[12]
Postmark: AV 1 ANGOVLESME
MS: British Library, Addit. MSS. 30877, 70–71.
Pub.: Almon, *Correspondence of the Late John Wilkes,* 5:9–16; Curtis, no. xxxiii.

1. ce sera bien pire] It will be a lot worse.

2. peste . . . vite] Lydia's typical lack of punctuation makes her intent problematic, but probably "it's a shame this young girl is giving us grand airs today[.] Let's abandon her (decamp) as quickly as we can." Curtis has "decompons"; Almon puts in the full stop and "Décampons."

3. égards . . . les filles] Consideration for women.—even less so, I would think, with respect to girls.

4. Smellfungus] Properly "Smelfungus," Sterne's name in *ASJ* for Smollett, whose ill-tempered *Travels* are an ironic target throughout that work; Lydia's attempt to capture her father's humorous tone in this letter is of interest, particularly given her comments on "wit" to Mrs. Montagu in letter xxxviii.

5. themselves ease . . . talking Bawdy] Cf. *TS,* IV.S.T.322, where Don Diego "eased his mind against the wall" with a poem; and the n. to the passage, 3:297, n. to 322.4, pointing to the probably "bawdy" meaning(s) behind "ease." Lydia may have learned more from her father than he might have wished.

6. sans façon] The opposite of the French expression "faire des façons" (to stand on ceremony), which underlies Lydia's phrase.

7. Angouleme] Elizabeth and Lydia lived in this ancient cathedral city until 1771, when they moved to Albi; it is in the modern department of Charente, some forty miles northeast of Bordeaux.

8. "Thus wisely . . . life away."] Lydia personalizes Pope's "Epistle to Miss Blount, with the Works of Voiture," where it is said of Voiture: "Thus wisely careless, innocently gay / Chearful he play'd the trifle, life, away" (ll. 11–12). In letter 77, Sterne cited the correspondence of both Pope and Voiture, in contrast to his own letters, none of which had been written, like their letters, "to be printed" (see n. 5).

9. his kind promise . . . fulfill it] Cf. Cash, *LY,* 348: "Her practical purpose in writing was to ask Wilkes to keep his promise to collaborate with Hall on a life of Sterne. Wilkes and Hall had told her that she and her mother could publish the biography and keep the profits, or they could include it in the edition of Sterne's letters which Lydia had been contemplating." Unfortunately nothing came of this project, as subsequent letters make clear. Instead, Lydia's edition of the *Letters* appeared in 1775, with an edited version of Sterne's own *Memoirs* prefixed to them.

10. in regard . . . into 6] The "8th edition" of *TS* was published in six volumes, a shared venture between Dodsley and Becket and Dehondt, in 1770, and reissued in 1777. Again, nothing seems to have come of the plan to have Lydia draw the frontispiece for each volume. When she indicates "already two done to my hands," she is clearly referring to Hogarth's illustrations of "Trim Reading the Sermon" and "Tristram's Christening." The other two suggestions did indeed become two of the most often illustrated episodes of *TS*, demonstrating the powerful grip of sentimentalism on the age; see esp. W. B. Gerard, "'All that the heart wishes': Changing Views toward Sentimentality Reflected in Visualizations of Sterne's Maria, 1773–1888," *SECC* 34 (2005): 231–69. Lydia's prescience in this regard is worth noting, since in 1769 no illustrations other than Hogarth's had yet appeared.

11. entre nous] Between ourselves.

12. single sheet] This long letter is definitely on two sheets rather than one, but saying on the cover it was but one sheet would have halved the postage—that is, if one got away with the lie.

xliv. *Lydia Sterne to John Wilkes*

Text: Ms.

angoulême [Monday,] Octr 24th 1769

how long have I waited with impatience for a letter from Mr Wilks in answer to that I wrote to him above two months ago!—I fear he is not well. I fear his own affairs have not allow'd him time to answer me.—in short I am full of fears,——hope defer'd makes the heart sick.[1]—three lines with a promise of writing Tristrams life for the benefit of his widow and Daughter would make us happy—a promise did I say?—that I already have but a second *assurance.* indeed my dear S^{r} since I last wrote we stand more in need of such an act of kindness—Panchaud's failure[2] has hurt us considerably——we have I fear lost more than we in our circumstances could afford to lose——do not do not I beseech you disapoint us—let me have a single <leaf> line from you—"I will perform my promise" and joy will take place of our sorrow.[3]——do write to me and tell me what I trust you will——write to Hall. in pity do. adieu dear S^{r} may you enjoy all the happiness you deserve may every wish of yours be granted as I am sure you will grant my request.—my Mother joins in best comp[ts]—our most cordial wishes attend you & the amiable Miss Wilks

believe me most truly
your faithful friend
and obed[t] humble serv[t]
L Sterne——

a Mad[lle] Mad[lle] Sterne angloise
chez. Monsr Bologne ruë Cordeliers
Angouleme
France

Address: To / John Wilks Esqr / Kings Bench Prison / in the Borough / London / Angleterre
Postmark: NO 3 ANGOVLESME
MS: British Library, Addit. MSS. 30877, 72–73.
Pub.: Almon, *Correspondence of the Late John Wilkes,* 5:16–17; Curtis, no. xxxiv.

1. hope defer'd . . . sick] Proverbs 13:12: "Hope deferred maketh the heart sick."

2. Panchaud's failure] Walpole reported the bankruptcy on July 19, 1769: "Panchaud, a banker from Paris, broke yesterday for seventy thousand pounds, by buying and selling stock . . ." (*Correspondence* 23:133).

3. joy will . . . sorrow] Perhaps another scriptural allusion from the daughter of a cleric; see John 16:20: "your sorrow shall be turned into joy"; cf. Job 41:22.

xlv. *Lydia Sterne to John Hall-Stevenson*

Text: Ms.

Angouleme [Monday,] Feb[y] 13 1770

dear S[r]

'tis at least six months since I wrote to you on an interesting subject to us namely to put you in mind of a kind promise you made me of assisting M[r] Wilk's in the scheme he had form'd for our benefit of writing the life of M[r] Sterne. I wrote also to him, but you have neither of you favour'd me with an answer. if you ever felt what hope defer'd occasions, you would not have put us under that painful situation.——from whom the neglect arises, I know not but surely a line from you dear S[r] would not have cost you much trouble——tax me not with boldness for using the word neglect. as you both promised out of the benevolence of your hearts to write my Father's life for the benefit of his Widow & Daughter and as I myself look upon a promise as sacred & I Doubt not but you do think as I do. in that case the word is not improper—in short dear S[r] I ask but this of you to tell me by a very short letter whether we may depend on your's & M[r] Wilks's promise.—or if we must renounce the pleasing expectation—but dear S[r] consider that the fulfilling of it may put £400 into our pockets & that the declining it would be unkind after having made us hope & depend upon that kindness.——let this plead my excuse—if you do not chuse to take the trouble to wait on M[r] Wilks send him my letter & let me know the oui ou le non.[1]——<but> still let me urge press & entreat M[r] Hall to be as good as his word—if he will interest himself in our behalf 'twill but be acting consistent with his character twill prove that Eugenius was the friend of Yorick—nothing can prove it stronger than befriending his Widow & Daughter—do then dear S[r] I beg you will. 'Tis the last request I shall ever make you———M[rs] James will send you this letter y[r] answer pleased to send to her & she will enclose it me.[a]

adieu dear S[r] believe me your
most obliged humble serv[t]
L Sterne

my mother joins in best <thanks> comp[ts]

PS

M[rs] James has some things to send us & your letter she will send by the same opportunity—Do favour me with an answer

---

Address: To / John Hall Stevenson / Esq[r] / London

MS: British Library, Addit. MSS. 30877, 78–79.

Pub.: Almon, *Correspondence of the Late John Wilkes,* 5:18–19 (without the postscript); Curtis, no. xxxv.

[a]do then . . . it me.] *om. Almon*

1. oui ou le non] Yes or no. Almon, 20, comments: "Neither of the gentlemen performed their promise"; presumably his use of the word "gentlemen" is ironic.

xlvi. *Lydia Sterne to Elizabeth Montagu*

Text: Ms.

Angouleme [Friday,] march 2^d 1770

my dear Cousin

I cannot defer writing to you any longer, but I will not be so negligent as not to give Mrs Montagu a direction which Mrs James tells me I omitted in my precedent letters.—sufficiently have I been punish'd by not hearing from you. a thousand anxieties took possession of our souls, sometimes we fear'd you was ill, or that Mr Montagu was so.—I will not weary my cousin with an account of every disagreeable thought, that made us so unhappy but beg leave to assure her that we rejoice to hear she is well. may she long continue so! suffer me to thank you a thousand times for the notes you was so kind as to give Mrs James for us.—the money came very seasonably for our attorney in York has neglected sending us our little remittances,[1] and we were short of money.—believe us truly grateful. but I will not hurt my dear cousin's delicacy by saying any more on the subject: sufficiently does she think herself paid in doing a benevolent action.—but I must not make you pay postage for a mere letter of thanks, I must give you some account of the place we are in—the town tho' ill built is situated most agreeably, the prospects fine, the walks beautiful.—but as to the inhabitants except a small number.——n'en disons rien.[2]—yet thus far I must speak in their praise, they understand eating, & play better than any people in the world.—the former is their study, their delight, a Capon stuff'd with trufles, or a Galantine sont des sujets inépuisables[3]—every day there is a great dinner, and every evening a supper.—we have 59 traiteurs[4] in this little town, that wear laced coats, & couteaux de chasse[5] and but one Bookseller, & he poor man is in want, & looks like Shakespear's starved apothecary.[6]—this gluttony renders the market very dear, nothing but Butcher's meat is reasonable fish, fowls &cc are extravagantly dear.—therefore we intend going a little further south[7] where we may live cheaper. civil as the people are to us, yet if we gave to eat we should be much better liked, but that is not our plan, and suits not our finances.—tho often invited out we seldom go because we do not chuse to return the compliment. I flatter myself my dear Cousin will favour me with a line if she knew the pleasure it would give us both she certainly would write—we are both of us much indisposed particularly myself. I haste to Bed as I have been bled this evening—Mrs James thinks herself highly honour'd with the civilities Mrs Montagu shew'd her.—& speaks of Mrs Montagu with enthusiasm.—but 'tis but a just tribute (which every one who is so happy as to know my Cousin pays her)——we hope Mr Montagu is well, & present our best comp^ts to him—my mother joins in most aff^e comp^ts

believe me dear Mad^m
y^r most obliged aff^e
L Sterne

A Mad^lle Mad^lle Sterne angloise ruë des Cordeliers Angouleme France

---

Address: To / Mrs Montagu / Hill street / Berkley square / London / Angleterre
Postmark: MR 12 ANGOVLESME
MS: Henry E. Huntington Library, San Marino, Calif., MO 1517.
Pub.: Blunt, *Montagu* (1923), 1:208–9; Curtis, no. xxxvi.

1. our attorney . . . remittances] John Graves (see letter xxvii, n. 1) was handling these remittances, which Curtis opines were "not so negligible as Lydia would imply" (455, n. 1); see letter xxviii, n. 5.

2. n'en disons rien] Let us say nothing about it.

3. or a Galantine . . . inépuisables] A Galantine [i.e., a cold dish consisting of boned meat or fish that has been stuffed, poached, and covered with aspic] is an inexhaustible subject for discussion. Cf. *TS,* VII.17.600: "the French love good eating——they are all *gourmands*——we shall rank high; if their god is their belly——their cooks must be gentlemen . . . ."

4. traiteurs] Restaurateurs; see *ASJ,* 134, and n. to 134.11, 6:358.

5. couteaux de chasse] Hunting knives.

6. Shakespear's starved apothecary] I.e., the apothecary in *Romeo and Juliet,* V.i.69–70: "Famine is in thy cheeks, / Need and oppression starveth in thy eyes."

7. a little further south] Elizabeth and Lydia would move to Albi in 1771, a few miles northeast of Toulouse on the Tarn, between Montauban and Castres in Languedoc.

xlvii. *Lydia Sterne to Jane Fenton*[1]

Text: Ms.

Angouleme [Friday,] March 23 1770

Dear Madam

'tis very true—I have not been as good as my word. I promised our kind friend to write to her as ^soon as^ I was fix'd in france and have not done it. my heart has reproach'd me a thousand times for my neglect,[2] and I deserve the mortification of your sending me back my letter without opening it but my dear Madam be not so severe tho' you should chance to wish you had after reading it keep that to yourself I beseech you. James[3] has scolded me most unmercifully for having been so idle, but my heart tells me that the good M[rs] Fenton will have seal'd my pardon as soon as she sees my name at the bottom of my paper.—for the first three months I defer'd writing in hopes to have something entertaining to write about, but was I to wait to eternity the eternal[4] sameness of the French will strike out nothing new, nothing I am sure worth waiting for, but all I can say in their praise shall not be omitted.—but first let me give you a description of the situation of Angouleme which requires a better pen than your humble servants to do it justice. but you must take the will for the deed.—the town in itself is ill built, but the walks are beautiful, the prospects fine, & romantick. a serpentine river which joins the Garonne at Bordeaux adds greatly to the prospect, there are little islands upon the River where in the heats of summer the inhabitants go and divert themselves 'tis in short the town in France the most beautifully situated.—from the publick walk which is much elevated you look down upon the River and see all round you Convents, gentlemen's seats, & most elegant Bridges the cattle and the people working in the Vineyard's appear very small, & puts one in mind of that fine description of Dover Cliff by Shakespear[5] | now as to the inhabitants I am sure they would not suit Mrs Fenton's taste no more than ours. gormandizing is their sole delight, and go into what company you will the conversation turns upon eatables & drinkables—a perigord pye which has been pronounced good is a subject not easily to have done with | in short they have no joy but eating nor no pleasure equal to talking about it | there are great suppers, & dinners every day, and 50 people compose the sett each striving to shew his abilities not in conversation but eating! we have many invitations but the picture is too odious to make such kind of society agreeable but there is another reason which makes us decline it <?w> 'tis this. Our circumstances will not permit us to return the compt and we do not chuse to lay ourselves under obligations to the French.—but do not imagine that all the french resemble those of Angouleme—heav'n forbid as we are destined to remain amongst them.—we spend our time agreeably notwithstanding the disadvantageous picture I have given you. what with reading musick walks, & the society of a few individuals more rational than the rest time slips away insensibly & not uncheerily.—how can it appear otherwise to me with such a mother as I am bless'd with? in her I find a tender affectionate parent, & at the same time a friend, a charming companion.—with her every situation is pleasing without her I know none that could be supportable | 50 Cooks in this town that fly from house to house to dress dinners &cc. & as are as rich as *one* <poo> unfortunate Bookseller is poor, you sentimental, sensible people of Angouleme much do you owe me for my panygerick. 'tis at your service.—It was with concern we heard that Mrs Roberts' your amiable Daughter[6] is not in so good a state of health as we wish.—I hope 'eer this reaches our dear friend she will be better.—heav'n grant she may.—now dear Madam do not punish me by a long silence, honour me with a line! and as soon as you can. what a feast would an hour's conversation <be to> with Mrs Fenton be to us in this land of folly | make us happy by a letter.—we leave this place in two months,[7] for a cheaper village. our situation obliges us to seek for the cheapest place we can hear of[a]. my mother joins with me in most aff[e] wishes for M[rs] Fenton & her Daughter. adieu

dear Mad[m] believe me y[r] most faithful obliged

L Sterne

please to direct a M[lle] Sterne M[lle] angloise angouleme France

---

Address: To / M[rs] Fenton / at M[r] Roberts's / Kings Arms Yard / Coleman street / London / Angleterre

Postmark: AP2

Endorsed: Mch: 1770 / Ly: Sterne

MS: Kenneth Monkman Collection, Shandy Hall.

Pub.: Kenneth Monkman, "A Letter by (and a Poem to?) Lydia, and a Letter by Elizabeth," *Shandean* 3 (1991): 167–82 (facsimile, fig. 53).

[a] of] off *MS*

1. *Jane Fenton*] See letter 63, n. 1.

2. neglect] Lydia and her mother had returned to France in the summer of 1769 (cf. Lydia's letter to Wilkes, no. xliii above), some eight months earlier.

3. James] Monkman, 177, rather improbably states that "'James' can surely be no other than Lydia's future husband-to-be," improbably because Lydia surely had enough French to know that *Jean* does not translate as *James,* and because Monkman's suggestion implies that Lydia talked about him to Mrs. Fenton in England in 1767, when Jean Medalle was only 15 years old. It is far more likely, especially in light of the very same mention of "James" in letter xlvi, that Lydia refers familiarly to Mrs. James, who had reminded her of her overdue correspondence.

As did her father, Lydia recycles the materials of one letter (to Montagu) in a second letter—and probably in other letters as well, if we knew her full correspondence.

4. eternal] Possibly "eternel," the French spelling, as in Monkman's text, but Lydia's vowels are often indistinguishable. Similarly, we have rendered Monkman's "gormondizing" as "gormandizing"; in both instances, we see "a" where he read the ms. differently.

5. Dover Cliff by Shakespear] In *King Lear,* IV.vi.11–18, Edgar describes the view from Dover Cliffs to his blinded father: "How fearful / And dizzy 'tis, to cast one's eyes so low! / The crows and choughs that wing the midway air / Show scarce so gross as beetles . . . / The fishermen that walk upon the beach / Appear like mice . . . ."

6. Mrs Roberts' . . . Daughter] As Monkman suggests, "from the address . . . it appears that Mrs Fenton and her daughter in 1770 lived with her son-in-law in Coleman Street." Nothing else is known about the Roberts family, although a Christopher Roberts, Esq. (1739–1810), subscribed to *Sermons* (1760, 1766); he was a director of the East India Company for many years, which may be the source of a connection to the Jameses.

7. in two months] See Monkman, 178: "It seems they did not move for at least a year. At the marriage [Lydia to Jean Medalle], it was stated that they had resided in Albi only since 25 April 1771."

xlviii. *Lydia Sterne to Elizabeth Montagu*

Text: Ms.

Albi [Thursday,] sept^{r} 26th 1771

my dear Cousin

my mother and myself were made happy some time ago by your kind affectionate letter which believe me dear Madam was a cordial to our souls. much were we concern'd to find that illness had deprived us of the pleasure of hearing from you. but hope that at present your health is as good as we wish it. Mrs James has inform'd us that you have been so kind as to remit her thirty pounds. a thousand thanks my dear Cousin. I wish I had the happiness to pay them in person. but I believe I should not be able to express all the gratitude I <have> ‸feel‸; indeed my dear Mrs Montagu we are both penetrated with a just sense of your goodness and both beg leave to thank you once more.—

to avoid an unnecessary expence we employ no Banker to receive our remittances. Mrs James receives all and sends us Bills on People at Paris.—the situation of this Village is pretty our little house is agreeable, but there is little society. and the little there is, is scarce worth the trouble of searching after.—both my mother and myself prefer Books to stupid conversation, and in such a little provincial Town as this the men are ignorant the women still more so except in the affair of the Toilet. but in general the french are good-natured and sometimes we go amongst them. and return with more pleasure to our Books—I remember my Father complain'd at Toulouse that by conversing much with the French his understanding diminish'd <dayly> every day.—my mother has had two narrow escapes from Death. about two months ago, she was awaken'd in the night by the Barking of a turn-spit, and getting up she perceiv'd a man coming down her chimney by the means of a Rope. she allarm'd the familly and the Villain ascended the Chimney. there was found upon the Tiles a large knife which was open, and the Rope still fasten'd round the Chimney. if my poor mother had not had a light in her room she would not have seen the Rope and in all probability would have been murther'd what a mercy it was that she was awaken'd by the Barking of the Dog!—we have got all the Chimneys grated, so that no one can descend. since that alass she has had an Epileptick fit and has continued ill ever since. may God restore her health. her loss would be irreparable to me.

I have ever found her a most affectionate mother a tender friend and her conversation with me is such as tends to form both my heart and my Head. I hope she has succeeded in the one, I mean as to my Heart.—you are very kind to tell me my dear Mrs Montagu that the subject of my health is interesting to you.—indeed I have very bad health and am very thin. I partake too much of my Father's constitution. when ever my dear Cousin favours me with a letter my direction is A Albi prés de[1] Toulouse en Languedoc. my mother joins with me[a] in most affectionate compliments and in prayers and wishes for your health and happiness—

I am my dear Cousin
your most obliged and
most affectionate God Daughter[b]
Lydia Sterne

Address: To / Mrs Montagu / in Hill street / London / Angleterres.
Postmark: OC 12
MS: Henry E. Huntington Library, San Marino, Calif., MO 1518.
Pub.: Blunt, *Montagu* (1923), 1:209–11; Curtis, no. xxxvii.

[a]with me] with *MS* [b]Daughter] Daugh [ms. torn]

1. prés de] Properly près de: near.

xlix. *Lydia Sterne to Elizabeth Montagu*

Text: Ms.

Albi [Monday,] March 23 1772.—

dear Madam. permit me to call you my dearest Cousin

pardon your affectionate God Daughter if she troubles you with a letter. it is of the utmost consequence to me and will not (to a heart like yours) appear the contrary. I have that confidence in your goodness that I fear not to impart to you, that I have had an Offer here of marriage[1] which tho' not advantageous, yet was far from disagreeable to me: my dear mother wish'd me rather to consider that an easy fortune was preferable to inclination, but seeing that the gentleman was far from displeasing to me, and not likely to render me unhappy has not absolutely opposed what I trust will be my happiness. seeing that he was no bigot to his Religion and has offer'd me and her every assurance that I shall be at full liberty to practice my own Religion.[2]—but his Father has insisted upon very hard terms.[3] namely that my mother should give up her estate immediately. whatever a woman brings in marriage in France 'tis the custom in france to secure her her fortune and no more. so she neither loses nor gains—my mother is willing almost to leave herself without ‸bread‸ for the advantage of her Lydia. my heart bleeds to think she should be under the necessity of reducing herself to so small a pittance: therefore my dear Mrs Montague permit me to plead for her to you. I here thrust my chair from me and write upon my <two> knees, consider her, and her alone, and withdraw not your bounty from her whilst she lives! I ask nothing for myself but shall feel doubly on her account if you grant my humble petition. Oh my dear Cousin she deserves your friendship by her Virtues, by her goodness. she has perform'd every duty in Life. as a Wife how has she conducted herself. when a Widow she acted nobly in regard to my Father's debts. as a mother she has acted too generously. and I may say without a boast I believe her One of the best of Women | I am sure she is the best of parents.—join dear Madam your consent to hers. but let me hope that what I so earnestly have beg'd will be granted. Merit has ever a claim with Mrs Montague. why should I doubt or fear? I do not | I plead for a parent for a tender mother. my dear Cousin's heart is susceptible of all that's great and good. my cause is gain'd!—may I flatter myself that you will favour me with an answer sent to Mrs James she will forward it—my mother has been and is very ill.[4] my health very indifferent. I inherit my father's constitution, <and> but I trust I inherit part of my mothers Virtues. she joins with me in most affectionate wishes for your health, and happiness | she honours and loves you. but so does every one who has the happiness to be acquainted with Mrs Montagu.—

I beg you to believe me my dear Cousin
your most obliged
affectionate God Daughter
Lydia Sterne

be so good as to present our compts to Mr Montagu and also to Mrs Scott.[5]—
à Albi pres de Toulouse en Languedoc France

Address: To / Mrs Montagu
MS: Henry E. Huntington Library, San Marino, Calif., MO 1519.
Pub.: Blunt, *Montagu* (1923), 1:211–12; Curtis, no. xxxviii.

1. an Offer here of marriage] The offer came from Jean-Baptiste-Alexandre-Anne Médalle (*b.* 1752) of Albi, son of Jean-François Medalle, a collector of the "décimes du clergé" (taxes imposed on the clergy by itself to pay expenses and debts), and an "advocat au parlement" (a lawyer authorized to argue cases before the Parliament of Toulouse). The banns were published on April 26; the marriage took place on April 28. The bridegroom's age is correctly given as "twenty years and some months"; Lydia's is understated as "twenty-one" (she had turned twenty-four three months earlier). What Lydia did not tell Mrs. Montagu was that she was five months pregnant, which gives rather special poignancy to her assertion toward the end of the letter that she inherited her "father's constitution" but "part of" her "mothers Virtues." A son, baptized Jean-François-Laurens, was born on August 6, 1772, and baptized the next day. See Cash, *LY,* 349–50, and Van R. Baker's two notes, "Laurence Sterne's Family in France," *N&Q,* n.s. 22 (1975): 497–501, and "Whatever Happened to Lydia Sterne?" *ECLife* 2 (1975): 6–11.

2. my own Religion] The wedding registration states unequivocally that the bride had renounced the Anglican faith and become a Roman Catholic.

3. very hard terms] See Cash, *LY*, 350; Elizabeth settled on the couple a dowry of 50,000 livres (about £2,200), reserving for herself the interest on her daughter's half. Jean-Baptiste's father settled upon them half his estate, but reserved the use of it for his lifetime. Elizabeth apparently managed to postpone her part of the arrangement, the Medalles not receiving the 50,000 livres until a year after her death; see next note.

4. my mother . . . very ill] As Cash, *LY*, 350, notes, Elizabeth did not attend the wedding, presumably because of illness. She died on July 11, 1773, "eleven months after the birth of her grandson. She had been confined nearly a year at No. 9, rue Saint-Antoine, the house of her physician and neighbour, Dr François Linières."

5. Mrs Scott] I.e., Sarah Scott; see letter 148, n. 1.

l. *Elizabeth Montagu to Lydia Sterne*

Text: Ms.[1]

[April 1772]

I cannot hesitate a moment to transfer entirely to your Mamma during her life the little Sum I used to send for your Mutual Service so that the Article of your letter which relates to this point is most easily answered, and with as much pleasure on my side as it can be received on yours. The more momentous Affair your Marriage I can ^not^ assent to with the same good will. What I shall say on this subject is not meant to offend the Gentleman who you have a desire to marry. I am a perfect stranger to his character, his Fortune, and even his name. You do not say any thing of them, all you give your Friends is that you are going to marry a man of a different Religion, and to reduce your Mother to almost Beggary, both these things you confess. You seem at the same time to declare stedfastness in Religion & Filial piety to your Parent. My dear cousin the Actions not the words are what shall decide the judgment of God and man. If your Husband has any zeal or regard for his religion he will be earnest to make you embrace it from regard to you and reverence to God, if he is void of Religion he will think such a Mark of your complaisance a trifle and the Authority of the Husband will interpose where faith stands Neuter. Your children must of necessity be . . . .[2]

MS: Henry E. Huntington Library, San Marino, Calif., MO 1520.
Endorsed: Copy of a letter / to Miss Sterne
Pub.: Blunt, *Montagu* (1923), 1:212–13; Curtis, no. xxxix.

1. Ms.] The entire fragmentary ms. is in a contemporary hand, not Mrs. Montagu's; the endorsement is in yet another hand.

2. be . . . .] The ms. stops abruptly at this point; how much longer Montagu could have continued her arguments against marrying outside one's faith may be suggested by Richardson's million words in *Sir Charles Grandison* (1753–54), the age's compendium, surely, for all such debates.

li. *Eliza Draper to Anne James*

Text: Ms.[1]

Bombay [Wednesday,] 15th April 1772.

. . . You say my dear, *that you ha<ve>~d~ "suffered much uneasiness at hearing that I thought you had not acted a friendly part by me in protecting two unfortunate People; and requesting me, to make a contribution amongst my friends in their Favor:—that, this Report touched you to the heart; tho' you disbelieved it, as it was inconsistent with my Humanity, my opinion of you, and the reverse of all my letters, and yet, when you found, that I had wrote to Becket, your Idea's were rather confused; for if I had, had a proper reliance on you; I need not have applied to him; as I might have supposed, you would find some means to secure my letters, if violent measures had been the Widows Plan, but, that you, was perfectly easy as to that matter; and imagined, I should have been the same; knowing you to be my Friend:—that there was a Stiffness, in my calling you Mrs James, which cut*[a] *you to the heart, particularly, whe<re>~n~ I said I could not accost you with my usual Freedom—What had you done to create reserve, & distance? and had my letter concluded in this*[b] *same style; you should have believed I was altered, not you."* I will endeavor to answer all this very plainly, and in the first place, I do assure you then (on my never forfeited word) that I neither by Thought, Word, or Action, ever gave the most distant Cause for such a Report—and how, or wherefore it was invented, & propagated, I know no more, than I do of any one finespun[c] Circumstance, yet unheard, or unthought of by me—it is certain my dear James, that so far from thinking unkindly of you, for your Patronage of the Sternes, that you never to me, appeared in so amiable a Light—strange, if you had not, as nothing but a sordid Principle, most narrowly selfish, could have induced me to dislike an Action which had its foundation in Generosity, and all the milder feminine Virtues—but my James, I will be very explicit with you, <as> ‸on this subject as‸ you have introduced <?this>~it~ yourself—the World, I fear, <?will not I fear,> ‸does not‸ see the beauty of a compassionate disinterestedness in the same Light that you, and I do. . . . You wonder my dear, at my writing to Becket—I'll tell you why I did so—*I had heard some Anecdotes extremely disadvantageous to the Characters of the Widow & Daughter, and that from Persons who said they had been personally acquainted with them, both in France & England—I had no reason to doubt the Veracity of these Gentlemen ‸Informants,‸ they could have no view in deceiving me, or motive of putting me on my Guard, but what arose from <?de>~A~ Benevolence, which I hope is common to the greatest part of Mankind—some part of their Intelligence corroborated, what I ha<ve>~d~ a thousand times heard, from the Lips of Yorick, almost invariably repeated—the Widow, I was assured, was occasionally a Drinker, a Swearer, venal & unchaste—tho' in point of Understanding, and finished Address, supposed to be inferior to no Woman in Europe*[d]—the Secret of my Letters being in her hands, had some how become extremely Public, it was noticed to me by almost every acquaintance I had in the Company's[e] Ships, or at this Settlement—this alarmed me—for ‸at that time‸ I had never Communicated the Circumstance, and could not suspect you of acting by me in any manner, which I would not have acted in ‸by‸ my self—One Gentleman in particular told me, that both you, & I, should be deceived, if We had the least reliance on the Honor or Principles of Mrs Sterne, for that, when she had secured as much as she could, for suppressing the Correspondence, she was capable of selling it to a Bookseller afterwards—by either refusing to restore it to you—or taking Copies of it, without our knowledge—and therefore He advised me, if I was averse to it's Publication[2] to take every means in my Power of Suppressing it—this influenced me to write to Becket, and promise Him a reward equal to his Expectations, if He would deliver the Letters to you. (I think I proposed ‸no other method to Him <but>~exc~ept‸ this, but I'm not sure) in case they were offered him for sale—I had a long Conflict in my own mind whether, I should, or should not, reveal every thing regarding this Business to you—at length, I determined to keep the Secret in my own breast—and that from a motive of Delicacy rather than good Judgment perhaps—for[f] well do I know, how harshly it grates, to have those we love, aspersed, whether with, or without Foundation—my Circumstances, as to this Family, were peculiar, and required the nicest Conduct—Interest, Jealousy, a thousand narrow motives, might be[g] supposed to stimulate me! as I could not with Honor, have disclosed my Authorities for advancing many things, I must have advanced, to say the half of what I had been told:—and as a real, or pretended respect, for myself had prompted the disclosure of them, it would have been something worse than ungenerous, to have subjected the Persons to ill Will, or being called upon to prove their Assertions when they had a <?>~moral~ Claim to my handsome treatment, at least, for whether their Intelligence, was founded on Truth, or falsehood, it is not to be conceived, that they meant I should suppose them influenced by unjust motives; consequently, it had all the Rights of well attested Facts, till I could disprove it——This I have never been able to do, tho' all my Enquiries, when Yoricks Widow or Daughter has been named have tended to this effect, in hopes of accomplishing my Wishes; for it cannot ^surely be^ supposed my dear James! that I am so fiendlike in my nature as to wish that any Woman of Sense & Character, might be proved vicious rather than virtuous, by the confirmations of Truth, <&>~or~ Chance.—it is True my friend! I love not these Ladies! and what is more, I think, I think! Excuse me my dear—that while I preserve my Rectitude and Sensibility, I never shall!—and I would not part with them for so paltry an Exchange, as the Acquisition of new Acquaintances. . . . You had told me that Sterne was no more—^I had heard it before, but this Confirmation of it^ <[illegible words]>~truely~ afflicted me; for I was almost an Idolator, of His Worth, while I fancied Him the mild, generous, Good Yorick, We had so often thought Him to be—to add to my regret for his loss—his Widow had my letters in her Power, (I never entertained a good opinion of her) and meant to subject me to Disgrace & Inconvenience by the Publication of them—you knew not the contents of these letters, and it was natural for you to form the worst judgment of them, when those who had seen 'em reported them, unfavorably, and were disposed to dislike me on that Account,—my dear Girl! had I not cause to feel humbled so Circumstanced—and can you wonder at my sensations communicating themselves to my Pen? you cannot, on reflection:—for such are the Emotions of the Human Heart, that they must influence human Actions, while Truth and Nature, are unsubdued—I do not, I assure you my dear James, I never did, think you acted by me, other than the kindest part throughout this whole Transaction with the Sternes—I lament your attachment to them, but I only lament it for your sake, in case Lydia, is rather speciously attached[h] than mildly amiable; w'ch I have heard, Insinuated.—whatever Cause, I may have to dislike them on my own account, I can have none to do so on yours—while they preserve an Empire in your Breast from their superiority in Merit principally—but beware, of Deceivers my dear Woman! the best Hearts are most liable to be imposed on, by them. . . . I ever speak of both Widow & Daughter as you or they, might wish me to speak, when expatiating on the subject,—for I have no Idea my James, that Eliza's Opinion, is to be the Standard of Other Peoples, well as I think of it in the Main—and however <?> Angry I may be with them, in my heart, I should be very sorry to have <?> People ∧I esteemed∧ think ill ∧of∧ them—as a proof of which, I'll transcribe for you, part of a letter I wrote ∧on the subject∧ the other Day, to Colonel Campbell[3] in Bengal—who is a great Favorite of mine, had sent me six hundred Rupees, which He had raised by Contribution for their use, and <?desired>~hinted~ his Wishes to know something of the Ladies—as He meant to visit England shortly.——"I sensibly feel the Exertions of your kindness in behalf of my Friends Widow & Daughter—and assure myself, if you ever know them, that your own Complacency will administer a Reward from the Consciousness of having served two very amiable Persons; as well Educated Women, of Talents, and Sensibility, are, I believe of all others, the most serious objects of a generous Compassion, when obliged to Descend from an Easy Elegance, their Native Sphere, to the Mortifying Vicissitudes of neglect

& pecuniary Embarrassments. The Ladies are no Strangers to your Character; and I please my self with the notion of their proving a very agreeable Addition to your Acquaintance, when you are at all disposed to cultivate Theirs. Mrs Sterne, I have heard spoke of as one of the most sensible Women in Europe—she is <?>~nearly~ related to the Mrs Montague, whose ∨Essay∨ ∧on the <Gen>∧ Writings and Genius of Shakespeare,[4] has reflected ∧so∧ much Honor, on the reputation of Female Judgment & Generosity—which circumstance renders it probable, that she ∧(Mrs Sterne)∧ may possess equal Powers, from Inheritance—Miss Sterne is supposed to have a portion of each Parents best Qualities—the Sensibility & frolic Vivacity of Yorick, most happily blended in her Composition—Lively by Nature, Youth & Education; she cannot fail to please every Spectator of capacious Mind; but much, I fear, that, the Shandy Race will be Extinct with this <?> ∧Accomplished∧ Young Woman—for She's of the Muses Train, and too much attached to them, & filial Duties, to think of a change of Name with much Complacency". . . . So much my Dear, for my discription of the Sternes to Colonel Campbell, tho' I've seen them not but with the Minds Eye:—be so good my dear, as to announce his name and Character to them, as it's probable He may find them out and make himself known to them—He has been very Assiduous in collecting above one half of the money I have sent Home for their use. . . . I am a good deal altered in my appearance James, since you used to view me with the Eyes of Kindness, due only, to a second self—but, my Head, and Heart; if self Love does not mislead me, are both, much improved and the Qualities of Reflection, and tenderness, are no bad substitutes for that clearness of Complection, and Je-ne-scai-quoi Air, which <[sentence illegible]> ∧my flatterers ∨used to∨ say entitled me to the Apellation of∧ Belle Indian. I read a great deal, I scribble much—and I daily ride on Horseback, bathe in the sea—and live most abstemiously—but I cannot manage to acquire confirmed Health, in this detested Country! and what is far worse, I cannot induce Mr Draper, to let me return to England; tho' He must be sensible, that both my Constitution and Mind, are suffering by the effects of a Warm Climate—I do, and must wonder that He will not,—for what good Purpose my Residence Here can promote, I am quite at a loss to imagine, as I am disposed to think favorably of Mr D's Generosity and Principles. My dear James, it is Evident to the whole of our Acquaintance, that our minds are not pair'd, and therefore I will not scruple informing *you*—that I neither do, or will any more, if I can help it, live with Him as a Wife . . . . *I cannot my dear, send you the six hundred Rupees, I received from Colonel Campbell for the use of the Sternes*[i] by this Ship, as none but Company's Servants are allowed Bills, on the Company, on their own Account.—Mr D— cannot swear, that this Money is his own Property—however, I will account to you, or them for it ∧with Interest∧—and if this Restriction as to Bills, is not taken off by the Mocha Ship,[5] I will lay out the Money in Pearl (as that I am told sells advantageously in England, very much so at present) and send it by Capt Jones, or somebody for their use; and by such means, they can <no>~in~ no way be losers, and I hope it will be no Inconvenience to them, to wait a few months longer for it, than I wished them to do—as I imagine th<?is>~eir~ Expectations from me, must have ceased, with the last Bill, I transmitted to England—O my dear Friend! for God Sake, pay them all the money of mine in your Hands—would it were twice as much!—the Ring too is much at Mrs Sternes Service—as should be every thing I have in the World, rather than I would freely owe the shaddow of an Obligation to Her—You say my dear, in your letter of May 29th ∧1771∧ dated from Eltham[6]—"I hope my Lydia's Letter did not give you pain, perhaps not Pleasure, but you must make some allowances, for she loves her Mother, who really is a good Woman—and even the Proposal, however kind the Intention in having Lydia live with you, yet the taking from Mrs Sterne her only Child, and only Comfort, and taking no notice of the Mother, was rather ill timed in my Eliza and threw some difficulties in my way"—Miss Sternes Letter, did indeed my dear, give me a great deal of pain—it was such a one, as I by no means deserved, in answer to one wrote in the true spirit of kindness, however it might have been construed.—Mr Sterne had repeatedly told me, that his Daughter was as well acquainted with my Character, as he was with my Appearance—in all his letters, wrote since my leaving England, this Circumstance is much dwelt upon—another too, that of Mrs

Sternes being in too precarious a state of Health, to render it probable that she would survive many months—her violence of Temper, (indeed James I wish not ∧to∧ recriminate or be severe just now) and the hatefulness of her Character, are strongly urged to me, as the Cause of his Indifferent Health, the whole of his Misfortunes, and the Evils that would probably shorten his Life—the visit Mrs Sterne meditated, some time antecedent to his Death, He most pathetically lamented, as an adventure that wou'd wound his Peace, and greatly embarrass his Circumstances—the former on account of the Eye Witness He should be, to his Childs Affections having been <?>~alienated~ from Him, by the artful misrepresentations of her Mother, under whose Tutorage she had ever been—and the latter, from the Rapacity of her Disposition—for well do I know, say's He,—"that the sole Intent of her Visit is to plague & fleece me—had I money enough, I would buy off this Journey, as I have done several others—but till my Sentimental <?>~Work~ is published, I shall not have a single sous more than will Indemnify People for my immediate Expences."[7] Soon after the receipt of this Intelligence I heard of Yoricks Death. The very first ship which left us afterwards, I wrote to Miss Sterne by—and with all the freedom which my Intimacy with her ∧Father & his Communications∧ warranted.—I purposely avoided, speaking of her Mother, for I knew nothing to her Advantage—and I had heard a great deal to the reverse—so circumstanced—How could I with any kind of Delicacy mention a Person, who was hateful to my departed Friend, when for the sake of that very friend—I wished to confer a <?Favor> ∧kindness∧ on his Daughter—and to inhance the value of it,—solicited her Society, & consent to share my Prospects, as the highest Favor, which could be shewn ∧to∧ myself?—indeed I knew not, but Mrs Sterne, from the Discription I had received of her, might be no more—or privately confined, if in Being; ∧owing to a Malady, which I've been told the violence of her temper subjects her to.∧ You, my dear, knew nothing of the Ladies at this time—my letter of Invitation was sent before I received Your's urging the Necessity of their Circumstances—and the worthiness of their Characters—but can they be thus worthy, when so ready to take part against a stranger—tho' that stranger is

<?her>~the~ friend <?>~of the~ Woman, they profess to Esteem & Admire, & has ever had the Advantage, of being described by ^her in an^ amiable light? Non Credo![8] . . . Miss Sterne, in her letter, tells me—*that her Father did sometimes misrepresent her mother, in order to justify his neglect of her*—I do not think highly of a Daughter, who could compliment a living Parent, however justly—at the expence of a Deceased one—but as this was Miss Sternes Opinion—she might in common justice to have supposed ^that Mrs Sterne had been misrepresented to me. this would have accounted for my silence on the subject & clearly evinced^ that I could not mean any kind of Disrespect to herself or mother by not naming her, in my letter of Invitation—indeed my dear—so far from it—that my silence on the subject, as I've hinted before, only proceeded from a Delicacy w'ch ^is^ natural to me, when I either wish or mean, to speak to the Affections—I have been strangely deceived in Miss Sternes—or she never could have perverted my Sentiments so much, as to suppose I did her an Injury, in addressing her as a kindred Spirit, and with all the freedom, I could wish to subsist between myself and a Sister of my Heart—the circumstance in particular, which you allude ^to^ was such as would of itself, have given me some reputation, in the Eyes of Discerning & kind sensibility; consequently it ought not to have obstructed, your <?> progress in my favor—nor would it my James—Excuse me! if these Rivals of mine, in your friendship—had been half as deserving, as <you> ^your^ absent Eliza—I cannot account for Mrs Sternes pique towards me from that, (as it proved[j]) unfortunate Letter—not on any one principle of goodness, my dear, can I account for it—for however the Woman might have been displeased, at my supposed Slight of her—the Mother I think, must have pleaded well for me, in a kind maternal breast—as she must have been sensible that I meant affectionate Services to her Child, however I'd fail'd in the Punctilo's due to herself, and th<?at>~e~ fond sensations, in such a Cause, must be lukewarm indeed <in>~if~ that could not counteract the effects of <my [illegible sentence]> ^Caprice—<?for> Reason, she had none, to be angry^ with me, knowing that my sole knowledge of her was derived from Yoricks Communications—and ^that^ such <?>, were not of the

favorable sort—I believed Sterne—implicitly, I believed him! *I had no Motive to do otherwise than believe him just generous & unhappy—till his Death gave me to know, that he was tainted with the Vices of Injustice—Meanness—& Folly*[k]—nothing had ever offered, to remove my prejudice against the Widows Character—till your Assurances made me wish to be divested of it. . . . A few words more, of the Widow & Daughter, and then I hope to have done with the subject forever—when I think of Miss Sterne's reply, to a letter, replete with kindness—for such I am sure it was, because such I meant it <to> ^should^ be—and the mothers starting any Difficulties to oblige me in a Point I had much at Heart—because I had neglected a mere Ceremony—which in my Case—could have meant just nothing at <the best> ^all, at the very best^——I can, and do pronounce from my very soul—that I think them as unworthy my Friendship—as any two Persons, I know, or ever yet, heard of—and it does indeed, wound both my Pride, and love, that the Woman in Life, I most Value—should bring them into Competition with myself, when she names me as her Friend—her Dear Eliza. . . .

E. Draper

MS: British Library, Addit. MSS. 34527, 47–70.
Pub.: Cross, *Journal to Eliza and Various Letters* (*Works,* 1904), 173–268; Curtis no. xl (in part).

[a]*cut*] *eat Cross, C* [b]*this*] *the Cross, C* [c]finespun] foreign *Cross, C* [d]*I had . . . Europe*] [no italics] *C* [e]Company's] C[ompany's] *Cross, C* [ms. worn] [f]for] so *Cross, C* [g]might be] might not be *C* [h]attached] attractive *Cross, C* [i]*I cannot . . . Sternes*] [no italics] *C* [j]proved] provide *C* [k]*I had . . . Folly*] [no italics] *C*

1. Ms.] This long, rambling, self-justifying, and unhappy letter of some 20,000 words is printed in its entirety in Cross (1904), but we have largely followed Curtis's condensed text, a selection based on relevance to Sterne's death and its aftermath. Cash, *LY,* 343–45, summarizes the relevant context: Eliza "had not allowed Anne [James] to negotiate with Elizabeth Sterne for the return of Eliza's letters; instead she had promised a reward to Becket if he would get them and turn them over to Anne for safekeeping. She was also at pains to explain how she could have invited Lydia to join her in India while ignoring her mother" (343).

Eliza's biographers are accurate in their assessment: "Eliza rambles on from topic to topic with little or no reference to the ordering of her matter. She wrote not a letter but a pamphlet, but it is a pamphlet which has no consistency or logical force. You read and wonder what the writer is driving at, and you end as you began in a state of perplexity as to the writer's real intention in occupying so much paper" (*Sterne's Eliza* 135); they quote considerable portions as well.

Eliza's handwriting is difficult, especially in determining her capitalization and punctuation; where questions existed, we have given more weight to modern "correctness" than we did for Sterne, and less weight to the earlier decipherings of Cross and Curtis; substantive variants are indicated, but the many variants in accidentals have not been. We have only a minimum of confidence that our readings of this particular letter are more accurate than those of the earlier editors.

2. averse to it's Publication] If Eliza is telling the truth, it certainly casts a dark pall over the Sterne women, who seem to be guilty of extortion. While we must assume that Eliza had some enabling hand in the publication of *Letters from Yorick to Eliza* (1773), the editor's lamentation "that Eliza's modesty was invincible to all the publisher's endeavours to obtain her answers to these letters" (xiv) may indicate her real interest in suppressing her portion of the correspondence. The release of Sterne's portion, moreover, might have been a preemptive strike; one suspects that the warmth of Sterne's letters and the probable coolness of Eliza's would have convinced even Lydia that nothing was to be gained by publishing her responses. Even if the letters had been returned to Eliza (or to Becket), Lydia could well have made copies before doing so—Eliza expresses precisely this suspicion.

3. Colonel Campbell] Curtis, 464, n. 1, suggests Donald Campbell (1751–1804), of Barbreck, Argyll, author of the popular *A Journey over Land to India* (1795), but it is highly unlikely that he would have been a colonel at the age of 21. What is perhaps more important to note is Eliza's manner of talking about him to her friend; there is a wink and a nod throughout the letter suggesting a romantic involvement with the Colonel, despite the feint toward match-making for Lydia; indeed, nine months after this letter, in January 1773, Eliza would abandon Draper for good, and almost certainly with the help of a male friend.

4. Essay . . . Shakespeare] Montagu's *Essay on the Writings and Genius of Shakespeare* was published anonymously in 1769, and was immediately successful as a patriotic defense of Shakespeare against the strictures of Voltaire; her authorship became known almost immediately. For a discussion of this work, see Elizabeth Eger, "'Out rushed a female to protect the Bard': The Bluestocking Defense of Shakespeare," *Reconsidering the Bluestockings*, ed. Pohl and Schellenberg, 127–51.

5. Mocha Ship] I.e., a ship that stopped at the Red Sea port of Mocha in its transit between India and Britain.

6. Eltham] Since 1759, the suburban home of the Jameses in southeast London, the borough of Greenwich.

7. the sole . . . Expences] Curtis, 387, prints this quoted material as a fragment of a Sterne letter (no. 207), dating it early August 1767. Sterne had been implying much the same thing about the impending visit of his wife and daughter since late June; see, e.g., *BJ*, 6:203–4 (June 20); and see also letters 220 (to Mrs. James) and 221 (to Hall-Stevenson).

8. Non Credo!] Unbelievable!

lii. *Lydia Sterne de Medalle to David Garrick*

Text: Medalle

DEDICATION[1]

To David Garrick, Esq.

When I was ask'd to whom I should dedicate these volumes, I carelessly answered to no one—Why not? (replied the person who put the question to me.) Because most dedications look like begging a protection to the book. Perhaps a worse interpretation may be given to it. No, no! already so much obliged, I cannot, will not, put another tax upon the generosity of any friend of Mr. Sterne's, or mine. I went home to my lodgings, and gratitude warmed my heart to such a pitch, that I vow'd they should be dedicated to the man my father so much admired—who, with an unprejudiced eye, read, and approved his works, and moreover loved the man—'Tis to Mr. Garrick then, that I dedicate these Genuine Letters.

Can I forget the sweet Epitaph[2] which proved Mr. Garrick's friendship, and opinion of him? 'Twas a tribute to friendship—and as a tribute of my gratitude I dedicate these volumes to a man of understanding and feelings[a]—Receive this, as it is meant—May you, dear Sir, approve of these letters, as much as Mr. Sterne admired you—but Mr. Garrick, with all his urbanity, can never carry the point half so far, for Mr. Sterne was an enthusiast, if it is possible to be one, in favour of Mr. Garrick.

This may appear a very simple dedication, but Mr. Garrick will judge by his own sensibility, that I can feel more than I can express, and I believe he will give me credit for all my grateful acknowledgements.

I am, with every sentiment of gratitude, and esteem, Dear Sir, Your obliged humble servant,

London, June, 1775. Lydia Sterne de Medalle

MS: Not located
Pub.: Medalle (1775), 1:v–ix.

[a]feelings] feeling *2d ed. (1776)*

1. DEDICATION] While this last item is not strictly "correspondence," we thought it a fitting tribute to Lydia Sterne Medalle to conclude these volumes of Sterne's correspondence with the dedication to her first edition of the letters. Given that we have often in our pages deplored her irresponsible approach to her editorial duties, it is only fair to acknowledge that, without her efforts, many of Sterne's letters might have been forever lost. We continue the work begun by Lydia.

2. the sweet Epitaph] Medalle prints the epitaph Garrick wrote for Sterne (xi): "Shall Pride a heap of sculptur'd marble raise, / Some worthless, un-mourn'd titled fool to praise; / And shall we not by one poor grave-stone learn, / Where Genius, Wit, and Humour, sleep with *Sterne?*"

INDEX

Because they are so frequently cited, Lydia Medalle's *Letters,* Lewis Perry Curtis's *Letters,* and Arthur Cash's *Early and Middle Years* and *Later Years* have not been indexed. Where a person or title is referred to in sequential notes, only the first reference is indexed. In most instances, the materials concerning the location and previous publication of each letter have not been indexed, except when discussed in the *Status* section. Roman-numbered pages refer to the front matter in volume 7, some of which is repeated (with different pagination) in volume 8. Page references in italics refer to illustrations.